models
& myths

in canadian sociology

models

&

myths

in

canadian

sociology

S. D. Berkowitz, editor

Department of Sociology
University of Vermont

Butterworths
Toronto

Models and Myths in Canadian Sociology

© 1984 Butterworth & Co. (Canada) Ltd.

Printed and bound in Canada

The Butterworth Group of Companies

Canada:
Butterworth & Co. (Canada) Ltd., Toronto and Vancouver
United Kingdom:
Butterworth & Co. (Publishers) Ltd., London
Australia:
Butterworths Pty Ltd., Sydney, Melbourne, Brisbane, Adelaide and Perth
New Zealand:
Butterworths of New Zealand Ltd., Wellington and Auckland
Singapore:
Butterworth & Co. (Asia) Pte. Ltd., Singapore
South Africa:
Butterworth Publishers (Pty) Ltd., Durban and Pretoria
United States:
Butterworth Legal Publishers, Boston, Seattle, Austin and St. Paul
D & S Publishers, Clearwater

Canadian Cataloguing in Publication Data
Main entry under title:
Models and myths in Canadian sociology

Bibliography: p.
Includes index.
ISBN 0-409-81361-3

1. Canada — Social conditions — Addresses, essays,
lectures. I. Berkowitz, S. D. (Stephen David), 1943-

HN103.5.M62 1984   971.06   C83-099241-3

Sponsoring Editor — J. Turner
Editor/Cover Design — D. Florkow
Production — J. Shepherd

To H. Marshall McLuhan,
author of *The Gutenberg Galaxy* and *Understanding Media*,
who so eloquently debated his critics
even when he could no longer speak.

For: My Parents
S. D. B.

Contents

Contributors

S. D. BERKOWITZ teaches sociology and is a member of the faculty of the Canadian Studies Program at the University of Vermont. He previously taught at the University of Toronto and the University of Saskatchewan, Regina. He is the author, together with Robert Logan, of a collection of essays on the Canadian unity issue. *Canada's Third Option* (1978), a book on the theory and practice of structural modeling, *An Introduction to Structural Analysis: The Network Approach to Social Research* (1982), and a variety of articles on economic structure and related problems. He was a principal investigator for a study, *Enterprise Structure and Corporate Concentration* (1976), conducted for the Royal Commission on Corporate Concentration, and is currently doing further research on Canadian market structure.

Y. MICHAL BODEMANN teaches at the University of Toronto and the Freie Universität Berlin. He is continuing his studies on the structure of Southern Italian society and labour migration. Recent publications also include work on changes in Jewish and German identity in the Federal Republic of Germany, the Marxist conception of class, as well as Marxist approaches to empirical social research.

ROBERT J. BRYM is Associate Chairman of the Department of Sociology at the University of Toronto. He is the author of *The Jewish Intelligentsia and Russian Marxism* (1978), *Intellectuals and Politics* (1980), the co-author (with Victor Zaslavsky) of *Soviet-Jewish Emigration and Soviet Nationality Policy* (1983), and the co-editor (with R. J. Sacouman) and a contributor to *Underdevelopment and Social Movements in Atlantic Canada* (1979). He is presently preparing a monograph on the development of sociology in Canada since the Second World War.

FREDERICK ELKIN is a Professor of Sociology at York University, Toronto. Formerly he taught at McGill University and the University of Montreal. In addition to several journal articles and contributions to edited works, he is the author of *Child and Society* (4th edition, 1984), *Family in Canada* (1964), *Rebels and Colleagues: Advertising and Social Change in French Canada* (1973) and co-editor of *Volunteers, Voluntary Associations and Development* (1981). He is a Molson Fellow of the Vanier Institute of the Family and serves on the Professional Advisory Committee of Dellcrest Children's Centre.

DENNIS FORCESE is Professor of Sociology and Anthropology and Dean of the Faculty of Social Sciences at Carleton University. He is the author of numerous books and articles including *The Canadian Class Structure* (Revised, 1980) and (with S. Richer) *Social Issues: Sociological View of Canada* (1982). His current interests include political sociology, social stratification and police studies.

P. KRISHNAN is Professor of Sociology at the University of Alberta. He was the founding editor of *Canadian Studies in Population* and served in that capacity until 1982. He was the Director of the Population Research Laboratory, University of Alberta, from 1972 through 1975. He is the author of numerous publications in the area of population and demography, a Fellow of the Royal Statistical Society (Eng.), a Fellow of the Human Biology Council, and a member of a variety of other scientific associations. He is currently continuing his research on various aspects of Canadian demography and on the historical demography of religious groups in India.

ROGER O'TOOLE is an Associate Professor of Sociology at the University of Toronto and a member of the faculty of the Graduate Centre for Religious Studies. He is the author of *The Precipitous Path: Studies in Political Sects* (1977), *Religion: Classical Sociological Approaches* (1984), several edited volumes and numerous articles on the sociology of religion. His current research areas include religion and politics, religion and social movements, the sociology of Roman Catholicism, and religion in Canadian society.

CHARLES E. REASONS has been a member of the Department of Sociology, University of Calgary, since 1974. His primary areas of teaching and research are social issues, the sociology of law, and criminology. He has published numerous articles and books including *Corporate Crime in Canada* (1978), with Colin Goff, *The Sociology of Law: A Conflict Perspective* (1978), with Robert Rich, *the Ideology of Social Problems* (1981), with W. D. Perdue, and *Assault on the Worker: Occupational Health and Safety in Canada* (1981), with Lois Ross and Craig Paterson.

TERRENCE H. WHITE is Dean of the Faculty of Arts, University of Alberta. He was formerly Chair of the Department of Sociology at the University of Alberta and Head of the Department of Sociology and Anthropology at the University of Windsor. His current research focuses on the changing meaning of work, organizational change, and white collar work.

Introduction

Five or six years ago, there was considerable speculation as to whether or not a distinctly "Canadian" sociology was "possible."[1] Two issues dominated the discussion: First, given the mass of material being produced throughout the world, is it possible to identify research *by* Canadians or *about* Canada that is particularly relevant to the Canadian experience? Second, given the pervasive influence of U.S. sociology, not only in Canada but in other countries as well, is there something unique about Canadian contributions to the development of the discipline?

These questions were intertwined with others — not the least of which was the controversy over the large number of foreign (principally American) sociologists hired to teach and do research at Canadian universities during the 1960s and 70s.[2] The fear was that sociologists who had been trained to look at the social world from the vantage point of Boston or Tulsa would apply substantially the same models in examining Halifax or Calgary. More often than not, however, this real issue got entangled with others: "quantitative" ("American") *vs.* "qualitative" ("Canadian") approaches, "conflict theory" ("American") *vs.* "consensualism" ("Canadian"), "ahistorical" ("American") *vs.* "historical" ("Canadian") models, and so on.[3]

With the passage of time, and a radical reduction in the rate of growth of sociology departments, most of these secondary issues have cooled. The key questions — those relating to the role of Canadian sociology within the discipline and within Canadian society — remain.

The essays presented here attempt to address these core issues directly. Each contributor has taken one of the principal research areas pursued by sociologists at Canadian universities and has provided us with a systematic overview of the key actors, contending approaches or paradigms, and important substantive results which have shaped the development of that sub-discipline during the course of the last several decades.

Some essays included here are, where subject matter warrants, largely descriptive. Until recently, it has often been difficult to disentangle work about Canada or by Canadians from the mass of research being produced in North America. As a rule, this problem has been especially acute in sub-areas of the discipline where there are relatively few Canadian practitioners or where the dominant research strategies demand cross-national comparisons. In these instances, contributors have judged that broad general overviews are most appropriate.

In sub-fields where there are large numbers of Canadian researchers, where empirical evidence is extensive, and where interpretive schools and paradigms are highly developed, the essays are more critical and analytic in tone and more clearly centered on specific theoretical issues. Here contributors have not tried to be encyclopedic — to reflect all of the subtle differences in the styles of work of different practitioners. Instead, they have sought to identify the principal intellectual currents within their areas and to relate these to the broader task of describing and analyzing Canadian social life.

The larger objective of this book, then, is not simply to present an overview — or even a critical overview — of Canadian sociology. It is not, moreover, simply to provide readers with a quick summary of the important social and economic factors which shape their lives. A variety of monographs, texts, and articles have addressed each of these tasks in isolation from the other. Our purpose here is to integrate the two: to present Canadian sociology in the context of Canadian society. The larger goal of this book, in other words, is to begin creating a "sociology of Canadian sociology": to help both students and practicing sociologists to become more aware of the unique ways in which Canadian political economy and social structure have affected the ways in which they go about the job of examining the society in which they live.

Each author whose essay appears in this volume is an active researcher in the sub-discipline about which he has written. In many cases, contributors themselves have been responsible for some of the "classic" work which they describe or critique. In another context this close association between a body of work and its criticism might be disadvantageous: after all, can we expect scholars, no matter how fair-minded, to be as sharply critical of their own research as they are that of others? But, in Canada, there are relatively few sociologists in each field or sub-discipline. Thus we do not have the luxury of being able to demand a studied distance between a contributor and his or her own work. Rather than attempt the impossible or impractical, we have opted here for the other obvious alternative: to select authors whose deep involvement in a particular area of Canadian sociology insures that they will have both an intimate knowledge of the common stock-in-trade of particular specialty groups and insights into points of passionate disagreement within these groups.

While this book does not assume previous knowledge of sociology — and readers may find some or all of it useful as an introduction to the field — it is not a conventional dry-as-dust text. It does not attempt, as most "modern" texts do, to present abstracted or bloodless Sociology which is divorced from the conditions under which it is produced. Rather, in C. Wright Mills's terms,[4] we have tried to convey not only the substance of our various areas of research, but also some of the flavor: to reflect not only what Canadian sociology *is,* but what it means to *do* sociology. We hope, in this fashion, to put readers in touch not only with a body of scholarship, but with a uniquely interesting form of human endeavor as well.

The editorial work involved in preparing this volume was greatly facilitated by the kind cooperation of Butterworths — in particular that of David Hogg and Janet Turner, our editors during various phases of the project. Shawn Berkowitz, Terry Berkowitz, Margot Bowlby and Lisa Handler deserve our thanks for their painstaking efforts in the preparation of the final copy. As always, H. G. McCann's careful help in proofreading was greatly appreciated.

The manuscript was produced through the use of the text-editing facilities of the Academic Computing Center, University of Vermont. We would like to thank Martin Blitz, Robert Bower, Norbert Charbonneau, Kim Lantman, Deb Thompson, David Whitmore and other members of the ACC staff for their patient and continuing aid in the completion of our work.

NOTES

[1]See, in particular, Felt, 1975; Stolzman and Gamberg, 1975; Ramu and Johnson, "Toward a Canadian Sociology," in Ramu and Johnson, 1976; and Mathews and Steele, 1969.

[2]See Symons, 1975.

[3]For a focused discussion of some of the issues involved, compare Clark, 1973, with Watson, 1975. Also see Shugarman and Butler, 1970, and Crowley, 1971.

[4]Mills, 1959.

Bibliography

Clark, S. D. "The American Takeover of Canadian Sociology: Myth or Reality." *Dalhousie Review* 53 (1973): 205-18.

Crowley, Terence. "Anti-Americanism and the Degeneration of Canadian Scholarship: A Rejoinder." *Journal of Canadian Studies* 6 (1971): 51-58.

Felt, Lawrence. "Nationalism and the Possibility of A Relevant Anglo-Canadian Sociology." *Canadian Journal of Sociology* 1 (1975): 377-79.

Mathews, Robin and James Steele. *The Struggle for Canadian Universities.* Toronto: New Press, 1969.

Ramu, G. N. and S. D. Johnson. "Toward a Canadian Sociology." In G. N. Ramu and S. D. Johnson, eds., *Introduction to Canadian Society: Sociological Analysis.* Toronto: Macmillan of Canada, 1976.

Shugarman, David and Michael Butler. "Canadian Nationalism, Americanization and Scholarly Values." *Journal of Canadian Studies* 5 (1970): 12-27.

Stolzman, James and Herbert Gamberg. "The National Question and Canadian Sociology." *Canadian Journal of Sociology* 1 (1975): 107-24.

Symons, T. H. B. *To Know Ourselves: The Report of the Commission on Canadian Studies.* Ottawa: Association of Universities and Colleges in Canada, 1975.

Watson, Llewelyn. "The Poverty of Sociology in A Changing Canadian Society." *Canadian Journal of Sociology* 1 (1975): 345-62.

CHAPTER 1

Models, Myths, and Social Realities: A Brief Introduction to Sociology in Canada

S. D. Berkowitz

BACKGROUND

Until recently, courses on "Canadian Society" usually began with a pious reminder that, soft drink and oil company signs to the contrary notwithstanding, Canada and the United States were not the same: that different forces and contexts had shaped the two and that, consequently, it was dangerous to assume that U.S.-made models and U.S.-based results could be easily extended to similar phenomena occurring within Canada.

This said, instructors faced a dilemma. With few exceptions there was only a scattering of relevant Canadian material in each of the sub-fields — economic development, family studies, community, and so on — on which societal surveys are usually focused.[1] Since some issues were not covered in the literature, confining the course to Canadian work would leave students with a disjointed impression of the discipline. Drawing heavily on outside sources, by contrast, would risk seriously distorting some aspect of Canadian society since most people assume that substantive findings, in particular, can be easily transposed from one societal context to another.

There was no really satisfactory solution to this problem. Some instructors hewed closely to the historical-developmentalist approach laid down by Harold Innis and other members of what is referred to as the Toronto School. This allowed them to exploit a rich vein of native scholarship.[2] By the late 1960s and early 1970s, however, many Toronto School studies no longer spoke directly to important contemporary trends and issues. Moreover, since explicitly sociological work within this genre was often more concerned with historical detail than with theory, it was difficult to extrapolate from such work to new contexts.

Another approach followed by some instructors during this period was to present the entire gamut of theoretical frameworks which might be used to interpret a given phenomenon — such as crime or modernization — and then to fill in gaps with small-scale examples of particular perspectives as applied to Canadian cases. This solution was not ideal, of course, because contrived examples could not convey the force of the analytic frameworks they were supposed to illustrate.

By the mid-1970s, Canadian sociology had matured to the point where these problems were greatly reduced: the number of sociologists in Canada had increased some twenty-fold since the 1950s, journals had been founded, and professional associations established. In simplest terms, this meant that more sociological research was being published and that, in the way of such things, this material reflected a wider range of theoretical interests and styles. Moreover, master's and Ph.D. programs begun at Canadian universities in the 1960s and early 1970s started to turn out significant numbers of graduates whose advanced training specifically prepared them to deal with Canadian problems and settings. This fact, together with a series of related institutional changes, led to a widening and deepening of the pool of expertise that instructors could draw upon in presenting theoretically coherent views of Canadian society.[3]

Canadianization: Competing Paradigms and Agendas

Ironically, it was only at the point where a theoretically broad-gauged sociology had begun to crystallize in the mid-1970s that many sociologists began to question the role that the study of Canadian society, *per se,* ought to play within their discipline. When research on Canadian topics had been sparse, it had seemed quite natural to treat "Canadian Society" as a disciplinary sub-specialty — much like an interest in deviance, theory, or historical sociology. At the point where significant Canadian work had appeared in virtually every specialty area — often reflecting a number of different perspectives — this kind of ghettoization no longer seemed possible. Moreover, if, *per force,* "Canadian Sociology" were nothing more than "sociology about Canada," could one even justify maintaining a separate "Canadian Society" sub-discipline? How, in principle, could one distinguish social research and teaching which was about Canada from that which properly formed part of the sociological study of "Canadian Society"?

By 1974, these and related questions had come to center stage in a series of debates taking place in sociology departments across the country. While the sides in these debates were not always clear, three reasonably well-defined positions had emerged. First, some sociologists clearly viewed societal-level analyses — and, among these, studies of Canadian Society — as secondary to research and teaching in sub-disciplines whose theoretical base is conceived to be universal and where, as a consequence, studies of specific national milieux are viewed as instances of a larger pattern, e.g., family studies, formal organization, stratification, interpersonal relations, and so on. Seen in this way, exclusively focusing on Canadian Society or Canadian Social Development would lead to hopelessly specific or redundant results and conclusions. This position was especially common, as a number of writers have observed, among researchers who explicitly or implicitly accepted the structural functionalist paradigm dominant in the United States in 1950s and 60s.[4]

Second, some parties to the debate contended that, given its long term relationship to political economy, Anglo-Canadian sociology had developed its own special emphases and traditions. Thus, while it had not grown up in a vacuum — and, indeed had strong familial ties to other sociological perspectives — Anglo-Canadian sociology had evolved in unique ways. In particular, they maintained, it had traditionally treated a range of societal-level problems which were typically given short shrift within internationally-dominant paradigms, e.g. nation-building, the formation of national consciousness, and the forces shaping national or regional character. These issues, they contended, ought to continue to form the irreducible core of the formal study of Canadian society if for no other reason than that they reflected the dominant perspective Canadians had used to interpret their social experience in the past.[5]

Finally, some observers held that Canadian sociologists ought to shy away from what C. Wright Mills unflatteringly referred to as the "Grand Theorizing" or "Abstracted Empiricism" of their American cousins.[6] They maintained, however, that the surest way to avoid these mistakes was to tie one's research and teaching closely to concrete, historically specific problems — and not become embroiled in searches for some wraith-like national consciousness or national character.

Given that they reflect radically different views not only as to how a discipline *ought* to develop, but also as to what it *is,* these divergent positions could not, of course, be easily reconciled. In practical terms, as long as Anglo-Canadian sociology departments continued to grow, opponents or proponents of each approach contented themselves with attempts to shape the future of the field by controlling the hiring of new faculty. This was critical since, by the early 1970s, it was clear that tenurable positions in university departments were rapidly being filled; in many cases by persons trained outside the country.

What had begun as a series of debates over the study of Canadian society, then, quickly got transformed into something quite different: The Canadianization Issue. At one time or another, it became the basis for factional disputes inside virtually every sociology department in the country. In the final analysis, it led to interventions by the Canadian Association of University Teachers, by the Association of Universities and Colleges in Canada, by at least two provincial government bodies, and by the Canadian Sociology and Anthropology Association.[7]

Since sociologists, like other human beings, are often poor observers of social movements in which they play a direct role, no attempt to resolve the

Canadianization issue would be fruitful here. However, whatever its ultimate sources, it is clear that the Canadianization controversy had at least one positive consequence: it sensitized most sociologists in Canada to the importance of theory and research relevant to the social environment in which they were living. In retrospect, it also probably helped to legitimate a variety of interests which might otherwise have remained the academic property of a few specialists.

Consolidation: The New Context

As Hiller and other critics have noted,[8] the cessation of large-scale hiring in sociology departments towards the middle of the 1970s led to an observable decline in the visibility of the Canadianization issue. This trend ran parallel to at least two important changes in the context within which Anglo-Canadian sociological research and teaching was being carried out. First, if it had remained simply one among many academic specialties within combined social science departments, it is unlikely that Anglo-Canadian sociology would have emerged as a fully formed discipline in its own right. After autonomous sociology departments were created in English Canada beginning in the early 1960s, the institutional basis was laid for the development of the kind of research and teaching practice needed for further development of the field. But, in another sense, Anglo-Canadian sociology was still a step-child of the other social sciences: they had been founded earlier, had been able to offer a wider range of courses, and had been more completely accepted by the academic establishment.[9] While anglophone sociologists were in a better position by the mid-1960s to exercise administrative control over their own work, they still lived in the shadow of these older disciplines. It was only after the rapid increase in faculty size which ended in the early to mid-1970s that these departments began to garner the share of university resources they needed to become fully institutionalized.

Second, this period of growth had often been turbulent. In many cases, conflicts within departments reflected differences in frameworks and intellectual styles associated with different faculty age-cohorts. As Tepperman observes, this left many sociology departments "stratified like rockbeds, with one ideological layer sitting on top of another."[10] Since younger faculty — many without Ph.D.s[11] — were disproportionately attracted to new approaches, this led to "an unfortunate congruence of rank and intellectual style... [which] served to limit the sharing of ideas between age-cohorts."[12] By 1980, however, these sedimentary layers were being pressed closer together through aging and through the progress through the ranks of younger members. This led to a diminution in conflict — or, at least, the opportunity for conflict — and to a more stable environment in which distinctive analytic styles could more readily emerge. While not quite paradigms — in the sense that they are not intended to be universal[13] — the interpretive schools that had begun to appear throughout the 1970s at Carleton, Alberta and various other universities had become sufficiently different, both from one another and from the mainstream Anglo-Canadian tradition, to constitute recognizably different approaches to social inquiry.

MODELS OF CANADIAN SOCIETY

By 1980, then, Anglo-Canadian sociology appeared ready to embark upon a new phase in its development.[14] Throughout much of its early history, Canadian sociology in the English-speaking provinces had principally been built around concerns derived from the Toronto School of political economy. This was no longer true. While the Toronto School continued to influence work in a number of areas, it no longer exercised the kind of hegemony it once had.[15] Canadian sociology was, by this time, far too large an enterprise to be dominated by any one school of thought or set of ideas. Rather, it closely reflected the diverse sets of substantive concerns and methodological styles characteristic of the discipline elsewhere in the world.

While clearly not a closed corporation on the old model, Anglo-Canadian sociology as it has begun to develop in the early 1980s is not completely eclectic or homogenized or Americanized or whatever: it has clear strengths, focal interests and characteristic biases. Although English Canada has produced or nutured some fine methodologists, Anglo-Canadian sociology as it has developed during the last two decades is not noteworthy for its contributions to research or teaching in this area: it is primarily concerned with substantive issues.[16] French Canada routinely trains highly skilled and creative demographers — but other areas requiring high levels of methodological skill are not as well supported.[17]

Canadian sociology is inventive: in ethnic studies,[18] crime and delinquency,[19] and studies of elites it has given birth to important theories and models. It has fostered the development of structural analysis,[20] a major theoretical and methodological development. Practitioners trained at Canadian universities during the 1970s have, in important cases, been able to reinterpret classic historical problems using theoretically and methodologically rigorous tools.[21]

Given all this vitality, why have Canadian sociologists remained preoccupied with their identity? Why are they still concerned with whether or not an Anglo-Canadian sociology is possible? Perhaps the best answer lies in history: for good or ill, Anglo-Canadian sociologists have been conditioned to expect large-scale interpretations of their social experience — along the lines provided by the Toronto School. Modern social theory — particularly its more formal variants — tends to shy away from global models because, with rare exceptions, they cannot be juxtaposed to, and compared with, bodies of detailed empirical evidence. Since they cannot ignore the environment in which they work, contemporary Anglo-Canadian sociologists experience a disjuncture between their own work — and the criteria by which it is evaluated — and the massive contributions of the "giants" of the past.

But is this a correct way of looking at things? When Tepperman (1978) points to vital and interesting research going on at various universities but feels compelled to note that it "is not particularly Canadian," he is reflecting this notion that contemporary social science not in the grand tradition is somehow less useful, less relevant to the Canadian experience, and therefore in this sense, less "Canadian." Is it an expression of "American scientism" to demand that Canadians conform to the broad canons of scholarly discourse and that they address an audience beyond their borders? Does it make a piece of work less relevant to the Canadian experience to do so?

Paradigms and Theory Groups: Interpreting Reality

It is a central thesis of this review that the search for a truly Canadian interpretation of Canadian society is misplaced and that this quest has, in the past, probably hampered more than helped the serious discussion of theoretical issues and the sustained pursuit of the empirical evidence needed to shed light on crucial dimensions of Canadian social and economic organization. The counter-argument offered here is that Canadian sociology is undergoing precisely those stages of growth we ought to expect given the structural constraints under which it came into being and the point at which it is in its developmental cycle.

The intellectual histories of scholarly or scientific groups can usually be broken down into a series of phases. In early stages of their development, these groups usually cluster around a few central figures whose work acts as a model for a set of colleagues and students. In some cases, this work provides the basis for a new way of looking at a set of problems, but follows well-trod theoretical or methodological paths. In other instances, the approach represented in this work makes a major break with past theorizing or methodology. In the first cases, we observe the establishment of what are referred to as interpretive schools and, in the second, paradigms. Initially, the work of successful groups — that is, ones whose influence persists over time — tends to be rather general since the function of such work is to lay out a set of problems, support a general approach to solving them, or to counteract the claims of different and competing groups. After this initial phase is complete, however, members of the group tend to shift their efforts to more specific and limited problems within the reach of the general model that has been laid down.[22]

We refer to groups pursuing a particular approach to understanding the social world as theory groups.[23] In cases where the theories put forward by sets of researchers only relate to one substantive area, theory groups will, in effect, be contained within substantive area groups. Other theory groups, by their very nature, will cross-cut the boundaries between areas, academic or research institutions, and nation-states. There is strong theoretical and empirical cause to believe that there is real interaction between the structure of these theory groups and the kind of work they produce.[24]

Anglo-Canadian faculty have historically been concentrated at a few large institutions. As Hiller notes, as late as 1956-57 "the faculty of the University of Toronto accounted for twenty per cent of all university teachers in Canada."[25] What this meant was that, during the earliest phase in the development of Anglo-Canadian social science, a few centers played a disproportionately large role in setting its agenda since faculties at outlying universities were often too small to sustain clusters of like-minded researchers.[26] After this initial incubatory stage, the pattern of top-down construction of faculties in English Canadian universities — that is, hiring a head who would then hire a staff — ensured the propagation of the ideas of metropolitan theory groups in outlying regions; but without the social support needed to challenge the prevailing orthodoxy.[27]

The avalanche of foreign-trained researchers which buried Canadian social science faculties during the period of rapid expansion broke this pattern. Since many of those hired were freshly-minted Ph.D.s, they naturally retained their ties to the theory groups which produced them. This resulted in a heterodoxy which was new to the Canadian context. Since central Canadian graduate programs were small, there was no offsetting influence from this source.[28] Thus, at a developmentally critical point in time, theory groups located in the large Anglo-Canadian training institutions were unable to effectively perpetuate themselves at newly established or newly expanded centers. This was true of the Toronto School proper, but also of its various offshoots, of the competing McGill tradition, and of ideas put forward by various other established groups.[29] The upshot was that after the dust had settled, the structure of the invisible colleges which link active researchers to one another was heavily biased toward north-south rather than east-west communication. It was this pattern which various investigators found when they began assessing the state of Canadian sociology in the late 1960s and early 1970s.[30]

Structural Change and Canadian Clusters

During the last several years, important changes have been going on in the way in which sociologists go about the task of describing and interpreting Canadian society. Underlying these changes are two profound shifts in the structure of Anglo-Canadian academic life. First, there has been a marked increase in the relative size of social science faculties at new or newly expanded universities in English Canada — many of these outside Ontario.[31] This has encouraged the establishment of localized clusters of social scientists pursuing similar problems at these universities and the consequent expansion of styles of academic work within the country as a whole. Second, some of the intellectual barriers between anglophone and francophone social science — engendered by their very different patterns of development and by language — have begun to crumble. Autonomous departments or institutes of sociology were established far earlier in French than in English Canada.[32] Until the 1960s, given a relatively more concentrated university system and greater familiarity of francophones with English than anglophones with French, sociology in Quebec was far more cohesive and integrated internally and, simultaneously, far more closely articulated with trends in the rest of the world than sociology elsewhere in Canada.[33] Changes in the structure of sociology as practiced in English Canada, which coincided with the beginnings of the Quiet Revolution in Quebec, are now facilitating greater knowledge on the part of both solitudes of the other's work.

The most important effects of these shifts are being felt in the range and quality of scholarly exchange currently going on about specific dimensions of Canadian social organization. At the point where there was little research on most aspects of Canadian society — or when such activity was confined to a few theory groups — it made little sense to talk about alternative models or scholarly exchange except in the limited sense of contentions between individual scholars. What is most symptomatic of the changes which have taken place in Canadian sociology over the last ten years is that there are now at least two, and often several, competing schools of thought among researchers in most sub-fields or disciplines.

Critical Groups

These different paradigms and interpretive schools, and the groups which are associated with them, will be discussed in detail in the chapters which follow. Briefly however, while there is, as we noted earlier, renewed interest in the Toronto School of political economy — and, in particular, in the implications of Innis' staples model as a schema for explaining the broad pattern of Canadian development — several quite different theory groups now lay claim to be carrying on in this tradition. One group — which centers around figures such as Abraham Rotstein, Mel Watkins, and Robert and James Laxer[34] — seems to draw sustenance from the political economy tradition, but uses it as a springboard for the discussion of contemporary issues as well. Most of those associated with this group are not sociologists by training, but come out of other disciplines, such as political science or history.[35] Paul Craven's recent study of the role of the state in the establishment of the pattern of industrial relations in Canada,[36] however, is a striking example of the way in which specifically sociological models can be applied to historical materials, to the enrichment of both disciplines.

Another theory group following in some ways in the footsteps of the political economy tradition is what is now generally referred to as the Carleton School. It consists of researchers drawn from a variety of backgrounds — most notably at the moment, Wallace Clement and Leo Panitch[37] — who are involved in extending and updating John Porter's work on the sources and consequences of social power in Canada. While Porter's earlier account[38] was heavily functionalist both in tone and substance, the writings of members of the Carleton School borrow much of the rhetoric, if not the form, of Marxist analyses.

The boundaries between these two theory groups, of course, are not firm and fast — and a variety of researchers draw upon and contribute to both of them. Thomas Naylor's model of the role of metropolitan elites in the process of Canadian development, for instance, bears certain familial resemblances to the work of both groups, but does not fit neatly or tightly into either one.[39] Leo Johnson, a Marxist historian, is frequently cited by both camps, but falls into neither.

Conventional Groups

In addition to these critical groups, there are a variety of more conventional ones which also provide interpretations of large-scale or global social processes. Two, in particular, bear mentioning here. The first is specifically formed around the issues of nation-building and the formation of national character — in modern words, political culture — which S. D. Clark brought into mainstream Canadian sociology from the Toronto School. The theoretical framework being assembled by this group, however, contains components which were not part of the stock-in-trade of the Innis tradition and, as such, its interpretation of the relationships between political ideology and social structure is far richer and more detailed than those of its predecessor. This new theory group — what might be called the New Toronto School — draws upon elements of European phenomenology and the sociology of knowledge,[40] from the American political modernization literature,[41] from symbolic interactionism,[42] and from a variety of other sources. David Bell and Lorne Tepperman's *The Roots of Disunity: A Look at Canadian Political Culture* is probably the most fully developed work in this genre, but we most certainly ought to view Herschel Hardin's *A Nation Unaware: The Canadian Economic Culture,* George Grant's *Lament for A Nation,* and Donald Smiley's *Canada in Question* as important contributions to the development of this framework as well.[43]

The second conventional group is probably the largest. It includes a variety of researchers who apply variants of functionalist models, principally as developed in the United States, to Canadian problems and issues.[44]

While less pervasive than it once was, functional analysis is probably still the single most influential paradigm in the field. As such, it tends to play a large role in the curriculum at most graduate schools and, hence, to crop up in the theories and empirical research of even the most uncompromisingly critical or unconventional practitioners. Thus, it is not surprising that a considerable number of Canadian sociologists incorporate strong functionalist elements into their models.

Given functionalism's broad impact on the way in which sociologists think about society, it is difficult to talk about a functionalist theory group without describing the field itself. Nonetheless, it is possible to specify those sub-disciplines where a particularly pure form of functionalism is prevalent, and to identify specific writers whose work best exemplifies this approach.

Functionalists view social structures as collections of discrete units which provide the essential building blocks for the larger social order. These building blocks — families, ethnic groups, occupations, status groups, or whatever — correspond to different but consistent patterns of social stratification which analysts may devise in order to interpret the observable world. Ethnic groups are therefore the units in systems of ethnic stratification, occupations the units in systems of occupational stratification, and so on. In any given case, functionalists maintain, these units are functionally interdependent, that is, they mutually regulate and mutually support one another as parts of a complex, organic whole. The functions that associate these basic units with one another are, moreover, universal throughout given societies and, if they persist, play a positive role in the integration of these societies. Some such functions, in fact, are indispensable and act as functional prerequisites for the formation of any social order.[45]

As we will see in detail in later chapters, models which rest on these assumptions are particularly commonplace in Canadian studies of crime, modernization, family and sex roles, and elites. John Hagan's influential interpretation of the implications of consensus and conflict theories of crime, for instance — i.e., that there are consensus crimes and conflict crimes and that each is best understood from the vantage point of its corresponding theory — is fully consistent with Coser's version of the functionalist paradigm.[46] The perspective on modernization[47] — the process(es) through which less developed societies change into more developed ones — that is advocated by Lorna Marsden and Edward Harvey is vintage functionalism in its emphasis on structural differentiation and integration as primary processes and in its interpretation of social disturbances (or similar phenomena) as simple by-products of uneven social change.[48] G. N. Ramu's *Courtship, Marriage and the Family in Canada* assumes the traditional functionalist framework as it applies to families and many of the articles included in his collection reflect this fact.[49] John Porter's *The Vertical Mosaic* treats social inequality as an inevitable consequence of the establishment of a complex social order. It therefore views the existence of elites and elite power as inevitable — a thoroughly functionalist interpretation of these phenomena.[50]

Smaller Groups

Beyond these major groupings, there are currently a variety of smaller, and usually more localized, theory groups active in Canada. Relatively compact clusters of this kind are often quite interesting since their work frequently foreshadows later developments within a field.

The most important theory group of this kind in Canada centers around the Structural Analysis Programme at the University of Toronto. Beginning in the mid-1950s, groups of researchers in Europe and North America began to explore ways of describing and analyzing highly complex and interrelated social structures. The result was a series of new analytic frameworks which gradually came to be known as structuralist.[51] Structural analysis, the predominant form of structuralism in North America, is thus "an approach to theorizing about, representing, and analyzing social processes which emphasizes their systemic character."[52]

Because of the complex nature of the phenomena they study, structural analysts frequently employ a number of sophisticated modeling techniques based on graph theory and algebra. Many social scientists, in fact, identify structural analysis with one of its most common tools and refer to it as network analysis. But, as a theoretical schema, structural analysis is not necessarily tied to any particular method or tool.

The cluster of structural analysts at the University of Toronto is noteworthy in several important respects. First, its members and former members have played an important role in creating and extending the paradigm. This has meant that graduate students at Toronto have been exposed to some of the most influential work going on in sociology during the last dozen years. Second, this cluster has acted as the organizational center for structural analysis since the mid-1970s — as the place where INSNA is housed and its internal journal, *Connections,* is published.[53] This has meant that Canadian efforts in the area have been well-recognized internationally. Finally, since many members of the program share common interests in problems of political economy or personal ties, this has meant, together with other factors, that a distinctive Toronto style has emerged within structural analysis and has been recognized as such.

Canadian structural analysts are currently examining a range of issues related to friendship and kinship patterns, corporate structure, hierarchy formation, patterns of political influence, systems of land tenure, international market formation, colonialism, and a variety of other topics.[54] In addition to Toronto, important structural analytic work is currently being done by faculty at York University, McMaster University, and the University of Victoria.

A second small theory group has historically been strong in the Canadian prairies and, at one time or another, has included a number of sociologists living or doing research in that region — notably, Arthur Davis, James McCrorie and Richard Ossenberg.[55] The approach it initially adopted bore strong filial resemblances to the Toronto School — in particular, to Innis' research on the CPR and Vernon Fowke's study of Western development.[56] This was compounded with concepts drawn from contemporary writers on the dual processes of development and underdevelopment — such as Andre Gunder Frank[57] — with the notion of dialectical opposition taken from Marx, and with elements of "orthodox structural-functionalism"[58] and Western populism. These were resolved into a framework in which the mainspring of Canadian history was seen to lie in confrontations between metropolis and hinterland and between hinterland and metropolitan groups. In these terms, western Canada (hinterland) is placed in fundamental opposition to central Canada (metropolis), anglophone Ontario (metropolis) to francophone Quebec (hinterland), northern populations (hinterland) to southern populations (metropolis), and so on. Canada, itself, forms a hinterland *vis-à-vis* a metropolitan United States.

The classical formulations of this metropolis-hinterland approach appeared over a decade ago[59] and were largely concerned with regional and region-based class confrontations. As Ossenberg's recent treatment of power and conflict in Canadian society demonstrates, however, the same essential framework can be extended to deal with phenomena as disparate as crime and sports activity.[60]

Finally, there is a small but influential Canadian section of the theory group referred to as ethnomethodology. Although ethnomethodology has roots in the European phenomenological tradition — particularly in the work of Alfred Schutz[61] — its primary development took place in the United States in the late 1950s and 1960s. The group's central intellectual concerns have to do with the ways in which everyday knowledge is acquired, used or invoked in ordinary encounters, and the processes which guide members of groups in interpreting situations.[62] Canadian ethnomethodologists have tended to be scattered around the university system, but have recently held appointments at the University of British Columbia, the University of Toronto and the Ontario Institute for Studies in Education, among other places, and have been training graduate students at these institutions.

Since departments of sociology typically include persons drawn from more than one theory group, each exerts influences on the others. In practical terms, this implies that, over time, the boundaries between groups are likely to become blurred and the intellectual affiliations of group members are likely to shift. Hence, any rigid classification of researchers or scholars into separate and airtight compartments will fail. This is especially true among Anglo-Canadian sociologists because individual departments tend to be large — and the opportunity for mutual influence commensurately greater — and because of the tumultuous nature of academic life during the last two decades. Since at least some of these pressures have recently diminished somewhat, however, the structure of Canadian theory groups should become more clearly defined in the 1980s.

CANADIAN SOCIOLOGY AND CANADIAN SOCIETY

The institutionalization of sociology since the mid-1960s has created new opportunities for the study of Canadian society. When the field included relatively few practitioners, and when these were concentrated in a few institutions, it was quite possible that only one or two specialists might be looking at any given problem. This was not ideal because it discouraged the kind of critical scrutiny necessary for the proper development of a body of scientific work. When scholarly communities accept findings or explanations simply because no one is in a good position to refute them, myths — popularly-held but counter-factual beliefs — can proliferate.

In the chapters which follow, each author will try to critically examine the literature relating to a specific aspect of Canadian society and to distinguish between models and myths — between those explanations and interpretations that are firmly rooted in well-considered theories and carefully assembled empirical evidence, and those which are not but are widely believed nonetheless.

In its relatively brief history as a separate discipline, Canadian sociology has produced more of both — more models and more myths — than one had a right to expect. Since people tend to feel comfortable with systems of explanation that reinforce their preconceptions, the latter are often better known and more generally accepted than the former. One important goal of this book is to identify firmly-held beliefs which we feel readers ought to question — or about which, at least, they ought to render a Scot's verdict of "not proven."[63]

The book begins with an essay by Robert Brym on social movements and third parties. Brym takes on a theoretically important problem — why the Canadian social milieu has been conducive to third party formation while the U.S. has not — and a pervasive and resilient myth — Canada's historically-conditioned toryism as a result of the influx of Loyalists fleeing the unbridled democracy of the American Revolution. Brym questions the cultural/institutional approach which attributes this Canadian propensity to foster third parties to the lingering effects of culturally transmitted values, such as liberalism and toryism. He finds that strands of supposed toryism in the Canadian political culture have been greatly exaggerated, that proponents of the cultural/institutional approach, in any event, cannot explain important cases of third party formation and ideology. Brym then considers the alternative structural approach which sees "the chief cause of third-party formation in Canada in concrete patterns of social economic and political relations." While he finds flaws in this as well, Brym suggests that variations on this approach which take into account the forces which produce popular culture are likely to yield far more complete and sustainable explanations of the characteristics and development of Canadian political and social movements.

Frederick Elkin's essay on the family and sex roles in Canada is quite different from Brym's in both form and intent. While there is a significant body of work on Canadian social movements and third-parties, the family literature is much larger. Consequently, instead of concentrating on one or two specific issues, Elkin has taken on the task of summarizing this enormous mass of material and highlighting areas where Canadian analysts have concentrated their efforts and where further research is likely to yield theoretical payoffs. Elkin sees Michael Katz's study of historic family patterns in Hamilton, Ontario, for instance, as a major contribution to our understanding of the evolution of modern family structure. Beyond this, he examines comparative data on contemporary family composition, studies of gender roles in francophone and anglophone families, ethnic patterns, courtship and mate selection, alternatives to conventional marriage, spouse abuse, divorce and remarriage, aging, and socialization for adult roles. In each case, he has been careful to demonstrate both the strengths and weaknesses of Canadian writings and how they fit into the broader context of sociological research on families going on elsewhere.

Roger O'Toole's chapter on religion and political culture is particularly interesting because of the historic stress that many social scientists have attached to the study of religious influences in Canadian life. While O'Toole sees few differences between the key concepts, classic literature, theoretical issues and methods employed by Canadian sociologists of religion and their counterparts in other countries, he recognizes that the existence of at least two powerful religious traditions — one in Upper and one in Lower Canada — makes the country as a whole a useful natural laboratory for historical comparisons. The dominant themes in Canadian studies of religious life, however — secularization of culture, demystification of religion, the establishment of a civic religion — are not substantially different from those advanced by sociologists in other contexts. With this in hand, O'Toole explores the relationship between traditional religion and political culture, the present role of religion in Canadian life, and a variety of contemporary projections or forecasts about the role it is likely to play in the future. O'Toole's essay is, however, not simply a summary of Canadian writings in the area: it is an active attempt to shed light on the classical concerns raised by the Toronto School and others about the relationship between religious organization and beliefs and the formation of political culture. As we will see in Y. Michal Bodemann's essay later in this volume, contentions about the relationship between the religious background of immigrants and their role in social development forms a central component in historical interpretations of Canadian settlement patterns.

In the next chapter, Dennis Forcese examines Canadian research on public participation in the political process. Canadian electoral patterns, Forcese contends, cannot be easily interpreted using classical models based on the notion of class interest. He suggests that potential class-based voting has not emerged in Canada as a result of the coincidence of at least two important social factors: "the divergent interests of class fractions" and "the persistence of ethnic/linguistic distinctions." Regionalism has exacerbated the effects of these factors, he argues, to the point where regional and continentalist interests and sentiments tend to override and mask the effects of class. He concludes from this that attempts to find simple evidence of class consciousness in Canadian electoral patterns reflect a fundamental misunderstanding of the forces shaping the political process.

P. Krishnan's essay on population studies proceeds in two stages. First he explores the central dynamics underlying changes in the structure of the population as a whole. Then he points to some important impacts that these changes have had or are having on Canadian political and social life. In the course of doing this he treats a variety of dramatic and theoretically important issues: the respective roles played by natural increase and immigration in the growth of Canada's population since Confederation, the "vital revolutions" in birth and death rates which mark the pattern of modernization, ethnic factors in population growth or decline, fertility differentials among parts of the population, and aging. He relates these to two socially critical issues which have been at the center of political controversies during the last decade: linguistic assimilation and migration.

Reasons' essay on deviance, crime and the state is probably one of the most sharply critical in this collection. Reasons maintains that Canadian research on deviance and criminology is dominated by a series of consensual frameworks which are designed to facilitate "studying deviants in order to better appreciate and/or correct their deviance." In the first instance, this engenders a focus on "deviant identities and subcultures" in isolation from the larger social and political forces which produce them. In the second, it encourages a kind of correctionalism in which the sources or characteristics of deviants acts or behavior are taken for granted and researchers confine their attention to finding and/or assessing the effectiveness of treatment programs — reinforcing prevailing state ideology with regard to the nature and importance of types of crime. Reasons then proposes a more broadly defined and less methodologically restricted approach to examining these issues — one which is rooted in the concrete material conditions under which Canadian society developed historically. He concludes that, despite recent evidence of change, "the study of crime and deviance in Canada has a long way to go before it sheds its provincial and parochial orientation."

Terrence White's contribution to this volume is a *tour de force* on three theoretically and practically important topics: industrial, work and organizational sociology. In recent years, issues related to these topics have been the occassion for numerous advisory board reports, Royal commissions, and studies by private groups or university researchers. White traces each area of work and ties it closely to the key issues raised by analysts examining the large-scale processes shaping Canadian society. He begins with industrialization and its impacts. He then turns to studies of the organization of occupations and professions, the "work world," job satisfaction, technological impacts on work, preparation for work, gender roles and women in the labor force, unions and unionization, strikes, bureaucratization, corporate organization, and quality of life. He finishes with a discussion of industrial democracy. In each area, he has provided us with a map showing how these apparently different studies relate to one another and to the larger task of interpreting trends in Canadian social organization.

Y. Michal Bodemann's essay on Canadian studies of community is much like Brym's in that it sharply focuses on what the author takes to be a few central or dominant themes. These are then related to the entire body of work in the area. Bodemann finds that Anglo-Canadian studies of community have historically been shaped by strong class-based ideological biases; in particular by what he calls a "commoditist" view of social relationships. Canadians, Bodemann asserts, conceive of Canada as "a piece of real estate" rather than a "consensual entity" composed of "disparate human elements." This view is reflected in Anglo-Canadian social science's fascination with "staples theory" as a framework for interpreting social development and, within the ambit of this approach, a propensity to treat immigrant groups as "human staples" whose "quality" and "fitness" for the tasks involved needs to be "graded." Together with an interpretation of Canadian society as "fragile" — and, hence, needing to be "guarded" — and with an "elitism" which justifies the perpetuation of power relationships between classes, this commoditist view has provided a powerful rationale for the maintenance of the *status quo* and has blinded Anglo-Canadian social scientists to the real dynamics and important problems facing their society. Bodemann concludes, moreover, that the Anglo-Canadian sociological mythology of community forms an important component of the ruling myth of Canada's dominant classes.

In the final essay, I specifically examine the large body of Canadian sociology which deals with corporate structure, corporate control and the formation of economic and social elites. The principal theoretical underpinnings of much of this work — even its radical variants — lie in the functionalist tradition. As such, theories put forward by researchers in this subfield often face precisely those difficulties encountered by other functionalist interpretations of social structure. Many "classic" Canadian studies of corporate structure and elites are, moreover, both empirically and methodologically suspect: they rest, in critical respects, on untested comparisons to and assertions about the American case and on wholly inadequate methods of data gathering or analysis. Only a few researchers have explicitly taken on the difficult tasks involved and the studies they have conducted have been extremely limited in scope. Ironically, I conclude, it is probably precisely those flaws in the current body of work which make it attractive to non-specialists.

A Final Word

Despite their broad scope, the essays included here cannot, of course, cover all models and myths in Canadian sociology in the same detail. There is, for instance, no separate chapter devoted to ethnicity and ethnic relations simply because the literature is too vast and because ethnicity is treated as an important dimension in studies in virtually every other subdiscipline. Hence, it seemed more appropriate to deal with it in these other contexts.

By focusing on only those specific models and myths which have had the greatest impact on the ways in which Canadian sociologists — and, particularly, Anglo-Canadian sociologists — have gone about the task of describing and analyzing their society, we hope to have been able to convey a more varied and fine-grained picture of the field than those provided by conventional texts. We hope, moreover, that the kind of critical approach taken here will enable people who are new to the discipline to see Canadian sociology as a living entity — as a dynamic series of research areas and theory groups — rather than a fixed and rigid collection of ideas set down by experts. If we have succeeded in doing this, and if readers are able to glean a richer image of Canadian society from the varied perspectives and styles of work presented here, then this book will have served the purpose for which it was created.

NOTES

[1]This situation was partially a result of sheer numbers — there were only 32 sociologists in Canada in 1956-57 — and partially a consequence of an Anglo-Canadian pattern of burying sociology inside combined social science departments. At the University of Toronto, in particular, this meant that a range of sub-disciplines did not develop until the 1960s. See Dennis Forcese and Stephen Richer, "Social Issues and Sociology in Canada," in Forcese and Richer, 1975:449-66; Hiller, 1982: 3-39.

[2]See especially Innis, 1930; Innis, 1940; Innis, 1971; Innis, 1956. For an excellent biographical account of Innis' contributions to the development of Canadian social science, see Creighton, 1957.

[3]von Zur Mehlen, 1977; Hiller, 1982: 33.

[4]For a discussion of the issues involved, see Baldus, et al., 1974; Felt, 1975. Watson, 1975, argues that this position is, numerically at least, the one adopted by the Anglo-Canadian "mainstream." The use of the term "paradigm" here follows Kuhn, 1970, in which he refers to codifications of social theory and research practice which "provide model problems and solutions to a body of practitioners." (Kuhn, 1970: viii.)

[5]Note that this definition of "Canadian sociology" excludes sociology as practiced in Quebec. This is the position which seems to undergird the argument in Clark, 1973, and Clark, 1975. Keyfitz, 1974, echoes many of the same sentiments when he argues that Canadians ought to focus on the social facts which make them "dif-

ferent" from their American cousins. This is a strange argument from Keyfitz, given his distinguished career in pursuit of scientific sociology. Can one be a positivist and a "Canadian exceptionalist" at the same time? As Rokeach observes in his commentary, Keyfitz is conflicted on the issue.

[6]By these terms he meant a tendency to either deal entirely in vague abstractions or examine empirical relationships without appropriate attention to theory. See Mills, 1959.

[7]For a more complete account of this issue, see Hiller, 1982: 36-39; Symons, 1975; CAUT, 1974; Shugarman and Butler, 1970; Crowley, 1971; Mathews and Steele, 1969.

[8]Hiller, 1982: xi; Felt, 1975: 382-83; Tepperman, 1978:435-37.

[9]Clark and other commentators attribute the relatively slow acceptance of sociology by Anglo-Canadian universities to British influence and, especially, to the strong emphasis in English universities on history and historical interpretations of current trends. See Clark, 1973; Hiller 1982. This explanation is not entirely adequate, however, since McGill — the only Anglo-Canadian university to develop an autonomous sociology department around the time they were being formed in the United States — was no less subject to British influence than the others. Hiller probably comes closer to the mark when he suggests that a combination of forces was at work — not the least of these being the strength of the political economy tradition at the University of Toronto and the central role which Toronto has played in setting the tone for the Anglo-Canadian academic hinterland. (Hiller, 1982: 15-17.)

[10]Tepperman, 1978: 435.

[11]In the 1973-74 academic year, more than a third of the faculty in sociology at the University of Toronto did not hold a doctorate.

[12]Tepperman, 1978: 435.

[13]See note 4.

[14]For a more complete discussion of the forces shaping periods in the development of Canadian sociology, see Hiller, 1982.

[15]Tepperman, 1978, notes a resurgence of interest in what he terms "the Innis 'staples approach'." But he also notes that, at the same time, little new concrete work had been done within that perspective beyond some articles included in Glenday, Guindon, and Turowetz, 1978. In referring to Innis et al. in this fashion, of course, he is employing an extremely limited definition of the Toronto School and its potential influence. See Drache, 1976. Bell and Tepperman, 1979, certainly reflects this tradition in its concern for political culture and in its search for the forces shaping national character. Clark, 1976, and Clark, 1978, are, if nothing else, exemplars of the Toronto School as it was transmitted to sociology by Clark himself. And many of the writings of the Carleton School, briefly referred to by Tepperman, show Innis's hand far more clearly than any other. Part of the difficulty here, of course, lies in the fact that, when a particular perspective has dominated an intellectual milieu for decades, its influence becomes so persuasive that it almost becomes invisible. For a further discussion of this issue, see S. D. Berkowitz, "Canadian Corporate Structure and Elites: Some Notes on the State of the Art," in Mizruchi and Schwartz, forthcoming a.

[16]This may change. As we will see in the chapters that follow, during the last decade researchers in a variety of sub-disciplines have been preoccupied with gathering certain kinds of basic information. At the point where at least a crude map of the social world exists, there should be more room for developing and refining interpretations of it — and, hence, methodology. There is evidence for this trend in Canadian studies of interlocking directorships and a few other areas.

[17]This account focuses on developments in English Canada for two reasons. First, the bulk of the literature described in succeeding chapters is in English. For unilingual readers, it is the most relevant. Second, the developmental histories of French and English Canadian sociology are so different that it would require much more space than we have available here to deal with both thoroughly. Thus, this review essay will only refer to Quebecois sociology when this is necessary for comparative purposes. Works cited here, however, will allow interested readers to fill in this gap.

[18]See, for example, Breton, 1964; Reitz, 1980.

[19]See, for example, Tepperman, 1978.

[20]See Berkowitz, 1982.

[21]E.g., Brym, 1978.

[22]See Kuhn, 1970, for the classic statement of the developmental logic of scientific specialty groups.

[23]Mullins, 1973.

[24]Mullins, 1968; Mullins, 1971; Mullins, 1973; Crane, 1969.

[25]von Zur Mehlen, 1977, as summarized in Hiller, 1982: 174.

[26]Mullins, 1973: 22-25.

[27]Speculatively at least, this ministry-like mechanism for building faculties accounts for the observably greater homogeneity in the quality of Canadian universities as compared with those in the United States. As a rule, Canadian university faculties tend to be — to use their favorite term — competent. But peaks of excellence are hard to find. By contrast, both peaks and troughs are present in great numbers in the United States.

[28]This reluctance — or inability — to train graduate students had a critical impact on the form taken by Canadian social science since training of students has historically been the mechanism through which theory groups are able to most effectively propagate their ideas.

[29]Hiller, 1982, provides an excellent summary of these early developments.

[30]Crane, 1969, and Crane, 1972, provide the best descriptions of the invisible college hypothesis. Also note that this phenomenon was not peculiar to sociology: see C. B. Macpherson, "After Strange Gods: Canadian Political Science 1973," in Guinsberg and Reuber, 1974. Also see C. B. Macpherson, "The Social Sciences," in Park, 1957.

[31]von Zur Mehlen reports that between 1956-57 and 1969-70 the proportion of Canadian faculty employed at the University of Toronto had decreased from 20% to 9.9%, despite increases in Toronto's faculty during that same period. See von Zur Mehlen, 1977.

[32]See Falardeau, 1967.

[33]See Falardeau, 1975. Some commentators attribute the very different courses followed by sociology in Québec and the rest of Canada to the differential influence of the French and British academic traditions, respectively, during a period of "European transference" (Hiller, 1982). Yet there is abundant evidence that Québécois sociologists have, historically, been able to draw upon theoretical and substantive work going on in the United States while incorporating it into their own genre in unique ways. Note, for instance, the impact of Everett Hughes' research or Horace Miner's study of St. Denis on sociology as practiced at francophone universities. Also note the impact of Jacques Dofny and other Québécois sociologists on areas of research in the United States. Thus, while Québec drew far fewer of its faculty from the United States during the build-up period than English Canada, the proportion of citations to American authors in its journals tends to be high: 33.5%.

But citations to Canadian sources — many, we may assume, Québécois — are even larger: 46%. See Fournier, 1974. A further analysis of citation data over a longer time period suggests that structural similarities between Québécois and American sociology probably promoted communication, while structural differences retarded communication with English Canada. See Berkowitz, forthcoming b.

[34]See, for example, Rotstein and Lax, 1972; Watkins, 1977; Craven, 1980; Laxer, 1973; Laxer, 1981.

[35]See Hutcheson, 1982-83, as an exemplar of the use of the Innis tradition as motif for discussions of this kind.

[36]Craven, 1980.

[37]See Clement, 1975; Clement, 1977; Panitch, 1977.

[38]Porter, 1965.

[39]See Naylor, 1972. Also see MacDonald, 1975. Richardson, 1982, provides an empirical critique of Naylor's "merchants against industry" model.

[40]See Mannheim, 1958.

[41]See Almond and Verba, 1965.

[42]Haas and Shaffir, 1978, provides good examples of the applications of this framework to Canadian issues.

[43]Hardin, 1974; Grant, 1970; Smiley, 1976.

[44]For a lucid and definitive statement of the functionalist position, see Merton, 1968: 73-136.

[45]See Merton, 1968: 79-91.

[46]Hagan, 1977; Coser, 1956.

[47]The term "modernization" itself, of course, derives from and implies the functionalist paradigm.

[48]Marsden and Harvey, 1979: 61.

[49]Ramu, 1979.

[50]Porter, 1965.

[51]For an interesting collection of articles which allows readers to compare these variants, see Blau and Merton, 1981.

[52]Berkowitz, 1982: vii.

[53]INSNA is the International Network for Social Network Analysis. *Connections* is edited by Barry Wellman and other members of the Structural Analysis Programme.

[54]For summaries of this work, see Berkowitz, 1982; Berkowitz and Wellman, forthcoming. Also see Lorrain, 1975.

[55]See Ossenberg, 1971.

[56]Fowke, 1957.

[57]Frank, 1969.

[58]A. K. Davis, "Canadian Society and History as Hinterland Versus Metropolis," in Ossenberg, 1971.

[59]In addition to Davis, 1971, see McCrorie, 1965.

[60]Ossenberg, 1980.

[61]Schutz, 1962; Schutz, 1964; Schutz, 1966.

[62]McHugh, 1968.

[63]Under Scottish criminal law, juries have this option in addition to the traditional ones of guilty and not guilty.

Bibliography

Almond, Gabriel and Sidney Verba. *The Civic Culture.* Boston: Little, Brown, 1965.

Baldus, B., S. Berkowitz, P. Craven, L. Felt, and J. Wayne. "Manifesto for a Relevant Canadian Sociology." Mimeograph. Toronto: Department of Sociology, 1974.

Bell, David and Lorne Tepperman. *The Roots of Disunity: A Look At Canadian Political Culture.* Toronto: McClelland and Stewart, 1979.

Berkowitz, S. D. *An Introduction to Structural Analysis.* Toronto: Butterworths, 1982.

_____. "Canadian Corporate Structure and Elites: Some Notes on the State of the Art." In Mark Mizruchi and Michael Schwartz, *The Structural Analysis of Business.* NY: Academic, forthcoming a.

_____. "Harry Hiller, *Society and Change: S. D. Clark and the Development of Canadian Sociology.*" Review in *American Journal of Canadian Studies,* forthcoming b.

Berkowitz, S. D. and Barry Wellman, eds. *Structural Sociology.* Cambridge and New York: Cambridge University Press, forthcoming.

Blau, Peter and Robert K. Merton, eds. *Continuities in Structural Inquiry.* Beverly Hills: Sage, 1981.

Breton, Albert. "The Economics of Nationalism." *Journal of Political Economy* 72 (1964): 376-86.

Brym, Robert. *The Jewish Intelligentsia and Russian Marxism.* London: Macmillan, 1978.

Card, B. Y. *The Expanding Relation: Sociology in Prairie Universities.* Regina: Canadian Plains Research Center, 1975.

CAUT, *CAUT Bulletin.* 22 (1974).

Clark, S. D. "The American Takeover of Canadian Sociology: Myth or Reality." *Dalhousie Review* 53 (1973): 205-18.

_____. "Sociology in Canada: an Historical Overview." *Canadian Journal of Sociology* 1 (1975): 225-34.

_____. *Canadian Society in Historical Perspective.* Toronto: McGraw-Hill Ryerson, 1976.

_____. *The New Urban Poor.* McGraw-Hill Ryerson, 1978.

Clement, Wallace. *The Canadian Corporate Elite.* Toronto: McClelland and Stewart, 1975.

_____. *Continental Corporate Power.* Toronto: McClelland and Stewart, 1977.

Coser, Lewis. *The Functions of Social Conflict.* Glencoe: The Free Press, 1956.

Crane, Diana. "Social Structure in a Group of Scientists: A Test of the 'Invisible College' Hypothesis." *American Sociological Review* 34 (1969): 335-52.

_____. *Invisible Colleges.* Chicago: University of Chicago Press, 1972.

Craven, Paul. *'An Impartial Umpire': Industrial Relations and the Canadian State, 1900-1911.* Toronto: University of Toronto Press, 1980.

Creighton, Donald. *Harold Adams Innis: Portrait of A Scholar.* Toronto: University of Toronto Press, 1957.

Crowley, Terence. "Anti-Americanism and the Degeneration of Canadian Scholarship: A Rejoinder." *Journal of Canadian Studies* 6 (1971): 51-58.

Davis, A. K. "Canadian Society and History as Hinterland Versus Metropolis." In Richard Ossenberg, ed. *Canadian Society: Pluralism, Change, and Conflict.* Scarborough, Ontario: Prentice-Hall Canada, 1971.

Drache, Daniel. "Rediscovering Canadian Political Economy." *Journal of Canadian Studies* 11 (1976): 3-18.

Falardeau, Jean-Charles. *The Rise of Social Sciences in French Canada.* Quebec: Department of Cultural Affairs, 1967.

_____., ed. *La Sociologie au Québec.* Québec: PUL, 1975.

Felt, Lawrence. "Nationalism and the Possibility of a Relevant Anglo-Canadian Sociology." *Canadian Journal of Sociology* 1 (1975): 377-79.

Forcese, Dennis and Stephen Richer. "Social Issues and Sociology in Canada." In Dennis Forcese and Stephen Richer, eds. *Issues in Canadian Society: An Introduction to Sociology.* Scarborough, Ont.: Prentice-Hall, 1975.

_____. *Issues in Canadian Society: An Introduction to Sociology.* Scarborough, Ont.: Prentice-Hall, 1975.

Fournier, Marcel. "La Sociologie Quebecois Contemporaine." *Recherches Sociographiques* 15 (1974): 167-200.

Fowke, Vernon. *The National Policy and the Wheat Economy.* Toronto: University of Toronto Press, 1957.

Frank, Andre Gunder. *Latin America: Underdevelopment or Revolution.* New York: Monthly Review Press, 1969.

Glenday, Daniel, Hubert Guindon, and Allan Turowetz, eds. *Modernization and the Canadian State.* Toronto: Macmillan of Canada, 1978.

Grant, George. *Lament for A Nation.* Toronto: McClelland and Stewart, 1970.

Haas, Jack and William Shaffir, eds. *Shaping Identity in Canadian Society.* Scarborough, Ontario: Prentice-Hall Canada, 1978.

Hagan, John. *The Disreputable Pleasures.* Toronto: McGraw-Hill Ryerson, 1977.

Hardin, Herschel. *A Nation Unaware.* Vancouver: J. J. Douglas, 1974.

Hiller, Harry H. *Society and Change: S. D. Clark and the Development of Canadian Sociology.* Toronto: University of Toronto Press, 1982.

Hutcheson, John. "Harold Innis and the Unity and Diversity of Confederation." *Journal of Canadian Studies* 17 (1982-83): 57-73.

Innis, Harold A. *The Cod Fisheries: The History of An International Economy.* New Haven: Yale University Press, 1940.

_____. *Essays in Canadian Economic History.* Edited by Mary Quayle Innis. Toronto: University of Toronto Press, 1956.

_____. *The Fur Trade in Canada.* New Haven: Yale University Press, 1930.

_____. *A History of the Canadian Pacific Railway.* Toronto: University of Toronto Press, 1971.

Keyfitz, Nathan. "Sociology and Canadian Society." In T. N. Guinsberg and G. L. Reuber, eds. *Perspectives on the Social Sciences in Canada.* Toronto: University of Toronto Press, 1974.

Kuhn, Thomas S. *The Structure of Scientific Revolutions.* 2d ed. Chicago: University of Chicago Press, 1970.

Laxer, James. *Canada's Economic Strategy.* Toronto: McClelland and Stewart, 1981.

Laxer, Robert, ed. *(Canada) Ltd.: The Political Economy of Dependency.* Toronto:

McClelland and Stewart, 1973.

Lorrain, François. *Reseaux Sociaux et Classifications Sociales.* Paris: Hermann, 1975.

McCrorie, James N. *In Union Is Strength,* Saskatoon: Saskatchewan Farmers Union, 1965.

MacDonald, L. R. "Merchants Against Industry: An Idea and Its Origins." *Canadian Historical Review* 56 (1975): 263-81.

McHugh, Peter. *The Organization of Meaning in Social Interaction.* Indianapolis: Bobbs-Merrill, 1968.

Macpherson, C. B. "After Strange Gods: Canadian Political Science 1973." In T. N. Guinsberg and G. L. Reuber, eds. *Perspectives on the Social Sciences in Canada.* Toronto: University of Toronto Press, 1974.

_____. "The Social Sciences." In Julian Park, ed. *The Culture of Contemporary Canada.* Ithaca, N.Y.: Cornell University Press, 1965.

Mannheim, Karl. *Ideology and Utopia.* New York: Harcourt Brace, 1936.

Marchak, Pat. *Ideological Perspectives on Canada.* Toronto: McGraw-Hill Ryerson, 1975.

Marsden, Lorna and Edward Harvey. *Fragile Federation: Social Change in Canada.* Toronto: McGraw-Hill Ryerson, 1979.

Mathews, Robin and James Steele. *The Struggle for Canadian Universities.* Toronto: New Press, 1969.

Merton, Robert K. *Social Theory and Social Structure.* New York: Free Press, 1968.

Mills, C. Wright. *The Sociological Imagination.* New York: Oxford University Press, 1959.

Mullins, Nicholas C. "The Distribution of Social and Cultural Properties in Informal Communication Networks Among Biological Scientists." *American Sociological Review* 33 (1968): 786-97.

_____. *The Art of Theory: Construction and Use.* New York: Harper and Row, 1971.

_____. *Theories and Theory Groups in Contemporary American Sociology.* New York: Harper and Row, 1973.

Naylor, R. T. "The Rise and Fall of the Third Commercial Empire of the St. Lawrence." In Gary Teeple, ed. *Capitalism and the National Question in Canada.* Toronto: University of Toronto Press, 1972.

Ossenberg, Richard J., ed. *Canadian Society: Pluralism, Change, and Conflict.* Scarborough, Ontario: Prentice-Hall Canada, 1971.

_____. ed. *Power and Change in Canada.* Toronto: McClelland and Stewart, 1980.

Panitch, Leo, ed. *The Canadian State: Political Economy and Political Power.* Toronto: University of Toronto Press, 1977.

Park, Julian, ed. *The Culture of Contemporary Canada.* Ithaca, N.Y.: Cornell University Press, 1957.

Porter, John. *The Vertical Mosaic.* Toronto: University of Toronto Press, 1965.

Pullman, Douglas R. "Roadside Notes: Establishing Sociology at the University of New Brunswick." Paper Presented at the Annual Meetings of the CSAA, Toronto, 1974.

Ramu, G. N., ed. *Courtship, Marriage and the Family in Canada.* Toronto: Macmillan of Canada, 1979.

Reitz, J. G. *The Survival of Ethnic Groups.* Toronto: McGraw-Hill Ryerson, 1980.

Richardson, R. J. "'Merchants Against Industry': An Empircal Study of the

Canadian Debate." *Canadian Journal of Sociology* 7 (1982): 279-95.

Rotstein, Abraham and Gary Lax, eds. *Independence: The Canadian Challenge.* Toronto: Committee for An Independent Canada, 1972.

Schutz, Alfred. *Collected Papers.* Edited by Maurice Natanson. The Hague: M. Nijhoff, 1962-66.

Shugarman, David and Michael Butler. "Canadian Nationalism, Americanization and Scholarly Values." *Journal of Canadian Studies* 5 (1970): 12-27.

Smiley, Donald. *Canada in Question.* 2d. ed. Toronto: McGraw-Hill Ryerson, 1976.

Symons, T. H. B. *To Know Ourselves: The Report of the Commission on Canadian Studies.* Ottawa: Association of Universities and Colleges in Canada, 1975.

Tepperman, Lorne. "Sociology in English-speaking Canada: The Last Five Years." *Canadian Historical Review* 59 (1978): 435-46.

von Zur Mehlen, Max. "The Full-time Faculty of Canadian Universities." Mimeographed. Ottawa: Statistics Canada, 1977.

Watkins, Mel. "The Staple Theory Revisited." *Journal of Canadian Studies* 12 (1977): 83-95.

Watson, G. Llewelyn. "The Poverty of Sociology in a Changing Canadian Society." *Canadian Journal of Sociology* 3 (1975): 345-62.

CHAPTER 2

Social Movements and Third Parties

Robert J. Brym

INTRODUCTION

Scores of collective attempts have been made — by farmers, workers, women, adherents of particular religions, ethnic traditions, and regional loyalties — to alter the conditions of social life in Canada. How can one assess in a short chapter the vast sociologically relevant literature on these protests against the *status quo?* In order to hone the task to manageable proportions I have chosen to discuss only those movements that have been (a) institutionalized as political parties closely aligned with neither the Liberals nor Progressive Conservatives; and (b) analyzed within at least one of the two major theoretical traditions that purport to explain political protest in this country. In the course of reviewing the application of these two theories I hope to show that one of them cannot adequately answer the questions it has raised while the second, although much more satisfactory in this regard, is still marred by several important conceptual flaws.

THE CULTURAL/INSTITUTIONAL APPROACH

It has frequently been asserted (and, with varying degrees of rigor, demonstrated) that the major federal political cleavages in Canada are based on region and ethnicity, not class: different parties are generally distinguished from one another by the degree to which they are supported by Maritimers or Westerners, francophones or anglophones, not working class or upper class people. Indeed, even by the most generous estimates,[1] Canada ranks, along with the U.S., as the country with the lowest class vote in the western world.

But the Canadian party system is also different from the American in many crucial respects, one of which I want particularly to emphasize here: third parties tend to be formed more frequently, exhibit greater longevity, and exercise more of an impact north of the 49th parallel. The U.S. has, and for a very long time has had, only the Democratic and Republican parties. Canada, in addition to its two 'establishment' parties, Liberal and Progressive Conservative, has the NDP and the Social Credit party, both of which originated as political protest movements.

In a highly influential work, Gad Horowitz (1968) has sought to explain, in cultural and institutional terms, why this is so. Specifically Horowitz asks why Canada has, in the NDP, a democratic-socialist party, while the U.S. does not. He locates the answer in the relatively unique clusters of beliefs, symbols, and values that were inherited from Europe and that congealed to form the political cultures of the two North American countries; and in the different electoral systems of the two countries.

Consider first the cultural side of his argument. Modifying somewhat a line of reasoning originally proposed by Louis Hartz and Kenneth McRae,[2] Horowitz asserts that American political culture was forged out of liberalism pure and simple; while that of Canada is an alloy, comprising, in addition to dominant liberal ideas, a strong admixture of toryism. Now liberalism and toryism conceive of society, and of people's relationships to society, in very different ways. Toryism maintains that, ideally, society is a real corporate entity consisting of hierarchically ordered classes, and that people's positions in the class system are relatively fixed once they enter certain classes at birth. Liberalism maintains that, ideally, society is simply a nominal agglomeration of individuals whose social locations are not fixed but determined by equality of opportunity, which allows them to rise (or fall) to a station that matches their natural capacities to succeed (or fail) in life.

Obviously, liberalism is the more radical and democratic set of ideas. It was in fact an important weapon in the fight of the thirteen American colonies against tory England — a fight that culminated in the American revolution. Not that all Americans subscribed to liberalism, notes Horowitz. As we know, some remained loyal to England and fled to British North America in the late eighteenth century. Moreover, almost a million, presumably non-liberal, Britons immigrated to British North America between 1815 and 1850. Thus, although Canada's political culture is most heavily indebted to liberalism, some toryism was firmly implanted on Canadian soil by the Loyalists and subsequent British immigrants.

What does all this have to do with the greater receptivity of Canada to democratic-socialist parties? Simply that, according to Horowitz, socialism can appear only where there is a history of liberalism *and* toryism. Socialism is, after all, an amalgam and extension of the egalitarian impulse contained in liberalism and the corporatist view of society contained in toryism. Its egalitarianism is evident in its insistence that, if true equality is to be achieved, equality of opportunity must be augmented by an equal distribution of those resources necessary to take advantage of available opportunities. Its corporatism is evident in its insistence that these resources can be more evenly distributed only if society as a whole has as its principal concern the welfare of its members and therefore takes the leading role in resource distribution. If, as in the U.S., liberalism is the only available set of political ideas, the socialist amalgam cannot develop since there exists no source of corporatist belief. If, as in Canada, strands of both liberalism and toryism are woven into the fabric of political culture, there exist sources of both egalitarianism and corporatism, so democratic-socialism can emerge.

In many essential respects this argument informs the work of the other major representative of the cultural/institutional school of thought, Seymour Martin Lipset.[3] Lipset, however, adds to Horowitz's theory by citing a number of formative historical events that reinforced the tory tendencies of Canada's political culture, and thus the likelihood of a democratic-socialist movement eventually being created. Following S. D. Clark[4] and others, Lipset notes that the U.S.'s failure to annex Canada in the war of 1812 represented a second defeat for liberalism in British North America (the first being the inability of the American Revolution to spread northward in 1776). Again, the 1837 rebellions in Upper and Lower Canada — movements of liberal democracy — were put down, and this entrenched still more deeply the values of toryism. For Lipset, then, Canada's counter-revolutionary tradition is patent. Like Horowitz, he can thus conclude that the value system of Canada, insofar as it contains elements of both liberalism and toryism, explains well the ideological content of at least its most important third parties, such as the United Farmers of Alberta, the CCF, and the NDP.

But, it must be emphasized, this is supposed to explain only the ideological content of some third parties, not the frequency with which they have been formed. How do Horowitz and Lipset account for the fact that the rate of third party formation is higher in Canada than in the U.S.? By examining the different political-institutional contexts within which social movements are constrained to operate: the American electoral system, they contend, makes it excedingly difficult for political protest movements to become institutionalised as third parties, while Canada's facilitates third party formation.

Two aspects of the Canadian and U.S. electoral systems appear to be particularly important in this regard. First, in Canada there is only one elective political arena at the provincial and federal levels — the legislatures — and seats in these legislatures are filled on a constituency-by-constituency basis. But in the U.S., aside from contests for state legislatures and the federal Congress, elections are also held for the executive branch of government — for governorships and the presidency — and these elections are state- or nation-wide. Thus, in a Canadian constituency in which radicals are highly concentrated it 'pays' to vote for a radical candidate since he or she stands a good chance of winning and therefore influencing government policy in the legislature. In voting for state governors or the President however, Americans must take into account the political complexion of a very large social unit that inevitably contains diverse interests, so that voting for a third party candidate is almost bound to be perceived as a wasted vote. In short, the separation of legislative from executive authority in the U.S. militates against the success of third parties, while Canada's centralized parliamentary government is conducive to their success.

A second way in which electoral systems affect third party strength has to do with the fact that the British parliamentary principle of party loyalty operates in Canada but not in the United States. In both state legislatures and the U.S. Congress, representatives vote according to their individual views as these are shaped by the desires of the people who support and elect them, and this is no way endangers the tenure of the administration. In Canada, disputes within a party are resolved in caucus, and once the representatives leave caucus and enter the legislature they are obliged to vote as a bloc: if the representatives of a governing party fail to do so they may very well cause the downfall of the government. In Canada, interests that are not satisfied with the policies of the existing parties thus have little alternative other than forming a third party. In the U.S., diverse interests can be accommodated within existing parties without major difficulties.

CRITIQUE

The most serious criticisms of the cultural/institutional theory include the following:
   (a) The content of Canadian political culture is not what Horowitz and Lipset take it to be.
   (b) Their theory does not make it clear when and why Canadian political culture congealed as it did.
   (c) Variations within Canada in the rate of third party formation and in the content of third party ideologies cannot be explained by the theory.

Criticism (a) is based, in the first place, on Horowitz's and Lipset's willingness to accept what is often called the 'tory myth'.[5] It is questionable that the Loyalists who came to British North American in the wake of the American Revolution, and who were supposedly responsible for injecting a substantial dose of toryism into Canadian political culture, were in fact tories. There had never been a strong tory tradition in the thirteen American colonies: without an entrenched aristocracy, American colonial life could not inculcate the respect for organic collectivism that, according to Horowitz and Lipset, must be present for democratic-socialism to develop at a later historical juncture. So it makes little sense to talk about the transmission of tory ideas northward. The Loyalists were not so much tories as people who had been bound up in one way or another with the colonial administrative apparatus, and what they transmitted northward was less tory culture than a reinforcement of British political intervention in North American affairs. If the British connection has had an influence on political life in Canada — and there can be little doubt that it has — this has more often involved the shaping of our political institutions and habits by British-connected ruling groups than it has the sympathetic and spontaneous evolution of tory values among Canadians.

If we push the story ahead a couple of centuries we continue to find evidence that Canadian political culture is less indebted to toryism than Horowitz and Lipset would have us believe. For example, one political scientist has developed a toryism-conservatism scale, applied it to samples of American and Canadian university undergraduates, and found that the Americans scored as high or higher than the Canadians: precisely the opposite of what the Horowitz-Lipset thesis would lead us to expect.[6] Two other political scientists[7] have shown that Progressive Conservative legislators in Ontario are no more collectivist in orientation than legislators in the Liberal party or the NDP. Since Horowitz[8] claims that the PC party is the "primary carrier" of toryism in Canada, this finding directly contradicts his argument. A social psychologist surveyed Canadian and American university students and discovered "no support... for Lipset's hypothesis."[9] Finally, two sociologists[10] report that in a survey conducted in one American and one Canadian town, Canadian respondents scored significantly *lower* on collectivity-orientation than the Americans.[11] While these studies may not be representative of the whole population and their measurement instruments may be imperfect, they do at least establish that there is no compelling reason to believe that toryism exists in Canada to a degree that would have a bearing on our receptivity to democratic-socialism.

The second major criticism of the cultural/institutional argument concerns the notion of congealment. It is a central thesis of Horowitz's book that, at a certain historical moment, Canadian political culture took on a relatively fixed form. But when did this happen? And why? Horowitz equivocates in answering the first of these questions and is silent on the second.

Horowitz originally[12] admitted that it was very difficult to "put one's finger on the point" when toryism and liberalism congealed. He suggested that congealment may have occurred at the time of the Loyalist migration, or when the million British immigrants came to Canada, or indeed not until British trade unionists with socialist ideas immigrated here in the late nineteenth and early twentieth centuries. But this argument left Horowitz open to the charge of equivocation: how could it be true that Canada's political culture stopped developing *and* that it has always assimilated new ideas from immigrants?[13] Nor did it help matters much when Horowitz[14] subsequently asserted that Canadian political culture has *always* been sufficiently congealed around tory ideas to enable new socialist ideas to 'fit' better here than in the United States. For our political culture, like any historical product, must have had origins in time. In short, it seems undeniable that no once-and-for-all congealment has occurred, and that waves of immigrants have been at least partly responsible for the continuous shaping of Canadian political culture.[15]

This is not to deny that some elements of Canadian political culture have become dominant. But if one wanted to know why, it would be necessary to leave aside the concern that Horowitz and Lipset have expressed with mass cultural values as causal agents and examine issues of power: how ruling groups of British origin, through their control over property, police, communications media, etc., have created a more or less general view of the world in their own image. But more of this later. For the moment let us move on to the third main criticism of the cultural/institutional theory.

Several scholars have pointed out that neither the supposedly strong trace of toryism in Canadian political culture, nor the adoption by Canada of the British parliamentary system of government, can explain variations within Canada in the rate of third party formation or in the ideological content of third parties.[16] According to Horowitz and Lipset, where toryism approaches parity with liberalism as a cultural influence, democratic-socialism will be strongest. Hence Canada has a stronger democratic-socialist tradition than the U.S. It follows that in those Canadian provinces where toryism is generaly regarded as strongest — such as New Brunswick, which was founded by the Loyalists and has experienced so little in-migration that there have been few new ideological influences brought in via this route — one would also expect a strong democratic-socialist tradition. But of course New Brunswick has one of the lowest rates of third party formation in the country. In its entire history it has elected only one federal third-party representative. In the other Atlantic provinces, also commonly regarded as bastions of toryism, there has been a similar rate of third-party formation. Even Ontario, with its strong Loyalist and British heritage, has, with the exception of a brief period in the 1920s, failed to produce a strong contingent of third-party candidates, especially at the federal level. Federal and provincial third parties have gleaned their greatest support in the ethnically heterogeneous Prairie provinces, in British Columbia, and more recently, in Québec. This, together with the fact that our parliamentary system exists in all provinces, and therefore cannot, logically, be the explanation for inter-provincial variations in support for third parties, leads inescapably to the conclusion that the cultural/institutional approach is of no value whatsoever in explaining differences among the provinces in rates of political protest.

The same holds true for variations over time. Protest movements in Canada have tended to come in waves — farmer and labor parties emerged almost everywhere from 1919-1925, right-wing populism and nationalism spread in Alberta and Québec in the second half of the 1930s, democratic-socialism in the form of the CCF made considerable progress in most parts of the country in the 1940s, and nationalist movements on the right and, even more so, on the left, came to the fore in Québec in the 1960s and especially in the 1970s. Again, constants (congealed values, the parliamentary system) cannot explain a variable (changes over time in the rate of third-party formation).

Mention of this diversity of ideologies prompts us to recognize yet another weakness of the cultural institutional thesis: it is one-sided in that it concentrates mainly on non-nationalistic, democratic-socialist parties. Yet right-wing populism, in the form of the Social Credit party of Alberta, or left-wing nationalism, in the form of the Parti Québécois, or right-of-center nationalism, in the form of l'Action Libérale Nationale, were or are important and established facts of Canadian political life. A theory that comes close to equating third parties with only the left-wing, non-nationalist variety leaves a great deal outside its explanatory ambit.

This shortcoming — and most of the others noted above — ultimately stem from the undue emphasis that Horowitz and Lipset place upon mass values as causes of political behaviour. However recent research demonstrates that mass values have only the most diffuse effect on the number and policies of political parties in Canada. For example, a study of politics in Atlantic Canada has shown that in the 1960s electors were more dissatisfied with political life than electors elsewhere in the country, yet they did not form any new parties to reflect their interests.[17] Several other studies have shown that, though electors may believe parties differ from one another in their policies on biculturalism, trade and resources, foreign affairs, and the distribution of wealth, the fact is that whichever party is in power, at both federal and provincial levels, does not affect government actions very much at all.[18] After reviewing much of the relevant literature, one political scientist was forced by the weight of evidence to conclude that "citizen attitudes, and the structures through which they are expressed, either do not have the influence on policy outcomes which they are thought to have, or they have an impact which is independent of any political intentions by the public expressing them."[19]

But if values do not determine the number and policies of parties to any significant degree, what does? In order to begin formulating an answer let us turn to the second major theory of third party formation.

THE STRUCTURAL APPROACH

The second theory I want to discuss may be termed structural in the sense that it locates the chief cause of third-party formation in Canada in concrete patterns of social, economic and political relations — not in the formal properties of political institutions or in the realm of culture. The theory is most closely associated with the names of C. B. Macpherson and Maurice Pinard.

Macpherson's[20] analysis of the Social Credit party in Alberta stresses two factors that led to the party's rise to power in 1935: the nature of Alberta's class structure and the relationship between its economy and eastern Canadian economic forces. Macpherson describes the class structure as essentially "petit bourgeois," by which he means that the largest class in the province consisted of farmers who owned comparatively small amounts of property. He describes the economic system as "quasi-colonial," by which he means that control over its major features was, especially through national tariff and transportation policies, exercised by capitalist interests in the East. The fact that the class structure was relatively homogeneous meant that most people in the province faced the same kinds of economic problems, had the same interests and were aware of them. The fact that small property owners constituted the major class meant that political protest was populist: unlike the socialism of propertyless workers, it supported capitalism, and unlike the liberalism typical of large property owners it pitted the "little man" against the evils of a plutocratic system. Finally, the fact that the economy was quasi-colonial meant that there was a highly visible enemy in the east which could be perceived as the major source of the population's disadvantaged position. In other words, there was a high degree of social cohesion *within* the major disadvantaged class and a high degree of segmentation *between* that class and external powers. This facilitated the emergence of a political party clearly expressing these views.

Macpherson undoubtedly over-emphasises the homogeneity of Alberta's class structure and fails to account for the emergence of different types of populist ideology in different Prairie provinces.[21] But it must also be noted that his work stimulated Maurice Pinard[22] to develop an account of the rise of the Quebec Social Credit party in the 1962 federal election that generalizes this argument to the point where Pinard is able to proffer an explanation that covers most cases of third-party formation in Canada. Cleavage between a quasi-colonial economy and a dominant, metropolitan economy is, Pinard submits, not the only form of social segmentation that is conducive to the rise of third parties. In fact, virtually any significant cleavage — between social classes, between ethnic groups, etc. — will suffice. Moreover, class homogeneity and solidarity among potential participants in a third party is not the only form of social cohesion that facilitates political protest. Strong social attachments among members of any disadvantaged group — through voluntary organizations, face-to-face contacts in small communities, common work contexts, etc. — will have much the same effect. Finally (and this is more an addition to, than a generalization from, Macpherson's study) a system of one-party dominance facilitates the rise of third parties. This last point requires elaboration.

When Pinard speaks of one-party dominance he refers to a situation where one of the two establishment parties receives less than a third of the vote for some considerable period of time, or where it suddenly has lost popular support as a consequence of, say, the revelation of flagrant corruption among party officials. In either case, only one of the establishment parties has a chance of forming the government. When seriously aggrieved segments of a population face a choice between a dominant establishment party and a very weak establishment party, they will be inclined to vote for neither. The dominant party is too closely identified with the sources of the population's grievances and the other establishment party is not seen as a realistic alternative since it is so weak. A third, alternative party is then likely to emerge.

Pinard claims that the importance of one-party dominance in accounting for the rise of third parties can scarcely be exaggerated. Thus, in 88 per cent of 33 provincial elections where the main opposition party was strong and received more than a third of the vote, third parties received 20 per cent of the vote or less. In 59 per cent of 22 provincial elections where the main opposition party was chronically weak and received less than a third of the vote, more than 20 per cent of the ballots were cast for the third party. And in 90 per cent of 10 provincial elections where the main opposition party was 'suddenly weak,' third parties received more than 20 per cent of the vote.

In a subsequent article, Pinard[23] made it clear that one-party dominance is in fact only one variant of a more general set of conditions that are conducive to the rise of third parties: the non-representation of social groups through the party system. That is to say, a strong, two-party or even multi-party system can fail as miserably as a system of one-party dominance in providing channels of expression and representation for aggrieved groups, and so may give rise to third parties. This may occur, for example, in times of crisis when establishment parties form a coalition, thereby preventing large groups which oppose the government from gaining representation. Or (and here Pinard agrees with the cultural/institutional theorists) it may happen more frequently when a party system is organized along British parliamentary lines and consequently inhibits the accommodation of diverse interests within existing parties.[24] In any event, this permits us to conclude that an unpolished summary of Pinard's views would argue that Canadian third parties have tended to emerge where members of disadvantaged groups are:

(a) bound together in dense social networks;
(b) highly polarized from advantaged groups; and,
(c) relatively unrepresented by existing parties.

CRITIQUE

It seems obvious that the structural theory matches the data on third parties and social movements much better than the cultural/institutional approach. The structural theory is not, however, beyond criticism. Specifically:

(a) Segmentation between, and solidarity within, conflict groups are not the only social-structural determinants of third-party formation, or more generally, of political protest.
(b) The state acts less independently to shape political protest than Pinard suggests.

(c) Both Pinard and Macpherson underestimate the range of state structures, policies, and interventions that help regulate such protest.

(d) Both authors obscure the role of culture in managing or facilitating
discontent.

I think it is undeniable that the greater the density of social ties among
potential members of a social movement or a third party, the more likely
they are to advance their goals. Nevertheless, other social-structural factors
are also important in deciding the likelihood of protest. Access to resources
— material (property, money, jobs), coercive (police, armed forces), and
normative (communications media, schools, etc.) — is at least as important
because the greater a protest group's access to resources, the more it can increase the benefits of participation to members and sympathizers and the
cost of opposition to its adversaries. Group size is a third (and less significant) influence on a group's capacity to engage in protest. All things being
equal, the larger the number of potential partisans of a social movement or
third party, the more likely protest activities are to occur. Thus, group size,
level of social organization, and access to resources determine how powerful a group is.[25] The greater the relative power of potential members of a
social movement or third party, the greater the likelihood of protest activities. Conversely, where authorities are significantly more powerful than
potential partisans, there is little chance of a third party of a social movement emerging — even if potential partisans are seriously aggrieved.

The importance of these considerations becomes clearer in light of my
second criticism of the structural theory. One of the most important institutions that classes and other groups employ to further their goals is the state,
which confers on them and their agents, and in proportion to the amount of
power they possess, the right to pass laws, dispense patronage, design
school curricula and take a variety of other, politically influential actions.
Although Pinard recognizes that at least one feature of the state — the electoral system — influences the rate of third party formation, he makes it
seem as if electoral systems simply 'happen' to exercise this influence,
thereby ignoring the fact that electoral systems themselves have social
origins. States otherwise, electoral systems (and other features of the state
mentioned below) are not independent, but intervening variables: they help
determine the likelihood of third party formation, but they, and the
representativeness of the party systems they help form, are in turn shaped
by the way in which power is distributed and, over time, redistributed in
society.[26] Historically, electoral institutions are stamped by the relative
power of various classes and other major groups when basic constitutional
arrangements are worked out. Consider, for example, the fact that opposing collective interests in the U.S. are played down as they are accommodated, homogenized, and therefore individualized within existing parties, while opposing collective interests in Canada cannot easily be accommodated in existing parties and are therefore recognized through the formation of third parties. What accounts for this difference? The Canadian elec-

toral system was modelled after the British pattern because Britain retained control over British North America well into the nineteenth century. And the British model, whose roots extend back to the era when the landed aristocracy reigned supreme, reflects the collectivism of that class. In contrast, American political institutions were formed in rejection of the British model and in a society overwhelmingly consisting of small capitalist landowners. The American model closely reflects the extreme individualism of that class. In other words, the electoral systems of Canada and the U.S. differ because they were created in the images of different, powerful classes at different times.

After initial constitutional decisions have been worked out, the distribution of power is bound to shift due to such developments as the expansion of agriculture, or at a later stage, industry. Such massive changes call into existence large, new classes and (through immigration) ethnic groups, while shoving others into the political background. This renders the party system less representative than it had been: the new classes and groups inevitably seek office as they become more numerous, organized and resourceful. This can of course take a long time if the old ruling circles are very powerful. For example, when Alberta and Saskatchewan were granted provincial status in 1905 the federal Liberal Party was in office and appointed the first Lieutenant Governors. The latter, in turn, summoned Liberal premiers who made exceedingly effective use of patronage in order to remain in office.[27] A sort of political bulwark was thus erected against the influx of farmers into the region because the Liberal Party, and the interests it represented, had enormous political resources at its disposal. It took one and a half decades in Alberta, and four in Saskatchewan, for the poorly represented farmers to bring third parties into office. Here too, we can plainly see how shifts in the distribution of power affect the representativeness of party systems and therefore their conduciveness to third-party formation.

But the nature of its electoral system is not the only feature of the state that influences the rate of third-party formation, and Pinard (and Macpherson) must also be criticized for failing to elaborate this point. Short of providing a full catalogue of influential state structures, policies, and interventions, it is useful to distinguish among three broad functions performed by the state in capitalist societies and ask how each function affects political protest.[28]

The coercive function exercises perhaps the most obvious impact: the police and the armed forces often have been used to quell discontent and teach Canadians that, in general, challenges to the *status quo* are costly and ought to be avoided. However, such interventions take place only in what political authorities regard as extreme situations; a more frequently employed means of minimizing discontent involves the state in its function of legitimizing the social order. Existing states of affairs are considered to be more or less just when citizens are taught to believe in the legitimacy of the social order and the illegitimacy of other possible orders. The state is one of the principal mechanisms through which those who benefit most from the *status quo* are able to inculcate a sense of legitimacy in the citizenry. For example, most school curricula in Canada systematically ignore the history of the agrarian and labor movements, thus teaching students (by omission) that class conflict has been relatively unimportant in our past and ought not to be considered a reasonable basis for political action in the present. Those who make ultimate decisions concerning the content of instruction thus wield enormous political power.

Finally, by facilitating the accumulation of capital the state subdues conflict in a more roundabout way. For example, a Crown corporation may be established out of tax revenues to provide a service — say, hydro-electricity — which entrepreneurs are unwilling or unable to furnish themselves. Some, however, benefit from this more than others: workers receive jobs and consumers electricity, but owners of industry are also able to reap large profits and avoid levels of unemployment that could cause social disorder. Thus, by providing an economic infrastructure the state lessens the likelihood of political unrest while simultaneously using public funds partly for private gain. Examples of the way in which the state, by facilitating capital accumulation, legitimizing the social order and coercing the unruly, influences the level of discontent in Canada, could easily be multiplied. What needs emphasis though (and further study), is the fact that these influences extend well beyond the electoral system to embrace a wide variety of control mechanisms.

My final criticism of the structural theory at first may seem quite out of place given the tenor of my earlier remarks on the cultural/institutional approach. Although I began this paper by criticizing Horowitz and Lipset for placing too much emphasis on culture as a cause of political behaviour, I now want to argue that both Pinard and Macpherson have done us a theoretical disservice by ignoring the ways in which culture helps shape our politics.

The paradox is removed once the term culture is clarified. By culture I do not mean abstract ideas like toryism or liberalism that were originally invented by statesmen and political philosophers and that are presumably adhered to by ordinary people centuries afterwards and oceans away. I strongly doubt that the political thinking of nurses in British Columbia or asbestos miners in Quebec is any more than tinged by such notions. Nurses and asbestos miners do, however, respond to the material constraints on their lives by learning and creating beliefs, symbols, and values that allow them to interpret their surroundings and engage in a host of everyday activities. And it is those ideas — ideas that give meaning and purpose to their lives — that form culture in the sense that I intend.

Once we recognize that more people in Canada play bingo, sing folk songs, and watch hockey games than read Gladstone, we are confronted with the problem of deciphering the political significance of this and related facts. It is a problem which has scarcely been explored,[29] yet one that demands inquiry. Suffice it to suggest here that two aspects of the issue bear special attention. On the one hand we need to know how the distribution and redistribution of power in society has produced elements of culture that constrain people's political vision, compels them to accede to existing authority, and divert attention away from pressing problems. On the other hand we need to know how the distribution and redistribution of power in society has produced elements of culture that enable people to reject the demands of authority and see the possibility of creating a better world for themselves. For culture is not just an epiphenomenal product of one's social environment. That is altogether too mechanical a view. Rather, culture is both a product of circumstances and the means by which men and women create their future. As such, it is the very stuff out of which social movements and third parties are created and deserves to be accorded greater attention by students of the subject.

NOTES

[1]Myles, 1979.
[2]Hartz, 1964.
[3]Lipset, esp. 1976.
[4]Clark, 1959.
[5]Bell and Tepperman, 1979: 43.
[6]Truman, 1977: 609.
[7]Winn and Twiss, 1977: 305.
[8]Horowitz, 1968: 19.
[9]Rokeach, 1974: 164.
[10]Crawford and Curtis, 1979.
[11]This was true at least for respondents less than 61 years of age; for those older the difference between Americans and Canadians was negligible. Crawford and Curtis also discuss the published results of three other studies that bear indirectly upon the subject of North Americans' collectivity orientations, and for the most part these invalidate the Horowitz-Lipset thesis.
[12]Horowitz, 1968: 15.
[13]McNaught, 1974: 419.
[14]Horowitz, 1978: 387-88.
[15]Horowitz's desire to trace Canadian democratic-socialism back to tory (and therefore British) roots leads him to underestimate the impact that non-Britons have had on the movement. Aside from the obvious role that Québécois workers are having on politics today, Scandinavians, Finns, Jews, Italians and Ukrainians in particular have at various times and places played a disproportionately important role on the left. See Black Rose Books Editorial Collective, 1975; Milner, 1978; Avery, 1979; Zakuta, 1964:31.
[16]Pinard, 1971: 66; Truman, 1971: 519. This criticism may not seem entirely fair

since Horowitz and Lipset set out to explain international, not interprovincial, differences. However, I can think of no logical reason why their argument should not apply interprovincially as well. Moreover, I strongly believe that theories ought to be critically examined not only for how well they explain, but also for how much they explain. Indeed, all of my criticisms of the structural theory, below, are of the 'how much' rather than the 'how well' variety.

[17]Brym, 1979 in Brym and Sacouman, 1979: 59-79.

[18]Winn and McMenemy, 1976.

[19]Shiry, 1976: 43.

[20]Macpherson, 1962.

[21]Brym, 1980.

[22]Pinard, 1971.

[23]Pinard, 1973.

[24]Pinard, 1973, also discusses the effects of party unrepresentativeness in one province on third party formation in neighboring provinces, and the effects of party unrepresentativeness at one level of government on third party formation at the other level.

[25]Bierstedt, 1974.

[26]White, 1973: 403. Lipset and Rokkan, 1967, have discussed this issue, but only as it applies to European political systems. See also Esping-Anderson, Friedland and Wright, 1976.

[27]Reid, in Gibbons and Rowat, 1976: 42-56.

[28]Panitch, 1977.

[29]See, however, Gruneau and Albison, 1976; Kealey, 1981; McKay, 1981; Palmer, 1981.

Bibliography

Abella, Irving. *Nationalism, Communism, and Canadian Labour: The CIO, The Communist Party, and the Canadian Congress of Labour, 1935-1956.* Toronto: University of Toronto Press, 1973.

Abella, Irving, ed. *On Strike: Six Key Labour Struggles in Canada.* Toronto: James Lewis and Samuel, 1974.

Alford, Robert. *Party and Society: The Anglo-American Democracies.* Chicago: Rand McNally, 1963.

_____. "Class Voting in the Anglo-American Political Systems." In S. M. Lipset and S. Rokkan, eds. *Party Systems and Voter Alignments.* New York: Free Press, 1967.

Allen, Richard. *The Social Passion: Religion and Social Reform in Canada, 1914-28.* Toronto: University of Toronto Press, 1971.

Avakumovic, Ivan. *The Communist Party in Canada: A History.* Toronto: McClelland and Stewart, 1975.

_____. *Socialism in Canada: A Study of the CCF-NDP in Federal and Provincial Elections.* Toronto: McClelland & Stewart, 1978.

Avery, Donald. *'Dangerous Foreigners'; European Workers and Labour Radicalism in Canada, 1896-1932.* Toronto: McClelland and Stewart, 1979.

Babcock, Robert H. *Gompers in Canada: A Study in American Continentalism Before the First World War.* Toronto: University of Toronto Press, 1974.

Bell, David and Lorne Tepperman. *The Roots of Disunity: A Look at Canadian Political Culture.* Toronto: McClelland and Stewart, 1979.

Bellamy, David J., Jon H. Pammett and Donald C. Rowat, eds. *The Provincial Political Systems.* Toronto: Methuen, 1976.

Bercuson, David. *Fools and Wisemen: The Rise and Fall of the One Big Union.* Toronto: McGraw-Hill Ryerson, 1978.

Betcherman, Lita-Rose. *The Swastika and the Maple Leaf: Fascist Movements in Canada in the Thirties.* Toronto: Fitzhenry and Whiteside, 1975.

Bierstedt, Robert. "An Analysis of Social Power." In *Power and Progress: Essays on Sociological Theory.* New York: McGraw-Hill, 1974.

Black Rose Books Editorial Collective, eds. *Quebec Labour,* 2d ed. Montreal: Black Rose Books, 1975.

Blais, André. "Third Parties in Canadian Provincial Politics." *Canadian Journal of Political Science* (6) 1973: 422-37.

Blake, Donald E. "The Measurement of Regionalism in Canadian Voting Patterns." *Canadian Journal of Political Science* 5 (1972): 55-81.

Bottomore, T. B. *Critics of Society: Radical Thought in North America.* London: George Allen and Unwin, 1967.

Breton, R. "The Socio-Political Dynamics of the October Events." *Canadian Review of Sociology and Anthropology. Special Issue: Aspects of Canadian Society* 1974: 37-60.

Brym, Robert J. "Regional Social Structure and Agrarian Radicalism in Canada: Alberta, Saskatchewan and New Brunswick." In Alex Himelfarb and James Richardson, eds. *People, Power and Process: A Reader.* Toronto: McGraw-Hill Ryerson, 1980.

Brym, Robert J. and James R. Sacouman, eds. *Underdevelopment and Social Movements in Atlantic Canada.* Toronto: New Hogtown Press, 1979.

Burnet, Jean. "Town-Country Relations and the Problem of Rural Leadership." *Canadian Journal of Economics and Political Science* 13 (1947): 395-409.

Cairns, Alan C. "The Electoral System and the Party System in Canada." *Canadian Journal of Political Science* 1 (1968): 55-80.

_____. "A Reply to J. A. A. Lovink, 'On Analysing the Impact of the Electoral System on the Party System in Canada.'" *Canadian Journal of Political Science* 3 (1970): 517-21.

Caplan, Gerald L. *The Dilemma of Canadian Socialism: The CCF in Ontario.* Toronto: McClelland and Stewart, 1973.

Clark, S. D. *Church and Sect in Canada.* Toronto: University of Toronto Press, 1948.

_____. *Movements of Political Protest in Canada, 1640-1840.* Toronto: University of Toronto Press, 1959.

_____. "Group Interests in Canadian Politics." In J. H. Aitchison, ed. *The Political Process in Canada.* Toronto: University of Toronto Press, 1963.

_____. "Movements of Protest in Post-War Canadian Society." *Transactions of the Royal Society of Canada* (Series IV). 8 (1970): 227-37.

Clark, Samuel D., J. Paul Grayson and Linda M. Grayson, eds. *Prophecy and Protest: Social Movements in Twentieth Century Canada.* Toronto: Gage, 1975.

Clarke, Harold D. *et al. Political Choice in Canada,* abridged ed. Toronto: McGraw-Hill Ryerson, 1980.

Cleverdon, Catherine. *The Woman Suffrage Movement in Canada.* Toronto: University of Toronto Press, 1974.

Conway, J. F. "Populism in the United States, Russia and Canada: Explaining the Roots of Canada's Third Parties." *Canadian Journal of Political Science* 11 (1978): 99-124.

_____. "The Prairie Populist Resistance to the National Policy: Some Reconsiderations." *Journal of Canadian Studies* 14 (1979): 77-91.

Craven, Paul. *'An Impartial Umpire': Industrial Relations and the Canadian State 1900-1911.* Toronto: University of Toronto Press, 1980.

Crawford, Craig and James Curtis. "English Canadian American Differences In Value Orientations: Survey Comparisons Bearing on Lipset's Thesis." *Studies in Comparative International Development* (1979): 23-44.

Creighton, Donald. *The Empire of the St. Lawrence.* Toronto: Macmillan, 1956.

_____. "The Economic Background of the Rebellions of 1837." In W. T. Easterbrook and M. H. Watkins, eds. *Approaches to Canadian Economic History.* Toronto: McClelland and Stewart, 1967.

Cross, Michael S., ed. *The Frontier Thesis and the Canadas: The Debate on the Impact of the Canadian Environment.* Toronto: Copp Clark, 1970.

Cuneo, Carl. "State Mediation of Class Contradictions in Canadian Unemployment Insurance, 1930-1945." *Studies in Political Economy* 3 (1980): 37-65.

Cuneo, Carl J. and James E. Curtis. "Quebec Separatism: An Analysis Of Determinants Within Social Class Levels." *Canadian Review Of Sociology and Anthropology* 11 (1974): 1-29.

Curtis, James E. and William G. Scott, eds. *Social Stratification: Canada,* 2d ed. Scarborough: Prentice Hall, 1979.

Dunham, Aileen. *Political Unrest In Upper Canada, 1815-1836.* Toronto: McClelland and Stewart, 1963.

Elkins, David J. "The Perceived Structure of The Canadian Party System." *Canadian Journal Of Political Science* 8 (1974): 502-24.

Erickson, Bonnie H. "Region, Knowledge, and Class Voting in Canada." *Canadian Journal of Sociology* 6 (1981): 121-44.

Esping-Anderson, Gosta, Roger Friedland, and Erik Olin Wright. "Modes of Class Struggle and the Capitalist State." *Kapitalistate* 4-5 (1976): 186-220.

Forbes, Ernest R. *The Maritime Rights Movement: 1919-1927.* Montreal: McGill-Queen's University Press, 1979.

Gibbons, Kenneth M. and Donald C. Rowat, eds. *Political Corruption In Canada.* Toronto: McClelland and Stewart, 1976.

Grayson, J. Paul and Linda M. Grayson. "The Social Base Of Interwar Political Unrest In Urban Alberta." *Canadian Journal Of Political Science* 7 (1979): 289-313.

Gruneau, Richard and John G. Albison, eds. *Canadian Sport: Sociological Perspectives.* Don Mills: Addison Wesley, Canada, 1976.

Gwyn, Richard *Smallwood: The Unlikely Revolutionary.* Rev. ed. Toronto: McClelland and Stewart, 1972.

Hallet, Mary "The Social Credit Party and The New Democracy Movement: 1939-1940." *Canadian Historical Review* 47 (1966): 301-25.

Hamilton, Richard and Maurice Pinard. "The Bases Of Parti Quebecois Support in Recent Quebec Elections." *Canadian Journal Of Political Science* 9 (1976): 3-26.

Hann, Russell. *Farmers Confront Industrialism.* Toronto: New Hogtown Press, 1975.

Hartz, Louis *The Founding Of New Societies.* New York: Harcourt and Brace, 1964.

Hiller, Harry H. "Internal Party Resolution and Third Party Emergence."

Canadian Journal of Sociology 2 (1977): 55-75.

Horn, Michiel. "The Great Depression: Past and Present." *Journal of Canadian Studies* 11 (1976): 41-50.

_____. "Academics and Canadian Social and Economic Policy In The Depression and War Years." *Journal of Canadian Studies* 13 (1978-79): 3-17.

_____. *The League for Social Reconstruction: Intellectual Origins of the Democratic Left in Canada, 1930-1942.* Toronto: University of Toronto Press, 1980.

Horowitz, Gad. *Canadian Labour In Politics.* Toronto: University of Toronto Press, 1968.

_____. "Notes On 'Conservatism, Liberalism, and Socialism In Canada.'" *Canadian Journal of Political Science* 11 (1978): 383-99.

Huxley, Christopher "The State, Collective Bargaining, and The Shape Of Strikes In Canada." *Canadian Journal of Sociology* 4 (1979): 223-39.

Irving, John A. *The Social Credit Movement In Alberta.* Toronto: University of Toronto Press, 1959.

Jamieson, Stuart. *Times Of Trouble: Labour Unrest And Industrial Conflict In Canada, 1900-66.* Study No. 22, Task Force On Labour Relations. Ottawa: Information Canada, 1971.

_____. *Industrial Relations In Canada.* 2d ed. Toronto: Macmillan, 1973.

Kay, B. J. "An Examination Of Class And Left-Right Party Images In Canadian Voting." *Canadian Journal of Political Science* 10 (1977): 127-44.

Kealey, Gregory S. *Toronto Workers Respond to Industrial Capitalism, 1867-1892.* Toronto: University of Toronto Press, 1980.

_____. "Labour and Working-Class History in Canada: Prospects in the 1980s." *Labour/LeTravailleur* 7 (1981): 67-110.

Kealey, Gregory S. and Peter Warrian, eds. *Essays In Canadian Working Class History.* Toronto: McClelland and Stewart, 1976.

Keddie, Vincent. "Class Identification and Party Preference Among Manual Workers." *Canadian Review of Sociology and Anthropology* 17 (1980): 24-36.

Kravnick, David. *Organized Labour and Pressure Politics: The Canadian Labour Congress 1956-1968.* Montreal: McGill-Queen's University Press, 1972.

Lambert, Ronald D. and Alfred A. Hunter. "Social Stratification, Voting Behaviour, and the Images of Canadian Federal Political Parties." *Canadian Review of Sociology and Anthropology* 16 (1979): 287-304.

Langdon, Steven. "The Emergence of the Canadian Working Class Movement, 1845-75." *Journal of Canadian Studies* 7, 2 (1972): 3-13 and 7, 3 (1972): 8-26.

Laxer, Robert. *Canada's Unions.* Toronto: James Lorimer, 1976.

Lipset, Seymour Martin. *Agrarian Socialism,* rev. ed. Berkeley: University of California Press, 1971.

_____. "Democracy In Alberta." *The Canadian Forum* 34 (1954): 175-77, 196-98.

_____. "Radicalism in North America: A Comparative View of the Party Systems in Canada and the United States." *Transactions of the Royal Society of Canada* (Series IV). 14 (1976): 19-55.

Lipsig-Mummé, Carla. "Quebec Unions and the State: Conflict and Dependence." *Studies in Political Economy* 3 (1980): 119-46.

Lipton, Charles. *The Trade Union Movement in Canada, 1927-1959.* Montreal: Canadian Social Publications, 1966.

Liversedge, Ronald. *Recollections of the On to Ottawa Trek.* Toronto: McClelland and Stewart, 1973.

Logan, H. A. *Trade Unions in Canada.* Toronto: McClelland and Stewart, 1948.

Lovink, J. A. A. "On Analysing the Impact of the Electoral System on the Party

System in Canada." *Canadian Journal of Political Science* 3 (1970): 497-516.

Macpherson, C. B. "Democracy in Alberta: A Reply." *The Canadian Forum* 34 (1955): 223-25.

_____. *Democracy in Alberta: Social Credit and the Party System.* 2d ed. Toronto: University of Toronto Press, 1962.

McCormack, A. Ross. *Reformers, Rebels and Revolutionaries: The Western Canadian Radical Movement, 1899-1919.* Toronto: University of Toronto Press, 1977.

McCrorie, James N. "Change and Paradox in Agrarian Social Movements: The Case of Saskatchewan." In Richard Ossenberg, ed. *Canadian Society: Pluralism, Change and Conflict.* Scarborough: Prentice-Hall, 1971.

_____., ed. *Canadian Review of Sociology and Anthropology.* (A Special Issue on Quebec) 15: (1978).

McDonald, Lynn. "Attitude Organization and Voting Behaviour in Canada." *Canadian Review of Sociology and Anthropology* 8 (1971): 164-84.

McKay, Ian. "Historians, Anthropology, and the Concept of Culture." *Labour/ LeTravailleur* 8/9 (1981): 185-241.

McNaught, Kenneth. "Comment." In John H. M. Laslett and Seymour Martin Lipset, eds. *Failure of a Dream? Essays in the History of American Socialism.* Garden City: Anchor, 1974.

Masters, D. C. *The Winnipeg General Strike.* Toronto: University of Toronto Press, 1950.

Miller, Richard U. and Fraser Isbester, eds. *Canadian Labour in Transition.* Scarborough: Prentice-Hall, 1971.

Mills, Allen. "The Canadian Forum and Socialism, 1920-34," *Journal of Canadian Studies* 13 (1978-9): 11-27.

Milner, Henry. *Politics in the New Quebec.* Toronto: McClelland and Stewart, 1978.

Morton, Desmond. "Aid to the Civil Power: The Canadian Militia in Support of Social Order, 1867-1914." *Canadian Historical Review* 51 (1970): 407-25.

Morton, W. L. *The Progressive Party in Canada.* Toronto: University of Toronto Press, 1950.

Myles, John F. "Differences in the Canadian and American Class Vote: Fact or Pseudofact?" *American Journal of Sociology* 84 (1979): 1232-37.

Myles, John F. and Forcese, Dennis. "Voting and Class Politics in Canada and the United States." In R. Tomasson, ed. *Comparative Social Research.* Greenwich, Conn.: JAI Press, 1980.

Neis, Barbara. "Competitive Merchants and Class Struggle in Newfoundland." *Studies in Political Economy* 5 (1981): 127-43.

Ogmundson, Rick. "On the Measurement of Party Class Positions: The Case of Canadian Federal Politics," *Canadian Review of Sociology and Anthropology* 12 (1975): 566-76.

_____. "Party Class Images and the Class Vote in Canada." *American Sociological Review* 40 (1975): 506-12.

_____. "Mass-Elite Linkages and Class Issues in Canada." *Canadian Review of Sociology and Anthropology* 13 (1976): 1-11.

_____. "On the Use of Party Image Variables to Measure the Distinctiveness of a Class Vote: The Canadian Case." *Canadian Journal of Sociology* 1 (1979): 169-77.

_____. "A Note on the Ambiguous Meanings of Survey Research Measures which use the Words 'Left' and 'Right'." *Canadian Journal of Political Science* 12: (1979): 799-805.

Ornstein, Michael, D., H. Michael Stevenson and A. Paul Williamson. "Region, Class, and Political Culture in Canada." *Canadian Journal of Political Science* 13 (1980): 227-71.

_____. "Liberal Ideology and the Study of Voting Behavior." *Canadian Review of Sociology and Anthropology* 17 (1980): 45-54.

Palmer, Bryan D. *A Culture in Conflict: Skilled Workers and Industrial Capitalism in Hamilton, Ontario, 1860-1914.* Montreal: McGill-Queen's University Press, 1979.

_____. "Classifying Culture." *Labour/LeTravailleur* 8/9 (1981): 153-83.

Panitch, Leo, ed. *The Canadian State: Political Economy and Political Power.* Toronto: University of Toronto Press, 1977.

Penner, Norman. *The Canadian Left: A Critical Analysis.* Scarborough: Prentice-Hall of Canada, 1977.

Pinard, Maurice. "Working Class Politics: An Interpretation of the Quebec Case." *Canadian Review of Sociology and Anthropology* 7 (1970): 87-109.

_____. *The Rise of a Third Party: A Study in Crisis Politics.* Englewood Cliffs: Prentice-Hall, 1971.

_____. "Third Parties in Canadian Revisited: A Rejoinder and Elaboration of the Theory of One-Party Dominance." *Canadian Journal of Political Science* 6 (1973): 439-60.

Pinard, Maurice and Richard Hamilton. "The Independence Issue and The Polarization of the Electorate: The 1973 Quebec Election." *The Canadian Journal of Political Science* 10 (1977): 215-59.

_____. "The Parti Québécois Comes to Power: An Analysis of the 1976 Quebec Election." *Canadian Journal of Political Science* 11 (1978): 739-75.

Posgate, Dale and Kenneth McRoberts. *Quebec: Social Change and Political Crisis.* Toronto: McClelland and Stewart, 1976.

Rawlyk, G. A. "The Farmer-Labour Movement and The Failure of Socialism in Nova Scotia." In Laurier Lapierre et al., eds. *Essays on the Left.* Toronto: McClelland and Stewart, 1971.

Resnick, Philip. *The Land of Cain.* Vancouver: New Star Books, 1977.

Richards, John and Larry Pratt. *Prairie Capitalism: Power and Influence in the New West.* Toronto: McClelland & Stewart, 1979.

Rinehart, James W. and Ishmael D. Okraku. "A Study of Class Consciousness." *Canadian Review of Sociology and Anthropology* 11 (1974): 197-213.

Rioux, Marcel. *Quebec in Question.* Toronto: James Lorimer, 1971.

Roberts, Wayne. *Honest Womanhood: Feminism, Femininity, and Class Consciousness Among Toronto Working Women, 1893-1914.* Toronto: New Hogtown Press, 1976.

Robin, Martin. *Radical Politics and Canadian Labour 1880-1930.* Kingston: Industrial Relations Centre, Queen's University, 1968.

Rokeach, Milton. "Some Reflections About the Place of Values in Canadian Social Science." In T. N. Guinsburg and G. L. Reuber, eds. *Perspectives on the Social Sciences in Canada.* Toronto: University of Toronto Press, 1974.

Ryerson, Stanley. *Unequal Union.* Toronto: Progress Books, 1973.

Saywell, John. *The Rise of the Parti Québécois, 1967-1976.* Toronto: University of Toronto Press, 1977.

Schreiber, E. M. "Class Awareness and Class Voting in Canada." *Canadian Review of Sociology and Anthropology* 17 (1980): 37-44.

Schwartz, Mildred A. *Politics and Territory.* Montreal: McGill-Queen's University Press, 1974.

Scott, Jack. *Canadian Workers, American Unions.* Vancouver: New Star Books, 1978.

Shiry, John. "Mass Values and System Outputs: A Critique of an Assumption of Socialization Theory." In Jon H. Pammett and Michael S. Whittington, eds. *Foundations of Political Culture: Political Socialization in Canada.* Toronto: Macmillan of Canada, 1976.

Simeon, Richard and David J. Elkins, "Regional Political Cultures in Canada." *Canadian Journal of Political Science* 7 (1974): 397-436.

Sinclair, Peter R. "Class Structure and Populist Protest: The Case of Western Canada." *Canadian Journal of Sociology* 1: (1975): 1-17.

_____. "Political Powerlessness and Sociodemographic Status in Canada," *Canadian Review of Sociology and Anthropology* 16 (1979): 125-35.

Skogard, Grace. "Agrarian Protest in Alberta," *Canadian Reviw of Sociology and Anthropology* 17 (1980): 55-73.

Smith, David E. "A Comparison of Prairie Political Developments in Saskatchewan and Alberta." *Journal of Canadian Studies* 4: (1969): 17-26.

Smith, Michael R. "The Transformation of Labour Relations in Quebec: An Analysis." In Katherina L. P. Lundy and Barbara D. Warme, eds. *Work in the Canadian Context: Continuity Despite Change.* Toronto: Butterworths, 1981.

Stein, Michael. *The Dynamics of Right-Wing Protest: A Political Analysis of Social Credit in Quebec.* Toronto: University of Toronto Press, 1973.

Stevenson, Garth. *Unfulfilled Union: Canadian Federalism and National Unity.* Toronto: Gage, 1982.

Stevenson, P. "Class and Left-Wing Radicalism." *Canadian Review of Sociology and Anthropology* 14 (1977): 269-84.

Strong-Boag, Veronica. *The Parliament of Women.* Ottawa: National Museums of Canada, 1976.

Taylor, K. Wayne and Nelson Wiseman. "Ethnic and Class Voting: The Case of Winnipeg, 1941." *Canadian Review of Sociology and Anthropology* 14 (1977): 174-87.

Teeple, Gary, ed. *Capitalism and the National Question in Canada.* Toronto: University of Toronto Press, 1972.

Tennyson, Brian D. "The Ontario General Election of 1919: The Beginnings of Agrarian Revolt." *Journal of Canadian Studies* 4 (1969): 26-36.

Thomson, Dale C., ed. *Quebec Society and Politics.* Toronto: McClelland and Stewart, 1973.

Torrance, Judith. "The Response of Canadian Governments to Violence." *Canadian Journal of Political Science* 10 (1977): 473-96.

Truman, Tom. "A Critique of Seymour Martin Lipset's Article, 'Value Differences, Absolute of Relative: The English-speaking Democracies'." *Canadian Journal Of Political Science* 4 (1971): 497-525.

_____. "A Scale for Measuring a Tory Streak in Canada and the United States." *Canadian Journal of Political Science* 10 (1977): 597-614.

van den Berg, Axel and Michael Smith. "The Marxist Theory of the State in Practice." *Canadian Journal of Sociology* 6 (1981): 505-19.

Walters, Vivienne. "State, Capital, and Labour: The Introduction of Federal-Provincial Insurance for Physician Care in Canada." *Canadian Review of Sociology and Anthropology* 19 (1982): 157-72.

_____. "Occupational Health and Safety Legislation in Ontario: An Analysis of its Origins and Content." *Canadian Review of Sociology and Anthropology* 26 (1983): 413-34.

White, Graham, "One Party Dominance and Third Parties: The Pinard Theory Reconsidered." *Canadian Journal of Political Science* 6 (1973): 399-421.

Whittaker, Reginald. *The Government Party: Organizing and Financing the Liberal Party of Canada 1930-1958.* Toronto: University of Toronto Press, 1977.

Wilbur, J. R. H. "H. H. Stevens and the Reconstruction Party." *Canadian Historical Review* 45 (1964): 1-28.

Wilson, John. "Politics and Social Class in Canada: The Case of Waterloo South." *Canadian Journal of Political Science* 1 (1968): 288-309.

_____. "The Canadian Political Cultures: Towards a Redefinition of the Canadian Political System." *Canadian Journal of Political Science* 7 (1974): 438-83.

Winn, Conrad and John McMenemy, eds. *Canadian Political Parties.* Toronto: McGraw-Hill Ryerson, 1976.

Winn, Conrad and James Twiss. "The Spatial Analysis of Political Cleavages and the Case of the Ontario Legislature." *Canadian Journal of Political Science* 10 (1977): 287-310.

Wiseman, Nelson and K. Wayne Taylor. "Ethnic versus Class Voting: The Case of Winnipeg, 1945." *Canadian Journal of Political Science* 7 (1974): 314-28.

_____. "Class and Ethnic Voting in Winnipeg During the Cold War." *Canadian Review of Sociology and Anthropology* 16 (1979): 60-76.

Young, Walter D. *The Anatomy of a Party: The National CCF, 1932-61.* Toronto: University of Toronto Press, 1969.

_____. *Democracy and Discontent: Progressivism, Socialism and Social Credit in the Canadian West.* Toronto: McGraw-Hill Ryerson, 1969.

Young, W. R. "Conscription, Rural Depopulation, and the Farmers of Ontario, 1917-1919." *Canadian Historical Review* 53 (1972): 289-320.

Zakuta, Leo. *A Protest Movement Becalmed.* Toronto: University of Toronto Press, 1964.

Zipp, John F. "Left-Right Dimensions of Canadian Federal Party Identification: A Discriminant Analysis." *Canadian Journal of Political Science* 11 (1978): 251-77.

CHAPTER 3

Family Studies in the Canadian Context

Frederick Elkin

INTRODUCTION

Our perceptions of major developments in family life are complicated by the fact that some of our awareness of current trends comes from our own experience or from reports in the popular media. Our ideas are also almost always affected by developments in other countries: in matters associated with family life or gender roles, Canada, in recent years, is very much a part of the Western world. We must add to such knowlege, of course, the more refined information which can be derived from the census, vital statistics or other government sources, and from academic research and analysis.

In seeking to understand and describe the major developments and trends in Canadian family studies it is appropriate to consider all such materials. It is also appropriate — since it is impossible to examine all aspects of family life simultaneously — largely to confine this discussion to those dimensions on which Canadian researchers have focused their attention and about which, as a consequence, we can be reasonably confident. Moreover, since, consciously or not, analysts select and examine problems within certain theoretical perspectives, it is also necessary to ask what these perspectives are and what consequences this has had for the kind of research on the family that has been done in Canada.

In this brief essay, we will first consider the place of the family in the larger social order. With this in mind, we will then look at man-woman and parent-child relationships. This will be followed by a brief discussion of family problems and family policy. In conclusion, I will present an overview of the state of our knowledge about the family in Canada and critically evaluate the theories and perspectives that have been applied to it.

THE FAMILY IN THE LARGER SOCIAL ORDER

Historical Studies

Until recently, except for scholars in Québec,[1] Canadian researchers have devoted little attention to the historical links between the family and the larger economic, political and social order. In the past decade, however, various scholars have broadened our vision. Michael Katz, for example, working with mid-nineteenth century archival data from Hamilton, Ontario, has added historical depth to our knowledge of Canadian family patterns.

Katz's work counters the popular image of the traditional extended family. As a rule, Katz discovered, older parents did not live with their grown children. In 1851, for example, only 15 per cent of households included any relatives. However, households often did serve as surrogate family settings for young immigrants: as many as 28 per cent of households — many headed by widows — took in boarders.[2]

Jane Synge, also working in Hamilton — but drawing on census data and life-history interviews of elderly residents — points out that, in the early twentieth century, adolescents moved smoothly, without any *rites de passage,* into the work world and, until they married, were active, financially-contributing members of their families.[3] She also concludes that the life of the elderly at the time was not a "period of ease and retirement."[4] Such studies are limited in context, but they point to a new direction in Canadian historical research relative to family structure.

Comparative Statistical Data

As sources of information of family life, nation-wide statistics that apply to all of Canada are extremely useful. They can be used to compare Canada with other countries, as well as to indicate broad trends going on within our borders. One such set of statistics points to our high standard of living. Relatively few Canadian households lack adequate food and shelter or such conveniences as electric refrigerators, telephones, radios or television sets. Over three out of four have washing machines, cars, record players and color TV sets.[5] All families, by right, also receive basic health care. Such items — although they conceal many pockets of poverty — have become part of the "standard package" of Canadian family life — a package matched by few other countries.

Another set of data points to the high value Canadians place on love and marriage. In a national survey of 3,288 respondents which focused on

values most closely associated with a quality of life index, the highest ranking domain, especially by married persons, was love/marriage. Leisure,
health or even the financial situation of the respondents were far behind.[6]

Without doubt the major source of change in the family in recent years
has been the women's movement. In several areas — legislation, education,
religion, media performers, voluntary organization leadership, everyday
customs, and the work world — women have sought and attained more
rights. Discrimination, undoubtedly with an ideological base,[7] continues to
exist in all these areas, but the trend has been towards greater equity and
equality of opportunity relative to men. The family, of course, is part and
parcel of this movement and these trends.

One major development often seen as a sign of liberation is the increasing proportion of married women entering the work force.[8] Whether or not
a wife works is associated with many factors including her husband's income, degree of education, opportunity for jobs, and especially the age and
number of her children. But the general trend in all categories and for all
social class groups is up.[9] In 1941 only four per cent of married women were
working for pay. In 1978, the percentage of the labor force was 60.3.[10] Of
all women in the labor force, almost three out of five were married.

This trend also applies to mothers. In 1976, over two out of five
mothers (in husband-wife families) with children under fifteen years of age
were working.[11] In recent years, even mothers of young children — who in
the past had almost always remained at home — have increasingly stayed in
the labor force. Lupri and Mills note that between 1967 and 1973, the participation rate of married women with preschool age children increased by
73 per cent; over seven times the growth rate for women in general.[12] Public
attitudes have changed accordingly. Gallup poll figures indicate an increase
in those who think married women with young children should take a job
outside the home: from 5 per cent in 1960 to 31 per cent in 1980. For those
under age 30, the proportion is 40 per cent.[13]

After World War II, many writers, following the work of Spitz[14] and
Bowlby,[15] argued that very young children without full-time mothering —
or, as later argued by others, at least considerable stimulation from
caretakers — would experience serious psychological problems. In recent
years, this general concern has receded into the background and has been
superseded by an emphasis on women's rights, including the right of a wife
and mother to participate in the labor force.

The type of work most women, including mothers, do, however, has
continued to fit a traditional mold. Working women tend to be
stenographers and typists, sales clerks, personal service workers, primary
school teachers, tellers, cashiers, nurses and textile factory workers. Most
of these occupations command low wages, provide low prestige, and offer
little opportunity for advancement.[16] As a general rule, wives with such jobs
earn considerably less than their husbands. Connelly, from another
perspective, views such women as part of a reserve labor force.[17]

Specific Studies of Family Structure

Family structure in Canada varies considerably by region, social class, and ethnicity. Except for occasional and incidental references, however, our data about these areas are scanty. Kohl's ethnographic study of family farm and ranch enterprises in southern Saskatchewan stresses the continuity that obtains with earlier patterns — including gender roles. Kohl suggests that, as in earlier generations, men concentrate their efforts on the farm or ranch; often taking over control from their fathers. Their wives participate in these enterprises while, at the same time, maintaining responsibility for household tasks and community activities. Over the years, women living in such settings have been gaining in education and opportunities — in some cases even inheriting and managing the farms. But the basic patterns have remained the same.[18]

Our knowledge of the relationship between social class and family structure derive less from specific research than from our common observations and national statistics. We know that families of different income and occupational levels have different life styles, and that children of the elite have better "life chances" than children from lower socio-economic groups.[19] Those with higher incomes tend to have higher educational levels and also fewer children.[20] On the lower end of the scale, many who have incomes below the poverty line are single mothers and elderly women.[21] Some specific research supports our notions that, compared to the well-to-do, working class families are more likely to maintain traditional husband-wife roles with a fairly sharp division of labor and the husbands remaining dominant.[22]

Studies of ethnic family groups are less consistent. The literature on the French-Canadian family has almost always stressed its uniqueness and its crucial importance in the maintenance of the traditional French-Canadian way of life. Families were large, kinship patterns were strong, women did not question their domestic assignments and served as mediators of moral values, and the family was closely linked to the Church and other conservative institutions.[23] In recent decades, as Québec and its economic, religious, and political institutions have been modernized, the family has as well. In terms of such indices as family size, divorce rates, the proportion of working wives, and attitudes towards sexual permissiveness, the rates in Québec are not out of line with those in other provinces. Over the years, there has been a convergence between patterns in French and English Canada, and whatever differences may still exist are likely to be more subtle. Although we have little research data to point to, we suspect that the family patterns among French Canadians, as elsewhere, also vary considerably by age, social class, region, and other dimensions.

Reports on other ethnic groups, such as Hutterites,[24] Dutch,[25] and Italians[26] point to a continuation of strong family traditions with patriarchal authority, a continued division of labor between males and females, and continuity in patterns of socialization in which families are strongly supported by community institutions. Other reports of Greek,[27] Polish,[28] and Mennonite[29] family patterns indicate decreasing patriarchy and movement towards a more modern Canadian model. General indices of ethnic group trends also point to a continuing loss of ethnic distinctiveness. Tavuchis, following a review of ethnic groups and family patterns, writes: "the thesis of convergence [that is, that various ethnic groups are moving toward common characteristics]... is with *certain qualifications,* applicable to a large if unknown proportion of Canadian families and together with other changes in Canadian society suggests the waning importance of ethnicity."[30] Tavuchis has qualified this statement due to fragmentary data, variations in ethnic trends, and differential rates of change in ethnic pockets. Yet, despite this, we can clearly see an overall trend towards the decreasing use of their "native tongue" by various ethnic groups and the increasing adoption of English or French in its stead.

Data of this kind are limited, however, in that they do not deal with some more sensitive aspects of ethnic family relationships — especially the sentiments which may temper the more obvious trends. Monica Boyd, for example, using Gallup poll data from 1964 to 1973, suggests that English and French Canadians hold similar egalitarian attitudes towards women, but once "mother" and "husband" images are invoked the French Canadians become more traditional; believing that women should remain at home and husbands should remain dominant.[31] Replies to the Gallup poll hardly get at the subtleties and complexities of such attitudes, yet here they do point to important questions regarding family and gender roles and suggest how limited our understanding of ethnic family groups really is.

MAN-WOMAN RELATIONSHIPS

Courtship and Mate Selection

Running through all observations of relationships between men and women is an increasing emphasis on the right of individuals to make their own decisions independent of conventions, family demands, and institutional pressures. In courtship, for example, the trend — according to both popular reports and academic studies — has been towards more liberal attitudes and freer sexual behavior. The prevalent pattern is what has been called the "love standard" or "permissiveness with affection," where unmarried men and women may have sexual relationships if they are sufficiently emotionally involved with one another. Older patterns — the double standard, which gives the man but not the women sexual freedom, and restraint until marriage for both partners — are considerably less evident than in the past.

Canadian research on courtship patterns is primarily based on responses to questionnaires administered to samples of university and technical school students. Reports on this research usually consist of summary statistics on the proportions of respondents who, under various circumstances, find behaviour such as premarital petting and sexual intercourse acceptable and/or have actually engaged in these behaviors themselves. Hobart, the most active researcher in this area, notes that in recent years (1977) certain convergences have taken place between the reported behavior and attitudes of the sample groups which have historically been used in making comparisons. First, Canadian students, who according to earlier reports were more conservative in their attitudes and behavior than their American counterparts, now show more similar patterns. Second, Canadian women students, who in earlier years were less permissive and less sexually experienced than men, have been "catching up." Finally, francophone students, who had been less permissive and less sexually experienced than anglophones, now more or less accept the "love standard," with accompanying changes in sexual behavior. For almost all respondents, the proportions of those who are more permissive and sexually experienced have increased.[32]

Marriage is the normal state for men and women in Canadian society. In 1971, 91.1 per cent of Canadian men and 92.6 per cent of Canadian women had at one time or another been married by age 50.[33] As in many other Western societies, Canadians tend to follow a mating gradient in their marriage choices; with men generally marrying down in the sense that they marry women who are younger, physically shorter, and have lower socioeconomic status.[34] We have actual supporting data, however, only for age: on average, men are a few years older than their wives — 2.3 years in 1976.

In recent decades, age at first marriage has declined. In 1941 men averaged 27.6 years of age when first married. In 1972, they averaged 24.7 In 1941 women averaged 24.7 years of age. In 1972, they averaged 22.2. More recent statistics, however, indicate a reversal of the long-term trend. In 1976, the average age for men rose to 25 and for women to 22.7.[35]

Marriage in Canada continues to follow something of an endogamous pattern, that is, men and women tend to marry within their class, religious, and ethnic groups. We have data, for instance, showing that husbands and wives have approximately the same number of years of education[36] — which is generally correlated with socio-economic status. We have additional information on religious and ethnic groups — although the rates vary considerably depending on such factors as the size of a specific population, its degree of segregation and cultural assimilation, and the strength of religious or ethnic identity. In general, the data show a continuation of endogamy, but decreasingly so in younger age cohorts. Young men and women, more mobile, more often acquainted with people from other ethnic groups, and more independent of traditions and family values, exert their right of free choice and more often marry outside of their religious and ethnic communities than their parents did. In the mid-twenties, less than six per cent of all Protestants, Catholics and Jews married spouses of a different religion.[37] In 1972, 25.3 per cent did. Among Roman Catholics in 1963, 87 per cent of brides married Roman Catholic grooms. In 1972, the rate had declined to 77.7 per cent. Among Jews, the rates for these years were down from 92 to 87.5 per cent. Among Protestants the comparable decline was from 81.1 to 70.3 per cent. The pattern was the same within Protestant denominations. Within the United Church, for example, in 1963 57.9 per cent of brides married United Church grooms. In 1972, the figure was down to 46.5 per cent. Data for the years 1974 to 1977 indicate a continuation of the same trend for major religious groups although not for intradenominational Protestant marriages.[38]

Among members of most ethnic groups there is a similar trend towards decreasing endogamy. In 1961, for example, 61.8 per cent of Ukrainian grooms married Ukrainian brides. In 1971, the proportion was 54 per cent. For Polish men, the corresponding figures were 49 and 43.2 per cent and for Scandinavians 31.2 and 26.9 per cent. In 1971, for the country as a whole, 24 percent of all family heads were married to wives of the same ethnic origin. The lowest intermarriage rates were among Jews (91.2 per cent endogamy), French (86.2 per cent), and British and Asian (80.9 per cent).[39]

In the light of recent interpretations which stress the trend towards individualism in ethnic group participation,[40] it would seem that even when men and women marry endogamously they are giving less weight than in the past to their cultures, institutional entrenchments, and family wishes. Rather, if they choose mates of the same religion and ethnic group it is because of their own present-day identifications, satisfactions, and emotional requirements and not because of blind adherence to group norms.

Alternatives To or In Marriage

The conventional family in Canada has historically consisted of a husband and wife living together with their young children. In 1967, 64.9 per cent of men and 63.4 per cent of women 15 years of age and over were married[41] and almost 90 per cent of children under 25 years of age were living in families with both parents present.[42] However, in recent years, men and women have been increasingly opting out of or, in some way or another, altering the conventional pattern. Several alternatives to, or variations on, this pattern, which do not carry the severe stigma of a generation ago, have appeared in recent years.

One alternative, especially for women, is really a non-family pattern: not to marry at all. From 1961 to 1971, the proportion of "never married" Canadian women 15 years and over rose from 23 to 25 per cent, and between the key ages of 20 to 24, from 40.5 to 43.5 per cent.[43] We cannot actually tell from these data whether these women are merely postponing marriage until a later date or if they intend to remain single. In a survey of 300 first year college students, Whitehurst discovered that 73 per cent of women said that they would stay single longer — but the meaning of longer is not clear.[44]

For women who are satisfactorily employed and remain single, the stigma of former days, of being an old maid, is considerably weaker. Single women are much freer today than a generation ago to compete for positions that were once not open to them, to travel and entertain, and to have sexual relationships or live intimately with a man or woman. Canadian research on single life styles is thin, and more work needs to be done before we can fully understand this pattern.

For the majority of men and women, there are also more alternatives and greater choice within marriage. We have already noted that increasingly more women — including young mothers — have been taking jobs for pay. Economic factors undoubtedly play a critical role in the decisions of many wives to work, but it also seems likely that many consider it important to protect a career, to avoid the stigma of being "just a housewife," or to seek the kinds of gratifications that come from being employed. Wives may also, of course, continue to work for reasons other than those which first led them into the labor market.

The increasing numbers of wives in the labor force raises many important questions. With regard to husband-wife relationships, for instance, do working wives gain more influence and power? Do their husbands take on more of the domestic obligations? Reports by researchers in other countries are contradictory. Two Canadian studies suggest that wives have made few gains in these areas. Brinkerhoff and Lupri, in a study of decision-making among 464 couples in Calgary, found — in contrast to "resource theory," which would argue that the greater a wife's contribution to family resources, the greater her influence — that working wives did not score higher in power than non-working wives.[45] Meissner and his colleagues, in a study conducted in Greater Vancouver, used a time budget technique to show that wives, whether working or not, tended to carry on the household tasks. Even among couples with young children, husbands of working wives only contributed one more hour per week to household maintenance.[46]

Since the family is an interacting unit — and a change in one person's behaviour inevitably influences that of others — we may also ask how the psychological health of a couple is affected when a wife takes a job. Burke and Weir conducted a study of 189 husband-wife pairs, 28 per cent of which included working wives.[47] They concluded that the working wives "appeared to be in better physical and emotional health, held more positive attitudes towards life in general, and towards marriage in particular." By contrast, the husbands of the working wives "were in poorer health, and... less content with marriage, work and life in general" than their counterparts whose wives remained in the home.[48]

What of women who remain housewives? In a suggestive study on the prestige of housewives conducted in the Kitchener-Waterloo area in the mid-1970's, Eichler notes that "housewife" is a medium prestige occupation, just below stenographer. A housewife, then, can raise her prestige in one of two ways: either enter a higher prestige occupation or marry a man holding a higher prestige position. Marrying a man with a lower prestige position lowers her prestige as a housewife.[49]

Another indication of expanded marital choice is the rising proportion of childless couples. Although only about five per cent of couples choose this pattern, the rates are increasing. Following her own research and a review of U.S. and Canadian literature, Veevers writes that "compared with the rest of the population, persons who deliberately avoid parenthood tend to live in large urban areas, to have been married for the first time at a late age, to have been married more than once, to be non-religious, to be college educated, and to have both husband and wife employed in relatively high income positions."[50] Childless couples — often following an initial postponement of pregnancy — tend to come to the decision to remain that way gradually. In the face of conventional norms regarding parenthood, they justify their decision to others and to themselves in terms of the greater freedom they enjoy and the burden that a child would bring.[51]

Spouse Abuse

In recent years, Canadian researchers have begun paying more attention to violence between spouses — in particular to "battered wives." A report of the Canadian Advisory Council on the Status of Women estimates that a woman is battered each year in one out of ten households by a husband or live-in lover.[52] From 10 to 30 per cent of all police calls in Canada are related to domestic disputes.[53] Despite this, research on husband-wife violence in Canada is still in its infancy. One intensive study of a small group of bettered wives in Toronto suggests that wife beating was an almost taken-for-granted part of their marital relationship. The wives, themselves, had a generally low self-esteem and were relatively isolated from sources of possible help.[54] With a greater emphasis in recent years on women's rights, it appears that this pattern of suffering in silence may be changing. In 1978, 12,000 women sought help from community transition houses in dealing with violent husbands or "lovers".[55]

Divorce and Remarriage

Perhaps the most widely publicized recent alternative for married couples is divorce. Since the Divorce Act of 1968, which, for the first time permitted divorce on the grounds of marriage breakdown as well as adultery and other limited grounds, the divorce rate has been rising rapidly; from

54.8 per 100,000 of population in 1968 to 243.4 in 1978.[56] Assuming the divorce rate for 1971 — 137.6 per 100,000 — nearly one quarter of Canadians marrying before the age of 26 will eventually divorce.[57] A more recent estimate, based on current rates, is that 40 per cent of marriages will end in divorce.

One important byproduct of this relatively high rate of divorce[58] is the number of children who are affected by it. The proportion of divorcing couples with children has been increasing in the last several years. It was as high, in 1975, as 57.6 per cent. The average number of children involved in these marriages was 1.17, compared to an average of 1.6 for all Canadian families.[59] As we might suspect, clinical studies — mostly in the U.S. — report that children of divorce experience psychological problems and "may have more emotional scars than children who have grown up in a happy and stable home."[60] They appear to fare no worse, however, than children of maladjusted, but lasting marriages.

As the rate of divorce in Canada has risen, so too has the rate of remarriage. Some 75 per cent of divorcees remarry; with higher rates for men than women. In 1966, of those marrying only 4.5 per cent of men and 4.3 per cent of women had been married before. In 1976, the comparable figures were 13.4 and 11.9 per cent. Remarriages occur relatively soon. In 1971, the average gap between divorce and remarriage was less than three years.[61]

The Middle Aged and Aged

Contemporary descriptions of the family often follow a "life cycle" approach: from courtship, through marriage and parenthood, to middle and old age. We have relatively little information on the family relationships of the middle aged and elderly in Canada. As parents get older, of course, their children become more independent and leave home. In two-parent Canadian families in which the husband is 45 to 54, about one out of four still have children at home. For those in which husbands are 55 to 64, the percentage drops to 7.3.[62]

In the past, sociologists tended to refer to the time when children leave home — usually middle age — as the period of the "empty nest;" implying that it was an especially difficult time for mothers whose attention and emotional life had centered on their children. In line with the women's movement, more recent writings are likely to stress the opportunities opened up for mothers rather than the "emptiness." Relatively little concrete research has been done on the subject, however.

Much more work has been done in recent years in Canada on the elderly — although relatively little of it specifically focuses on family relationships. The increasing number of elderly in our population stems from an increase in life expectancy (approximately 70 for males and 77 for females) and high birth rates and high immigration in the past. In 1961, 7.6 per cent of the Canadian population was 65 or older. In 1976, it had risen to 8.7 per cent.[63]

A decreasing proportion of the elderly in Canada are living with relatives. In 1971, only 15.5 per cent of women and 6.3 per cent of men over 65 lived with kin. Over two out of three elderly men lived with their wives, while only 35.9 per cent of elderly women did.[64] Since women usually marry older men, and they also live longer, the proportion of widows in Canada is high — roughly 4.5 widows for every widower. Almost all of these women live alone.

Leaving aside the serious economic and medical problems faced many of the elderly, family questions are probably best seen in terms of roles — the elderly as grandparents, or retired, or widowed. In each instance, we can consider the transition to the role in question and ask what expectations others (and the elderly themselves) have of the new positions. Problems often arise because transitions to these roles may be difficult to make and the expectations may be ambiguous, inconsistent, or even conflicting. With the exception of demographic data, most relevant literature on the elderly in a family setting (although probably less so for widows)[65] derives from studies done in the United States.[66]

PARENTS AND CHILDREN

According to the 1976 census, close to 90 per cent of Canadian children under 25 years of age lived with their parents. In the following five years, however, the situation changed considerably. The number of single parents grew by 27.6 per cent and 20 per cent of all households consisted of a single person. Along with the increasing age of marriage, these figures suggest that fundamental changes are occurring in Canadian family life.[67]

Over the years, Canadian families have become smaller. The average number of persons per family in 1971 was 3.7. In 1976, it was 3.5 The sharpest decline occurred in Quebec, where the number of persons per family dropped from 3.9 to 3.5.[68]

This decrease in family size directly reflects the smaller number of children per family. In 1961, the average was 1.9. In 1971, it was 1.8, and in 1976, 1.6:[69] not enough in itself to maintain a stable population. There is also a trend toward what Wargon calls the "younging" of parenthood: couples having their children at earlier ages.[70] This, along with smaller families, longer life expectancy, and a propensity for children to leave home at younger ages, means that many couples — to continue a trend of recent decades — will be spending a longer time alone after their children have left home.[71]

One especially significant trend in recent years is the increase in the proportion of lone-parent families: from 8.2 per cent in 1966 to 9.8 in 1976.[72] In over 80 per cent of these families the lone parent is the mother.

Most have only one child at home and of those with older children, a high proportion are widows. Without long-term studies, we can only speculate on the significance of this trend.[73]

The two parent nuclear family, as we have noted, is still the most common family arrangement in Canada. Over the last several decades, there has been a corresponding decrease in the number of three generation families or family households containing additional persons. From 1971 to 1976, the percentage of households including children-in-law decreased by 30.7 per cent, the number of grandchildren by 22.1 per cent, the number of parents-in-law by 27.3 per cent, and the number of unrelated members by 43 per cent.[74]

Gender Role Socialization

Perhaps most Canadian research about the relationships between parents and children focuses, in one way or another, on gender role socialization. Two recent reviews[75] of Canadian and some American literature present a general picture of children who become aware of gender role stereotyping quite early and who have an image of males with more freedom, prestige, and power than females. Research indicates that this process of stereotyping begins in the family and is then reinforced in books geared to young audiences,[76] by the behavior of school teachers,[77] by popular magazines,[78] and by general social relationships. Acceptance and recognition of these patterns continues through adolescence and into young adulthood.[79]

Research done on this subject in Canada is consistent, plausible, and in line with our educated observations — as well as with similar research done in the U.S. In the area of gender role socialization, the general U.S. and Canadian patterns are by and large the same. But ethnicity is, in some important respects, more salient in Canada than in the U.S. While it is difficult to generalize because of the limited data we have available on variations among and within particular ethnic groups, there is evidence of the persistence of more traditional family relations within ethnic pockets or enclaves in Canada. In the recent past, reports on the Hutterites, Mennonites, Dutch, Greeks, Italians, and Poles suggest that traditional male and female roles were very much accepted, as evidenced in dress, family rituals, assigned tasks, schooling, and work opportunities. Girls were expected to help around the house, to become skilled at domestic activities, to take a subordinate role in major family decisions, and to look forward to becoming housewives and mothers. Boys were expected to do masculine-defined tasks, prepare for a role as breadwinner, and later to assume community leadership roles. Girls were encouraged and expected to identify with their mothers and other women, and boys with their fathers and other men. Children were not often presented with other alternatives, either in the family or in their ethnic communities. This is not a very different picture from that in the English and French communities in Canada a few generations ago.

Some more recent reports of studies of Canadian ethnic groups, however, present a more complex picture. Sturino speaks of the encouragement some Italian parents give to their sons to study for technical and professional, but not academic careers.[80] Danziger, in another study, found that girls from Italian families, after being in Canada for a few years, became more willing to express their feelings to their parents.[81] Anderson and Driedger report that an egalitarian family is emerging among more liberal, young Mennonite families.[82] And Radecki in regard to Poles,[83] Chimbos to Greeks,[84] and Ishwaran and Chan to the Dutch,[85] all point to the same rejection of traditional patriarchal ways.

Gender role socialization is typically affected not only by ethnicity, but also by social class. Radecki suggests that working class Poles encourage higher education only for males, while the middle class encourages education for both males and females.[86] In Montreal, Taylor, Frasure-Smith and Lambert studied 80 husband-wife sets.[87] The parents were asked to respond to tape recorded versions of a six-year-old child in various family interaction episodes. They observed that working class parents, in general, were more severe than middle class parents in their reactions to temper outbursts and were more restrictive of the child's bid for autonomy or requests to have a guest over to play. Less common, but also signficant, were observed differences between English and French Canadians: the English tended to give tougher and more restrictive replies. Differences in parents' responses by the gender of the child were not apparent.[88] These findings were consistent with those from one study comparing grade 8 and grade 12 boys and girls in private schools in Vancouver. The researchers discovered little difference between the younger male and female pupils in "fear of success," a difference which has been commonly cited as one effect of differential gender role socialization.[89]

FAMILY POLICY AND FAMILY PROBLEMS

Problem areas associated with the family differentially concern particular groups of people: the elderly, poor, parents in need of daycare, battered wives, or handicapped or abused children. Governments and welfare agencies always have policies of one kind or another toward such groups, although these policies are not always explicit. Family policy as such, however, has not been developed as an area of systematic study either in Canada or the U.S.[90] We do not have any recognized criteria for establishing family well-being, any clear conception of the effects of particular policies on families, or much analysis that directly links these problem groups with family relationships.

In questions concerning the family, there can be no sharp line between matters of policy, social problems and social trends. We have observed, for example, that in recent years, an increasing number of children are being raised by separated, divorced or unmarried parents, mostly mothers. These parents, besides being younger than comparable parents a generation ago, also tend to be at the lower end of the economic scale,[91] and many are on welfare.[92] Such a situation raises policy questions, for both our socio-economic system and governments.

Similarly, when researchers point to the high proportion of elderly women with incomes below the poverty line,[93] to the school and peer group problems of children of alcoholics,[94] to marital violence,[95] to the increasing rate of child abuse,[96] to the increasing number of teen-age unmarried mothers who are keeping their children,[97] to inconsistencies in the country in the handling of abortion,[98] to the relatively small proportion of children of working mothers in day care centers,[99] to psychological problems among the children of divorce,[100] to dilemmas experienced by widows,[101] or even to the income differentials between divorced and separated women and their male counterparts,[102] policy questions are implied.

As a rule, particular interest groups in Canada have been more active in systematically developing the area of family policy than academic research-ers and scholars. The Vanier Institute of the Family often raises issues for public discussion.[103] The Canadian Council on Children and Youth has been a spokesman for numerous issues concerned with the condition and rights of children.[104] The Canadian Advisory Council on the Status of Women has initiated numerous reports on behalf of particular groups of women.[105] Finally, the Canadian Council on Social Development has issued reports on foster care, housing for the elderly, homemaker services, abused children, one parent families, family planning, and numerous other topics associated with family welfare.

Federal, provincial, and local governments — through direct assistance to individuals, and through funding of various agencies — are the prime framers of family policy. Given this, it is appropriate to ask what ideologies they follow, what values and pressures enter into their decisions, how their policies affect families and family relationships, and what ties exist between government policymakers and interested business and voluntary organiza-tions. These issues have not, for the most part, been systematically explored in Canada.

We find one prominent exception to the rule that the formulation of Canadian family poicy has not been preceded by systematic analysis: the area of family law. Federal and provincial law reform commissions, follow-ing studies and analyses of family issues and problems, have rather thoroughly analyzed — at least from a legal point of view — the implica-tions and inequities of earlier statutes and, with recent trends in mind, have made recommendations to their respective governments. The legislation which has followed regarding such matters as the distribution of family property, family courts, maintenance obligations, and child custody are much more in line with current norms, values, and current views than in the past.[106] Many of the questions raised by social scientists, however, remain untouched.[107]

CONCLUSION

Inevitably, there will be large gaps in our knowledge about the Canadian family. Relationships within families — and between the family and the larger social order — are complex and constantly changing. Consequently, neither Canada nor any other country has the resources to study the wide and varied range of relevant topics in detail. Necessarily, then, there must be a selection of problems for study and research.

Our basic knowledge about the family in Canada is provided by the census, vital statistics, labor force surveys, and other government reports. In periods of rapid change, however, these data may not indicate the latest shifts and national surveys and polls may be more useful as sources of information about attitudes and behavior.

With basic source materials like these in hand, we must then be selective in the subjects we choose to study or analyze. Two broad criteria seem to have been used by Canadian researchers in making this selection. First, for reasons of human interest, humanitarianism, and social policy, we find that many researchers have been concerned with social problems: one-parent families, the elderly, child abuse, battered wives, and family law.

Second, in line with the changing position of women in society, we find numerous studies associated in one way or another with changing gender roles: women in the work force, socialization patterns, divorce, premarital sex relations, and childless couples.

Beyond this, we have a range of materials generated as a by-product of studies originally primarily concerned with population growth, language, continuity of ethnic patterns, historical development, leisure, women in the work world, or other research not specifically concerned with the family. In many cases, the conclusions reached in these studies tend to bear out what we suspect from our own experience and from reports in the popular media. This, of course, in no way belies their value.

In many important respects, Canada — with its distinctive history, education, political system, media, ethnic populations, and public policies — is different from any other country. In most trends directly associated with family and family relationships, however, there seems to be little that sets us apart from major trends in the United States and Western Europe. All over the industrialized world, the church and kinship groups have lost some of their conservative influence. Birth rates have generally been decreasing, more women have been obtaining access to higher education and following new careers, divorce rates are higher, premarital sex is more openly accepted, pressures are strong to reduce differences in the socialization of boys and girls, and there is greater acceptance of less conventional family forms.

This is not to say, however, that there is uniformity in the ways in which these trends have been manifest in various countries. Canada, for example, has been and continues to be more conservative than the United States: the age at marriage is higher, the birth rate is higher, the divorce rate is lower, and the proportion of wives working for pay is smaller. Yet major trends in behaviour and attitudes in both countries appear to be the same. Similarly, there are important observable differences within Canada. The Atlantic provinces, particularly Newfoundland, are the most conservative. Families are larger, divorce rates are lower, and fewer women are in the labor force. Ontario and the Western provinces — particularly, British Columbia and Alberta — represent the opposite pole. But the Atlantic provinces represent a relatively small part of Canada's total population and, in some respects, their patterns are regional. Thus in general, "We may anticipate the gradual eclipse and disappearance of the more traditional types of family constellations found there."[108]

Compared to the United States and England, we have relatively fewer studies of many specific issue areas associated with the family. We do have, however, a limited literature dealing with clearly distinctive aspects of and trends in Canadian family life: those dealing with regional variations, language differences, ethnic relationships, or political socialization in the Canadian context.

Despite the variations we observe, we must also recognize that the Canadian family remains, in many respects, a conservative institution and force for stability. Most Canadians still choose marriage and a husband-wife nuclear family unit. Relatively few married couples choose not to have children. Divorced men and women are likely to remarry. Parents are expected — through their life styles, the educational opportunities they offer their children, and inheritance — to give their children the best life chances they can.

Theory has not been given a high priority in Canadian family studies. Researchers have usually begun their studies with specific substantive problems in mind and then asked what bodies of theory — or more often, what concepts and perspectives — are likely to be most helpful in understanding the phenomena in question. Most often, Canadian researchers have undertaken their work either in a comparative or social change context.

In recent years, Canadian family scholars have not sought to develop complex models which seek to integrate a range of studies on particular topics as some of their American counterparts have.[109] Considering the scope of the field, our limited data, the many problems of immediate interest, and the rapid changes that are occurring, it does not seem likely that theory or model building will become a major preoccupation of Canadian sociologists. Rather, using basic demographic data and everyday knowledge and insight, Canadian family specialists are likely to continue to be eclectic in perspective and most interested in illuminating problem areas, explaining social change, and comparing Canadian trends with those in other countries — or among the regions of this vast and diverse nation.

NOTES

[1] Garigue, 1962; Lavigne and Stoddart, 1977.

[2] Katz, 1975. For a recent review of socio-historical studies of the family, see Nett, 1981. For a selection of articles, see Parr, 1982.

[3] Synge, 1979.

[4] Synge, 1980.

[5] Statistics Canada Daily, Nov. 5, 1979.

[6] Atkinson and Murray, 1979.

[7] Smith, 1975. For a recent feminist review, see Wilson, 1982.

[8] Boyd et al., 1976.

[9] Nakamura et al., 1979.

[10] Women's Bureau, 1980.

[11] Statistics Canada, Oct. 1979.

[12] Lupri and Mills, 1979.

[13] *Toronto Star,* Feb. 27, 1980.

[14] Spitz, 1945.

[15] Bowlby, 1952.

[16] Armstrong and Armstrong, 1978.

[17] Connelly, 1977.

[18] Kohl, 1976.

[19] Porter, 1965; Porter, Porter and Blishen, 1979; Anisef and Okihiro, 1982.

[20] Statistics Canada, 1976.

[21] National Council on Welfare, 1979.

[22] Crysdale, 1968; Lambert, 1969; Gaskell, 1975.

[23] Garigue, 1962: Elkin, 1964.

[24] Peter, 1976.

[25] Ishwaran, 1977.

[26] Boissevain, 1976; Danziger, 1975; Sturino, 1980.

[27] Chimbos, 1980.

[28] Radecki, 1980.

[29] Anderson and Driedger, 1980.

[30] Tavuchis, 1979: 131.

[31] Boyd, 1975.

[32] Hobart, 1979.

[33] Basavarajappa, 1978: 24. See Krishnan, this volume, for a general discussion of marriage and fertility patterns.

[34]Veevers, 1977: 8.

[35]Statistics Canada, Oct. 1979.

[36]Kalbach and McVey, 1976; Kalbach, 1983.

[37]Ramu, 1979: 5.

[38]Veevers, 1977: 18; Kalbach, 1983: 46.

[39]Veevers, 1977: 19; Kalbach, 1983: 43.

[40]Burnet, 1976.

[41]Statistics Canada, Sept. 1979.

[42]Wargon, 1979: 15.

[43]Basavarajappa, 1978: 117.

[44]Whitehurst, 1977.

[45]Brinkerhoff and Lupri, 1978.

[46]Meissner et al., 1975: 436.

[47]The husbands were engineers and accountants, the jobs of the wives were not given.

[48]Burke and Weir, 1976: 284-85.

[49]Eichler, 1977.

[50]Veevers, 1979: 10.

[51]Veevers, 1980.

[52]Canadian Advisory Council on the Status of Women, 1980.

[53]Schlesinger, 1979a.

[54]Chan, 1978.

[55]Canadian Advisory Council on the Status of Women, 1980.

[56]Statistics Canada Bulletin, Sept. 4, 1979.

[57]Basavarajappa, 1978: 50-59.

[58]Divorce rates vary considerably within Canada. The highest are in the west. In 1980, the rate per 100,000 of population was over 350 in Alberta and British Columbia. Ontario's rate was the same as Canada's overall rate, 259, and Quebec's was somewhat lower. In general, higher divorce rates are associated with urban residence, Protestantism, and especially teenage marriage. From 1969 to 1979, 42.4% of divorcing wives were 20 years of age or less.

[59]Ambert, 1980: 40.

[60]Ambert, 1980: 170.

[61]Statistics Canada, Oct. 1979.

[62]Wargon, 1979: 84.

[63]Statistics Canada, March 1979.

[64]Dulude, 1978.

[65]Vachon, 1979.

[66]Marshall, 1980.

[67]Wargon, 1979: 15.

[68]Statistics Canada, Oct., 1979.

[69]Statistics Canada, Oct., 1979.

[70]Wargon, 1979: 17.

[71]Statistics Canada, Oct., 1979.

[72]Wargon, 1979: 82.

[73]Wargon, 1979: 16.

[74]Davids, 1980.

[75]Mackie, 1979; Nett, 1979.

[76]Pyke, 1975.

[77]Russell, 1978.

[78]Wilson, 1976.

[79]Hobart, 1973.

[80]Sturino, 1980.

[81]Danziger, 1976.

[82]Anderson and Driedger, 1980.

[83]Radecki, 1980.

[84]Chimbos, 1980.

[85]Ishwaran and Chan, 1980.

[86]Radecki, 1980.

[87]Half had 6-year-old sons and half had 6-year-old daughters. Half were English-Canadian half French-Canadian. And half were working class and half middle class.

[88]Taylor, Frasure-Smith and Lambert, 1978.

[89]Kimball, 1977.

[90]Giele, 1979; Redekop, 1978.

[91]Wargon, 1979: 87.

[92]Schlesinger, 1979b.

[93]Dulude, 1978.

[94]Cork, 1969.

[95]Chan, 1978; Chimbos, 1978; Canadian Advisory Council on the Status of Women, 1980.

[96]Van Stolk, 1978.

[97]Lipovenko, 1980.

[98]Greenglass, 1976.

[99]Hepworth, 1975.

[100]Ambert, 1980.

[101]Vachon, 1979.

[102]Boyd, 1977.

[103]Vanier Institute of the Family, 1974; 1977.

[104]Canadian Council on Children and Youth, 1978.

[105]Canadian Advisory Council on the Status of Women, 1979; 1980; Pearson, 1979.

[106]Law Reform Commission of Canada, 1974.

[107]Elkin, 1975.

[108]Wargon, 1979: 18.

[109]Burr et al., 1979.

Bibliography

Ambert, Anne-Marie. *Divorce in Canada.* Don Mills, Ont.: Academic Press Canada, 1980.

Anderson, Alan and Leo Driedger. "The Mennonite Family: Culture and Kin in Rural Saskatchewan." In K. Ishwaran, ed. *Canadian Families: Ethnic Variations.* Toronto: McGraw-Hill Ryerson, 1980.

Anisef, Paul and Norman R. Okihiro. *Losers and Winners.* Toronto: Butterworths, 1982.

Armstrong, Pat and Hugh Armstrong. *The Double Ghetto.* Toronto: McClelland and Stewart, 1978.

Atkinson, Tom and Michael Murray. "Values, Domains and the Perceived Quality of Life." Downsview, Ontario: York University, Institute for Behavioural Research, Quality of Life Project, Working Paper, No. 1, 1979.

Basavarajappa, K. G. *Marital Status and Nupitality in Canada.* Ottawa: Statistics Canada, 1978.

Boissevain, Jeremy. "Family and Kinship among Italians in Montreal." In K. Ishwaran, ed. *The Canadian Family.* Rev. ed. Toronto: Holt, Rinehart and Winston, 1976.

Bowlby, John. *Maternal Care and Mental Health.* Geneva: World Health Organization, 1952.

Boyd, Monica. "English-Canadian and French-Canadian Attitudes Towards Women: Results of the Canadian Gallup Polls." *Journal of Comparative Family Studies* 6 (1975): 153-69.

_____. "The Forgotten Minority: The Socioeconomic Status of Divorced and Separated Women." In Patricia Marchak, ed. *The Working Sexes.* Vancouver: Institute of Industrial Relations, University of British Columbia, 1977.

Boyd, Monica, Margrit Eichler and John R. Hofley. "Family: Functions, Formation, and Fertility." In Gail C. A. Cook, ed. *Opportunity for Choice.* Ottawa: Statistics Canada, 1976.

Brinkerhoff, M. B. and E. Lupri. "Theoretical and Methodological Issues in the Use of Decision-Making as an Indicator of Conjugal Power: Some Canadian Observations." *Canadian Journal of Sociology* 3 (1978): 1-20.

Burke, Ronald J. and Tamara Weir. "Relationships of Wives' Employment Status to Husband, Wife and Pair Satisfaction and Performance." *Journal of Marriage and the Family* 38 (1976): 279-87.

Burnet, Jean. "Ethnicity: Canadian Experience and Policy." *Sociological Focus* (1976): 199-208.

Burr, W. R., R. Hill, R. I. Nye, and I. L. Reiss. *Contemporary Theories about the Family.* Vol. 1. New York: Free Press, 1979.

Canadian Advisory Council on the Status of Women. *Women in the Public Service: Barriers to Equal Opportunity.* Ottawa, 1979.

_____. *Wife-Battering in Canada: The Vicious Circle.* Ottawa, 1980.

Canadian Council on Children and Youth. *Admittance Restricted: The Child as Citizen in Canada.* Ottawa, 1978.

Chan, Kwok Bun. *Husband Wife Violence in Toronto.* Ph.D. dissertation, York University, 1978.

Chimbos, Peter. *Marital Violence: A Study of Interspouse Homocide.* San

Francisco: R. and E. Research Associates, Inc., 1978.

_____. "The Greek-Canadian Family: Tradition and Change." In K. Ishwaran, ed. *Canadian Families: Ethnic Variations*. Toronto: McGraw-Hill Ryerson, 1980.

Clifford, Howard. "Infant Group Care: the Stepchild of Day Care." *Canada's Mental Health* 27 (1979): 23-25.

Connelly, M. Patricia. "The Economic Context of Women's Labour Force Participation in Canada." In Patricia Marchak, ed. *The Working Sexes*. Vancouver: Institute of Industrial Relations, University of British Columbia, 1977.

Cork, R. Margaret. *The Forgotten Children*. Toronto: Paperjacks, 1969.

Crysdale, Stewart. "Social and Occupational Mobility in Riverdale: A Blue-Collar Community." In W. E. Mann, ed. *Canada: A Sociological Profile*. Toronto: Copp Clark, 1968.

Danziger, Kurt. "Differences in Acculturation and Patterns of Socialization among Italian Immigrant Families." In Robert M. Pike and Elia Zureik, eds. *Socialization and Values in Canadian Society*. Vol. II Toronto: Carleton Library, Macmillan, 1975.

_____. "The Acculturation of Italian Immigrant Girls." In K. Ishwaran, ed. *The Canadian Family*. Rev. ed. Toronto: Holt, Rinehart and Winston, 1976.

Davids, Leo. "Family Change in Canada, 1971-1976." *Journal of Marriage and the Family* 42 (1980): 177-83.

Dulude, Louise. *Women and Aging: A Report on the Rest of Our Lives*. Ottawa: Canadian Advisory Council on the Status of Women, 1978.

Eichler, Margrit. "The Prestige of the Occupation Housewife." In Patricia Marchak, ed. *The Working Sexes*. Vancouver: Institute of Industrial Relations, University of British Columbia, 1977.

Elkin, Frederick. *The Family in Canada*. Ottawa: Vanier Institute of the Family, 1964.

_____. "Review of 'Studies on Family Property Law'." *Social Sciences in Canada* 3 (1975): 19

Garigue, Phillipe. *La vie familiale des Canadiens Francais,* Montréal: Presses de l'Université de Montréal, 1962.

Gaskell, Jane S. "The Sex-Role Ideology of Working Class Girls." *Canadian Review of Sociology and Anthropology* 12 (1975) 453-61.

Giele, Janet Z. "Social Policy and the Family." In A. Inkeles, J. Coleman and R. H. Turner. *Annual Review of Sociology* 5 (1979): 275-302.

Grayson, J. Paul. "Male Hegemony and the English Canadian Novel." *Canadian Review of Sociology and Anthropology* 20 (1983): 1-21.

Greenglass, Esther R. *After Abortion*. Don Mills, Ont.: Longman Canada, 1976.

Hepworth, Philip E. *Day Care Services for Children*. Ottawa: Canadian Council for Social Development, 1975.

Hobart, Charles W. "Attitudes towards Parenthood among Canadian Young People." *Journal of Marriage and the Family* 35 (1973): 71-81.

_____. "Courtship Process: Marital Sex." In G. N. Ramu, ed. *Courtship, Marriage and the Family in Canada*. Toronto: Macmillan, 1979: 37-58.

Howard, Irving. *The Family Myth: a Study of Relationships Between Married Couples and Their Parents*. Toronto: Copp Clark, 1972.

Ishwaran, K. *Family, Kinship and Community: A Study of Dutch Canadians*. Toronto: McGraw-Hill Ryerson, 1977.

_____. ed. *The Canadian Family*. Rev. ed. Toronto: Holt, Rinehart and Winston, 1976.

Ishwaran, K. and Kwok Chan. "Time, Space and Family Relationships in a Rural Dutch Community." In K. Ishwaran, ed. *Canadian Families: Ethnic Variations*. Toronto: McGraw-Hill Ryerson, 1980.

Kalbach, Warren E. "The Canadian Family: A Profile." In K. Ishwaran, ed. *The Canadian Family.* Toronto: Gage, 1983.

Kalbach, Warren E. and Wayne W. McVey, Jr. "The Canadian Family: A Demographic Profile." In Lyle E. Larson, ed. *The Canadian Family in Comparative Perspective.* Scarborough, Ontario: Prentice-Hall, 1976.

Katz, Michael B. *The People of Hamilton, Canada West.* Cambridge, Mass.: Harvard University Press, 1975.

Kimball, Meredith M. "Women and Success: A Basic Conflict?" In Marylee Stephenson, ed. *Women in Canada.* Rev. ed. Don Mills, Ontario: General Publishing, 1977.

Kohl, Seena. *Working Together: Women and Family in Southern Saskatchewan.* Toronto: Holt, Rinehart and Winston, 1976.

Lacasse, François. "Women at Home: The Cost to the Canadian Economy of the Withdrawal From the Labour Force of A Major Proportion of the Female Population." *Studies of the Royal Commission on the Status of Women.* Ottawa: Information Canada, 1971.

Lambert, Ronald D. *Sex Role Imagery in Children.* Ottawa: Information Canada, 1969.

Lavigne, Marie and Jennifer Stoddart. "Women's Work in Montreal at the Beginning of the Century." In M. Stephenson, ed. *Women in Canada.* Rev. ed. Don Mills, Ont.: General Publishing, 1977.

Law Reform Commission of Canada. *Reports and Working Papers on Family Law.* Ottawa: Information Canada, 1974.

Lipovenko, Dorothy. Toronto: *Globe and Mail,* Jan. 31, 1980.

Lupri, Eugen and Donald L. Mills. "The Changing Roles of Canadian Women in Family and Work: An Overview," In E. Lupri, ed. *The Changing Roles of Women in Family and Society: A Cross-cultural Comparison.* Leiden: E. J. Brill, 1979.

Mackie, Marlene. "Gender Socialization in Childhood and Adolescence." In K. Ishwaran, ed. *Childhood and Adolescence in Canada.* Toronto: McGraw-Hill Ryerson, 1979.

Marshall, Victor W., ed. *Aging in Canada: Social Perspectives.* Toronto: Fitzhenry and Whiteside, 1980.

Meissner, Martin, Elizabeth W. Humphreys, Scott M. Meis and William J. Scheu. "No Exit for Wives: Sexual Division of Labour." *Canadian Review of Sociology and Anthropology* 12 (1975): 424-39.

Nakamura, Alice, Masao Nakamura and Dallas Cullen. *Employment and Earnings of Married Females.* Ottawa: Statistics Canada, 1979.

National Council on Welfare. *Women and Poverty.* Ottawa, 1979.

Nett, Emily M. "Socialization for Sex Roles." In G. N. Ramu, ed. *Courtship, Marriage and the Family in Canada.* Toronto: Macmillan, 1979.

_____. "Canadian Families in Socio-Historical Perspective." *Canadian Journal of Sociology* 6 (1981): 239-60.

Ornstein, Michael. "The Impact of Marital Status, Age, and Employment on Female Suicide in British Columbia." *Canadian Review of Sociology and Anthropology* 20 (1983): 96-100.

Palmer, Sally E. "Reasons for Marriage Breakdown: A Case Study in South Western Ontario." *Journal of Comparative Family Studies* 23 (1971): 251-62.

Parr, Joy, ed. *Childhood and Family in Canadian History.* Toronto: McClelland and Stewart, 1982.

Pearson, Mary. *The Second Time Around: A Study of Women Returning to the Work Force.* Ottawa: Canadian Advisory Council on the Status of Women, 1979.

Peter, Karl. "The Hutterite Family." In K. Ishwaran, ed. *The Canadian Family.*

Rev. ed. Toronto: Holt, Rinehart and Winston, 1976.

Peters, John F. "A Comparison of Mate Selection and Marriage in the First and Second Marriages in a Selected Sample of the Remarried Divorced." *Journal of Comparative Family Studies* 7 (1976): 483-90.

Porter, John. *The Vertical Mosaic.* Toronto: University of Toronto Press, 1965.

Porter, Marion, John Porter and Bernard Blishen. *Does Money Matter?* Toronto: Macmillan, 1979.

Pyke, S. W. "Children's Literature: Conceptions of Sex Roles." In Elia Zureik and Robert M. Pike, eds. *Socialization and Social Values in Canada.* Vol II. Toronto: McClelland and Stewart, 1975.

Radecki, Henry. "The Polish-Canadian Family: A Study in Historical and Contemporary Perspectives." In K. Ishwaran, ed. *Canadian Families: Ethnic Variations.* Toronto: McGraw-Hill Ryerson, 1980.

Ramu, G. N., ed. *Courtship, Marriage and the Family in Canada.* Toronto: Macmillan of Canada, 1979.

Redekop, John H. "Social Policy; the Role of the Governing Party." In Shankar A. Yelaja, ed. *Canadian Social Policy.* Waterloo, Ontario: Wilfred Laurier University Press, 1978.

Russell, S. *Sex Role Socialization in the High School: A Study of the Patriarchal Culture.* Ph.D. dissertation, University of Toronto, 1978.

Schlesinger, Benjamin. "Women and Men in Second Marriages," In S. Parvez Wakil, ed. *Marriage, Family and Society: Canadian Perspectives.* Toronto: Butterworths, 1975.

_____. *Families: Canada.* Toronto: McGraw-Hill Ryerson, 1979a.

_____. *One in Ten: The Single Parent in Canada.* Toronto: Faculty of Education, University of Toronto, 1979b.

Smith, Dorothy E. "Ideological Structures and How Women are Excluded." *Canadian Review of Sociology and Anthropology* 12 (1975): 353-69.

Spitz, R. A. "Hospitalism: An Inquiry into the Genesis of Psychiatric Conditions in Early Childhood." *Psychoanalytic Study of the Child I* (1945): 53-74.

Statistics Canada. *Canada's Elderly.* Ottawa: March, 1979.

_____. *Canada's Population: Demographic Perspectives.* Ottawa: Sept. 1979.

_____. *Divorce, Law and the Family in Canada.* Ottawa: 1983.

Sturino, Franc. "Family and Kin Cohesion among Southern Italian Immigrants in Toronto." In K. Ishwaran, ed. *Canadian Families: Ethnic Variations.* Toronto: McGraw-Hill Ryerson, 1980.

Synge, Jane. "The Transition from School to Work: Growing Up Working Class in Early 20th Century Hamilton, Ontario." In K. Ishwaran, ed. *Childhood and Adolescence in Canada.* Toronto: McGraw-Hill Ryerson, 1979.

_____. "Work and Family Support Patterns of the Aged in the Early Twentieth Century." In Victor W. Marshall, ed. *Aging in Canada: Social Perspectives.* Toronto: Fitzhenry and Whiteside, 1980.

Synnott, Anthony. "Little Angels, Little Devils: A Sociology of Children." *Canadian Review of Sociology and Anthropology* 20 (1983): 79-95.

Tavuchis, Nicholas. "Ethnic Perspectives." In G. N. Ramu, ed. *Courtship, Marriage and the Family in Canada.* Toronto: Macmillan of Canada, 1979.

Taylor, Donald M., Nancy Frasure-Smith, and Wallace E. Lambert. "Psychological Development of French and English Canadian Children: Child-Rearing Attitudes and Ethnic Identity." In Leo Driedger, ed. *The Canadian Ethnic Mosaic: A Quest for Identity.* Toronto: McClelland and Stewart, 1978.

Timson, Judith. "Teensex," *Maclean's.* March 31, 1980.

Vachon, Mary L. S. *Identity Change over the First Two Years of Bereavement: Social Relationships and Social Support in Widowhood.* Ph.D. thesis, York University, 1979.

Van Stolk, Mary. *The Battered Child in Canada.* Rev. ed., Toronto: McClelland and Stewart, 1978.

Vanier Institute of the Family. *Some Policy Approaches of the Vanier Institute of the Family,* Ottawa, 1974.

_____. *A Statement of Contemporary Familial Life Styles.* Ottawa, 1977.

Veevers, J. E. *The Family in Canada.* Ottawa, Statistics Canada, 1977.

_____. "Voluntary Childlessness: A Review of Issues and Evidence" *Marriage and Family Review* 2 (1979): 1-24.

_____. *Childless by Choice.* Toronto: Butterworths, 1980.

Wargon, Sylvia T. *Children in Canadian Families,* Ottawa: Statistics Canada, 1979.

Whitehurst, Robert N. "Youth Views Marriage: Awareness of Present and Future Potentials in Relationships." In Roger W. Libby and Robert N. Whitehurst, eds. *Marriage and Alternatives: Exploring Intimate Relationships.* Glenview, Illinois: Scott, Foresman and Co., 1977.

Wilson, S. *The Changing Image of Canadian Women as Reflected in Popular Magazines — 1931-1970.* Ph.D. dissertation, University of Toronto, 1976.

_____. *Women, the Family and the Economy.* Toronto: McGraw-Hill Ryerson, 1982.

Women's Bureau, Labour Canada. *Women in the Labour Force, Facts and Figures.* 1977 ed. Ottawa, 1980.

CHAPTER 4

Some Good Purpose: Notes on Religion and Political Culture in Canada[1]

Roger O'Toole

INTRODUCTION

During recent decades, sociologists have sought after many strange gods.[2] Crazes and cults have come and gone as theoretical and methodological prophets have scrambled for hegemony.[3] Meanwhile, the fortunes of particular subdisciplines have waxed and waned in response to the magnetic power of funds.

Amidst the uproar, at least one sociological subdiscipline has remained relatively undisturbed. The sociology of religion has, at least in Canada, remained unembarrassed by riches: whether in the shape of numerous zealous recruits, in the guise of inflammatory intellectual blueprints, or in the more prosaically tangible form of coin of the realm. This has proven a mixed blessing. On the one hand, practitioners within the discipline have perhaps been spared the unreadable plethora of trivia that appears to be a frequent consequence of current practices in large-scale research support; and have likewise been denied the dubious benefits of the dogmatic tracts of academic faddists and transients. On the other hand, their position on the academic sidelines of sociology has placed them in danger of intoxication from the stale air of the cloister.

Like their counterparts in other lands, Canadian sociologists of religion repress the doubts and complexes accompanying their status deprivation[4] by repetition of the first article of their creed, which affirms that the scientific study of religion is an enterprise which is, not merely intrinsically interesting, but central to the discipline of sociology as a whole.

The present essay participates in this act of faith, and does so, furthermore, by noting the degree to which Canadian society affords a particularly hospitable environment for analysis of the socio-cultural importance of the phenomenon of religion. In this regard, the discussion which follows also contains the ingredients of an act of hope. It attempts, under separate headings, to outline the scope of the sociology of religion in Canada: to explore the links between traditional religion and Canadian political culture; and to consider the present significance of religion in Canadian life from a number of theoretical perspectives.

THE SCOPE OF THE SOCIOLOGY OF RELIGION IN CANADA

In this brief essay, it is impossible to provide full characterization, let alone a critical synthesis, of all the diverse strands of research and teaching which might appropriately be labelled a "Canadian Sociology of Religion."[5] Scrutiny of a mass of publications and conference proceedings, together with relevant bibliographical sources,[6] reveals, however, that the work of Canadian scholars is a fairly typical product of the subdiscipline considered as an international enterprise. With few exceptions, Canadian sociologists of religion are indistinguishable from their American, British, French and German colleagues with respect to their perceptions of key concepts, classic literature, and theoretical issues; as well as their past and present empirical concerns and the methods by which these are exploited.[7]

Thus, Canadian sociologists of religion build upon foundations laid primarily by Weber and Durkheim (and to a lesser extent by Marx).[8] They exhibit a methodological bias towards quantitative survey research, while providing occasional and useful exceptions to this rule in the form of qualitative "participant-observation" studies.[9] Focusing primarily on institutional forms of religion,[10] they explore the links between formal religious affiliation and the social, economic and cultural attributes of individuals and groups.[11] Having scrutinized religious virtuosi or professionals,[12] and traced the fortunes of sundry churches, denominations and sects, they now exhibit fascination with the "new religious consciousness" manifested in various, largely imported, sects and cults of recent vintage.[13] More rarely, they take the broader view, ruminating theoretically upon general social or social-psychological aspects of religion,[14] and posing again the question that is the alpha and omega of their subdiscipline: what *is* religion?[15]

Despite the breadth and variety of such Canadian work in recent decades, an explicit or implicit common underlying theme may be discerned. Predictably, it is the same theme which dominates the analysis of religion in the rest of the Western world: *secularization,* the process whereby, in Bryan Wilson's succinct definition, "religious thinking, practice and institutions lose social significance."[16]

That Canadian sociologists have been drawn to the concept of secularization, despite its eloquent critics, should surprise no one.[17] The delayed decline of organized religion in this country has been characterized by a bewildering swiftness and intensity which has tempted more than one observer to discern "the end of a religion."[18] Indeed, so taken for granted is the tightening grip of secularization, even (and perhaps especially) in the formerly "priest-ridden" province of Québec, that dissenters to this orthodoxy snatch at straws in their haste to proclaim "the return of the sacred,"[19] hanging their weighty thesis upon the extremely fragile peg of "the new religious consciousness."[20]

The bemusement with which sociologists have apprehended this Northern *Götterdämmerung* underscores a fundamental point that is in danger of neglect. In their anxiety to understand a world in which documentation and analysis of traditional religious organizations appears akin to recording the qualities of exotic endangered species, observers of the Canadian religious scene may be inclined to forget to what extent in the very recent past such phenomena appeared as natural, and perhaps even necessary, elements of Canadian life.

Notwithstanding this danger, the rapid disenchantment of Canadian society has contributed to the demystification of many students of religion. However, by causing them to pause and take their theoretical bearings through renewed intellectual meditation on the nature of religion, this demystification has engendered a receptivity to perspectives requiring painful re-thinking and demanding arduous re-exploration of the definitional labyrinth. For example, the response to Luckmann's provocative "invisible religion" thesis, may, whatever the merits of its attendant debate, be understood and appreciated in this light.

This informed and wary openness to theoretical innovation — fused with a sophisticated sensitivity to the impact of secularization — is the prime requisite of the Canadian sociologist of religion in the closing decades of the present century. But, as previously observed, awareness of actual and potential changes in traditional religion, alertness to the possibility of novel species of religiosity, or even the capacity to visualize the nature of a society without religion are not, of themselves, sufficient. These qualities require, as their foundation, thorough appreciation of the vital role played by institutional forms of religion in the creation and development of this society.[21]

Nurturing such an appreciation appears, moreover, to be of more than academic importance: it is an undertaking relevant to all citizens of a nation perched precariously on the brink of political, regional, social and economic fragmentation.

TRADITIONAL RELIGION AND CANADIAN POLITICAL CULTURE

It is possible to ascertain the distance which Canadians have travelled along the road of secularization by attempting to recall "a time, not long ago in some places, when religion was a major and even decisive factor in the lives of Canadian individuals and communities."[22] As John Webster Grant has observed, such a time must already "seem to some of the young either a projection of nostalgic fantasy or a truism that can only be stated but no longer imagined in concrete detail."[23] Even the memory of religious vitality, fervor and certitude (accompanied by barricades, battles and bigotry) appears to be dimming in a country whose recent English-Canadian prime minister's historically unusual profession of both Progressive Conservatism and Roman Catholicism passed largely unnoticed during this brief interregnum.

Traditional religion has rapidly, and probably irredeemably, been edged to the margin of real life in Canada,[24] so that if a scholar is intrigued by the presence of religious foundations in the social and political philosophy of Pierre Elliott Trudeau,[25] the ordinary citizen is surprised and even offended on encountering religious activity out of context. In stark contrast, religion in pre-secular times was ubiquitous, reaching unavoidably into all areas of life, so that "no real understanding of the forms and values of Canadian society is possible without a knowledge of the diverse religious convictions, organizations and experience that have substantially shaped this society."[26] The very pervasiveness of religion for previous generations entails the necessity of cautious selectivity on the part of its modern investigator. Thus, in the present essay it is clearly both impossible and undesirable to document *all* aspects of the role of religion in shaping a Canadian national identity.[27] Religious influence on, for example, the economy, the family, education and the arts is, therefore, neglected, while attention is focussed primarily upon the importance of organized religion in the development of political culture, perhaps the key element in what is sometimes termed our "national character."[28] The impact of religion on specifically political orientations — attitudes towards the political system and its various parts, and attitudes towards the role of the self in the system — has been varied and complex, but it is, nonetheless, undeniable.[29]

As the research of a number of sociologists and church historians makes plain, the "presidency"[30] exercised by organized religion over social life was acutely evident in the strategically crucial realm of politics until recent times. Thus, the formation of national political culture can only be fully understood if due consideration is given to the diverse ways in which the influence, and at times outright power, of organized religion was exercised within the broad context of governmental and state affairs, at both national and regional levels. Emphasis on such influence is not intended as a denigration of the role of other, possibly more important, elements involved in the formation of Canadian poltical culture — for example, those dissected in the work of Seymour Martin Lipset[31] or Louis Hartz.[32] Nor does it deny the importance of purely secular political ideas and interests. It merely underlines the importance of religion, among and combined with other factors, and brings into prominence the fact that the absence of any mention of religion in the original Canadian constitution — the British North America Act of 1867 (now known as the Constitution Act, 1867) — belies the crucial relevance of the sacred in the evolution of "peace, order and good government" in this dominion.[33] It may be suggested that the distinctiveness of political culture in the Canadian nation (or nations) is in considerable measure due to a "religious factor"[34] which has acted as a force for both stability and change in political life as well as in society as a whole. Advancing "the influence of religious issues on the whole Canadian political tradition"[35] as a neglected but worthy theme for Canadian historical writers, John Webster Grant notes that "from few books on Canadian history...would one gather to what extent our political parties have crystallized upon lines of cleavage originally ecclesiastical...."[36] In a brief sketch of the interplay between the churches and the Canadian character, Grant offers a number of insights which provide an excellent basis for the present discussion. Examining the origins of religious influence upon politics in the dawn of French and English settlement, he views transplanted advocacy of the conception of the "established church" as the first assault in the battle waged by religious bodies to define the parameters of politics and the proper obligations of the state. Such a conception assumed a "Christian society," in the most partisan and intolerant sense of the term, such a society being "conceived as a unified entity within which religious, social and political structures could be distinguished."[37] For proponents of establishment, "church and state were alike sacred, alike Christian and their interaction betokened not the interference of one with the other but the harmonious operation of a single enterprise."[38] A Christian nation without an established church was, thus, a contradiction in terms.

Grant is surely correct in viewing the doctrine of religious establishment as common to both founding "races," and in perceiving its impact on both French and English Canada. The Roman Catholic church has retained an only recently eroded establishment status in the heartland of French Canada.[39] But this special status should not be confused with political conservatism. It should not be forgotten that, transplanted to another setting, the theocratic ideas of the Québec church provided a foundation for rebellion rather than preservation of the *status quo*.[40] In English Canada, establishmentarianism never lacked eloquent opponents and had run its course by the middle of the last century. But it was, nonetheless, a paramount ideological factor in the uneasy periods following the American Revolution and the War of 1812. If the Church of England could be termed "the Tory party at prayer," its colonial representatives would have found little to quibble with in such a description.

If the legacy of church establishment in French Canada is manifest, its imprint on English Canada is less obvious. Thus, while commentators have differed in their interpretation of the role of the church in Québec, none has doubted its importance. Indeed, so natural has its hegemony appeared until recently that the very notion of a secular Québec must seem as incomprehensible to some observers as a nationalism which is not stage-managed by the clergy. The Gallican fusion of church and politics transported to New France persisted under British rule and was, indeed, intensified after the failed revolt of 1837. A rigid Ultramontanism belligerently confronting all the political anathemas of the *Syllabus of Errors* permeated political thought in Québec throughout the second half of the nineteenth century. It persisted into the present century even after the Second World War. During this time, the church encouraged, legitimated and sustained state conservatism, authoritarianism and reaction even to the point of flirtation with neo-Fascism.[41] Canadian and American scholars, inspired by the work of Max Weber, have been primarily intrigued by the influence of religion upon *economic* activity in Québec. It is clear, however, that such influence is no less interesting in a *political* context.[42]

In English Canada, the monopolistic attempt of Anglicanism to impose itself as a national church was thwarted by the resistance of nonconformity led by such spokesmen as Egerton Ryerson. The failure of establishmentarianism came too late, however, to prevent it infusing some pungent ingredients into the political atmosphere, particularly in Upper Canada. Its proclamation that the Anglo-Saxon burden of Empire, monarchy, aristocracy, and British constitutionalism were part of a sacred scenario and, by the same token, its condemnation of mass democracy, egalitarianism, republicanism and revolution as the work of the devil left an indelible mark on English-Canadian political life. It appears reasonable to suppose that the conservative, counter-revolutionary, "law-and-order" identity which some observers detect and perceive as characteristically and distinctively English-Canadian, is at least in some measure, the legacy of Bishop Strachan and his fellow Churchmen.[43]

A final suggestion regarding the importance of both English and French establishment traditions "not only in forming the Canadian character but in distinguishing the Canadian identity" may be made by again invoking Grant. Examining the situation in the United States, he notes that the "formative years" of the American churches were marked by both "the Puritan attempt to create a new commonwealth of saints and by the enlightenment faith in the possibilities inherent in human nature."[44]

In this combination lay the inspiration for Americans to conceive their country "as a new creation superior to the static society of Europe precisely because of its ability to innovate."[45] In Canada, by contrast, the new society was regarded "as a replica, or even extension, of England and France; or...as a mosaic of all the cultures imported into it. A sense of continuity rather than of novelty was the establishment contribution...."[46] In view of this interpretation, consideration of the centrality of notions of continuity and tradition in our national political thinking, and of their likely *religious* origins, would appear worthwhile.[47] If Roman Catholicism and Anglicanism shared an emphasis on continuity, a sense of mission was also common to both Catholics and Protestants in the nineteenth century. This crusading zeal, most notable among the various bodies of religious dissent, is perceived by Grant as "more influential in the long run than the establishment principle in shaping the Canadian character...."[48] The sense of obligation "to extend the sway of Christ over every part of the world and over every segment of life both personal and social"[49] made a separation of religion and politics indefensible and added an extra religious ingredient to the emerging political life of British North America. For, while assuring that traditional values must be upheld and reinforced, missionaries envisioned a new society to be created in a spirit of otherworldly asceticism, a unique Christian nation with its own special political mission. Whether Grant is correct in perceiving the roots of "the concept of a special role for Canada either abroad in promoting peace and mutual aid or at home in developing an alternative to the materialistic society of the United States"[50] in the conceptions held independently by both the British and French that they constituted religiously elect nations is open to discussion.[51] Likewise, his insightful contention that the interpretation of Canadian national identity as a quest rather than an endowment originated in the "missionary impulse" of these chosen people requires careful scrutiny.[52] What appears undeniable, however, is that the militant, quasi-millenarian religious crusades were also socially and politically divisive, and that a contemporary judgement which ascribed the basic rift in Canadian identity more to religious than to ethnic differences contained a measure of truth. Thus, while André Siegfried's assertion that "religious questions are at the root of all Canadian differences and divisions" may have been unduly sweeping, it emphasized forcefully that religious enthusiasm could be politically disruptive as well as integrative in its effect.[53]

Leaving aside the obvious case of the French-English political division, a pertinent illustration of the validity of such a perspective may be found in N. Keith Clifford's discussion of the Protestant vision of Canada as "His Dominion" in the decades between Confederation and the Second World War.[54] For, although conceived as a means of integrating Canadians into a Protestant Christian community which would constitute a "Canadian version of the Kingdom of God," this religious movement evolved into a bigoted, paranoid, reactionary, and disruptive crusade against "foreign" immigration. Grounded in a homogeneous ethnic and political heritage, Canadian Protestantism "was unable to articulate an ideology of Canadianism which was acceptable to those who did not share [it.]"[55] As Clifford notes:

> The failure of their missions in French Canada, the failure of much of their prohibitory legislation, and the legacy of tension, bitterness and hatred which their bid for Protestant cultural hegemony in Canada had created in the educational system and in the relations between Anglo-Saxons and other ethnic groups, especially during the two world wars of the twentieth century, indicated that whatever shape the Kingdom of God might take in a Canadian context, it was not going to be realized in the terms elaborated by those who had fashioned the broad Protestant coalition and consensus in the period following disestablishment in the 1850's. The pluralistic nature of the political, social, and religious dimensions of Canadian society were such that the millennial dreams of any particular group were an inadequate basis for the elaboration of an ideology which would be acceptable to all.[56]

Nonetheless, it appears unlikely that those who sought, with such perseverance, to build "His Dominion" should have bequeathed no political legacy. Thus, it may be suggested that an English-Canadian nationalism which embraces protectionism and justifies ethnic prejudice — while simultaneously condemning immigration, Americans, and francophones — is, to an extent unrealized by its proponents, the inheritor of a political perspective embedded in the religious foundation of Protestant, evangelical, missionary and millennial fervor.

Consideration of the ways in which religion has permeated political consciousness in this country must acknowledge the various and complex metamorphoses involved as well as their frequently unintentional nature. This insight is implicit in the work of S. D. Clark which, drawing on both Frederick Jackson Turner's celebrated "frontier thesis"[57] and H. Richard Niebuhr's conception of the transition from sect to denomination,[58] has attempted, on the basis of a wealth of historical data, to appraise the influence of religion on Canadian political life, and more specifically the role of the religious sect in Canadian politics.[59] Immersion in the study of movements of political protest in this country leads Clark to challenge the widely assumed view that "evangelistic religious movements, through the support of radical programs of political reform, have made substantial contributions to liberal thought" and to condemn it as "based upon a superficial examination of the facts."[60] Denying that the political activities of the evangelical churches have derived from "a deeply embedded political philosophy," he asserts that "the real contribution to the development of religious principles of government" is to be found in "the peculiar role of the religious sect" from which such churches have evolved.[61] Adapting from Niebuhr a cyclical view of sectarianism — in which sects come to terms with the world, develop into churches and thereby spawn new dissenting sects — Clark is alert to the complex nature of the sect's interaction with the wider society and its ambivalent link with political life. Thus, though they are born of protest and revolt, the long-term political influence of sects is perceived by Clark as less than radical. This view is exemplified in the classic case of William Aberhart's Alberta Social Credit movement which, after emerging from its founder's Prophetic Bible Institute and preaching radical monetary reform, evolved into an established political party favored by big business interests.[62] In Clark's estimation, Canadian religious sects have, in the process of compromise with the world, largely been transformed into evangelical churches whose influence in political life has been, at its worst, "to produce a citizen body politically illiterate or unprincipled."[63] As he observes:

> An indifference to politics which religious sectarianism engendered has checked the growth of political thought, and the weakness of political thought, in turn, in contributing to a political opportunism on the part of evangelical church leaders, has checked the growth of political statesmanship.[64]

Clark's bluntly expressed views have found many critics but still provide suggestive topics for future research.[65] For example, his contention that "the maintenance of a successful federal system... has depended upon the strength of forces of decentralization" among which may be counted religious sects,[66] is worthy of note. In this context, the historic opposition of sects to the "unholy alliance" of churches and the state takes on a wider and timely political significance.

The conviction, expressed by Clark, that it is the "persistence of the sectarian spirit in religious organizations which has given religion its dynamic force in society [and] has exerted a decisive influence upon determining the relation of the church to the state and thereby upon determining the contribution of religion to political thought,"[67] appears relevant to a number of instances where the impact of religion on politics is widely acknowledged. Its application, for example, to the "Social Gospel" movement of the early years of the present century, and to the rise of agrarian socialism under the banner of the Co-operative Commonwealth Federation in Saskatchewan, raises important issues regarding the precise nature of the impact of religion on politics in these cases.[68]

Although the preceding discussion has provided only the briefest sketch of the role of religion in the formation of Canadian political culture, it has perhaps succeeded in indicating the wide-ranging nature of these effects. The influence of religion may be detected, for example, in the insular reactionary authoritarianism of Québec before the "Quiet Revolution," in the prejudice and conservatism of English Canada, as well as in the national legacy of political and social reform. Furthermore, conceptions of the sacred have shaped the opinions of the powerful and the powerless, the secure and the dispossessed, and their impact has been politically integrative and disintegrative; conducive to both change and stability. Finally, while religion may have contributed vital elements to our "national character," these cross-cut particular political, ethnic, regional, and denominational perspectives, and thereby underline the pluralistic aspect of Canadian political culture at the same time as they bespeak its distinctiveness.[69]

THE PRESENT SIGNIFICANCE OF RELIGION IN CANADIAN LIFE

In the first paragraph of his *Politics,* Aristotle observes that "every state is an association of persons formed with a view to some good purpose"[70] and that "as all associations aim at some good, that one which is supreme and embraces all others will have also as its aim the supreme good. That is the association which we call the State, and that type of association we call political."[71] It is readily apparent that, in no small degree, the "good purpose" or "supreme good" for which political associations exist has been defined, until recently, by avowed religious organizations. Thus, shortly after the Second World War, S. D. Clark still felt able to declare forcefully:

> Canada has been, and remains, a fundamentally religious nation. No great political or social upheaval in the country has served to break the close ties with a past which placed a great emphasis upon religious values of life.[72]

Three decades later, it is impossible to be sanguine regarding the assured place of traditional religion in the national life, or even about the survival of those "ties with a past" in which religion dominated men's lives. The reality of secularization confronts even the theologians. John W. Grant sums up matters aptly when he remarks:

> The collapse of the nineteenth-century Christian programme for Canada is so recent that even now we are too much under its shadow to be able to sift out what is significant in the contemporary reaction to it. What is certain, however, is that in a well-developed technological society we have been involved in a process of disengagement from the hegemony of the churches... It is scarcely surprising that many Canadians regard their religious heritage as a brake upon the growth of the nation and that they are almost pathetically eager to demonstrate that they have emancipated themselves from the tutelage of the churches... The vision of a Christian society, whether conceived as a replica of the old Christendom or as an anticipation of the promised millennium, has clearly lost its power to inspire.[73]

A similar perspective has not only been embraced but formally promulgated by leading politicians. Thus, a decade and a half ago Mr. Trudeau, then Minister of Justice, proclaimed:

> We are now living in a social climate in which people are beginning to realize, perhaps for the first time in the history of this country, that we are not entitled to impose the concepts which belong to a sacred society upon a civil or profane society. The concepts of the civil society in which we live are pluralistic and I think... it would be a mistake for us to legislate into this society concepts which belong to a theological or sacred order.[74]

There is little reason to doubt that the decline of religious hegemony in political life has been accompanied by a similar process in other spheres of Canadian society. Yet, so striking and crucial is the increasing irrelevance of religious bodies to the politics of the nation and to the formulation of its ultimate goals, that it merits far more attention than has so far been accorded it. The degree of survival of religious elements,[75] however transmogrified, and the means and sources of their replacement in our political culture are worthy topics for investigation and analysis.

The disenchantment of Canadian political life deserves study both as a topic of intrinsic importance and as a revealing paradigm for the secularization of social institutions. A post-mortem on the decline of religious influence in political life necessarily entails discussion of those "good purposes" which underlie political thought and action. It thereby involves consideration, not merely of the state of the nation, but of the society as a whole. Thus it is relevant not only to the sociological subdisciplines of religion and politics, but also to social theory in general. Within this context, the wider applicability of perspectives generated within the sociology of religion becomes apparent and the centrality of their sociological concerns is underscored.[76] Faced with the apparent decline of its traditional forms, Canadian students of religion have, in varying degree, begun to adopt or consider a number of perspectives which, though (somewhat typically) originating in Europe and the United States, are nonetheless adaptable in principle to Canadian circumstances.

Return of the Sacred

The first of these perspectives may usefully be evoked by Daniel Bell's phrase "the return of the sacred."[77] Although it would be unfair to identify Bell with all the diverse individuals and groups who, for whatever reason, detect a "return" of religion, he does provide a useful "umbrella term" for a certain perspective — although his own arguments are specifically at odds with many of these other interpretations. Not all such observers, moreover, would necessarily endorse Bell's specific arguments, but none, once aware of it, would doubt his conclusion.

Those who perceive such a return of, or to, the sacred, espouse a cyclical rather than a linear view of history in which the evening of the Age of Secularization heralds the dawn of a new Age of Religion. Religion, they argue, has changed in form and content — but it has not declined. If the perceived revival of fundamentalist "old time" Christianity illustrates the irrelevance of established denominations, the "new religious consciousness" provides a preview of forms of religiosity appropriate to the future and to sophisticated, contemporary human needs. Its mysticism, manipulationism, pentecostalism, enthusiasm and exoticism cross traditional boundaries, and find expression not only in the predictable multitude of sects and cults, but also in decidedly mass settings. It is noteworthy that proponents of most versions of the "return of the sacred" perspective do not require any broadened, innovative or convoluted definition of their key term. Though their conceptions of the sacred are not uniform, their thesis may be expressed on the basis of a narrow, largely substantive, social rather than sociological, definition of religion. It should also be noted that their perspective is not without a certain functionalist aspect, although Bell himself would undoubtedly disapprove.[78]

If those who preach the return of the sacred to Canada are proven correct, political life would appear likely to experience a renewed infusion of religious ideas from a number of directions at once. The revival of notions of a "Christian Nation" might well be accompanied by pressure to develop a new political consciousness rooted in the insights of the East. There is, in fact, little evidence to suggest that such a process is underway. Indeed, the precipitate quality of "return of the sacred" prophecy is bluntly illustrated in the realm of Canadian politics. A religious revival confined largely to the young, the alienated, and the marginal might conceivably be the harbinger of a new religious age. The odds, however, appear to be very much against it.[79]

Functionalism

The second perspective is perhaps more properly regarded as a series of linked perspectives, each calling for separate treatment, but united by the common theme of functionalism. The first variant on this theme minimizes the impact of secularization by definitional fiat rather than empirical evidence. It falls back on the persisting mainstream American structural-functionalist approach to religion, which for so long has allowed scholars to have their cake and eat it. Never noted for clarity or consistency in terminology, structural-functionalist discussions of religion frequently vacillate in their use of the term. Nonetheless, by their implacable hostility to substantive definitions of the concept, and by reiteration of the formula "religion *is* what religion *does*," latter-day adherents of this doctrine are able to discern religion in the strangest places. Tracing their pedigree from Durkheim, and from his conception of religion as "a unified system of beliefs and practices relative to sacred things...which unite into one single moral community...all those who adhere to them,"[80] they emphasize the integrative, cohesive consequences of religion to such degree that it is seen as "a requisite of all social systems — a dominant force which binds men together and provides the basic cognitive, evaluative and expressive guidelines for the stable operation of the society."[81] In short, they argue that while religion is a social phenomenon, society is also a *religious* phenomenon, and that if a society exists it must therefore, *ipso facto* possess a religion.[82] In this sense, religion is viewed as a social universal, the source of the most general guidelines for human action and the means by which societies hold together.

Somewhat inconsistently in terms of this definition, functionalists have also responded to the decline of traditional, organized religion in modern industrial societies, by a quest for its "functional alternative." Accordingly, they locate the "grounds of meaning" and cohesive agency in social systems in "secular religion," "quasi-religion," "political religion" or "civic religion."[83] In this regard, the most influential thinkers in an American context have been the theologian, Will Herberg[84] and the sociologist Robert Bellah.[85]

Civic Religion

Herberg's analysis of the changing role of the traditional religious

bodies in the U.S. remains provocative in according them a merely supportive or secondary role in the maintenance of American society. What he
terms "the sweeping secularization of American life"[86] has resulted in
religious belonging becoming essentially "a mode of defining one's
American identity."[87] At the same time, he maintains, conventional
religion "has been integrated into the 'common religion' of the American
Way and made to serve a non-religious function" and, as such, it has grown
increasingly vacuous.[88] For Herberg, this tripartite religion is "thoroughly
secularized and homogenized, a religion-in-general that is little more than a
civic religion of democracy, the reification of the American Way." In a
functionalist sense, therefore, the *real* religion of American society — its
"ground of meaning" and prime cohesive agency — is the "American
Way" itself.[89] Herberg notes that

> Americans, by and large, do have their 'common religion' and that that 'religion' is
> the system familiarly known as the American Way of Life. It is the American Way of
> Life that supplies American society with an 'overarching sense of unity' amid conflict.
> It is the American Way of Life about which Americans are admittedly and unashamedly
> 'intolerant'. It is the American Way of Life that provides the framework in terms of
> which the crucial values of American existence are couched. By every realistic criterion
> the American Way of Life is the operative faith of the American people.[90]

The notion of civic religion (or civil religion) has most recently been
associated with the name of Robert Bellah — although, of course, the term
itself may be traced to Rousseau's *Social Contract*.[91] Bellah argues that
while the "American Way of Life" is, indeed, celebrated by both church
and synagogue: "few have realized that there actually exists alongside of
and rather clearly differentiated from the churches an elaborate and well-
institutionalized civil religion in America."[92] This religion is "a collection
of beliefs, symbols, and rituals with respect to sacred things and institutionalized in a collectivity."[93] It is "neither sectarian nor in any specific
sense Christian" but it has "borrowed selectively from the religious tradition in such a way that the average American [sees] no conflict between the
two," and in this way has been "able to build up... powerful symbols of national solidarity and to mobilize deep levels of personal motivation for the
attainment of national goals."[94] Thus, though permeated by biblical
elements, the American civil religion is, in Professor Bellah's view"...ge-
nuinely American and genuinely new [with] its own prophets and its own
martyrs, its own sacred events and sacred places, its own solemn rituals and
symbols."[95]

Given the wide readership these authors have enjoyed in Canada, and
the widespread acceptance of variants of a functionalist interpretation of
religion, it is surprising that greater efforts have not been made to adopt the
views of Herberg and Bellah to the Canadian experience.[96] Interestingly,
Reginald Bibby has given very recent consideration to the Herberg thesis,
but though attention is directed to the "Canadian situation" in his article,
no attempt is made to consider Herberg's views in an explicitly Canadian

context.[97]

It is, of course, questionable to what extent Herberg's postulate of the emergence of a Protestant-Catholic-Jewish religious ascendance is transposable to Canada with its distinct religious history and its dissimilar approach to ethnic pluralism. Yet, at a time of "sweeping secularization," an image of Canadian religious bodies playing second fiddle to, and providing legitimation for, some secular political conception of "The Canadian Way," does not necessarily appear outlandish. If people of varied backgrounds have, in fact, reached the point of desiring to identify themselves as "Canadians," then in a situation where ethnicity stresses the "hyphenated" or "mosaical" aspect of Canadian life, organized religious affiliation would seem a possible mode of defining such an identity. Whether such a process is underway, or, if not, whether religious bodies will long be capable of initiating it — and whether in either case they would have the will or the resources to sustain it — are questions worth posing. Certainly, Herberg's insights suggest one possible line of inquiry into what Grant has termed "the emergence of a new phase in the relation of religion to the national life."[98]

It is again puzzling that Canadian scholars have shown such reluctance to consider the possible utility of the concept "civil religion" in the context of their own country.[99] During the last two decades, Canadians have witnessed unprecedented governmental efforts to engender national unity on the basis of supposedly emotive national symbols. At the same time, numerous diagnosticians of Canadian identity have shared the public limelight with the advocates of various brands of Canadian nationalism, while in academia a growing stress has been placed upon Canadian Studies and Canadian content — particularly in the fields of literature, the arts, history and the social sciences.[100]

In a different national context, these observations, of course, apply *a fortiori* to Québec. Scepticism regarding the likely existence of a Canadian Civil Religion is no excuse for neglecting to explore the strengths and weaknesses of the concept of civil religion in national or regional Canadian contexts, or for a failure to ponder the possibility of its emergence in the future. It is surely not impossible, given the significant influence of religion upon Canadian politics, that (as Bellah observed in the U.S.) a civil religion may exist — though few may realize the fact. Furthermore, it is conceivable that the legacy of religious influence on political life might take the form of a civil religion, especially at a time when politicians seek to formulate "some good purpose" for the state without the advice of formal religious practitioners.

Thus, while Canadian scholars have been willing to espouse functionalism in general, and to adopt its broad non-substantive definitions of religion, they have been less eager to utilize some of its more specific formulations. This seems a pity, for with only one major exception the future contribution of functional analysis appears to lie (and perhaps always lay) in its more specific treatment of social institutions rather than in its excursions into Grand Theory.[101]

Invisible Religion

The specific exception noted above constitutes a variant of functionalism whose pedigree is unashamedly mixed. Luckmann's "invisible religion" thesis[102] owes little to American structural-functionalism, something to European phenomenology, and much to Weber and Durkheim. Indeed, it may be regarded as the logical conclusion, or less favorably, the *reductio ad absurdum,* of the Durkheimian analysis of religion. Defining religion as the capacity of the human organism to transcend its biological nature through the construction of objective, morally binding, all-embracing "universes of meaning,"[103] Luckmann proposes the most inclusive of all functional definitions by identifying the religious with the human. As a means of acknowledging the force of secularization while simultaneously denying the demise of "religion," his work is ideal. Not only does it emphasize the universality and almost eternal quality of religion in its anthropological sense, it does so without the necessity of demonstrating its integrative or cohesive social functions. Indeed, in shifting emphasis from institutionalized or church-oriented religion to religion as an increasingly subjective or private affair in the contemporary situation, Luckmann attempts a revolutionary re-orientation of the sociology of religion. Portraying a world in which individuals are free to construct not only their own personal identities but personalized systems of ultimate significance, however "syncretistic and vague," he perceives the emergence of secondary institutions that "attempt to articulate the themes arising in the 'private sphere' and re-transmit the packaged results to potential consumers" in such forms as newspaper advice columns, popular psychology, *Playboy* philosophy, positive thinking and the lyrics of pop songs.[104] Designed specifically for the "religious" needs of their consumers, these products must themselves be regarded as religious in nature. Therefore, where the individual decides what is ultimately significant, religious phenomena may take somewhat unfamiliar or profane forms.[105]

Luckmann's unrepentant crusade to rescue religion from the clutches of the churches has provoked scholars to review their fundamental suppositions in the light of a reanimated functionalism. While it has generated a greater response in Canada than the work of either Herberg or Bellah, the invisible religion thesis has not ignited the blaze of reaction and controversy which it merits. However, at least one student of religion has imaginatively used Luckmann's work to demonstrate the religious aspect of ice-hockey in this country,[106] and although, in fact, he misinterprets Luckmann's argument,[107] he nonetheless indicates its potential utility in the study of Canadian society. For the Canadian sociologist, *The Invisible Religion* provides possible insight, not only into the potential variety of new "religious" forms in secular society, but into the nature of the society which gives them birth. Like his conception of religion itself, Luckmann's themes of identity, subjectivity, privatization, and consumerism have wide social and political significance, and may be seen as relevant to the discussion of such matters as mass society, political apathy, the decline of community, nation building, consensus, propaganda and public opinion.[108] In taking up issues raised by Luckmann, Canadian sociologists of religion can give their sub-discipline a wider interest and relevance than it normally enjoys, without necessarily sharing his conclusions.

Epitaph to Religion

The third perspective worth recording has found little explicit favor among sociologists of religion in this country, although it is possible that it is implicitly accepted by many. In a sense, this is the perspective of classic sociology in which, albeit prematurely, the epitaph to religion was written and social thinkers contemplated how society would be organized without it.[109] Assuming that religion is of declining social significance and that it makes sense to assert that man is becoming less religious or even non-religious, exponents of this perspective prefer a substantive and narrow definition of religion, close to everyday use of the term.

Regarding a concern with a "supernatural" or "super-empirical" transcendent reality to which the natural or empirical world is subject, as the hallmark of religion,[110] they argue that "society does not, in the modern world, derive its values from certain religious preconceptions which are then the basis for social organization and social action."[111] Agreeing with Herberg that modern forms of religion merely reflect and provide secondary legitimation for "the values which stem from social organization itself," they refuse to accord these "values, norms, conventions and orientations to the world laid deep in the socialization process" a religious character in the functionalist manner.[112] "Good purposes," then, may be, but are not necessarily, religious in their origin, and the cohesion of modern society is not to be sought, by definition, in religion. It is, rather, to be discovered in "the complex dovetailing of our institutional arrangements ...the mixture of inducement and coercion which prevails within the work order of our society... the largely autonomous body of duly instituted law [and] the elaborate interaction of supply, demand, knowledge of the market and knowledge of consumers, which structure much of the provision of a modern economy...."[113] In short, in order to understand a complex, modern society, proponents of this perspective invoke the Durkheim of *The Division of Labor* rather than of *The Elementary Forms of The Religious Life.*[114] In adopting such a perspective, Canadian sociologists of religion enter a dangerous but fertile land. In penning the epitaph to religion, they may also eventually write the obituary for their subdiscipline. But, in refusing to preserve religion by definitional sleight-of-hand, and by entertaining (ideal-typically) the notion of a purely secular society, they may contribute much to our knowledge of emerging elements in Canadian political culture and the sources of cohesion in this highly pluralistic society. Finally, they may also, in a Canadian context, teach us more about the nature of religion itself.

CONCLUSION

Whether the viewpoints outlined above on the influence of religion in Canadian politics, or on the place of religion in a secularized society, are best regarded as models or myths will be a matter of dispute. Their final worth, however, will be judged, not on their correctness, but on their provocation of subsequent inquiry.

By asserting the historical importance of religious influence in politics, and by implication, in other areas of Canadian life, this essay stresses the formerly crucial public aspect of religion; while in observing its retreat into an increasingly circumscribed and private sphere, it underlines a significant transformation in Canadian society.[115] Thus, consideration of the decline or absence of organized religion in its traditional forms, raises broad theoretical questions concerning the workings of society as a whole. For this reason, the deliberations of sociologists of religion regarding secularization, the end (or future) of religion, and even the interminable definitional debate, possess more than a subdisciplinary relevance, and should be regarded as central to the sociological enterprise in Canada. Moreover, such deliberations are surely relevant to analyses of the political future of this fragile federation.[116] If Canadian sociologists of religion will undertake, in these deliberations, to use the analysis of what we *were* as a basis for discerning what we *are,* they may make a significant contribution to helping us know what we may *become.*

NOTES

[1]This is a slightly revised version of an essay first published in *The Annual Review of the Social Sciences of Religion* 6 (1982): 177-217.

[2]Professor C. B. Macpherson has used this phrase for political scientists. See C. B. Macpherson, "After Strange Gods: Canadian Political Science 1973," in Guinsburg and Reuber, 1974: 52-76.

[3]For overviews, see for example, McNall, 1979; Rex, 1974; and Ions, 1977.

[4]This is David Martin's phrase. See Martin, 1966: 353-59.

[5]Useful bibliographical sources and overviews include Crysdale and Montminy, 1974; Crysdale, 1977; Hiller, in Ramu and Johnson, 1976: 394-400.

[6]See Stryckman, 1977; Falardeau, 1950-51: 127-42; Falardeau, 1962: 209-28; Dumont, 1958; Fallding, "Canada," in Mol, 1972: 101-15; Bibby, 1977a; Hiller, 1976; Stryckman, 1977b: 145-83. This article contains a helpful bibliography.

[7]A useful enterprise involving inventory of the teaching of courses with religious subject matter in Canadian universities was unfortunately discontinued. See Anderson and Nosanchuk, 1967; and Anderson, 1969. Useful historical sources are Clifford, 1969 and Clifford, 1980.

[8]On Weber, see primarily Weber, 1963 (first published in German, 1922); Weber, 1930 (first published, 1904-5). See also Weber's studies of the religions of China, India and ancient Judaism. On Durkheim, see Durkheim, 1915 (first published in French, 1912); and W. S. F. Pickering, 1975. On Marx, see Marx and Engels, 1958; and McKown, 1975.

[9]A useful indication of the main biases of the sociology of religion in Canada may be found in Crysdale and Wheatcroft, 1976. Ten of the selections in this volume utilize sample surveys while three utilize the method of participant-observation. See pp. 40-41 and *passim*. For a useful bibliography of survey research on religion in Canada see Bibby, 1977.

[10]In the sense which Luckmann attacks as a "church-oriented" conception of religion. See Luckmann, 1967 (first published in German, 1963). For a further discussion of Luckmann, see below.

[11]See for example, the useful summary by Mol, "Major Correlates of churchgoing in Canada," in Crysdale and Wheatcroft, 1976: 241-54.

[12]See, for example, Stryckman, 1970; Stryckman and Gaudet, "Priests Under Stress" in Crysdale and Wheatcroft, 1976: 336-45; and Stryckman and Gaudet, 1971.

[13]The Crysdale and Wheatcroft collection and the Crysdale and Montminy bibliography provide evidence of the range of studies on various churches, denominations and sects. On the "new religious consciousness", see Glock and Bellah, 1976; Wuthnow, 1976. For Canadian material, see Whitworth and Shiels, "From Across the Black Water: Two Imported Varieties of Hinduism," in Barker, 1982: 155-72; Bird, "A Comparative Analysis of the Rituals Used by Some Contemporary 'New' Religious and Para-Religious Movements," in Slater, 1977: 447-69; Paper, "A Shaman in Contemporary Toronto," in Slater, 1977: 471-89; Bird and Reimer, "New Religious and Para-Religious Movements in Montreal," in Crysdale and Wheatcroft, 1976: 307-20.

[14]See for example, Mol, 1979: 379-89; Mol, 1976; Fallding, 1974; Hiller, 1969; Warburton, 1975; Warburton, mimeographed; and Beals, 1978: 147-62. Of course, differences between Canada's "two sociologies" (French and English), as Hubert Guindon has termed them, must not be overlooked. Crysdale and Wheatcroft, 1977: 42-44, offer some useful comments on this matter, but see also the Crysdale and Montminy bibliography, cited above.

[15]Of the many discussions of the definitional dilemma, see Spiro, "Religion: Problems of Definition and Explanation," in Banton, 1966: 85-126; Horton, 1960: 201-26; Goody, 1961: 142-64; Berger, 1969: 175-77; Berger, 1974: 125-33, Streng, 1972: 219-37. The classic problem of definition is posed by Weber in *The Sociology of Religion* and the most controversial recent re-definition of the concept is in Luckmann, 1967. For recent Canadian excursions into this labyrinth, see Richard, 1978 and Blasi, 1980.

[16]See Wilson, 1969: 14; Wilson, 1976. The literature on secularization is vast, but the

following are useful sources: Macintyre, 1967; Martin, 1978; Fenn, 1978; and Glasner, 1977.

[17]For such criticism, see Martin, "Towards Eliminating the Concept of Secularization," in Gould, 1965: 169-82; Greeley and Baum, 1973; and Greeley, 1972.

[18]See Moreux, 1969. For a discussion of the decline of traditional religion in Canada, see Crysdale, 1976: 137-48; MacLeod, 1979; Bibby, 1979a: 1-17; Bibby, 1979b: 105-16; Bibby, "Religion," in Hagedorn, 1980: 422-25; Bibby, "The Nature of Religiosity in Canada," in Crysdale and Beattie, 1977; and Crysdale, "Religion and Secularization," in Crysdale and Beattie, 1973: 267-90.

[19]The phrase is Daniel Bell's. See Bell, 1977: 419-49. Also see the discussion of this matter below.

[20]See Glock and Bellah, 1976.

[21]It is necessary to consider, for example, whether there is any Canadian historical parallel to de Tocqueville's view of American religion as an "institution which powerfully contributes to the maintenance of a democratic republic...." See de Tocqueville, 1948: 300.

[22]Grant, 1973.

[23]*Ibid.*

[24]Certainly, hope of its regaining its "former dominant role" in national life appears to have been largely abandoned. See, for example, John Webster Grant, "Religion and the Quest for a National Identity: The Background in Canadian History," in Slater, 1977: 19. The extent to which traditional religion "has become socially less and less significant" has been emphasized by Bryan Wilson who notes that, in modern secular society, "religious thinking, practices and institutions have but a small influence in the everyday life of modern man." See Wilson, 1969 and Wilson, 1976.

[25]See Whitaker, 1980: 5-31.

[26]Symons, 1975: 108.

[27]Analysis of our "national identity" has become a virtual cottage industry over the past decade, but the following are worthy of note: Blishen, Jones, Naegele and Porter, 1968: 1-18; Smith, 1970: 247-75; McKillop, 1974: 533-47; Cook, 1972; Russell, 1972; Morton, 1961; Grant, 1970.

[28]John Webster Grant has recently made use of the term "national character" in preference to the term "national identity." See his "Religion and the Quest for a National Identity," 1977: 8-9. On the concept of "political culture," see Almond, "Comparative Political Systems," in Almond, 1965; and Kavanaugh, 1972. For a recent discussion of the term in a Canadian context, see Bell and Tepperman, 1979, especially pp. 1-39. In the present essay, use of the term "political culture" does not necessarily imply any "functionalist" or "consensualist" perspective. To speak of "Canadian political culture" is not to assume a uniform Canadian political culture. (Almond and Verba themselves emphasize that the concept of political culture "helps us to escape" from "the assumption of homogeneity," 1965: 13). But, while a monolithic consensual view is clearly unrealistic, it is likewise unwarranted to assume that elements of political consensus are totally lacking in this nation.

[29]Almond and Verba, 1965: 12.

[30]This is Bryan Wilson's term.

[31]See Lipset, 1964; Lipset, 1967 (see especially Chapter Seven "Value Differences, Absolute or Relative: The English-Speaking Democracies," pp. 284-312); Lipset, 1970; Lipset, 1968; and Lipset, 1976: 19-54.

[32]See Hartz, 1953; Hartz, 1964; and Hartz, "A Comparative Study of Fragment

Cultures," in Graham and Gurr, 1969: 100-17. See also McRae, 1978: 17-30.

[33]This absence is noted by Norman, 1968: 9, 73.

[34]Gerhard Lenski's phrase is borrowed here. See Lenski, 1963. But also see Clark, 1947: 89-103.

[35]Grant, 1955: 102.

[36]*Ibid.*

[37]Grant, "Religion and the Quest for a National Identity," in Slater, 1977: 12.

[38]*Ibid.,* p. 10. See also E. R. Norman, 1968, on the question of establishment.

[39]See for example Falardeau, 1952: 214-29; Falardeau, "The Role and Importance of the Church in French Canada," in Rioux and Martin, 1964: 342-57; Moreux, 1969; Miner, 1939; Hughes, 1943; Guindon, 1960; Barnes, 1961: 52-76; and Dumont, 1961: 47-65.

[40]See Flanagan, 1979.

[41]See Hughes, "Action Catholique and Nationalism: A Memorandum on the Church and Society in French Canada, 1942," in Crysdale and Wheatcroft, 1976: 173-90; and Trofimenkoff, 1973; Trofimenkoff, 1975.

[42]For discussions inspired by Weber and Tawney, see Lower, "Two Ways of Life: The Primary Antithesis of Canadian History," in Berger, 1967: 15-28 (1943); Porter, 1965: 98-103, 511-19; and see Ryan, 1966.

[43]See Henderson, 1969a; and Henderson, 1969b.

[44]Grant, "Religion and the Quest for a National Identity," in Slater, 1977: 12.

[45]*Ibid.*

[46]*Ibid.*

[47]Analysis of the currently politically fashionable term "mosaic" might prove particularly interesting in this regard, while it might be equally rewarding to devote serious attention to John Moir's comment: "Whenever military, economic, political or cultural absorption by the United States threatened...Canada has turned to its counter-revolutionary tradition for inspiration. And ecclesiasticism is a traditional part of that tradition." Moir, "The Sectarian Tradition in Canada," in Grant, 1963: 132. For a discussion of the connection between this "counter-revolutionary tradition" and violence in Canada, see Torrance, 1978; Torrance, 1975; and Torrance, 1977: 473-96.

[48]Grant, "Religion and the Quest for a National Identity," in Slater, 1977: 13.

[49]*Ibid.*

[50]*Ibid.,* p. 16.

[51]The Biblical notion of the "elect nation" or "chosen people" has most commonly been applied in the context of the United States. Thus, the colonists of seventeenth century Virginia were, in the view of John Rolfe, "a peculiar people, marked and chosen by the hand of God." See Bellah, 1975. The British and French in North America have also regarded themselves as "peculiar people" with special missions and it would be interesting to consider the legacy of this fact. As a beginning, see, for example, Rousseau, "Recit Mythique des Origines Québecoises," in Slater, 1977: 43-60.

[52]See Grant, "Religion and the Quest for a National Identity," in Slater, 1977: 16.

[53]See Siegfried, 1966 (1907).

[54]See Clifford, "His Dominion: A Vision in Crisis," in Slater, 1977: 24-41.

[55]*Ibid.,* p. 35.

[56]*Ibid.,* p. 35.

[57]See Hofstadter and Lipset, 1968. For some Canadian variants on the theme see Oliver, 1930; Careless, 1954; and Zaslow, 1948.

[58]See Niebuhr, 1957 (1929).

[59]Clark's most important works in the present context are: Clark, 1948; Clark, 1959; Clark, 1945: 207-16; Clark, 1946: 439-53; Clark, 1944: 86-96; and Clark, 1947: 89-103. All the above articles, together with other pertinent material are reprinted in Clark, 1968. The last mentioned article has been re-titled "The Religious Influence in Canadian Society." For an appraisal and bibliographical inventory of the work of S. D. Clark in this area see Hiller, 1976-77: 415-27.

[60]Clark, 1968: 130.

[61]*Ibid.,* p. 130.

[62]*Ibid.,* p. 139-40. In this context, see also Irving, 1959.

[63]*Ibid.,* p. 144.

[64]*Ibid.*

[65]See, for example, Grant, 1955; Clifford, 1969; Walsh, 1954: 78; and Hiller, 1976-77. However, for a study which explicitly attempts to continue Clark's work, see Mann, 1955.

[66]Clark, "The Religious Sect in Canadian Politics," in Clark, 1968: 145.

[67]*Ibid.,* 146.

[68]See, for example, Lipset, 1968; McNaught, 1959; Allen, 1971; Allen, 1975; and Baum, 1980.

[69]It is worthwhile considering the impact of religion, particularly in the context of discussions which devote little attention to it. In particular, it is worth speculating on the role of religion when appraising literature which deals with Canadian "national identity" or with the forms of political authority and integration in this country. For very recent discussions, see Friedenberg, 1980; and *Canadian Review of Studies in Nationalism/Revue Canadienne des Etudes sur le Nationalisme* 7 (1980) (Special issue On Anglo-Canadian Nationalism and Social Communications). See also Taylor, 1970.

[70] Aristotle, 1962: 25.

[71] *Ibid.*

[72]Clark, "The Religious Influence in Canadian Society," in Clark, 1968: 182. Elsewhere in the same essay Clark notes: "In few countries in the Western world has religion exerted as great an influence upon the development of the country as it has in Canada" (p. 168); and "At no time has religion assumed an insignificant role in the life of the Canadian community. On occasion it has been a force of dominant importance" (p. 169).

[73] Grant, "Religion and the Quest for a National Identity," in Slater, 1977: 18-19.

[74]Speech to the House of Commons, Ottawa, quoted in Whitaker, 1980.

[75]It is obvious, of course, that the values and norms of secular societies "owe, in origin and development, much to religious conceptions of society in the past." See Wilson, 1969: 257. Wilson observes that the "secular society of the present, in which religious thinking, practices and institutions have but a small part, is nonetheless the inheritor of values, dispositions and orientations from the religious past. The completely secularized society has not yet existed." See Wilson, 1969: 262.

[76]As David Martin notes: "... we cannot live by unexamined sociological faiths in a closed world. Other disciplines may try to live in sealed off compartments but it is the task of sociology and of the sociology of religion in particular to think in terms of dialectic and synthesis." Martin, 1966: 539.

[77]See Bell, 1977.

[78]See Bell, 1977.

[79]Bryan Wilson has condemned "those who should know better" than to predict a new age of religion on the basis of the evidence of marginal sects and cults: "... what then is to [be] understood by 'the return of the sacred'? Anything more than the likelihood that certain groups are likely to espouse special interpretations of the world? And that the groups most disposed to do so are typically comprised of those least enmeshed in the role structure of the economic system — the students and the young, or those in independent occupations and small businesses? If that is all, who will quarrel? But is that a return of the sacred?" Wilson, 1979: 280.

[80]Durkheim, 1915: 62

[81] See the excellent discussion in Robertson, 1970: 15-24, 36-42. See also Williams, 1952: 312.

[82]This is essentially a Durkheimian position. Parsons observes: "Not on the basis of the definition alone, but rather on that of the whole argument of Durkheim's theory it may be maintained not only that those who have a common religion constitute a moral community, but that, conversely, every true moral community, that is every 'society', is characterized to a certain degree by the possession of a common 'religion'. For without a system of common values, of which a religion is in part a manifestation, a system adhered to in a significant degree, there can be no such thing as a society" (Parsons, 1937: 434).

[83]The great totalitarian movements of the present century have frequently been labelled "religious" in this sense, particularly where they may be seen to constitute "state religions." Likewise, scientific and even formally "anti-religious" organizations may be perceived to perform "religious" functions. See, for example, Macrae, "The Bolshevik Ideology," in Macrae, 1961: 181-97; Constas, 1961: 282-98; Budd, "The Humanistic Societies: The Consequences of a Diffuse Belief System," in Wilson, 1967: 377-405. For interesting recent discussions relevant to the question of "secular religion" see the papers in Moore and Myerhoff, 1977; and see Bergeson, 1978: 19-29.

[84]See especially Herberg, 1960; Herberg "Religion in a Secularized Society: Some Aspects of America's Three-Religion Pluralism" reprinted in Schneider, 1964: 591-600; and Herberg, "America's Civil Religion: What It Is and Whence It Comes," in Richey and Jones, 1974: 76-88.

[85]See especially Bellah, "Civil Religion in America" reprinted in Richey and Jones, 1974: 21-44 (originally published in *Daedalus,* Winter 1967); "American Civil Religion in the 1970's" in Richey and Jones, 1974: 255-272; and Bellah, 1975.

[86]Herberg, "Religion in a Secularized Society," 1964: 599.

[87]*Ibid.,* p. 599.

[88]*Ibid.*

[89]*Ibid.,* p. 600.

[90]*Protestant-Catholic-Jew,* 1960: 75.

[91]It may be found in Chapter 8, Book 4.

[92]Bellah, 1974.

[93]*Ibid.,* p. 29. Note the Durkheimian ring to this passage.

[94]*Ibid.,* p. 31, pp. 34-35.

[95]*Ibid.,* pp. 40-41.

[96]Exceptions are Blumstock, 1977; Stahl, 1981; and John Simpson, "Ethnic Groups

and Church Attendance in the United States and Canada," in Greeley and Baum, 1979.

[97]See his chapter "Religion," in Hagedorn: 422-25 and compare the article by Simpson cited above. Some thoughts on the genesis of civil religion which might be useful in a Canadian context are provided by Cole and Hammond, 1974: 177-89.

[98]Grant, "Religion and the Quest for a National Identity," in Slater, 1977. For some thoughts along these lines, see two other papers in the Slater collection: Antoni Gualtieri, "Towards a Theological Perspective on Nationalism," pp. 508-25; and Michel Despland, "Religion and The Quest for National Identity: Problems and Perspectives," pp. 526-51. (The latter is the more sophisticated treatment.)

[99]With the exceptions of Blumstock and Stahl. For some non-American discussions relevant to the notion of "civil religion", see Shils and Young, 1953: 63-81; Birnbaum, 1955: 5-23; and Vogt and Abel, "On Political Rituals in Contemporary Mexico," in Moore and Myerhoff, 1977: 173-88; and McDowell, 1974: 265-79. In an American context, see Richey and Jones, 1974; Cherry, "American Sacred Ceremonies" in Hammond and Johnson, 1970: 303-16; Hammond, "Further Thoughts on Civil Religion in America" in Cutler, 1968; Stauffer, 1973: and Lipsitz, 1968: 527-35.

[100]Discussions of "Canadian Identity" have been noted above. In an academic context, relevant documents are: Mathews and Steele, 1969 and Symons, 1975. The nearest approaches to a concern with civil religion emerge, interestingly, in work which for literary, religious or anthropological reasons, exhibits a concern with myth. Such analyses, in fact, may easily be incorporated into, or used to complement, functionalist interpretations. See the following in the Slater collection: Rousseau, pp. 43-63; Michel Campbell, "Les Bruits de la Mer: Essaie hermeneutique religieuse d'un mythe de l'original dans les chansons populaires québécoises," pp. 353-82; William Klassen, "Two Wise Men from the West: Canadian Identity and Religion," pp. 271-88; and Peter Slater, "Religion as Story: the Biography of Norman Bethune," pp. 289-314. See also McKillop, 1974: 539-40.

[101]This term was coined by C. Wright Mills. See Mills, 1959.

[102]See Luckmann, 1967.

[103]*Ibid.,* p. 49-50. It might be stated that where there is "culture" in an anthropological sense, there is "religion" in Luckmann's "anthropological" sense of the term.

[104]*Ibid.,* p. 104.

[105]*Ibid.,* p. 105. The notion of a "free market" in such choices is important here. On the profane or unfamiliar forms of religion which can emerge under Luckmann's definition, Bryan Wilson has remarked: "Unlike some sociologists of religion, I do not regard the Rolling Stones, because of the enthusiasm they engender, as the modern-day equivalents of Moody and Sankey. Nor do I believe that washing the car, even if done religiously every Sunday morning, constitutes a religious act — or that it is an expression of man's 'ultimate concern' in the modern world. I do not accept the idea that the human search for affection, including sexual gratification, is to be seen as modern man's 'invisible religion'." (Wilson, 1976: 4.)

[106]See Tom Sinclair-Faulkner, "A Puckish Reflection on Religion in Canada," in Slater, 1977: 383-405.

[107]Sinclair-Faulkner's analysis of ice-hockey is really closer to a structural-functionalist interpretation, though even in this regard it is not as novel as it appears, for see Cohen, "Baseball as a National Religion," in Cohen, 1946: 334-36 (originally published 1919). See also John Badertscher, "Response to Sinclair-Faulkner," in Slater, 1977: 407-20.

[108]For example, compare its thesis with that in Kornhauser, 1959. For parallel discussion, see Stauffer, 1973; and Fenn, 1972: 16-32. For an American attempt to apply Luckmann's thesis, see Machalek and Martin, 1976: 311-21.

[109]This is true of all the great nineteenth-century "classic thinkers" of sociology, even though some provided "secular religions" of their own as their legacy. For a brief defense of the view that "the founding fathers of sociology subscribed to the idea of secularization, and saw the decline of religion as an implicit part of the general process of social evolution..." see Wilson, 1979.

[110]See Robertson, 1970: 46-47 for a defense of such usage in a sociological context. As noted above, such a definition has been implicit in the present essay, not merely because of the author's preference, but in order to contrast sharply a commonly-accepted use of the term in historical, political, and much sociological literature with its more unusual application in certain sociological contexts. The ambiguities of the term "secularization" are thereby also underlined. See the literature on the definitional problem cited above.

[111]Wilson, 1969.

[112]*Ibid.*, pp. 256-57.

[113]*Ibid.*, p. 257.

[114]See Durkheim, 1933 (first published 1893).

[115]It might be argued that in recent years many social activities have ceased to be private, and have, in current phraseology, come "out of the closet" and even "gone public". The reverse has been true of religious activity which is now in the private rather than the public domain.

[116]See Marsden and Harvey, 1979. The authors have adopted Mordecai Richler's description of Canada as "a fragile, loosely knit confederation."

Bibliography

Alford, Robert R. *Party and Society.* Chicago: Rand McNally and Company, 1963.
_____. "The Social Bases of Political Cleavage in 1962." In John Meisel, ed. *Papers On The 1962 Election.* Toronto: University of Toronto Press, 1964.
Allen, Richard. *The Social Passion: Religion and Social Reform in Canada, 1914-28.* Toronto: University of Toronto Press, 1971.
_____. ed. *The Social Gospel in Canada: Papers of the Inter-disciplinary Conference on the Social Gospel in Canada.* Ottawa: History Division Paper No. 9, National Museums of Canada, 1975.
Almond, Gabriel and Sidney Verba. *The Civic Culture.* Boston: Little, Brown and Co., 1965.
_____. "Comparative Political Systems." In Gabriel Almond. *Political Development,* Boston: Little, Brown and Co., 1970.
Anderson, C. P. and T. A. Nosanchuk, eds. *The 1967 Guide to Religious Studies in Canada.* np: Canadian Society for the Study of Religion, 1969.
Anderson, C. P., ed. *The 1969 Guide to Religious Studies in Canada.* np: Canadian Society for the Study of Religion, 1969.
Anderson, Grace M. "Voting Behaviour and the Ethnic Religious Variable: A Study

of a Federal Election in Hamilton, Ontario." *Canadian Journal of Economics and Political Science* 32 (1966): 27-37.

Aristotle. *The Politics.* Translated by T. A. Sinclair. Harmondsworth: Penguin Books, 1962.

Badertscher, John. "Response to Sinclair-Faulkner." In Peter Slater, ed. *Religion and Culture in Canada.* Waterloo, Ont.: Wilfred Laurier University Press, 1977.

Barker, Eileen, ed. *New Religious Movements: A Perspective for Understanding Society.* New York and Toronto: The Edwin Mellen Press, 1982.

Barnes, Samuel H. "Quebec Catholicism and Social Change." *Review of Politics* 23 (1961): 52-76.

Baum, Gregory. "Social Catholicism in Nova Scotia." In Peter Slater, ed. *Religion and Culture in Canada.* Waterloo, Ontario: Wilfred Laurier University Press, 1977.

_____. *Catholics and Canadian Socialism: Political Thought in the Thirties and Forties.* Toronto: James Lorimer, 1980.

Beals, Ralph C. "Religion and Identity." *International Yearbook for the Sociology of Knowledge and Religion* 11 (1978): 147-162.

Bell, Daniel. *The End of Ideology: On the Exhaustion of Political Ideas in the Fifties.* Glencoe: The Free Press, 1960.

_____. "The Return of the Sacred? The Argument on the Future of Religion." *British Journal of Sociology* 28 (1977): 419-49.

Bell, David V. J. "The Loyalist Tradition in Canada." *Journal of Canadian Studies* 5 (1970): 22-33.

Bell, David, and Lorne Tepperman. *The Roots of Disunity.* Toronto: McClelland and Stewart, 1979.

Bellah, Robert N. "Civil Religion in America." In R. E. Richey and D. G. Jones, eds. *American Civil Religion.* New York: Harper and Row, 1974. (Originally published in *Daedalus,* Winter, 1967.)

_____. *The Broken Covenant: American Civil Religion in Time of Trial.* New York: Seabury Press, 1975.

Bendix, Reinhard. *Max Weber: An Intellectual Portrait.* London: Heinemann, 1960.

Berger, Carl. *The Writing of Canadian History: Aspects of English-Canadian Historical Writing, 1900-1970.* Toronto: Oxford University Press, 1976.

Berger, Peter. *The Sacred Canopy.* Garden City, N.Y.: Doubleday-Anchor Books, 1969.

_____. "Some Second Thoughts on Substantive Versus Functional Definitions of Religion." *Journal for the Scientific Study of Religion* 13 (1974): 125-133.

_____. *The Heretical Imperative: Contemporary Possibilities of Religious Affirmation.* Garden City, N.Y.: Doubleday-Anchor Press, 1979.

Bergeson, Albert James. "A Durkheimian Theory of 'Witch Hunts' with the Chinese Cultural Revolution of 1966-1969 as an Example." *Journal for the Scientific Study of Religion* 17 (1978): 19-29.

Bibby, Reginald W. "Numbers and Northerners: Survey Research in the Sociology of Religion in Canada." Paper presented at the Annual Meeting of the Society for the Scientific Study of Religion, Chicago, Illinois, 1977.

_____. "The Nature of Religiosity in Canada." In Stewart Crysdale and Christopher Beattie, eds. *Sociology Canada: Readings.* 2d ed. Toronto: Butterworths, 1977b.

_____. "Religion and Modernity: The Canadian Case." *Journal for The Scientific Study of Religion* 18 (1979a): 1-17.

_____. "The State of Collective Religiosity in Canada." *Canadian Review of Sociology and Anthropology* 16 (1979b): 105-116.

_____. "Religion." In Robert Hagedorn, ed. *Sociology.* Toronto: Holt, Rinehart and Winston, 1980.

Bird, Frederick. "Comparative Analysis of the Rituals Used by Some Contemporary 'New' Religious and Para-Religious Movements." In Peter Slater, ed. *Religion and Culture in Canada.* Waterloo, Ontario: Wilfred Laurier University Press, 1977.

Bird, Frederick and William Reimer. "New Religious and Para-religious Movements in Montreal." In Stewart Crysdale and Les Wheatcroft, eds. *Religion in Canadian Society.* Toronto: Macmillan, 1976.

Birnbaum, Norman. "Monarchs and Sociologists: A Reply to Professor Shils and Mr. Young." *Sociological Review* 3 (1955): 5-23.

Blasi, Anthony J. "Definition of Religion and Phenomenological Approach Towards a Problematic." *Cahiers du CRSR* 3 (1980): 55-70.

Blumstock, Robert. "Civil Uncivility: Non-Civil Religion in Canada." Paper presented to the Annual Meeting of the Society for the Scientific Study of Religion, Chicago, 1977.

Bowen, Desmond. *The Protestant Crusade in Ireland, 1800-70.* Dublin: Gill and Macmillan, 1978.

Budd, Susan. "The Humanistic Societies: The Consequences of a Diffuse Belief System." In B. R. Wilson, ed. *Patterns of Sectarianism.* London: Heinemann, 1967.

Cahnman, Werner Jacob and Alvin Boskoff, eds. *Sociology and History: Theory and Research.* New York: The Free Press, 1964.

Campbell, Douglas F. "Religion and Values Among Nova Scotia College Students." *Sociological Analysis* 27 (1968): 80-93.

Campbell, Douglas F. and Dennis W. Magill. "Religious Involvement and Intellectuality Among University Students." *Sociological Analysis* 29 (1968): 79-93.

Campbell, Michel. "Les Bruits de la Mer: Essaie herméneutique religieuse d'un mythe de l'original dans les chansons populaires québécoises." In Peter Slater, ed. *Religion and Culture in Canada.* Waterloo, Ontario: Wilfred Laurier University Press, 1977.

Canadian Review of Studies in Nationalism/Revue Canadienne des Etudes sur le Nationalisme 7 (1980). (Special Issue on Anglo-Canadian Nationalism and Social Communications.)

Careless, J. M. S. "Frontierism, Metropolitanism and Canadian History." *Canadian Historical Review* 35 (1954): 1-21.

Cherry, Conrad. "American Sacred Ceremonies." In Phillip E. Hammond and Benton Johnson, eds. *American Mosaic: Social Patterns of Religion in the United States.* New York: Random House, 1970.

_____. *God's New Israel: Religious Interpretations of American Destiny.* Englewood Cliffs, N. J.: Prentice-Hall, 1971.

Christianson, Paul. *Reformers in Babylon: English Apocalyptic Visions from the Reformation to the Eve of the Civil War.* Toronto: University of Toronto Press, 1978.

Clark, S. D. "Religious Organization and The Rise of The Canadian Nation, 1850-1885." In *Report of the Annual Meeting of the Canadian Historical Association* (1944): 86-96. (Reprinted in *The Developing Canadian Community,* 115-130.)

_____. "The Religious Sect in Canadian Politics." *American Journal of Sociology* 51 (1945): 207-16. (Reprinted in *The Developing Canadian Community,* 130-46.)

_____. "The Religious Sect in Canadian Economic Development." *Canadian Journal of Economics and Political Science* 12 (1946): 439-53. (Reprinted in *The Developing Canadian Community,* 147-66.)

_____. "The Religious Factor in Canadian Economic Development." In *The Tasks of Economic History,* supplement to the *Journal of Economic History* (1947): 89-103. (Reprinted in *The Developing Canadian Community* under the title

"The Religious Influence in Canadian Society.")

_____. *Church and Sect in Canada.* Toronto: University of Toronto Press, 1948.

_____. *Movements of Political Protest in Canada, 1640-1840.* Toronto: University of Toronto Press, 1959.

_____. *The Developing Canadian Community.* Rev. and expanded ed. Toronto: University of Toronto Press, 1968.

_____. *Canadian Society in Historical Perspective.* Toronto: McGraw-Hill Ryerson, 1976.

Clifford, N. Keith. "Religion and the Development of Canadian Society: An Historographical Analysis." *Church History* 38 (1969): 506-23.

_____. "His Dominion: A Vision in Crisis." In Peter Slater, ed. *Religion and Culture in Canada.* Waterloo, Ont.: Wilfred Laurier University Press, 1977. (Originally published in *Studies in Religion/Sciences Religieuses* 2 (1973).

_____. "History of Religion in Canada." *The Ecumenist* 18 (1980): 65-69.

Cohen, Morris R. "Baseball as a National Religion." In *The Faith of a Liberal.* New York: Henry Holt, 1946. (Originally published in 1919 in *The Dial* 67 (1919): 57.)

Cole, William A. and Phillip Hammond. "Religious Pluralism, Legal Development and Societal Complexity: Rudimentary Forms of Civil Religion," *Journal for the Scientific Study of Religion* 13 (1974): 177-89.

Constas, Helen. "The U.S.S.R. — From Charismatic Sect to Bureaucratic Society," *Administrative Science Quarterly* 6 (1961): 282-98.

Cook, Ramsay. *The Maple Leaf Forever.* Toronto: Macmillan of Canada, 1972.

Crysdale, Stewart. *The Industrial Struggle and Protestant Ethic in Canada: A Survey of Changing Power Structures and Christian Social Ethics.* Toronto: Ryerson Press, 1961.

_____. *The Changing Church in Canada: Beliefs and Social Attitudes of United Church People.* Toronto: United Church of Canada Publishing House, 1965.

_____. "Religion and Secularization." In S. Crysdale and C. Beattie, *Sociology Canada: An Introductory Text.* Toronto: Butterworths, 1973.

_____. "Some Problematic Aspects of Religion in Canada." *Sociological Focus* 9 (1976): 137-48.

_____. "Historical, Change and Conflict Perspectives in the Sociology of Religion in English-Speaking Canada." Paper presented at the Annual Meeting of the Society for Scientific Study of Religion, Chicago, Illinois, 1977.

Crysdale, Stewart and Jean-Paul Montminy. *Religion in Canada/La Religon au Canada: Annotated Inventory 1945-1972.* (Histoire et Sociologie de la Culture, No. 8) Downsview and Québec. York University and Les Presses de l'Université Laval, 1974.

Crysdale, Stewart and Les Wheatcroft, eds. *Religion in Canadian Society.* Toronto: Macmillan of Canada, 1976.

Despland, Michel. "Religion and the Quest for National Identity: Problems and Perspectives." In Peter Slater, ed. *Religion and Culture in Canada.* Waterloo, Ontario: Wilfred Laurier University Press, 1977.

Dumont, Fernand, "La Sociologie religieuse au Canada Français," In *Sociologie Religieuse, Sciences Sociales, Actes du IVe Congrès International.* Paris: Éditions Économie et Humanisme, 1955.

_____. *La situation presente de la theorie dans la sociologie des religions.* Ottawa Editions du Musée de l'Homme, 1958.

_____. "Réflexions sur l'histoire religieuse de Canada française." In *L'Eglise et le Québec.* Montréal: Éditions du Jour, 1961.

_____. "La Sociologie et le renouveau de la theologie." In Lawrence K. Shook and Guy-M. Bertrand. *La Renouveau de la Theologie.* Montréal: Editions Fides, 1969.

Durkheim, Emile. *The Division of Labor in Society.* Translated by Simpson. New

York: The Macmillan Co., 1933. (First published 1893.)

————. *The Elementary Forms of The Religious Life.* Translated by Swain. London: George Allen and Unwin, 1915. (First published 1912.)

Falardeau, Jean-Charles. "The Parish as an Institutional Type." In *Canadian Journal of Economics and Political Science* 15 (1949): 365-71.

————. "The Role and Importance of The Church in French Canada." In M. Rioux and Y. Martin, eds. *French Canadian Society.* Toronto: McClelland and Stewart, 1964. (Originally published in French in *Esprit* (1952): 214-29 under the title "Role et Importance de l'Église au Canada Français.")

————. "The Seventeenth-Century Parish in French Canada." In S. Crysdale and L. Wheatcroft, eds. *Religion in Canadian Society.* Toronto: Macmillan, 1976.

————. "Les Recherches de Sociologie Religieuse au Canada." In *Lumen Vitae* 6 (1950-51): 127-42.

————. "Parish Research in Other Countries: Canada." In Neuse and Harte, eds. *Sociology of the Parish.* Milwaukee: Bruce Publishing Co., 1951.

————. "Les Recherches Religieuses au Canada Français." *Recherches Socio-graphiques* 3 (1962): 209-28.

Fallding, Harold. "Canada." In Hans Mol, ed. *Western Religion: A Country by Country Sociological Inquiry.* The Hague: Mouton, 1972.

————. *The Sociology of Religion.* Toronto: McGraw-Hill Ryerson, 1974.

————. "Mainline Protestantism in Canada and the United States of America: An Overview." *Canadian Journal of Sociology* 3 (1978): 141-60.

Fenn, Richard K. "Toward A New Sociology of Religion." *Journal for the Scientific Study of Religion.* 2 (1972): 16-32.

————. *Toward a Theory of Secularization.* Society for the Scientific Study of Religion Monographs, No. 1, 1978.

Flanagan, Thomas. *Louis "David" Riel: "Prophet of the New World."* Toronto: University of Toronto Press, 1979.

Friedenberg, Edgar Z. *Deference to Authority: The Case of Canada.* White Plains, N. Y.: M. E. Sharpe, Inc., 1980.

Geertz, Clifford. *The Interpretation of Cultures.* New York: Basic Books Inc., 1973.

Glasner, Peter E. *The Sociology of Secularization: A Critique of a Concept.* London: Routledge and Kegan Paul, 1977.

Glock, Charles Y. and Robert N. Bellah, eds. *The New Religious Consciousness.* Berkeley and Los Angeles: University of California Press, 1976.

Goody, Jack. "Religion and Ritual: The Definitional Problem." *British Journal of Sociology* 12 (1961): 142-64.

Grand-Maison, Jacques. "Nationalisme et Religion." *Nationalisme et Révolution Culturelle* 12 (1961): 142-64.

Grant, George. *Lament for a Nation.* New ed. Toronto: McClelland and Stewart, 1970.

Grant, John Webster. "Asking Questions of the Canadian Past." *Canadian Journal of Theology* 1 (1955): 98-104.

————. "Canadian Confederation and The Protestant Churches." *Church History* 38 (1969): 327-37.

————. *The Church in the Canadian Era.* Toronto: McGraw-Hill Ryerson, 1972.

————. "Religion and Canada: A Historical Perspective." Paper presented to the Canadian Society for the Study of Religion, Kingston, Ontario, 1973.

————. "At Least You Knew Where You Stood With Them: Reflections on Religious Pluralism in Canada and the United States." *Studies in Religion* 2 (1973): 340-51.

————. "Religion and the Quest for a National Identity: The Background in Canadian History." In Peter Slater, ed. *Religion and Culture in Canada.* Waterloo, Ontario: Wilfred Laurier University Press, 1977.

Greeley, Andrew. *Unsecular Man: The Persistence of Religion.* New York: Schocken Books, 1972.

Greeley, Andrew and Gregory Baum, eds. *The Persistence of Religion.* New York: Herder and Herder, 1973.

Gualtieri, Antonio R. "Towards a Theological Perspective on Nationalism." *Anglo-Welsh Review* 22 (1973). Reprinted in Peter Slater, ed. *Religion and Culture in Canada.* Waterloo, Ontario: Wilfred Laurier University Press, 1977.

Guindon, Hubert. "The Social Evolution of Quebec Reconsidered." *Canadian Journal of Economics and Political Science* 26 (1960): 533-51.

Guinsberg, T. N. and Grant Reuber, eds. *Perspectives on the Social Sciences in Canada.* Toronto: University of Toronto Press, 1974.

Hagedorn, Robert, ed. *Sociology.* Toronto: Holt, Rinehart & Winston, 1980.

Hammond, Phillip E. "Further Thoughts on Civil Religion in America." In Donald R. Cutler, ed. *The Religious Situation.* Boston: Beacon Press: 1968.

———. "The Sociology of American Civil Religion: A Bibliographic Essay." *Sociological Analysis* 37 (1976): 169-82.

Hartz, Louis. *The Liberal Tradition in America.* New York: Harcourt Brace, 1953.

———. *The Founding of New Societies.* New York: Harcourt Brace, 1964.

———. "A Comparative Study of Fragment Cultures." In H. D. Graham and T. R. Gurr, eds. *Violence in America: Historical and Comparative Perspectives.* New York: Signet Books, 1969.

Henderson, J. L. H., ed. *John Strachan: Documents and Opinions.* Toronto: McClelland and Stewart, 1969a.

———. *John Strachan, 1778-1867.* Toronto: University of Toronto Press, 1969b.

Herberg, Will. *Protestant-Catholic-Jew: An Essay in American Religious Sociology.* Garden City: Doubleday Anchor Books, Revised Edition, 1960.

———. "Religion in a Secularized Society: Some Aspects of America's Three-Religion Pluralism." In Louis Schneider, ed. *Religion, Culture and Society.* New York: John Wiley and Sons, 1964.

———. "America's Civil Religion: What It Is and Whence It Comes" in R. E. Richey and D. G. Jones, eds. *American Civil Religion.* New York: Harper and Row, 1964.

Hiller, Harry H. "The New Theology and The Sociology of Religion." *Canadian Review of Sociology and Anthropology* 6 (1969): 179-87.

———. "Alberta and The Bible Belt Stereotype." In S. Crysdale and L. Wheatcroft, eds. *Religion in Canadian Society.* Toronto: Macmillan of Canada, 1976.

———. "The Sociology of Religion in Western Canada: An Assessment." Paper presented at the Annual Meeting of the Canadian Sociology and Anthropology, Quebec City, 1976.

———. "The Sociology of Religion in Canadian Context." In G. N. Ramu and S. D. Johnson, eds. *Introduction to Canadian Society: Sociological Analysis.* Toronto: Macmillan, 1976.

———. "The Contribution of S. D. Clark to the Sociology of Canadian Religion." *Studies in Religion* 6 (1976-77): 415-27.

———. "Continentalism and the Third Force in Religion." *Canadian Journal of Sociology* 3 (1978): 183-207.

Hofstadter, Richard and S. M. Lipset, eds. *Turner and The Sociology of the Frontier.* New York: Basic Books, 1968.

Horowitz, Gad. "Conservatism, Liberalism, and Socialism in Canada: An Interpretation." In *Canadian Labour in Politics.* Toronto: University of Toronto Press, 1968.

Horowitz, Irving Louis. "The Hemispheric Connection: A Critique and Corrective to the Entrepreneurial Thesis of Development with Special Emphasis on the

Canadian Case." *Queen's Quarterly* 80 (1973) 327-59.

Horton, Robin "A Definition of Religion and its Uses." *Journal of the Royal Anthropological Institute* 90 (1960): 201-26.

Hughes, Everett C. *French Canada in Transition.* Chicago: University of Chicago Press, 1943.

_____. "Action Catholique and Nationalism: A Memorandum on the Church and Society in French Canada, 1942" in S. Crysdale and L. Wheatcroft, eds. *Religion in Canadian Society.* Toronto: Macmillan, 1976.

Hutchinson, Roger C. "Religion, Morality and Law." In Peter Slater, ed. *Religion and Culture in Canada.* Waterloo, Ont.: Wilfred Laurier University Press, 1977.

Ions, Edmund. *Against Behaviouralism.* Oxford: Basil Blackwell, 1977.

Irving, John A. *The Social Credit Movement in Alberta.* Toronto: University of Toronto Press, 1959.

Kalbach, Warren E. "Religious Characteristics." In *The Impact of Immigration on Canada's Population.* Ottawa: Dominion Bureau of Statistics, 1970.

Kalbach, Warren E. and Wayne McVey. *The Demographic Bases of Canadian Society.* 2d ed. Toronto: McGraw-Hill Ryerson, 1979.

Kavanaugh, Dennis. *Political Culture.* London: Macmillan, 1972.

Klassen, William. "Two Wise Men from the West." In Peter Slater, ed. *Religion and Culture in Canada.* Waterloo, Ont.: Wilfred Laurier University Press, 1977.

Kornhauser, William. *The Politics of Mass Society.* New York: The Free Press, 1959.

Krauz, Ernest. "Religion as a Key Variable." In Elizabeth Gittus, ed. *Key Variables in Social Research.* [Vol. 1, Religion, Housing, Locality.] London: Heinemann (for the British Sociological Association), 1972.

Laponce, J. A. "The Religious Background of Canadian M.P.'s." *Political Studies* 6 (1958): 253-58.

Legaré, Jacques. "Les religieuses du Canada: Leur evolution numérique entre 1965 et 1980." *Recherches Sociographiques* 10 (1967-68/1969): 7-21.

Lenski, Gerhard. *The Religious Factor.* Garden City: Doubleday Anchor Books, 1963.

Lipset, Seymour Martin. "Canada and the United States — A Comparative View," *Canadian Review of Sociology and Anthropology* 1 (1964): 173-85.

_____. *The First New Nation: The United States in Historical and Comparative Perspective.* Garden City: Doubleday Anchor Books, 1967.

_____. *Agrarian Socialism: The Co-operative Commonwealth Federation in Saskatchewan.* Garden City: Doubleday-Anchor Books, 1968. (First published 1950 by University of California Press.)

_____. *Revolution and Counterrevolution.* Garden City: Doubleday-Anchor Books, 1970.

_____. "Radicalism in North America: A Comparative View of the Party Systems in Canada and the United States." *Transactions of the Royal Society of Canada.* Series 4. 14 (1976): 19-54.

Lipset, Seymour Martin and Richard Hofstadter. *Sociology and History: Methods.* New York: Basic Books, 1968.

Lipsitz, Lewis. "If, as Verba says, the State functions as a religion, what are we to do to save our souls?" *American Political Science Review* 62 (1968): 527-35.

Lower, Arthur M. "Two Ways of Life: The Primary Antithesis of Canadian History." In Carl Berger, ed. *Approaches to Canadian History.* Toronto: University of Toronto Press, 1967.

Lucas, Rex. *Minetown, Milltown, Railtown.* Toronto: University of Toronto Press, 1970.

Luckmann, Thomas. *The Invisible Religion: The Transformation of Symbols in Industrial Society.* New York: The Macmillan Company, 1967. (1963.)

Machalek, Richard and Michael Martin. "'Invisible' Religion: Some Preliminary Evidence." *Journal for the Scientific Study of Religion* 15 (1976): 311-21.

Macintyre, Alasdair. *Secularization and Moral Change.* Oxford: Oxford University Press, 1967.

MacLeod, Henry. "The Religious Situation in Canadian Society." Paper presented at the Annual Meeting of the Canadian Sociology and Anthropology Association, Saskatoon, 1979.

Macpherson, C. B. "After Strange Gods: Canadian Political Science 1973." In T. N. Guinsberg and G. L. Reuber, eds. *Perspectives on the Social Sciences in Canada.* Toronto: University of Toronto Press, 1974.

Macrae, Donald G. *Ideology and Society.* London: Heinemann, 1961.

Mann, William E. *Sect, Cult and Church in Alberta.* Toronto: University of Toronto Press, 1955.

Marsden, Lorna and Edward B. Harvey. *Fragile Federation: Social Change in Canada.* Toronto: McGraw-Hill Ryerson, 1979.

Martin, David. "The Sociology of Religion: A Case of Status Deprivation?" *British Journal of Sociology* 17 (1966): 353-9.

_____. "Towards Eliminating the Concept of Secularization." In Julius Gould, ed. *Penguin Survey of the Social Sciences.* Harmondsworth: Penguin Books, 1965.

_____. *A General Theory of Secularization.* New York: Harper and Row, 1978.

Marx, Karl and Frederick Engels. *On Religion.* Moscow: Foreign Languages Publishing House, 1958.

Mathews, Robin and James Steele, eds. *The Struggle for Canadian Universities.* Toronto: New Press, 1969.

McDonald, Lynn. "Religion and Voting: A Study of the 1968 Canadian Federal Election in Ontario." In *Canadian Review of Sociology and Anthropology* 6 (1969): 129-44.

McDowell, Jennifer. "Soviet Civil Ceremonies." In *Journal for the Scientific Study of Religion* 13 (1974): 265-79.

McKillop, A. B. "Nationalism, Identity and Canadian Intellectual History." *Queen's Quarterly* 81 (1974): 533-47.

McKown, D. B. *The Classical Marxist Critiques of Religion: Marx, Engels, Lenin, Kautsky* The Hague: Martinus Nijhoff, 1975.

McNall, Scott G., ed. *Theoretical Perspectives in Sociology.* New York: St. Martins Press, 1979.

McNaught, Kenneth. *A Prophet in Politics: A Biography of J. S. Woodsworth.* Toronto: University of Toronto Press, 1959.

McRae, Kenneth D. "Louis Hartz' Concept of the Fragment of Society and its Application to Canada." *Études Canadiennes* 5 (1978): 17-30.

Meisel, John. "Religious Affiliation and Voting Behaviour" in *Canadian Journal of Economics and Political Science.* 22 (1956): 481-96.

_____. *The Canadian Federal Election of 1957.* Toronto: University of Toronto Press, 1962.

_____. ed. *Papers on the 1962 Election.* Toronto: University of Toronto Press, 1964. (See especially papers by George Perlin, pp. 3-18; S. Peter Regenstrief, pp. 235-52; and the conclusion.)

Millet, David. "A Typology of Religious Organizations Suggested by the Canadian Census," *Sociological Analysis* 30 (1969): 108-19.

Mills, C. Wright. *The Sociological Imagination.* New York: Oxford University Press, 1959.

Miner, Horace. *St. Denis: A French-Canadian Parish.* Chicago: University of Chicago Press, 1939.

Moir, John S. *Church and State in Canada West: Three Studies in the Relation of Denomination and Nationalism, 1841-1867.* Toronto: University of Toronto

Press, 1959.

_____. "The Sectarian Tradition in Canada." In John W. Grant, ed. *The Churches and The Canadian Experience.* Toronto: Ryerson Press, 1963.

_____. *The Church in the British Era: From the British Conquest to Confederation.* Toronto: McGraw-Hill Ryerson, 1972.

Mol, Hans, ed. *Western Religion: A Country by Country Sociological Enquiry.* The Hague: Mouton, 1972.

_____. "Major Correlates of Churchgoing in Canada." in S. Crysdale and L. Wheatcroft, eds. *Religion in Canadian Society.* Toronto: Macmillan of Canada, 1976.

_____. *Identity and The Sacred: A Sketch for a New Social Scientific Theory of Religion.* Agincourt: The Book Society of Canada, 1976.

_____. "The Origin and Function of Religion," *Journal for the Scientific Study of Religion* 18 (1979): 378-89.

Montminy, Jean-Paul and Stewart Crysdale. *Religion in Canada/La Religion au Canada: Annotated Inventory 1945-1972.* (Histoire et Sociologie de la Culture, No. 8) Downsview and Québec: York University and Les Presses de l'Université Laval, 1974.

Moore, Sally F. and Barbara G. Myerhoff, eds. *Secular Ritual.* New York: Humanities Press, 1977.

Moreux, Colette. *Fin d'une religion?* Montréal: Les Presses de l'Université de Montréal, 1969.

_____. "The End of a Religion?" In Gerald L. Gold and Marc-Adelard Tremblay, eds. *Communities and Culture in French Canada.* Toronto: Holt, Rinehart and Winston, 1973.

Morton, W. L. *The Canadian Identity.* Toronto: University of Toronto Press, 1961.

Naegele, Kaspar D. "Modern National Societies." In B. Blishen, F. E. Jones, K. D. Naegele and J. Porter, eds. *Canadian Society.* 3rd ed. Toronto: Macmillan, 1968.

Niebuhr, H. Richard. *The Social Sources of Denominationalism.* New York: Meridian Books, 1957. (First published 1929.)

Norman, E. R. *The Conscience of the State in North America.* Cambridge: Cambridge University Press, 1968.

Nosanchuk, T. A. "Dimensions of Canadian Religiosity: A Preliminary Survey." *Journal for the Scientific Study of Religion* 7 (1968): 109-10.

Oliver, E. H. *The Winning of the Frontier.* Toronto: Ryerson Press, 1930.

O'Toole, Roger. "Review of Thomas Flanagan, *Louis 'David' Riel: Prophet of the New World." Journal for the Scientific Study of Religion* 19 (1980): 310-12.

Paper, Jordan. "A Shaman in Contemporary Toronto." In Peter Slater, ed. *Religion and Culture in Canada.* Waterloo, Ontario: Wilfred Laurier University Press, 1977.

Parsons, Talcott. *The Structure of Social Action.* Glencoe: The Free Press, 1949 (1937).

Pickering, W. S. F. "The Church in a Changing Society." *Bulletin of the Council for Social Service* No. 187, Toronto: Anglican Church of Canada, 1963.

_____. *Durkheim on Religion.* London: Routledge and Kegan Paul, 1975.

Pickering, W. S. F. and J. E. W. Jackson. "A Brief Sociological Examination of Local United and Anglican Churches." *Canadian Journal of Theology* 14 (1968): 249-61.

Porter, John. *The Vertical Mosaic.* Toronto: University of Toronto Press, 1965.

Regenstrief, S. Peter. "Some Aspects of National Party Support in Canada." *Canadian Journal of Economics and Political Science* 29 (1963): 59-74.

Rex, John, ed. *Approaches to Sociology.* London: Routledge and Kegan Paul, 1974.

Richard, Reginald. "Le Concept de Religion: Specificité ou Homologie." *Les*

Cahiers du CRSR 2 (1978): 3-17.
Richey, Russell E. and Donald G. Jones, eds. *American Civil Religion*. New York: Harper and Row, 1974.
Rioux, Marcel and Yves Martin, eds. *French-Canadian Society*. Toronto: McClelland and Stewart, 1964.
Robertson, Roland. *The Sociological Interpretation of Religion*. New York: Schocken Books, 1970.
Rousseau, Louis. "La Naissance du Récit Mythique des Origines Québécoises." In Peter Slater, ed. *Religion and Culture in Canada*. Waterloo, Ontario: Wilfred Laurier University Press, 1977. (Originally published in *Studies in Religion/Sciences Religieuses* 3 (1973).)
Russell, Peter, ed. *Nationalism in Canada*. Toronto: McGraw Hill Ryerson, 1972.
Ryan, William F. *The Clergy and Economic Growth in Québec 1896-1914*. Québec Les Presses de l'Université Laval, 1966.
Schwartz, Mildred. *Public Opinion and Canadian Identity*. Berkeley: University of California Press, 1967.
Seeley, John R., Alexander Sim, and E. W. Loosley. *Crestwood Heights*. Toronto: University of Toronto Press, 1956.
Shils, Edward and Michael Young. "The Meaning of the Coronation." *Sociological Review* 1 (1953): 63-81.
Siegfried, André. *The Race Question in Canada*. Toronto: McClelland and Stewart, 1966. (First published in English, 1907.)
Silverstein, Sandford. "Occupational Class and Voting Behaviour: Electoral Support of a Left-Wing Protest Movement in a Period of Prosperity." In S. M. Lipset, *Agrarian Socialism*. Garden City: Doubleday Anchor Books (updated ed.), 1968.
Simpson, John H. "Ethnic Groups and Church Attendance in the United States and Canada." In Andrew Greeley and Gregory Baum, eds. *Ethnicity*. New York: Seabury Press, 1979.
Sinclair-Faulkner, Tom. "Hockey in Canada: A Puckish Reflection on Religion in Canada." In Peter Slater, ed. *Religion and Culture in Canada*. Waterloo, Ontario: Wilfred Laurier University Press, 1977.
Sissons, C. B. *Church and State in Canadian Education*. Toronto: Ryerson Press, 1959.
Slater, Peter, ed. *Religion and Culture in Canada/Religion et Culture au Canada*. Waterloo, Ontario: Wilfrid Laurier University Press, 1977.
_____. "Religion as Story: Norman Bethune." In Peter Slater, ed. *Religion and Culture in Canada*. Waterloo, Ontario: Wilfred Laurier University Press, 1977.
Smith, Allan. "Metaphor and Nationality in North America." *Canadian Historical Review* 51 (1970): 247-75.
Sociological Analysis 37 (1976). (Special Issue on Civil Religion.)
Spiro, Melford E. "Religion: Problems of Definition and Explanation." In Michael Banton, ed. *Anthropological Approaches to the Study of Religion*. London: Tavistock Publications, 1966.
Stahl, William A. "Civil Religion and Canadian Confederation." Doctoral dissertation, Graduate Theological Union, Berkeley, Calif., 1981.
Stauffer, Robert E. "Civil Religion, Technocracy and the Private Sphere: Further Comments on Cultural Integration in Advanced Societies." *Journal for the Scientific Study of Religion* 12 (1973): 415-25.
Streng, F. J. "Studying Religion: Possibilities and Limitations of Different Definitions." *Journal of the American Academy of Religion* 40 (1972): 219-37.
Stryckman, Paul. *Les prêtres du Québec d'aujourd'hui*. Québec: Université Laval Centre de Recherches en Sociologie Religieuse, 1970.
_____. "Theory and Research in Quebec: Qualitative Appraisal and Perspectives."

Paper presented at the Annual Meeting of the Society for the Scientific Study of Religion, Chicago, Illinois, 1977a.

_____. "Reflexions et Perspectives sur le Sociologie de la Religion au Québec," *Les Cahiers du CRSR* 1 (1977b): 145-83.

Stryckman, Paul and Robert Gaudet. *Priests in Canada, 1971: A Report on English-Speaking Clergy.* Québec: Centre de Recherches en Sociologie Religieuse, Université Laval, 1971.

_____. "Priests Under Stress." In S. Crysdale and L. Wheatcroft, eds. *Religion in Canadian Society.* Toronto: Macmillan, 1976.

Studies in Religion 6 (1976-77). (Special Issue on Canadian Religion.)

Symons, T. H. B. *To Know Ourselves: The Report of the Commission on Canadian Studies.* Ottawa: Association of Universities and Colleges in Canada, 1975.

Taylor, Charles. *The Pattern of Politics.* Toronto: McClelland and Stewart, 1970.

Tocqueville, Alexis de. *Democracy in America.* 2 vols. New York: Alfred Knopf, 1948.

Torrance, Judy. "Cultural Factors and The Response of Governments to Violence." Ph.D. thesis, York University, Canada, 1975.

_____. "The Response of Canadian Governments to Violence." *Canadian Journal of Political Science* 10 (1977): 473-96.

_____. "The Canadian Government, Social Movements and Violence." Paper presented to the Annual Meeting of the Canadian Sociology and Anthropology Association, London, Ontario, 1978.

Trofimenkoff, Susan Mann. *Abbé Groulx: Variations on a Nationalist Theme.* Toronto: Copp Clark, 1973.

_____. *Action Française: French Canadian Nationalism in Québec in the 1920's.* Toronto: University of Toronto Press, 1975.

Vogt, Evon Z. and Susan Abel. "On Political Rituals in Contemporary Mexico". In S. F. Moore and B. G. Myerhoff, eds. *Secular Ritual.* Assenc/Amsterdam: Van Gorcum, 1977: 173-88.

Walsh, H. H. "Canada and The Church: A Job for the Historians." *Queen's Quarterly* 61 (1954): 71-79.

Warburton, T. Rennie. "Critical Theory and The Sociology of Religion." Paper presented to the Annual Meeting of the Society for the Scientific Study of Religion, Milwaukee, Wisconsin, 1975.

_____. "Religion and The Control of Native Peoples." In S. Crysdale and L. Wheatcroft, eds. *Religion in Canadian Society.* Toronto: Macmillan of Canada, 1976.

_____. "A Dialectical Theory of Religion." Mimeographed.

Weber, Max. *The Protestant Ethic and The Spirit of Capitalism.* Translated by Parsons. London: George Allen and Unwin, 1930. (First published 1904-05.)

_____. *The Sociology of Religion.* Translated by Fischoff. Boston: Beacon Press, 1963 (1922).

Westhues, Kenneth. "The Established Church as an Agent of Change." *Sociological Analysis* 34 (1973): 106-23.

_____. "The Adaptation of the Roman Catholic Church in Canadian Society." In S. Crysdale and L. Wheatcroft, eds. *Religion in Canadian Society.* Toronto: Macmillan, 1976.

Whitaker, Reginald. "Reason, Passion and Interest: Pierre Trudeau's Eternal Liberal Triangle." *Canadian Journal of Political and Social Theory* 4 (1980): 5-31.

Whitworth, John and Martin Shiels. "From Across the Black Water: Two Imported Varieties of Hinduism." In Eileen Barker, ed. *New Religious Movements: A Perspective for Understanding Society.* New York and Toronto: The Edwin Mellen Press, 1982.

Whyte, Donald. "Religion and The Rural Church." In M. A. Tremblay and W. J. Anderson, eds. *Rural Canada in Transition.* Ottawa: Agricultural Economics Research Council of Canada, 1966.

Williams, John R. "Religion in Newfoundland: The Churches and Social Ethics." In Peter Slater, ed. *Religion and Culture in Canada.* Waterloo, Ontario: Wilfred Laurier University Press, 1977.

Williams, Robin. *American Society: A Sociological Interpretation.* New York: Alfred A. Knopf, 1952.

Wilson, Bryan R. *Religion in Secular Society: A Sociological Comment.* Harmondsworth: Penguin Books, 1969.

_____. *Contemporary Transformations of Religion.* Oxford: Oxford University Press, 1976.

_____. "The Return of the Sacred." *Journal for the Scientific Study of Religion* 18 (1979): 268-80.

Wise, S. F. "God's Peculiar Peoples." In W. L. Morton, ed. *The Shield of Achilles.* Toronto: McClelland and Stewart, 1968.

Wuthnow, Robert. *The Consciousness Reformation.* Berkeley and Los Angeles: University of California Press, 1976.

Zaslow, Morris. "The Frontier Hypothesis in Recent Historiography." *Canadian Historical Review* 29 (1948): 153-67.

CHAPTER 5

Canada's Politics: Class, Region, and Continentalism

Dennis Forcese

INTRODUCTION

Since 1867, there have been 32 general elections in Canada — 13 of these since 1945. Recent elections have involved on the order of 1,000 candidates per campaign, representing several political parties. Nominally at least, Canadians have considerable political choice available to them. In fact, there has been considerable stability in electoral outcomes over time. Since 1945, 9 of 13 governments have been formed by the Liberal Party. Of the four Progressive Conservative Party governments, in only the one that came to power in 1958 did the government have a majority in Parliament. The 1979 government lasted a mere six months before it was succeeded by a new Liberal majority.[1]

Satisfying explanations of these electoral patterns have eluded generations of observers. Analyses have been proffered, only to founder on a plethora of potential explanatory factors or on the apparent irreconcilability of empirical findings and theoretical or ideological projections. It is striking, for instance, that voting behavior in federal elections bears little or no relationship to social science's most cherished variable, social class. This empirical finding has been examined and re-examined, operationalizations modified and re-modified, one data set succeeded by another, but the finding endures.[2]

No doubt some researchers will persist in trying to invent a satisfactory way of associating class and voting. However, it has recently been suggested that this quest may be futile in that Canadians do not seem to respond to left-right politics or to class distinctions.[3] Others have chosen to blame Canadian political parties, which have, uncooperatively, failed to develop class or ideological identities despite social science insistence, or the Canadian public for not realizing that the existing parties really do represent different class interests.[4]

Both of the latter arguments are premised on some conception of "class consciousness" and its apparent maldevelopment in Canada. The problem has accordingly been shifted to an attempt to understand the forms of socio-political organization that have apparently deterred class consciousness and class voting in Canada. It has also been observed that the formal electoral system of single member population-based constituencies, and the consequent character of national political parties with their centrist appeals, would lead in this direction.[5]

This essay will focus on the relationship between voter response in federal elections and several factors that seem to account for an organized Canadian pattern of electoral choice. I will argue that available data suggest that social class interests have not been overtly expressed in Canadian federal politics because of a coincidence of social factors: most prominently, the divergent interests of class fractions and the persistence of ethnic/linguistic distinctions. The effects of these forces have been enhanced by the fact that the Canadian political economy has engendered very strong regional economies — and, hence, regional consciousness — and not unrelated to this, continentalist interests and sentiments.

I would like to stress that the account which follows should not be considered a repudiation of either the reality or political relevance of social classes and class conflict. Elsewhere I have forthrightly argued that social classes provide the fundamental basis for social action.[6] But insofar as one particular manifestation of political action — federal voting response — is concerned, I take the empirically sustained view that class interests are obscured by other affiliations and influences.[7] In particular, I will argue that regions provide the clearest basis for overt cleavages in Canada, subsuming but not explaining class and ethno-linguistic oppositions. Public consciousness of inequality in Canada is less oriented around classes than regions. Dissatisfactions are more often attributed to competition between regions and to a Canadian federation that imposes unnatural lines of commerce and development — in opposition to a "natural" north-south pattern of integration — than they are to any other factor.

Ironically, the sheer magnitude of the existing pattern of transnational economic integration acts to reinforce regional antagonisms and to thwart awareness of class oppositions. Political factors such as regionalism and continentalism reflect critical dimensions of national and transnational economic organization and class structure.[8] Hence, when one discusses language groups, regions, social classes, and continent-wide social and economic organization, in a sense one is considering wheels within wheels within wheels which are fundamentally embedded within an institutionalized structure of economic and political inequality. It is the interface among these dimensions that I will consider here.

SOCIAL CLASS

Social classes have been defined and measured in a variety of ways.

One may choose to designate classes, for instance, with reference to capital and labor, or as essentially occupational strata.[9] Each mode of defining them, whether following the Marxian or Weberian traditions, acknowledges differences among important class fractions — as, for example, distinctions between unionized skilled workers and unorganized unskilled workers, or state bureaucrats and capitalist entrepreneurs.

One might reasonably expect that "classes," however conceived, would be manifest in disparate political responses consistent with their particular interests. In fact, there are expressions of class-based political protest and conflict — such as strikes. But classes in Canada have not, in any consistent way, been demonstrably related to political choice, especially at the national level. Whatever one's operationalizations of class or political choice, there is no convincing evidence of class voting: the majority of members of all social classes, including the working class, vote for the Liberal Party.[10]

This fact, I submit, is fundamentally attributable to the nature of the so-called "social classes" in Canada. The problem is not that these groups are mere artifacts of social science measurement. But, for various reasons, social classes in Canada are not homogeneous and conscious collectivities, subsuming other bases of allegiance and organization: they are heterogeneous in both social composition and attitudes.[11]

Apparent interests of members of social classes are not always reconcilable. Actions which are to the short-term economic advantage of some sub-group within a class are frequently in conflict with those of others. Consider, for instance, the contrasting interests of organized labor and those of unskilled or unemployed workers. Or consider the differences between the economic goals of farmers and merchants.

Members of a class will often perceive themselves, first and foremost, as sharing common interests with other kinds of groups defined on the basis of non-class criteria. For example, the cultural aspirations of ethnic minority populations, although often related to economic status, may not be consciously thought of in these terms. Or, economic dissatisfactions and interests may be real enough, but they may be associated with non-class criteria of group definition. If, for example, all of the shopkeepers and landlords in a small town are drawn from one ethnic group and their working class customers are from another, the tendency will be for class antagonisms to become focused around ethnicity rather than class.

Canadian regional identifications provide another example of this sort of thing. Many Western farmers have historically seen their interests as fundamentally opposed to those of the grain merchants and financiers involved in the wheat trade. But because these merchants and financiers are located "down East" (in central Canada), farmers — and the populist organizations they have created — have tended to see these conflicts in regional, rather than class terms.

Similarly, many class-related organizations, such as unions or business associations, cut across national boundaries. In the course of doing this, they tend to deter a sense of national class-like consciousness and interest within a given nation-state. Thus, for example, it may well be that American-based corporations and American-based employee organizations act to dilute Canadian nationalism and, at the same time, the opposition of class interests within Canadian society.

In sum, while classes may be real, they are by no means precise, homogeneous, and articulate collectivities in Canada. Because of contending interests within classes and important competing bases for group consciousness and loyalty, class-based voting has not been a conspicuous feature of Canadian political life. If we wish to adequately explain patterns of federal political support, we will have to look elsewhere.

LANGUAGE GROUPS

Both popular writers and social scientists have stressed the salience of ethnic identity in Canadian society.[12] In terms of political behavior, the most persistent and marked cleavage may be more usefully seen as linguistic rather than ethnic: there are marked differences in the federal voting behavior of francophone and anglophone Canadians. This split in voting does not directly fall along ethnic lines because the anglophone group includes people drawn from a plethora of ethnic origins.

The notion of francophones as "second class citizens" has been a persistent theme in Canadian politics since at least the 1920s. English-speaking members of "non-Charter" ethnic groups have invoked the counter-claim that they have faced discrimination because they are not of English *or* French origins, especially in Western Canada.[13] Francophones, in recent years — as we discuss later — have overwhelmingly supported the Liberal Party, with minor support for Le Railliement des Créditistes du Québec through the 60s and 70s.[14] Anglophone support has been split — depending on regional interests and issues — among the Liberal, Progressive Conservative, and New Democratic parties. In Atlantic Canada, both the Progressive Conservatives and the Liberals have been well-represented, with the majority of their seats swinging between the two old parties. Similarly, these same two parties divide federal electoral support in Ontario, and trade majority status from election to election. There is also a modest and teasing intrusion into Ontario by the New Democratic Party — which, after winning a seat in 1945 and 1953, reached a high of 11 federal seats in Ontario in 1972.[15] In the West, anglophone support is divided among three major political parties. Since 1957, the majority of seats have gone to the Progressive Conservatives, but the New Democratic Party has been strong, and the Liberal Party has had some support, especially in British Columbia.[16]

Some recent research tentatively suggests that this pattern of split electoral support among anglophones has allowed at least some slight class-based voting in the West — at least to the extent that major occupational groupings such as non-manual, manual or farm workers can be used to indicate class.[17] Other researchers discern a rural-urban split in anglophone voting patterns.[18]

What is clear in all this is that anglophone voting varies in party support, while francophone voting does not. In practice, this means that francophones have been disproportionately effective in securing governments which reflect their point of view. Francophone support of the Liberal Party, moreover, has overridden class divisions. A partial exception is the eight-year Créditiste deviation which attracted rural and small town petit bourgeois and working class support.[19]

The bulk of this francophone vote is concentrated in Québec, but the same pattern of support for the Liberal Party obtains in areas outside of the province — such as in Cape Breton, New Brunswick, and Manitoba — in heavily francophone ridings. In modern history, the Progressive Conservative Party has only succeeded once — in 1958 — in breaking this voting pattern; winning 50 of 75 seats in Québec. In later elections, even with the Créditistes entering into the picture, francophone voters continued to give a majority of their support to the Liberals.[20]

While this pattern of differential party support by ethno-linguistic groups has played an important role in determining the course of Canadian federal elections, it is not the whole tale by any means: no party can command a majority in Parliament simply on the basis of the francophone vote. Moreover, since francophones are heavily concentrated in Québec, even the francophone/anglophone split has a heavy regional component associated with it.

REGION

The data suggest that the overriding historical basis for political divisions within Canada has been regional sentiments or loyalties. Regional patterns are historically vested in the constitution and in economic realities, and reflect "different patterns of socio-political evolution" and development in different parts of the country.[21] In Canada, the federal nature of the state system, differential patterns in ethnic settlement, clear geographic boundaries, and variable resource bases within provinces have all coalesced to produce distinct regions. Conflicts between these regions have, thus, tended to summarize economic inequities and senses of affiliation and interest.[22] For example, Macpherson premised his explanation of Social Credit in Alberta on divergent economic interests that may be summarized within politically delimited regions, that is, provinces. He, in effect, suggested that the "quasi-colonial" West's subordination to central Canada moderated within-region and national class conflict in favor of confrontation or competition between regions. Class inequality was, therefore, subsumed within regional inequality.[23] In recent years, regional conflict has increasingly centered around control over non-agricultural resources; with regions and their respective governments seeking to use control over scarce natural products, such as petroleum, gas, and potash, as a source of economic and political leverage.[24]

In broad outline, this type of confrontation is not new. Regional boundaries in Canada have tended to be quite stable over time due to the distinct social and economic evolutionary histories of each region. Moreover, since regional boundaries tend to coincide with the political boundaries between provinces — the border between Ontario and Manitoba, for instance, or between Alberta and British Columbia — regions have had some degree of political autonomy in the form of provincial governments which are able to intervene formally to represent their population *vis-a-vis* the national collectivity and the federal state.

This stability in the boundaries between regions has also tended to engender relatively distinct regional subcultures. These have been reinforced by a high degree of geographic immobility in the Canadian population. In an age when migration is supposed to be unusually high, there is evidence to suggest that Canadians tend to remain within their provinces or regions. By one estimate, in the period from 1966 to 1977, only 5 per cent of Canadians emigrated from Canada and only 5 per cent migrated to another province.[25] Even travel tends to take place within regions and there is evidence that out-of-region travel by Canadians tends to be north-south or cross-national, rather than between national regions.[26]

The boundaries between anglophone and francophone Canada have been extremely stable due to language isolation. This stability, moreover, has, as we have seen, been expressed in a consistent pattern in federal voting which has been especially potent because the francophone vote is largely concentrated within a single province. This undiluted support has virtually guaranteed the Liberals approximately 50 safe seats from Québec. This provides the Liberals with such an advantage that a Liberal Party government is "normal," while a Progressive Conservative federal government is an aberration. In effect, this fact has enabled the Liberal Party to become, in the 20th century, the "government party."[27]

There is no convincing class-based explanation of electoral support within regions. In Québec, especially with the demise of the Créditistes, electoral support for the Liberal Party is overwhelming among all social classes. In Canada's most industrialized province, Ontario, working class support is dispersed among all three national political parties, with the majority going to the Liberals. In the Atlantic provinces, all social classes fluctuate in their support for the two old parties with only a minor and erratic pocket of working class support for the New Democratic Party in Cape Breton, and, more recently, in Newfoundland.

Western voting patterns are strikingly different. Except for tiny outcroppings of Liberal support in francophone ridings in Manitoba — such as

St. Boniface — and sporadic support in parts of British Columbia, voting is consistently anti-Liberal. Westerners typically split their vote between Progressive Conservatives and New Democrats in Manitoba, Saskatchewan, and British Columbia. Since the demise of the national Social Credit Party, voting has been uniformly Conservative in Alberta. Clearly, regional voting patterns in the West — especially in the Prairies — ought to be seen as a repudiation of the eastern Canadian Liberal Party.

The reasons for this are both historical and structural. Western alienation from eastern Canada and from eastern Canadian interests has historically been expressed in prairie populist social movements. These movements have spawned third parties such as the Cooperative Commonwealth Federation (CCF) in Saskatchewan and Manitoba and the Social Credit Party in Alberta. Over time, traditional populist ideology has been coopted by the Progressive Conservative Party — especially the Progressive Conservative Party of John Diefenbaker — and surfaces in continuing support for the New Democratic Party in Manitoba, Saskatchewan, and British Columbia. In the case of the NDP, agrarian petit bourgeois support for a "socialist" party is still extremely strong and stands in marked contrast to the NDP's relatively ineffectual appeal to organized labor in central and Atlantic Canada.

Federal Parties and Regional Loyalties

If one thinks of the national parties as loose federations of provincial groups, then all three major parties have succeeded in capturing and mobilizing regional loyalties.[28] Moreover, parties have been successful in doing this because of distinct appeals to regional priorities and attitudes. There are clear differences, for instance, between the western and Ontario wings of the Progressive Conservative and New Democratic parties. In Ontario, the Conservatives are clearly identified with and linked to the large corporations and banks. In Saskatchewan, support for the Progressive Conservatives often comes from rural areas where populist sentiment often identified business interests and banks as "the enemy." In Saskatchewan, social reform issues often predominate in NDP party conventions. In Ontario, bread-and-butter labour issues tend to come to the fore. For these reasons, it has been suggested that the western components of both parties have historically been more progressive or change-oriented than their eastern counterparts.[29]

Consistent with regional voting preferences, it is clear that people in different parts of Canada most strongly identify with regional units. Public perceptions of the efficacy of politics and government — especially expressions of approval — tend to center on provincial rather than federal units. Whether this is due to the fact that, in terms of genuine autonomy and symbols of nationhood, Canada is a relatively "new" country or, more importantly, to fundamental regional divergences in economic conditions, there is evidence to suggest that the loyalty of Canadians is as much regional as national.[30] For example, a survey conducted in 1968 indicated that high school students in Manitoba, Ontario, and Québec consistently preferred their provincial governments to the federal government. The only exceptions were anglophones in Québec.[31] This is consistent with Pammett's results from the 1974 National Election Study of 2562 Canadian adults. Western respondents in particular, Pammett observes, were most likely to think in regional rather than national terms.[32] Gregg and Whittington, working with a national sample of 5842 school children found that Ontario children identified more frequently with the federal than the provincial government, in marked contrast to children from other provinces/regions. As they put it, the "center" in effect favors the center's government, while the "hinterland's" population tends to favor their provincial governments.[33] Gregg and Whittington also find that partisan children — that is, children claiming party commitment — are less common in the West than elsewhere. This is consistent with a divergence of choice and ticket-splitting in the West; in contrast to more stable voting preferences in central and eastern Canada.[34] Related data indicate that Canadians have a clear conception of regional power: the majority tend to identify central Canada as most powerful.[35]

These public perceptions are reasonable reflections of the extent to which different regions are represented in Parliament. For example, after both the 1979 and 1980 elections, much was made of the underrepresentation of certain regions in the federal Cabinet — Québec in the first instance of short-lived Conservative government, and the West in the Liberal government which followed. Regional voting allegiances are obviously reflected at the Cabinet level, and it is equally clear that the prevailing trend has been towards increased representation of the center — including Québec — and reduced representation of the periphery, especially the West, but also the Atlantic provinces. As Table 5-1 indicates, Ontario and Québec's representation in the Cabinet has almost doubled in the 1962-1976 period when com-

TABLE 5-1

Average number of Federal Cabinet Members by Region*

	Atlantic	Quebec	Ontario	Prairies	British Columbia	West
1945-1962	2.6	5	6.5	3.4	1.9	5.3
1963-1975	3.4	10	10	1.9	2.1	4

*Adapted from Colin Campbell, *Canadian Political Facts, 1945-1976,* Toronto: Methuen, 1977, p. 32.

pared with the period 1945-1962. At the same time, Prairie representation, always small, has been halved.[36] There has been a clear increase in central Canadian domination of the Cabinet, at the expense of the West.

Cabinet representation aside, it is clear that the West tends not to support the winning political party, that is, the Liberals. By contrast, Québec and the Maritimes do, and Ontario as a swing province fluctuates in supporting the government-forming political party.[37] Fewer than 50 per cent of prairie voters supported the governing party except during the 1958 Diefenbaker sweep and the 1979 election.[38] John Diefenbaker's victory in 1958 was unique in post-World War II Canadian politics. Even the so-called "Trudeaumania" of the 1970s did not overshadow the Diefenbaker all-region and cross-language group majority.

Seen in this light, Western voters usually seem to be casting a protest vote *vis-a-vis* domination by central Canada. Historically Western subordination has been economic. Periphery status was part of the initial national design for the west. As Phillips remarks, "within the national policy, the West was fully expected to be a staple economy, for which St. Lawrence financial and commercial capital acted as intermediary with Europe."[39] Moreover "the West was to be a captive market for the manufacturers not only of central Canada but also of the Maritimes."[40] Hence the present gulf between Westerners and central Canadians is not accidental: it is the realization of a historical political-economic design. Despite publicized western prosperity in the past decade, and even with present growth rates, economic parity with industrialized central Canada would "not be reached until the year 2039," according to one set of estimates.[41] Moreover, as Western economic power, based on resource exploitation, grows, an unadjusted Canadian federalism may be viewed as even more exploitative and contrary to Western interests. Whatever the economic gains, Western perceptions of hinterland status will be aggravated. A growing consequence of this may well be an increasingly open and serious pursuit of Western separatism.

In sum, the pattern of regional cleavage in Canada today, which is rooted in economic and linguistic interests, is a realization of the founding character of the federal state. This is as true of the "alienated" West — seeking to escape its hinterland staple economy status — as it is of the Québécois — reacting to conquest-based economic and cultural subordination. Given Québec's relatively greater impact on the federal government, it is in the West that patterns of political and economic subordination remain most congruent.

It is, therefore, not remarkable that Westerners perceive that the federal government acts in the interests of central Canada. Patterns of immigration brought ethnic populations to the prairies who either were markedly different from the two charter groups, or United Kingdom emigres who were ideologically committed to variants of European socialism. The agricultural economy was not diversified, as in central Canada, and was consequently subject to enormous fluctuations. Central Canadian industrial, financial

and political intervention has incrementally contributed to western resent-
ment of the political party most identified with "the East," that is, the
Liberals, and the federal government that the Liberal Party generally
forms. A stubborn polarization of federal political support has crystallized
in Canada — a polarization not primarily based on social class, but region.

CONTINENTALISM

There is an additional ingredient that mixes with regional attitudes and
economics in order to yield the nationwide pattern of electoral support we
have been examining throughout this chapter: continentalist attitudes and
economic organization. Canadian regionalism must be considered within
the context of a continental and not simply a national political economy. In
the same way that some economists suggest that the Canadian economy
must be analyzed as a series of regional components within a continental
and not a national economic system, so too political responses may be
understood as regional manifestations of a larger continental pattern.[42]

The voting responses we have examined here are well-established
historically, and have persisted with relatively minor deviations. They are,
moreover, related to patterns of social stratification, but are not simply or
obviously class-based: the link is to be found within the pattern of regional
and continental economic organization.

Continentalist links, as Clement and others have argued, reinforce Ontario's domination of peripheral regions and are reflected in economic exchange and political representation. Not remarkably, Ontario is therefore
the locus of key fractions of the dominant class in Canadian society.[43] As
Marchak remarks, we find "the larger part of an owning and directing class
has its territorial base in the metropolitan...center."[44] The concentration
of capital and secondary manufacturing in southern Ontario, evolving
historically in conjunction with geographically proximate industrial sectors
in the United States, continues to dominate the Canadian reality, despite recent resource advantages accruing to the West.[45]

Given central Canadian economic integration with the United States,
corporate and labor oganizations operating in Canada — especially those
that purport to be national in scope — are less Canadian than American:[46]
"big business" in Canada has become American-controlled business,
achieving clear ascendancy since World War Two.[45]

Canadian labor, although influenced by the international unions, has
gradually shifted since World War Two from a situation where a majority
of union members where in internationals, to one where a reported 47.4 per
cent of all members were in 1978.[48] Yet, because many of the Canadian
unions are unaffiliated — and despite a majority of national unions in the
Canadian Labour Congress — it is a fair inference that labor still tends to
concentrate in the internationals, especially the major industrial unions, as

contrasted with "middle class" nationals such as the Canadian Union of Public Employees.[49] The principal economic actors in Canada, whether business or labor, are therefore, continental in orientation. At least since the early post-World War II period, and markedly after the 1950s, economic continentalism has, in effect, been encouraged by federal government policies. As Phillips puts it, rather than a national policy, there has been "a continentalist (anti-national) policy which relies on American multinationals, particularly in the resource industries," to provide the capital investment, initiative, and direction for economic growth.[50] Moreover, monetary policies, as indicated by interest rates, are allowed to follow American policies, perhaps inevitably given the high degree of economic dependence upon American economic units.

So too, political socialization, as indicated by awareness of political leaders, is American as much as Canadian. For example, data from a 1968 survey of high school students — today's voting adults — in Québec, Ontario, and Manitoba, found that an overwhelming majority of francophone and anglophone respondents chose as "great men" American figures. Fewer than 10 per cent of first choices, by either anglophone or francophone respondents, were English or French Canadian historical figures:[51] Canadian political heroes, and fantasies, seem to be American. There are not national heroes to bridge the regional sentiments, but American heroes that establish continentalist sentiments.

In some sense, continentalism may be seen as a "key to Canadian politics".[52] The continentalist ties reflected in economic organization and in socialization and perceptions interact with regional decentralization. Coherent national economic responses are deterred, and regional interests and non-class conflict are reinforced.

Continentalist attitudes interface with and vary by region. One analysis suggests that favorable public attitudes towards close ties with the United States are stronger in the Atlantic provinces and in Québec than in other parts of the country.[53] But such views have also been a traditional part of Western political culture as evidenced in free trade sentiment and opposition to "Eastern" tariff policies. Western Canadian economic dissatisfaction has been expressed not only in protest movements and separatist rhetoric, but also in an explicit, albeit extremely small minority, interest in political affiliation with the United States. For example, after the 1980 federal election, a few Western Canadians returned to the idea of union with the United States as preferable to either continued federation with Canada or Western independence. On March 11, 1980, the former leader of the Saskatchewan Progressive Conservative Party declared himself an independent, devoted to organizing a movement for Western Canadian union with the United States.[54] After this initial declaration, a poll revealed that 90 per cent of 600 respondents in Alberta wished the province to remain within Confederation. However, 68 per cent of respondents complained that their interests were not represented by the federal government.[55]

Aspirations towards union with the United States may be somewhat eccentric and unrepresentative of Western Canada's views. However, it is an historically recurrent notion in the Prairies and in British Columbia, reinforced by geography, trade and travel. Moreover, it is a sentiment that is apt to gain in popularity and plausibility if the Liberal Party — and central Canadian interests — continue their monopoly of the federal government.

CONCLUSION

There are, therefore, dominant and persisting regional political preferences in Canada. They have their historical origins in ethnic/linguistic and regional economic conditions and subsequent political socialization. They relate, in turn, to continental ties that reinforce patterns of economic privilege by region. As a consequence, social classes have been less salient than language groups or regions insofar as federal political response is concerned. Moreover, Canada's formal Parliamentary system, with single member constituencies and pragmatic non-ideologically oriented parties, has ensured that only dominant or majority political preferences will be represented in federal politics. After the 1979 and 1980 elections, much public attention was directed toward electoral reform, with the suggestion that a system of proportional representation would allow minority sentiments in each region to be more adequately reflected in Parliament. Such a system would be a concession to a persisting Canadian reality. Another proposal — for a free trade area — was seen as one way of reorganizing continental links that presently reinforce the historical headstart of industrially developed central Canada.

Barring such formal changes, regional economic disparities may be diminished if peripheral regions are able to take advantage of their control over scarce natural resources. But regional cleavages in political expression and federal power are apt to persist. This will be manifested by well-demarcated regional clusters in federal voting and in marked conflict between provincial and federal governments. In a system of emergent sovereignty-associations, class voting and most other expressions of direct class political action may occur within regions. But it is more likely that all class interests and politics will be subordinated to the consuming politics of redefining an increasingly decentralized federal union of distinctive regions.

NOTES

[1]Beck, 1968; Campbell, 1977.
[2]Alford, 1963; 1967; 1968; Ogmundson, 1975; Myles, 1979; Erickson, 1979;

Lambert and Hunter, 1979; Myles and Forcese, 1980.

[3]Lambert and Hunter, 1979: 303.

[4]Ogmundson, 1975: 511; Erickson, 1979.

[5]Alford, 1968; Schwartz, 1974; Engelmann and Schwartz, 1975; Meisel, 1975.

[6]Forcese, 1980.

[7]Myles and Forcese, 1980.

[8]Myles and Forcese, 1979; Forcese, 1979.

[9]Forcese, 1980: 13-20.

[10]Ogmundson, 1974; Myles, 1979; Myles and Forcese, 1980; Forcese, 1980: 117-22.

[11]Macpherson, 1953: 227-28.

[12]Porter, 1965.

[13]Beck, 1968: 365.

[14]Support for the Créditistes peaked at 26 seats in 1962 and disappeard in the 1980 federal election. See Campbell, 1977: 91.

[15]Campbell, 1977: 92.

[16]Campbell, 1977: 92.

[17]Cheal, 1978: 329-30.

[18]Beck, 1968.

[19]Ogmundson, 1975.

[20]Beck, 1968: 324; Campbell, 1977: 91-92.

[21]Cheal, 1975: 337; Marsden and Harvey, 1979: 148-62.

[22]Forcese, 1980: 36-43.

[23]Macpherson, 1953: 23-28; 237-250.

[24]Richards and Pratt, 1979: 279-329.

[25]Bell and Tepperman, 1979: 154.

[26]Bell and Tepperman, 1979: 154-55; 159-67.

[27]Whitaker, 1977.

[28]Smith, 1963: 100.

[29]Smith, 1963: 127.

[30]Simeon and Elkins, 1974; Gregg and Whittington, 1976.

[31]Forbes, 1976: 305.

[32]Pammett, 1976: 87.

[33]Gregg and Whittington, 1976: 82-83.

[34]Gregg and Whittington, 1976: 78-79.

[35]Cuneo, 1978: 147.

[36]Campbell, 1977: 32.

[37]Schwartz, 1974: 58-59.

[38]Englemann and Schwartz, 1975: 188.

[39]Phillips, 1979: 7.

[40]Phillips, 1979: 7.

[41]Oake, 1980.

[42]Phillips, 1979: 8.

[43]Clement, 1977: 295-98; 1979: 94-99.

[44]Marchak, 1979: 100.

[45]Chorney, 1977: 123-24; Marchak, 1979: 1.

46Clement, 1977; Smucker, 1980: 111-20; 182-87; 194-213.
47Clement, 1977.
48Smucker, 1978: 205.
49Smucker, 1980: 204; 208-13.
50Phillips, 1979: 12.
51Forbes, 1976: 297.
52Redekop, 1978: 28-57.
53Cuneo, 1976: 62-63.
54Canadian Press, March 18, 1980, p. 1.
55Canadian Press, March 17, 1980.

Bibliography

Alford, Robert. *Party and Society.* Chicago: Rand McNally, 1963.
_____. "Class Voting in the Anglo-American Political System." In S. M. Lipset and S. Rokkan, eds. *Party Systems and Voter Alignments.* New York: The Free Press, 1967.
_____. "The Social Bases of Political Cleavage in 1962." In B. Blishen, ed. *Canadian Society.* 3rd ed. Toronto: Macmillan, 1968.
Beck, J. Murray. *Pendulum of Power: Canada's Federal Elections.* Scarborough, Ont.: Prentice-Hall, 1968.
Bell, David, and Lorne Tepperman. *The Roots of Disunity.* Toronto: McClelland and Stewart, 1979.
Campbell, Colin. *Canadian Political Facts, 1945-1976.* Toronto: Methuen, 1977.
Campbell, Kenneth. "Regional Disparity and Interregional Exchange Imbalance." In Daniel Glenday, Hubert Guindon and Allan Turowetz, eds. *Modernization and the Canadian State.* Toronto: Macmillan, 1978.
Canadian Press. "West better off joining U.S., says former Sask. P.C. leader." *Ottawa Journal,* March 17, 1980: 8.
_____. "Most Albertans favour staying part of Canada: Poll," *Ottawa Journal,* March 17, 1980: 8.
_____. "Second P.C. switches to Western separatism." *Ottawa Journal,* March 18, 1980: 1.
Cheal, David. "Models of Mass Politics in Canada." *Canadian Review of Sociology and Anthropology* 15 (1978): 325-38.
Chorney, Harold, "Regional Underdevelopment and Cultural Decay." In Craig Heron, ed. *Imperialism, Nationalism, and Canada.* Toronto: New Hogtown Press, 1977.
Clement, Wallace. *Continental Corporate Power.* Toronto: McClelland and Stewart, 1977.
_____. "A Political Economy of Regionalism in Canada." In Daniel Glenday, Hubert Guindon and Allan Turowetz, eds. *Modernization and the Canadian State.* Toronto: Macmillan, 1978.
Cuneo, Carl. "A Class Perspective on Regionalism." In Daniel Glenday, Hubert Guindon and Allan Turowetz, eds. *Modernization and the Canadian State.*

Toronto: Macmillan, 1978.

_____. "The Social Basis of Political Continentalism in Canada." *Canadian Review of Sociology and Anthropology* 13 (1976): 55-70.

Engelmann, F. C., and M. A. Schwartz. *Canadian Political Parties.* Scarborough: Prentice-Hall, 1975.

Erickson, Bonnie. "Region, Knowledge, and Class Voting in Canada." Mimeographed. Department of Sociology, University of Toronto, July, 1979.

Forbes, H. Donald. "Conflicting National Identities among Canadian Youth." In Jon Pammett and Michael Whittington, eds. *Foundations of Political Culture.* Toronto: Macmillan, 1976.

Forcese, Dennis. *The Canadian Class Structure.* 2d ed. Toronto: McGraw-Hill Ryerson, 1980.

Gregg, Allan, and Michael Whittington. "Regional Variations in Children's Political Attitudes." In David Bellamy, Jon Pammett and Donald Rowat, eds. *The Provincial Political Systems.* Toronto: Methuen, 1976.

Lambert, Ronald, and Alfred Hunter. "Social Stratification, Voting Behaviour, and the Images of Canadian Federal Political Parties." *Canadian Review of Sociology and Anthropology* 16 (1979): 287-304.

Macpherson, C. B. *Democracy in Alberta.* Toronto: University of Toronto Press, 1953.

Marchak, Patricia. *In Whose Interests.* Toronto: McClelland and Stewart, 1979.

Marsden, Lorna, and Edward Harvey. *Fragile Federation: Social Change in Canada.* Toronto: McGraw-Hill Ryerson, 1979.

Meisel, John. *Working Papers on Canadian Politics.* 2d ed. Montreal and London: McGill-Queen's University Press, 1975.

Myles, John. "Differences in the Canadian and American Class Vote: Fact or Pseudo-fact?" *American Journal of Sociology* 84 (1979): 1232-37.

Myles, John, and Dennis Forcese. "Voting and Class Politics in Canada and the United States." In R. Tomasson, ed. *Comparative Social Research* Vol. 4. Greenwich, Connecticut: JAI Press, 1980.

Oake, George. "Western Canada still 'hinterland' in political power." *The Citizen,* Ottawa (Southam News Service) March 5, 1980: 99.

Ogmundson, Rick. "Party Class Images and the Class Vote in Canada." *American Sociological Review* 40 (1975): 506-576.

Pammett, Jon. "Public Orientation to Regions and Provinces." In David Bellamy, Jon Pammett and Donald Rowat, eds. *The Provincial Political Systems.* Toronto: Methuen, 1976.

Phillips, Paul. "The National Policy Revisited." *Journal of Canadian Studies* 14 (1979): 3-13.

Porter, John. *The Vertical Mosaic.* Toronto: University of Toronto Press, 1965.

Redekop, John. "Continentalism: The Key to Canadian Politics." In J. Redekop, ed. *Approaches to Canadian Politics.* Scarborough, Prentice-Hall, 1978.

Richards, John, and Larry Pratt. *Prairie Capitalism: Power and Influence in the New West.* Toronto: McClelland and Stewart, 1979.

Schwartz, Mildred. *Politics and Territory.* Montreal: McGill-Queen's University Press, 1974.

Smith, Denis. "Prairie Revolt, Federalism, and the Party System." In Hugh Thornburn, ed. *Party Politics in Canada.* Toronto: Prentice-Hall, 1963.

Simeon, Richard, and David Elkins. "Regional Political Cultures in Canada." *Canadian Journal of Political Science* 7 (1974): 397-437.

Smucker, Joseph. *Industrialization in Canada.* Scarborough: Prentice-Hall, 1980.

Whitaker, Reg. *The Government Party: Organizing and Financing the Liberal Party of Canada, 1930-1958.* Toronto: University of Toronto Press, 1977.

CHAPTER 6

Population

P. Krishnan

INTRODUCTION

Canada is a large country. It occupies nearly 10 million square kilometers (3.9 million square miles); stretching between the Atlantic and Pacific Oceans, and between the United States in the South and the Artic Circle in the North. Although the second largest country in the world,[1] its population is a rather small proportion of the world total. The 1976 Canadian mini-census enumerated 23 million people at a time when the world population stood at nearly 4 billion. For a large country with a population density of only 2.3 persons per square kilometer (approximately 6 persons per square mile), however, the characteristics of the Canadian population are highly variegated. Here we will look at some of the dynamics of this population and how it influences important aspects of socio-political life in the country.

GROWTH OF POPULATION

At the time of Confederation, Canada's population stood at around 4 million. At the turn of this century, it was some 5 million. Over these 30 years, then, it increased by only 25 per cent. Between 1901 and 1976, in three-quarters of a century, the population grew from 5 million to 23 million — a four fold increase. Table 6-1 shows the total population at the time of various censuses.[2] The annual per cent change was highest between 1901 and 1911, second highest from 1911 to 1921, and lowest between 1931 and 1941.

Knowledge of the factors which underlie population growth is essential for studying changes in growth rate. Consider two points in time, T_1 and T_2, and let the population of Canada be enumerated through the census operations at these points. If P_1 and P_2 are the populations at these points, P_2-P_1 is the change in the population during this span. We can then compute the growth rate from the population change (P_2-P_1) and the original base population P_1.

TABLE 6-1

Components of Population Growth in Canada, 1901-1976

Census Year	Population ('000)	Change over the preceeding census ('000)	Per cent Change	Natural Increase ('000)	Net Immigration ('000)
1901	5,371	538	11.1		
1911	7,207	1835	34.2	1025	810
1921	8,788	1581	21.9	1270	311
1931	10,377	1589	18.1	1360	230
1941	11,507	1130	10.9	1222	-92
1951	14,009	2503	21.8	1972	169
1956	16,081	2072	14.8	1473	598
1961	18,238	2157	13.4	1675	482
1966	20,015	1777	9.7	1518	259
1971	21,568	1553	7.8	1090	463
1976	22,993	1424	6.6	924	500

Source: George, M. V. (1976), Table 1.

A population's growth rate is usually expressed in terms of the annual addition to the population for every 100 members. There are two ways of calculating this. If the growth rate is slow, a linear approximation is used. If there are n years separating two censuses, then the growth rate is given by

$$\left[\frac{P_2 - P_1}{P_1} \right] \times \frac{100}{n}$$

Thus, as shown in Table 6-1, in the period from 1901 to 1911 a simple approximation to the growth rate would be $34.2/10 = 3.42\%$ per annum.

A better approximation would be obtained if the growth were assumed to follow the compound interest law. If r is the rate of interest for every dollar compounded at every instant in time, then the capital P_1, together with its compound interest, yields after n years an amount $P_2 = P_1 \exp(rn)$. Replace dollars by population counts, then the growth rate is given by

$$\frac{1}{n} \log_e \left(\frac{P_2}{P_1} \right)$$

From here, we get a rule for the doubling of a population. $\text{Log}_e 2$ is nearly 0.70. Then

$$r = \left(\frac{0.70}{n}\right) \quad \text{or} \quad n = \left(\frac{0.70}{r}\right)$$

Thus a population growing at one per cent ($r = 0.01$), doubles in 70 years, and one growing at three per cent ($r = 0.03$), doubles in 23 years.

But our aim is to break ($P_2\text{-}P_1$) down into its components. The base population P_1 is depleted when some members die, increases when babies are born and when people immigrate into Canada, and decreases when some people in Canada leave for (emigrate to) other nations. Immigrants can also, in due course, account for births and deaths as well. Hence we write:

$$P_2\text{-}P_1 = (B\text{-}D) + (I\text{-}E)$$

where B stands for the total number of births, D the total numbers of deaths, I the total number of immigrants and E the total number of emigrants during the time interval ($T_2\text{-}T_1$). The expression given above which relates these factors to one another is called the "balancing equation." The component ($B\text{-}D$) is the balance of births over deaths and is called the natural increase and the segment ($I\text{-}E$), the balance of immigration over emigration, is referred to as net immigration. Decade-wise natural increase and net immigration are also shown in Table 6-1. Note that in the decade from 1931 to 1941, Canada lost population through net emigration while, for all other time intervals, natural increase exceeded net immigration.

The figures given for natural increase and net immigration (Table 6-1) are crude. In order to understand the situation better, we need measures that are independent of population size. Demographers use the notion of "rates" for this purpose.[3] In this case, we construct what are called the crude birth rate (CBR) and crude death rate (CDR). These indicate the number of babies born and deaths that occur in a year for every 1,000 of population. Then, CBR-CDR yields the rate of natural increase (RNI): the balance of births over deaths for every 1,000 members of the population. A net immigration rate can also be calculated in a similar manner.

Table 6-2 shows the CBR and the CDR for Canada for the period from 1921 to 1976. These data are drawn from Vital Statistics records of births and deaths, which came into being only after the Dominion Bureau of Statistics was created in 1918. In the late 19th and early 20th centuries, one must estimate birth and death rates from the census or rely on data gathered by some provinces (e.g., Québec).

TABLE 6-2

Crude Birth and Death Rates, Canada 1921-76

Year	CBR	CDR	RNI
1921	29.3	11.6	17.7
1926	24.7	11.4	13.3
1931	23.2	10.2	13.0
1936	20.3	9.9	10.4
1941	22.4	10.1	12.3
1946	27.2	9.4	17.8
1951	27.2	9.0	18.2
1956	28.0	8.2	19.8
1961	26.1	7.7	18.4
1966	19.4	7.5	11.9
1971	16.8	7.3	9.5
1976	15.7	7.3	8.4
1978	15.3	7.2	8.1

Source: Vital Statistics, 1976, and Statistics Canada Daily, January 8, 1980.

VITAL REVOLUTIONS

Table 6-2 reveals that both the Canadian birth and death rates have shown a tendency to decline over time. The birth rate in the early part of the 19th century was over 50 per 1,000. Available data on Québec and Ontario reveal that the Québec CBR in 1831 was 55 per 1,000, while Ontario's in 1837 to 1846 was almost 67 per 1,000. A CBR of over 50 per 1,000 corresponds to 8 to 10 children per couple. Based on a detailed study of genealogical data, Charbonneau[4] calculates that couples married before the Québec census of 1681 had an average of 7.7 children.[5] And where is Québec now? It has the lowest birth rate in Canada and the all-Canada rate, itself, is low. Thus we see that a major revolution in reproduction has taken place: it has moved from a high level to almost below replacement.[6]

Another revolution is also noticeable: a complete change in the pattern of death and diseases. Canadians had a very high death rate — over 25 per 1,000 — in the 17th and 18th centuries. The average that a new-born baby could hope to live was only 35 years.[7] Now life expectancy is over 70.

These two types of revolutions — when both the death and birth rates move from a high to a low — have taken place in all Western societies. It took almost more than a century to make this transition. In a majority of cases, the decline in mortality occurred first and the decline in reproduction lagged behind.

Thompson[8] and Notestein[9] first observed this pattern in the English,

Welsh, French, German and U.S. cases. It is known as the "the demographic transition."[10] Here we will develop a simple index of the extent of demographic transition experienced by Canada in the early and middle part of this century. Bogue[11] has developed a formula to estimate the per cent demographic transition completed for the have-not nations of the world.[12] This formula ignores mortality. The modified version suggested here, incorporates measures of both reproduction and mortality. Let us take Québec's 1831 CBR (i.e., 55 per 1,000) as the highest and the 1976 CBR (i.e., 15.7 per 1,000) as the lowest. Similarly, Québec's death rate of around 1700 (28 per 1,000) may be taken as the highest and Canada's in 1976 (i.e., 7.3 per 1,000) as the lowest. Then, if CBR_t and CDR_t are the birth and death rates in Canada at time t, the per cent demographic transition completed at time t is given by

$$100 \times \left[\frac{1}{2} \left(\frac{55 - CBR_t}{39.3} \right) + \frac{1}{2} \left(\frac{28 - CDR_t}{20.7} \right) \right]$$

Table 6-3 reports the per cent demographic transition completed at different time points. From here we see that, gradually at first but rapidly in the last two decades, Canada has moved towards completing the demographic transition.

TABLE 6-3

**Per Cent Demographic Transition
Completed, Canada 1921-1976**

Year	Per Cent Transition Completed
1921	72.3
1926	78.6
1931	83.5
1936	87.9
1941	84.7
1946	80.3
1951	81.3
1956	82.2
1961	86.3
1966	94.8
1971	98.6
1976	100.0

Source: Author's Computations.

TRANSITION AND MODERNIZATION

Simply recording the movement of a society from high to low fertility and mortality oversimplifies the many changes that take place in a population under these circumstances. This decline in birth and death rates was associated with a variety of changes in Canadian society, generally. There was, for instance, massive rural-urban migration. Family structures were transformed. Agriculture became mechanized and less dependent on human labor power. Industrial and tertiary economic sectors began to employ most people. Life-styles also changed accordingly. An explanation for the demographic transition lies here: it is really part and parcel of the pattern of modernization that characterized Canada and other Western nations in the nineteenth and early twentieth centuries.

Determinants of Mortality in Canada

Until now we have confined our discussion to changes in Canada's "vital situation." The sections which follow will examine the factors which underlie these shifts.

Let us look at mortality first. We know that different age, occupational, religious and sex groups are subject to different death rates. In view of these differentials,[13] the CDR is not a useful index of mortality conditions. Population scientists employ the life table method to develop life expectancies at different ages. These indices are best used comparatively.

TABLE 6-4

A. Expectation of Life in Years at Birth, Canada 1931-71

Year	Male	Female
1931	60.0	62.1
1941	63.0	66.3
1951	66.3	70.8
1956	67.6	72.9
1961	68.4	74.2
1966	68.8	75.2
1971	69.3	76.4

B.   Expectation of Life in Years, Provinces/Regions 1931 and 1971

Region	1931		1971	
	M	F	M	F
Atlantic	60.2	61.9	69.1	76.6
Quebec	56.2	57.8	68.3	75.3
Ontario	61.3	63.9	69.6	76.8
Prairies	63.5	65.5	70.6	77.2
British Columbia	62.2	65.3	69.9	76.7

Source: Statistics Canada (1976), Vital Statistics 1974, Vol. III.

Expectation of life at age zero (i.e., at birth) is, for instance, most sensitive to infant mortality. Table 6-4 presents life expectancies at birth by sex for Canada for the period from 1931 to 1971. Two observations emerge from this data set: (1) life expectancy has increased for both sexes, but considerably more for females; and (2) the male-female gap which was nearly two years in the thirties is now nearly seven years.[14]

Panel B in Table 6-4 brings out regional differentials in mortality. The western provinces, especially the prairies, seem to be endowed with more favorable conditions for long life than Québec, Ontario and the Atlantic provinces. While observed differences were striking in the thirties, and have narrowed sharply in the seventies, they still persist.

In order to understand the reasons for reductions in mortality, one has to look at the major causes of death: (a) death due to infectious and parasitic disease; and (b) chronic and degenerative diseases. In the early twentieth century, Canada was a playground of diseases of type (a). Tuberculosis, diphtheria, and other lung diseases took the major toll. With the advent of inoculation, vaccination, and other public health measures, infectious diseases were largely eliminated. Improved nutrition, water filtration, pasteurization of milk and better heating reduced many of the oldest sources of premature death. Life expectancy naturally rose. Medical discoveries and health-care programs began to show their influence on mortality in the recent decades. Now, Canadians do not die because of infectious diseases, but because of chronic and degenerative diseases: cancer and heart disease — closely followed by motor vehicle accidents.

The major sources of chronic disease are related to life-style:[15] eating too much high protein and high calorie food; excessive drinking; smoking; lack of exercise; and the stress created by the "achievement orientation" syndrome. A study of the Mormon population of Alberta by Jarvis[16] clearly shows that their incidence of death from all causes is much less than that for the Alberta population as a whole.[17]

Mormons religiously proscribe drinking alcoholic beverages, coffee, or tea; smoking; and eating excessive amounts of meat. Their life-styles differ a great deal from those of the general population. Seventh Day Adventists encourage vegetarianism.[18] Both of these groups, therefore, provide excellent comparisons for assessing the impacts of life-style related diseases on mortality. No study has been done, however, of Canadian Seventh Day Adventists.

TABLE 6-5

Age Standardized Death Rates by Sex for Selected Canadian Ethnic Groups, 1961

Ethnic Group	Male	Female
British	10.8	8.2
French	11.1	9.2
German	8.2	7.0
Netherlands	9.1	7.1
Scandinavian	8.8	6.7
Hungarian	9.5	7.2
Polish	8.8	7.0
Russian	8.4	5.8
Italian	8.5	7.0
Ukrainian	9.5	8.1
Native Indian	14.3	12.4

Source: Kalbach, W. and W. McVey, 1979: 82.

Ethnic Factors

Given the impact of ethnicity on a range of attitudes and behaviors, sociologists would expect markedly different mortality for members of different groups. Kalbach and McVey[19] present age standardized death rates for males and females by ethnic group for the years 1951 and 1961. The 1961 figures are shown in Table 6-5 in order to drive home the fact that the differentials in mortality among ethnic groups are not small.

It is clear from this table that, for the groups shown, Native Indians have the highest incidence of mortality for both males and females.[20] Non-French and non-British European males have lower mortality than their French of British counterparts. Among females, Russians and Scandinavians have the lowest mortality.

Mortality data by ethnic group membership are hard to come by. Estimates of the mortality of Native Indians and Inuit are known from studies conducted by Bracher,[21] Legaré and Desjardins,[22] Piché and George,[23] and Romaniuc and Piché.[24] Obviously, the levels for these groups are high. Since mortality data for other ethnic groups are not immediately available, Krishnan and Rowe[25] used age data for some ethnic groups from the 1971 Census of Canada and estimated the life expectancy through the use of some mathematical models.[26] They found that Scandinavians had the highest life expectancy, followed by the Germans. The results of this preliminary study are compatible with the Kalbach-McVey findings and those of others for some U.S. ethnic groups. Scandinavians seem to do well everywhere: the Scandinavian countries have always led the others in life expectancy. This persistent result — in spite of generational change, intermarriage, and adaptation to a new environment — leads us to conclude that there may be some cultural and hereditary factors which affect mortality.

Determinants of Fertility in Canada

Mortality is an easy phenomenon to interpret: everybody wants to live longer and, hence, anything that helps reduce mortality is acceptable to almost everyone. But fertility[27] is a very personal and sensitive aspect of human life. It cannot be easily changed or manipulated by external forces. Moreover, it is necessary to understand people's motivational framework in order to effect changes in fertility at the individual or national levels.

Fertility, though a biological phenomenon, is socially determined. Otherwise the number of children born to a typical family in Bangladesh and Canada would be the same. Even in Canada, Hutterities, Native Indians and Inuit have more children on average than white Canadians. Mormons also have high fertility. Infertility is fairly constant from country to country. Then why are there fertility differentials between countries and, within countries, among sub-populations?

Fertility, as we observed, is ultimately dependent on an element of personal choice. This personal element is shaped by societal values and norms. If a society is threatened with extinction, it will demand higher fertility from its members and reward them for it. That is the reason why, in the early stages of the demographic transition, high fertility goes hand in hand with high mortality.

All cultural, environmental and biological factors affecting fertility, then, are modified and filtered by social organization. In a pioneering paper, Davis and Blake[28] identified eleven social structural factors through which the various determinants of fertility operate to fix the final level of reproduction in a society. These eleven "intermediate variables" are listed in Table 6-6. For Canadian society, as with all Western societies, the single most powerful intermediate variable is contraception. Voluntary control of family size has been possible with the use of the various birth control methods that were and are available to populations.

The use of contraception is personal and is affected by economic conditions, aspirations, and the religious and other affiliations of couples. If a majority of couples accept the idea of controlling their own fertility, national fertility tends to decline. This is what has happened in Canada. In order to appreciate this better, let us look at the Canadian CBR over time.

TABLE 6-6

The Davis-Blake Intermediate Variables

I. Factors affecting exposure to intercourse ("intercourse variables").
  A. Those governing the formation and dissolution of unions in the reproductive period.
    1. Age of entry into sexual unions (legitimate and illegitimate).
    2. Permanent celibacy: proportion of women never entering sexual unions.
    3. Amount of reproductive period spent after or between unions.
      a. When unions are broken by divorce, separation, or desertion.
      b. When unions are broken by death of husband.
  B. Those governing the exposure to intercourse within unions.
    4. Voluntary abstinence.
    5. Involuntary abstinence (from impotence, illness, unavoidable but temporary separations).
    6. Coital frequency (excluding periods of abstinence).
II. Factors affecting exposure to conception ("conception variables").
    7. Fecundity or infecundity, as affected by involuntary causes.
    8. Use or nonuse of contraception.
      a. By mechanical and chemical means.
      b. By other means.
    9. Fecundity or infecundity, as affected by voluntary causes (sterilization, medical treatment, etc).
III. Factors affecting gestation and successful parturition ("gestation variables").
    10. Fetal mortality from involuntary causes.
    11. Fetal mortality from voluntary causes.

Source: Davis and Blake, 1956: 211-35.

Table 6-2 shows that the CBR reaches a low in 1936 and then begins to rise, reaching a peak in 1956. It then falls off rapidly. The decline is gradual until 1931, but sharp between 1931 and 1936. Here, fertility behavior would have been better delineated if we had shown the time series in greater detail and used better age standardization measures (e.g., TFR).[29] Note, however, that the Great Depression hit Canada during the early 1930s. Poor economic conditions forced Canadians to resort to all sorts of methods for reducing their fertility. Some postponed marriage.[30] Those who married did not opt to have a child immediately. Those who were married and had children did not add to them. Remember that, at this time, the Canadian age structure was very suitable for high fertility.[31] Despite this, fertility fell. But when economic conditions improved, people began to make up for this loss: fertility began to rise and continued to remain at high levels for the next decade. Note that by this time the age structure of the Canadian population was most unsuitable for high performance. Despite this, fertility reached a peak level of almost four children per woman by 1956 and 1961.

We refer to this unusual surge of births following the Depression and World War II as the "baby boom." Following the baby boom, Canadian fertility began to decline due to various factors. Now we have reached a situation where not enough children are being born to replace the parent generation. Grindstaff[32] aptly calls this the "baby bust."

There are various reasons for the baby boom, that is, the continuation of high fertility for a little over a decade following the Depression. In order to understand it, we have to broadly distinguish between two groups of women: those entering into family building for the first time after the War, and those who had begun childbearing before it but had few children. The pattern of timing of births by the two groups creates fluctuations in the total number experienced in any given year. The first group, which had been imbued with small family norms, had their children quickly. The second group — with larger family size expectations and whose members were accustomed to long intervals between births — also had their children as per schedule. In view of a combination of these two birth-timing patterns, we had a large number of births in the period from 1946 to 1961. Given this, why did the young mothers change to an early childbearing pattern?

The answer to this lies, again, in changing life-styles. The War led to an economic boom and industrial expansion. Owing to manpower shortages, women took jobs in factories.[33] Though initially women out of the reproductive age group were the first to join the labor force, the demand was high and the benefits were such that women in childbearing years were also induced to join the labor force. The income these women earned encouraged higher levels of consumption. Couples, thus, had to choose between having children and acquiring various consumer goods.[34] Further, the roles of worker and mother were not fully compatible: something had to be done to curb a potential loss in income. Since effective birth control methods were becoming available, couples opted in favor of contraception. All these choice patterns led to small family size norms and early child bearing.

Easterlin's[35] analysis had been somewhat simplified here. Life-style changes have been so dramatic, however, that one segment of the population does not want to have children at all,[36] does not want to marry legally, but wishes to live together. The incidence of voluntary childlessness seems to have decreased considerably in Canada,[37] even though some differentials by types are noteworthy.

FERTILITY DIFFERENTIALS

Various census monographs have examined fertility differentials in Canada.[38] Employing rigorous demographic techniques, these studies have unravelled some complex relationships between fertility and a variety of social characteristics of the population. Since their analyses were based on census data, however, the researchers involved were not able to utilize the various attitudinal and behavioral attributes of the population in interpreting their findings: detailed field surveys are needed to gather the relevant data. Even though a few local studies have been undertaken,[39] there has yet to be a national fertility survey of Canada of this kind.[40] Hence, we are forced to use the results of those studies done between 1968 and 1973 for exploring the relationship between attitudinal and behavioral factors and reproductive activity in Canada.

These surveys reveal high use of contraceptives by Canadian women. Eighty-five per cent of married women in Toronto under 45 years of age had used contraceptives at one time in their lives. This was true of 75 per cent of young married women under 35 in Québec, and 80 per cent of the women 18 to 54 in Edmonton. The pill was most often the preferred method. Differences were observed between the fertility of Catholics and non-Catholics; between women in and those not in the labor force; between native-born and foreign-born women; between those who had fewer and those with more years of schooling.[41]

Ethnic Differences

Differences in fertility were also observed among members of various ethnic groups. These varied somewhat independently from attitudes toward abortion. Even though the women sampled in all three surveys generally held liberal views towards abortion, approval for aborting a fetus for socio-economic reasons (e.g. career, economic hardship) was rather low. Approval for abortion for health reasons, however, was phenomenal.[42]

There have been various attempts to explain differences in fertility among ethnic groups. Beaujot[43] presents a detailed discussion of the two approaches to this issue. The so-called "characteristics" or "assimilationist" school holds that if the socio-economic and demographic characteristics of two groups are similar, or made similar, there should be no differences in fertility between them. The other school maintains that even if characteristics are made similar, the ethnic variable may still influence fertility; though to a lesser extent. Beaujot[44] and others are still able to see fertility differences between ethnic groups after removing the effects of socio-economic characteristics. In the absence of other possible explanatory factors, one is left to conclude that the residue left behind is the real ethnic fertility effect.

Unfortunately, ethnicity is poorly measured in Canadian censuses and those surveys which adopt the census definition of it.[45] No attempt is being made to rectify the situation by asking people to identify themselves. Even if present day census data are reasonably good, descendants of the earlier immigrants will not find it meaningful. Intermarriage with members of other groups has also seriously eroded ethnic identity.[46]

Another useful approach to getting at the same sort of dimension is to classify the population by mother tongue.[47] Even this is being eroded, however, as we shall see in a later section on language assimilation. There is a great need, in any event, to bring together the dimensions of ethnicity, mother tongue, and home-language use for really assessing the role of cultural factors in fertility.

It is important to note that all studies done so far in Canada reveal only small differentials in fertility among various groups. Given present day social and environmental conditions, and high levels of contact between groups, we ought to expect a great deal of similarity in behavioral patterns. Over time, social structural factors are likely to become less relevant to fertility differentials in Canada or in other industrial societies. We will probably have to search for various psychological factors in greater depth to understand narrower differences in fertility.

AGING OF THE CANADIAN POPULATION

One of the major consequences of the low fertility in recent years is that the age structure is seriously distorted. This, along with the high life expectancy and the baby boom children now in their early 30s, makes the situation worse.

The Canadian age structure has a narrow base consisting of children and a heavy top consisting of older people. Let us consider the broad age groups to be: under 15 years, 15-64 years, and 65 and above. If the birth rate is low, the part of the population in the group below 15 years should be around 25-30 per cent, and that over 65 years over 8 per cent. For Canada, the broad age structure for 1901 and 1976 shows that the percentage of older persons increased from 5.0 to 8.7. The proportion of children decreased from 34.4 per cent in 1901 to 25.6 per cent in 1976. A population is said to be demographically aged when the proportion of population 65 years and over is above 7 per cent.

Aging is defined in many ways depending on the discipline from which one views the issue. To a physiologist or physician, a person is aging right from the instant of birth: the human body undergoes changes and decay all the time. Sociologists tend to think in terms of the role relations connecting members of a society: as a person gets older, retires, and has a different life pattern, society expects a different type of role behaviour from him or her. Psychologists look at a person's intelligence, behavior, and self-esteem or self-image in determining whether he or she is "aged" or still "young." All these aspects of aging are interrelated.

In all these cases, the disciplines involved focus on individuals. Population scientists, by contrast, tend to look at the total population and the number of older people — conveniently defined in terms of the retirement age — which it contains. The simplest index of aging is the proportion of population 65 years of age and over, and is known as the coefficient of old age (COA).[48] The United Nations (1956) considers a population to be "young" if the COA is less than 4, "mature" if the COA is 4 to 6 per cent, and "aged" if it is more than 7 per cent. By this criterion, Canada had a "young" population at the turn of this century, which became aged by 1951.

The main reason for the demographic aging of Canada is her declining birth rate: when the birth rate declines, the age/sex pyramid[49] gets dented at the base. Since mortality is already low and people live longer, this "denting" at the base pushes the top and flattens it. If fertility, which is already below replacement level, declines further, then the base will get narrower. When the baby boom group reaches retirement age, there will be a large number of retired people in Canada.

There are important economic implications of this aging of the population right now, and there will be more in the next few decades. These economic implications can be assessed by means of a complex simulation model such as the one devised by Denton and Spencer.[50] They can be illustrated, however, in a simpler way. Statistics Canada projects the population of Canada under several different assumptions.[51] Let us use the highest projection here. The population values by broad age groups are noted in Table 6-7. From this extract, the total number of senior citizens aged 65 years and over would exceed 3 million by 1996.

TABLE 6-7

Population Projections,* 1981-2001, Canada

Year	Total Population (mill)	Population 65 + (mill)
1981	24.57	2.31
1986	26.33	2.62
1991	28.09	2.99
1996	29.64	3.28
2001	30.98	3.46

Source: Statistics Canada, 1974.

* The projections used here are those under assumption 1

Now let us look at the Canada pension plan. At the present rate of nearly $6,000 per annum per capita, we need (in 1980 dollars) $18 billion to distribute as pensions to the senior citizens of 1996. (No inflation factor is built into this calculation.) Where will this money come from? At the present time, every member of the labor force contributes under $200 to the Canadian pension plan. We hope to have (assuming full employment) a maximum of 18 million people in the labor force in the year 1996. his means that the per capita contribution to the plan has to be raised to $1,000 per annum, a five-fold increase. One wonders where we are heading, in the years to come, in this one area alone.

The health-care plan, living arrangements, and other social services needed for the elderly would also be quite enormous. The dependency ratio depicts very clearly the burden placed on the shoulders of the working people for supporting both older and younger segments of society. Dependency ratios for the years 1881 to 1976, and estimated ones for the latter part of the 20th century, are shown in Table 6-8. Juxtapose this with Table 6-2: as fertility declines, old age dependency rises. In 1976, every 100 members of the work force had to support 13 older persons, and this is number is going to increase to 18 or 19 by the year 2000.

TABLE 6-8

Dependency Ratios,* Canada 1901-2001

Year	Young Dependency Ratio	Old Dependency Ratio	Total Dependency Ratio
1901	56.8	8.3	65.1
1911	52.9	7.5	60.3
1921	56.6	7.9	64.4
1931	50.3	8.8	59.2
1941	42.4	10.2	52.6
1951**	49.0	12.5	61.5
1961	58.1	13.1	71.2
1966	55.5	13.0	68.4
1971	47.5	13.0	60.4
1976	39.1	13.3	52.3
1981	23.1	15.2	38.3
1991	23.7	17.3	41.0
2001	22.1	18.0	40.1

Source: Kalbach, W. and W. McVey, 1979: 171. Statistics Canada, 1974.
*   From projected figures under assumption 1.
** Newfoundland is included.

A low birth rate implies a reduced labor force in the long run. It is this labor force that has to man the economy and support the pension plan. How can we increase the labor force? A slight increase in fertility is needed. Is that possible? Only time can tell. If fertility does not increase, Canadian society may have to depend more on immigration to take care of its labor force needs. Given that most western nations are in the same plight in regard to fertility, much of this immigration may have to come from the have-not nations.

LINGUISTIC ASSIMILATION IN CANADA

Canada is officially a bilingual country. Besides the official languages, i.e., the ethnic languages of the two "Charter groups," we have several non-official languages — the ethnic languages of the other cultural communities. The census of Canada collects information on the mother tongue of every inhabitant of this country. Since every ethnic group is distinguished by its own language, a comparison of the number of those who claim to belong to an ethnic group with those who report the ethnic language as mother tongue reveals how we fare in regard to maintaining the various languages.

Joy[52] showed that the French language is disappearing from Canada.[53] He demonstrated that Canada would be unilingually French in Québec and English elsewhere, with the city of Montreal and the area around Ottawa somewhat bilingual. There are more sophisticated studies carried out by Lieberson,[54] The Royal Commission on Bilingualism, Lamy[55] and others. But it is not simply French that is being lost through assimilation: the other ethnic languages are also disappearing, as demonstrated by Krishnan.[56]

Ethnic languages are the single most important trait in the Canadian mosaic. If these languages disappear soon, Canada can no longer claim that its "integration" policy is successful. We would like to inquire into the causes of linguistic assimilation. Obviously, this assimilation is into English. In a social correlates analysis attempted by Krishnan,[57] the degree of institutional completeness[58] and degree of urbanization of an ethnic group were negatively related to assimilation, while the degree of scattering of a group was positively related. The influence of the English language is inescapable as it is the language of business, technology, educational institutions, etc. The only plausible way in which ethnic languages can be preserved is by increasing the scope of bilingual educational programs in the school systems, since children are the ones to lose their mother tongue fastest.

MIGRATION

Migration occurs when people from one geographical area move to another with the idea of settling down. If this movement occurs within a nation-state, we refer to the phenomenon as "internal migration." If the movement is between nations, we call it "international migration." We will briefly touch on both here.

When Canada was in the early stages of demographic transition, most of its population was agricultural and rural. But over time, with the onset of modernization, the economy began to be less agrarian (in terms of employment) and more industrial. Since employment opportunities were concentrated in urban areas, migration to cities and towns began. In 1851, only 13.0 per cent of Canada's population lived in urban areas. In 1976, almost 75.5 per cent of the population was urban. The least urbanized province in 1976 was P.E.I. (37.1 per cent). The Atlantic provinces are less urbanized compared to the western provinces — excluding Saskatchewan.

Even though urbanward migration had been on the increase from the early part of this century, it cannot be said that all internal migration has been urbanward. Since cities are now congested, highly polluted, and not "a good place to raise children," some have a desire to move back to the quiet of the countryside. The 1971 census indicates that between 1966 and 1971, 25 per cent of movers (aged five years and above) wended their way to the countryside from the census metropolitan areas.

TABLE 6-9

Rates of Natural Increase and Net Migration,*
Provinces and Territories

Province	1931-1941		1961-1971	
	Natural Increase	Net Migration	Natural Increase	Net Migration
Newfoundland	—	—	222	- 90
P.E.I.	105	- 28	127	- 62
Nova Scotia	109	10	127	- 59
New Brunswick	132	- 18	144	- 85
Quebec	139	8	132	4
Ontario	72	27	124	86
Manitoba	94	- 53	125	- 55
Saskatchewan	126	-155	137	-136
Alberta	132	- 47	162	38
B.C.	46	118	101	190
Yukon & NWT	124	99	297	46

Source: Statistics Canada (1976), 1971 Census of Canada, Bulletin 5, 1-1, Table 11, 34.

* Rate per 1000 average population of the decade.

The provinces have grown over time along with Canada as a whole. But, looking at the components of growth, we see that migration between provinces is quite extensive. Table 6-9 presents rates of natural increase and net migration for the provinces and territories for the periods from 1931 to 1941, and 1961 to 1971. It is clear from this that Ontario, B.C., Québec, and the Territories are all net gainers of population in the time spans considered; the Atlantic provinces and the Prairies (other than Alberta), the losers. Saskatchewan has usually lost population. But between 1971 and 1976, Saskatchewan[59] lost only 0.5 per cent of its population. Given that Alberta and Saskatchewan were important oil producers, there were more opportunities in these provinces. Alberta experienced a heavy influx of migrants for these reasons.

Experts have found that economic opportunities are the prime motivating factor behind migration. In that case, Saskatchewan is likely to experience substantial immigration soon. Internal migration in Canada has been westward and Ontario-ward. But in the eighties, it is likely to be mostly westward. Between 1971 and 1976, Québec lost more members than it gained through migration. The formation of the P.Q. Government in 1976, and the stipulation of French language only at place of work, and the lack of employment opportunities may be pointed out as causes of increased out-migration from Québec in recent years.

Before we proceed to look at some of the social, political, and other ramifications of migration, let us briefly look at international migration, which is a very important determinant of population growth in Canada. There are some commendable studies on immigration policies, or lack of policies, the impact of immigration on Canada's population, the assimilation of post-war immigrants in Canada, and migration between the U.S. and Canada.[60] Though a country with heavy immigration at certain points in time, as noted elsewhere, Canada lost population by net emigration, particularly during the Depression. Like fertility, immigration is highly sensitive to economic conditions in the receiving country.

Canadian policies regarding immigration are *ad hoc.* Racial barriers were removed in 1962, and emphasis was placed on education, training, skills, etc. A point system was introduced in 1967 to back up these requirements.[61] The point system helped immigrants from Third World countries to enter Canada in greater numbers, resulting in net immigration accounting for 33 per cent of total growth, for the period 1966 to 1975. According to Statistics Canada, in 1976 net immigration accounted for over a third of all population growth. The influx of "visible immigrants" brought great public pressure on the Government of Canada to bring in a Green Paper on Immigration for public discussion. The new Immigration Act was passed in August 1977 and implemented in April 1978.

Immigration quotas are now based on the economic opportunities available in the country. Roughly about 100,000 immigrants are admitted and nearly 40,000 of those living in Canada emigrate. Hence, there is a net addition of 60,000 immigrants into Canada annually. Fixing of immigration quotas is still very poorly done, as there is very little policy research on fertility and economic and social trends to back up the estimates.

Migration, internal and international, has ramifications on the social scene. Even though considerable research has been done on immigrant adaptation and assimilation, very little research is available on the political implications of migration. Will the migration from Québec, the Maritimes, and Saskatchewan into Alberta alter the political scene? We don't know. It is claimed that the immigrants are normally supporters of the Liberal party. Is this true? The recent flow of immigrants from non-European countries, and South-East Asian refugees has already triggered off race relations questions. Canada has always admitted refugees, sometimes under international pressure. The Hungarian and the Czechoslovakian refugees did not face much of a "discrimination" problem. But others are likely to face this, sooner or later.

Demography of Ethnic and Other Small Groups

Canada, though founded by two main ethnic groups, is a country of various small and large cultural, religious, and linguistic groups. There are Hutterites, Mennonites, Jews, Inuits, Metis, various Indian bands, West Indians, Indo-Pakistanis, etc. Most of these groups have not been analyzed for their population characteristics and their implications. Hutterites have a unique demography of their own. Laing (1975) has presented a demographic profile of Hutterites in Alberta, and Gaudette et al. (1978) have written on the mortality due to cancer among them. Detailed studies of this type are needed to elucidate the inter-relationship between social and demographic factors of these minority groups. The Inuit, and the Indian bands, the French in anglophone Canada, all need to be looked into.

FUTURE PROSPECTS

Canadian fertility is now below replacement level. This does not mean that the population is at zero growth. If fertility declines further and the birth and death rates become equal, then we may reach zero population growth. Therefore, the crucial factor in future growth is the fertility level — since mortality is already at its lowest possible level. If we ever reach a zero population growth situation, the socio-economic structure of the country will be completely dependent on net immigration.

NOTES

[1]Second to the Soviet Union.

[2]Censuses are conducted in Canada on a decennial basis. Canada follows the U.K. pattern of having its censuses in the year after the end of the decade. But unlike those in Britain, Canadian censuses are *de jure* (i.e., enumeration by usual place of residence), rather than *de facto* (i.e., enumeration by actual place of residence). Since 1951, mini-censuses have been conducted every five years after the main census.

[3]In population studies, there are two notions — incidence and prevalence. Incidence indicates the occurrence of new events (e.g., babies, new cases of illness) and prevalence refers to all cases of events, new and old. A rate is computed to indicate the number of events that may happen to 1000 members of the population who are likely to experience that phenomenon (the risk population). Thus the crude birth rate (CBR) is given by CBR = 1000 (number of live births in a year) over estimated mid-year population for that year. Similarly CDR. These are crude rates in view of the poor risk population employed. Demographers employ better measures of birth incidence, etc. For details, consult any standard methods book in population analysis. Barclay, 1958,is one of the best.

[4]Charbonneau, 1975.

[5]A group of people born in a given time span — usually a year — is known as a "cohort." Here we have a group of couples marrying at a particular point in time — a "marriage cohort." What Charbonneau is referring to is the number of children ever born to the marriage cohort "before 1681."

[6]It has been shown that, if 1000 Canadian women have 2100 children during their lifetime, the population of Canada will just replace itself. This does not take into account the immigration-emigration factor.

[7]The most rigorous methodology for analyzing mortality is the "life table technique." The life table presents, after extensive computations, the mortality history by age of a group of people (usually one sex at a time) born at the same time and continuing on the march of life until all its members die. The last column of the table gives the life expectancy at a given age and denotes the probable number of years that the male/female can hope to live after attaining that age, provided that present day (i.e., the reference time of the data employed) mortality conditions do hold.

[8]Thompson, 1929.

[9]Notestein, 1945.

[10]For a discussion of the demographic transition, see Petersen, 1975.

[11]Bogue, 1969.

[12]Bogue employs two refined measures of incidence of births to develop the per cent demographic transition. The total fertility rate (TFR) moved from 7500 to 2200, the general fertility rate (GFR) from 235 to 175 per 1000, when the Western nations completed the transition. Thus, the Bogue Index is given by:

$$100 \left[\frac{1}{2} \left(\frac{235\text{-GFR}}{175} \right) + \frac{1}{2} \left(\frac{7500\text{-TFR}}{5300} \right) \right]$$

[13]The phenomenon of different population groups experiencing different levels of mortality is called differential mortality. In Canada, as elsewhere in the West, females live longer than males. The married (males/females) have the lowest death rates as to compared to single, widowed and divorced. Different regions in Canada

experience different levels of mortality. The prairies have the lowest death rate in Canada. A detailed look at the differentials helps to detect the etiology of illnesses and mortality.

[14]The poor nations of the world have higher male life expectancy. As these countries modernize, female life expectancy converges towards that for males and later exceeds it.

[15]Lalonde, 1976 presents this very clearly.

[16]Jarvis, 1977.

[17]Jarvis compares causes of death among Alberta Mormons with those for the populations of both Alberta and Canada. The data below are for 1970-72 for Canada and Alberta, and 1967-75 for Mormons.

Death Rate per 100,000		Cancer	Heart Disease
Males	Canada	162.7	413.2
	Alberta	137.8	345.0
	Mormons	76.6	212.2
Females	Canada	129.5	312.1
	Alberta	101.1	223.7
	Mormons	71.4	174.9

[18]Sidney Katz, 1979 presents some useful information on vegetarianism. Also see Wynder et al., 1959; Lemon et al., 1964.

[19]Kalbach and McVey, 1979. The age structure (i.e., the distribution of people in the various age categories) of a population has an influence on mortality, as the death rates for specific ages are low for the early age groups, and high for older ones. Thus a population which has a higher percentage of youths will have lower mortality. In order to compare populations, one has to control age structure. This is called age standardization and is done by taking one age structure as standard (here the British age structure) and using the age-specific death rates for this structure in computing a standardized death rate for all. For details, see Barclay, 1958.

[20]It appears that these are comparable to those for the Inuit.

[21]Bracher, 1975.

[22]Legaré and Desjardins, 1975.

[23]Piché and George, 1973.

[24]Romaniuc and Piché, 1972. Piché and George estimate the death rate has declined from 10.9 to 7.5. The infant mortality rate has declined from 81.5 per 1000 in 1960 to 34.9 per 1000 in 1970. Bracher utilized the data on the Inuit from the Department of Indian Affairs to fit a quasi-stable model to the age structure. His estimates of the Inuit birth rate and the death rate are 54.9 per 1000 and 15.9 per 1000 respectively.

[25]Krishnan and Rowe, 1978.

[26]Krishnan and Rowe employed a regression model, developed from the West Model Life tables to generate the estimates of life expectancies from the age data for 1971 of selected ethnic groups. They are as follows:

	Life Expectancy	
Ethnic Group	Males	Females
Scandinavian	75.9	89.9
German	67.5	77.4
Japanese	70.9	64.7
Italian	53.1	74.7

[27]"Fecundity" is the term used for the biological ability to reproduce. The term "fertility" is used to refer to the actual production of children.

[28]Davis and Blake, 1956.

[29]Vital Statistics publications may be consulted for in-depth analysis.

[30]Krishnan, 1978 analyzes the marriage situation in Canada in relation to the Depression and War. It shows that practically every Canadian male and female born between 1911 and 1946 married; though, during the Depression, marriage tended to be postponed until later. But the male and female cohorts of 1946-1950 (now in their thirties) are experiencing a decline in the incidence of marriage. One may take this as evidence for a new life-style — living together, experimenting, and later deciding whether to marry or not.

[31]If age standardized birth rates are calculated, these results become clear.

[32]Grindstaff, 1975.

[33]For an interesting discussion of this and the related issue of women's liberation, see Weeks, 1978: 271-90.

[34]Treating children as consumer goods was first proposed by Becker, 1960. Blake, 1968, is vehemently opposed to this. For an overview of the issues involved, see Namboodiri, 1972.

[35]Easterlin, 1968.

[36]See Krishnan and Krotki, 1976, for the point of view that some couples (nearly 4.2 per cent) do not want to have children at all and that is why they approve of the use of contraception.

[37]Voluntary childlessness in Canada has been analyzed in great detail by Veevers in a series of articles. This finding emerges from her research. See Veevers, 1972, 1980.

[38]Charles, 1948; Henripin, 1972; Balakrishnan, Ebanks and Grindstaff, 1979.

[39]Balakrishnan, Kantner, and Allingham, 1975; Krishnan and Krotki, 1976; Henripin and Lapierre-Adamcyk, 1974.

[40]The Toronto fertility survey was conducted in 1968 and sampled 1,632 married women aged 45 and below. The Québec survey, carried out in 1971, included 1,745 married women aged between 18 and 65. The Edmonton survey was conducted in 1973 on the basis of a sample of 1,045 women from 18 to 54.

[41]The average ideal family size from these surveys is given below.

Surveys	Catholic	Non-Catholic
Edmonton	2.81	2.57
Toronto	3.25	2.88

[42]Per cent approving abortion as reflected in the surveys under certain conditions:

	Toronto	Québec	Edmonton
Health of mother in danger/endangered mother's life	87	75	81

[43]Beaujot, 1978; 1975.

[44]Beaujot, 1975.

[45]A person's ethnicity is obtained from the answer to the census question: "To what ethnic, or cultural group did you or your ancestor (on the male side) belong on coming to this continent?"

[46]See Elkin, this volume.

[47]In the census, "mother tongue" is defined as "the language a person first learned in childhood and still understands."

[48]There are various other indicators of demographic aging of a population: median age, proportion of children in the population, a ratio of aged population to youth, and the old age dependency given by the ratio,

$$\left(\frac{\text{Proportion 65 years and older}}{\text{Proportion 15-64}}\right) \quad x \quad 100$$

are some of the measures used. If we use the median age of the population, over time this has to go up. For Canada, the median age in 1901 was 22.7 years and in 1976, it stood at 27.8 years. Let us take the proportion of children, i.e., population under 15 years. This was 34.4 per cent in 1901, and in 1976, this had declined to 25.6. If the old age dependency ratio is considered, there was an increase from 8.3 in 1901 to 13.3 in 1976.

[49]Age/sex pyramid is the diagram of histograms of either the actual number of/or proportion of males and females on the horizontal axis and age on the vertical axis. Conventionally, the male histograms are on the left and the female ones on the right side of the vertical axis.

[50]Denton and Spencer, 1975.

[51]For details, consult Population Projection for Canada Provinces, 1972-2001, Statistics Canada, 1974.

[52]Joy, 1974.

[53]Joy takes the difference between "Ethnic origin French" and "Mother tongue French" (expressed as a per cent of ethnic origin French) as a measure of linguistic assimilation. If M_i is the number reporting i as the mother tongue (language of the ethnic group i) and E_i the number reporting i as ethnicity, then the Joy Index of Assimilation is $J = (1 - M_i/E_i) \times 100$ M_i/E_i is the mother tongue retention rate.

[54]Lieberson, 1970.

[55]Lamy, 1977.

[56]Krishnan, 1977. Krishnan has computed Joy Index J for the other ethnic groups and has shown that, *ceteris paribus*, all would disappear from the Canadian scene by the year 2041.

[57]Krishnan, 1977.

[58]The notion of institutional completeness is due to Breton, 1964.

[59]For excellent analyses of internal migration in Canada see Anderson, 1966; George, 1970; Kasahara, 1966; Stone, 1969; and Stone and Fletcher, 1977.

[60]Hawkins, 1972; Kalbach, 1970; Richmond, 1967; Samuel, 1969; Lavoie, 1972.

[61]Potential migrants are graded on nine factors. Of 100 points, about half are assigned to economic factors: skills, whether a job is already pre-arranged, what is the demand for the migrant's occupational skills. The rest of the points were assigned to the migrant's capability to establish oneself in Canada's socio-economic environment (e.g., years of education, knowledge and fluency in the official languages, having a relative in Canada and lastly, the immigration officer's judgment on the applicant's personality, adaptability, etc.).

Bibliography

Anderson, I. B. *Internal Migration in Canada, 1921-1961*. Economic Council of Canada (Staff Study 13). Ottawa: The Queen's Printer, 1966.

Balakrishnan, T. R., G. E. Ebanks and C. F. Grindstaff. *Patterns of Fertility in Canada.* Ottawa: Ministry of Supply and Services, 1979.

Balakrishnan, T. R., J. F. Kantner, and J. D. Allingham. *Fertility and Family Planning in a Canadian Metropolis.* Montreal: McGill-Queen's University Press, 1975.

Barclay, G. W., *Techniques of Population Analysis.* New York: John Wiley and Sons, 1958.

Beaujot, R. P. "Canada's Population: Growth and Dualism." *Population Bulletin* 23 (1978): 3-46.

Beaujot, R. P. *Ethnic Fertility Differentials in Edmonton.* Ph.D. thesis, Edmonton: University of Alberta, Dept. of Sociology and the Faculty of Graduate Studies and Research, 1975.

Becker, G. S. "An Economic Analysis of Fertility." In *Demographic and Economic Change in Developed Countries.* Princeton: National Bureau of Economic Research, 1960.

Blake, J. "Are Babies Consumer Durables? A Critique of the Economic Theory of Reproductive Motivation." *Population Studies* 22 (1968): 5-25.

Bogue, D. J. *Principles of Demography.* New York: John Wiley and Sons, 1969.

Bracher, M. "Estimates of Vital Rates of the North West Territories Inuit." Western Canada Series Report 2, Edmonton: University of Alberta, Population Research Laboratory, 1975.

Breton, R. "Institutional Completeness of Ethnic Communities and the Personal Relations of Immigrants." *American Journal of Sociology* 70 (1964): 193-205.

Charbonneau, H. *Vie et Mort Des Nos Ancestres: Etude Demographique.* Montréal: Presses de l'Université de Montréal, 1975.

Charles, E. *The Changing Size of Family in Canada.* Ottawa: The Queen's Printer, 1948.

Davis, K. and J. Blake. "Social Structure and Fertility: an Analytic Framework." *Economic Development and Cultural Change* 4 (1956): 211-35.

Denton, F. and B. Spencer. *Population and the Economy,* Farnborough (Eng): Saxon House, D.C. Health Ltd., 1975.

Easterlin, R. A. *Population, Labor Force, and Long Swings in Economic Growth.* New York: National Bureau of Economic Research, 1968.

Gaudette, L. A., T. M. Holmes, L. M. Laing, K. Morgan and M. G. A. Grace. "Cancer Incidence in a Religious Isolate of Alberta, Canada, 1953-74." *Journal of the National Cancer Institute* 60 (1978): 1233-36.

George, M. V. *Population Growth in Canada.* 1971 Census Profile Studies. Ottawa: Statistics Canada, 1976.

George, M. V. *Internal Migration in Canada: Demographic Analysis.* 1961 Census Monograph. Ottawa: Dominion Bureau of Statistics, 1970.

Grindstaff, C. F. "The Baby Bust: Changes in Fertility Patterns in Canada." *Canadian Studies in Population* 2 (1975): 15-22.

Hawkins, F. *Canada and Immigration: Public Policy and Public Concern.* Montreal: McGill-Queen's University Press, 1972.

Henripin, J. *Trends and Factors Of Fertility in Canada,* Ottawa: Information Canada, 1972.

Henripin, J. and E. Lapierre-Adamcyk. *La Fin de la Rivanche des Berceaus: Q'uen Pensent Les Québécoises?* Montreal: Presses de l'Université de Montréal, 1974.

Jarvis, G. K. "Mormon Mortality Rates in Canada." *Social Biology* 24 (1977): 294-302.

Joy, R. *Languages in Conflict: The Canadian Experience.* Toronto: McClelland and Stewart, 1972.

Kalbach, W. E. *The Impact of Immigration on Canada's Population.* 1961 Census

Monograph. Ottawa: The Queen's Printer, 1970.

Kalbach, W. E. and W. W. McVey. *The Demographic Bases of Canadian Society.* 2d ed. Toronto: McGraw-Hill Ryerson Ltd., 1979.

Kasahara, Y. "Mobility of Canada's Population, 1956-61." *Canada Yearbook, 1966.* Ottawa: The Queen's Printer, 1966.

Katz, S. "How to Live Longer." *Quest: Canada's Urban Magazine* 8 (1979): 18-22.

Krishnan, P. "War and Depression Effects on Canadian Marriage Rates: A Macro-Analysis." *Population et Famille* 44: (1978): 89-102.

Krishnan, P. "Linguistic Assimilation in Canada: The Case of the Non-French." Paper Presented at the Annual Meetings of the Canadian Population Society, Fredriction, New Brunswick, 1977.

Krishnan, P. and K. Krotki. *Growth of Alberta Families Study.* Edmonton: University of Alberta, Population Research Laboratory, 1976.

Krishnan, P. and G. Rowe. "Ethnic Differentials in Mortality, Canada 1971." Paper Presented at the Annual Meetings of the Canadian Population Society, London, Ontario, 1978.

Laing, L. *Population Growth Patterns Among Alberta Hutterites.* M.A. thesis. Edmonton: University of Alberta, Dept. of Sociology and the Faculty of Graduate Studies and Research, 1975.

Lalonde, M. *A New Perspective on the Health of Canadians.* Ottawa: Health and Welfare Canada, 1976.

Lamy, P. *Language Maintenance and Language Shift in Canada: New Dimensions in the Use of Census Language Data.* Ottawa: University of Ottawa, 1977.

Lavoie, Y. *L'Emigration des Canadiens aux Etats-Unis avant 1930.* Montréal: Presses de L'Université de Montréal, 1972.

Legaré, J. and L. Normadeau-Desjardins. "Infant and Child Mortality Among Canadian Inuit." *Canadian Studies in Population* 2 (1975): 101-10.

Lemon, F. R., R. T. Walden, and R. W. Woods. "Cancer of the Lung and Mouth Among Seventh Day Adventists." *Cancer* 17 (1966): 486-97.

Lieberson, S. *Language and Ethnic Relations in Canada.* New York: John Wiley and Sons, 1970.

Namboodiri, N. K. "Some Observations on the Economic Framework for Fertility Analysis." *Population Studies* 26 (1972): 185-206.

Notestein, F. W. "Population — The Long View." In T. W. Schultz (ed), *Food for the World.* Chicago: University of Chicago Press, 1945.

Petersen, W. *Population.* 3d ed. New York: Macmillan Co., 1975.

Piché, V. and M. V. George. "Estimates of the Vital Rates for the Canadian Indians." *Demography* 10 (1973): 351-66.

Richmond, A. H. *Post-War Immigrants in Canada.* Toronto: University of Toronto Press, 1967.

Romaniuc, A. and V. Piché. "Natality Estimates for the Canadian Indians by Stable Population Models, 1900-1969." *Canadian Review of Sociology and Anthropology* 9 (1972): 1-20.

Samuel, T. J. *The Migration of the Canadian-Born Between Canada and the United States of America, 1955-68.* Ottawa: Dept. of Manpower and Immigration, 1969.

Statistics Canada. *Population Projections For Canada and Provinces, 1972-2001.* Ottawa: Statistics Canada, 1974.

Stone, L. O. *Migration in Canada: Regional Aspects.* 1961 Census Monograph, Ottawa: The Queen's Printer, 1969.

Stone, L. O. and S. Fletcher. *Migration in Canada, 1971.* Census of Canada Profile Studies, Bulletin 5: 1-5. Ottawa: Statistics Canada, 1977.

Thompson, W. S. "Population." *American Journal of Sociology* 34 (1929):

959-75.

United Nations. *The Aging of Population.* Population Studies No. 26. New York: The United Nations, 1956.

Veevers, J. "Factors in the Incidence of Childlessness in Canada: An Analysis of Census Data." *Social Biology* 19 (1972): 266-74.

_____. *Childless By Choice.* Toronto: Butterworths, 1980.

Weeks, J. R. *Population: An Introduction to Concepts and Issues.* Belmont: Wadsworth, 1978.

Wynder, E. L., F. R. Lemon and I. J. Bross. "Cancer and Coronary Artery Disease Among Seventh Day Adventists." *Cancer* 12 (1959): 1016-28.

CHAPTER 7

Deviance, Crime, and the State

Charles E. Reasons

INTRODUCTION

In a recent review, a criminologist bemoaned the fact that there really is no specifically Canadian criminology:

> Canadian criminologists have too often relied upon theories grounded in U.S. race and ethnic relations, urban settlement patterns, and an obscurantist liberal ideology. Sub-cultural explanations not only do not suffice as analytical tools, they tend to blame the poor for social problems which are more properly seen as being the result of the activities of the rich.[1]

It should be added that when theories are imported they are often the kind of largely consensual frameworks which emphasize studying deviants in order to better appreciate and/or correct their deviance. This orientation is rife in Canadian studies of deviance, generally, and in Canadian criminology in particular. The brief essay which follows will begin by examining some of the implications of this dominant consensual approach to the study of deviance in Canada. It will then juxtapose to this a series of alternative frameworks which capture some of the underlying dimensions and root sources of deviant activity. Finally, it will draw conclusions about the directions which Canadian studies of deviance are likely to follow in the future, and it will evaluate the appropriateness of the various frameworks discussed for addressing the important questions which are likely to arise.

CANADIAN NUTS, SLUTS, AND PERVERTS

In the early 1970s, Alexander Liazos (1972) took American students of deviance to task for their focus on deviant identities and subcultures, their lack of analysis of deviant behavior by economic and political elites, and their failure to deal with the significant power relations involved in the designation of what is considered "deviant." Liazos was reacting to a number of studies which, while trying to "humanize" and "normalize" deviant persons, were written from the point of view "zookeepers" who were simply fascinated with those who are considered "different."

These criticisms are particularly true of Canadian work. For example, one recent book about deviants' life styles in Canada is entitled *Hookers, Rounders and Desk Clerks.* In their introduction, its authors (Prus and Irini) tells us that "It's a book about hookers and strippers, bartenders and cocktail waitresses, bouncers and desk clerks, bar patrons and rounders."[2] It is almost entirely devoid, however, of any critical or political analysis. Its stories about people and their lives are fascinating, but it lacks any sense of social structure, any historical dimension, and any appreciation for political dynamics. It simply "describes." In this sense, it is typical of a whole genre of work.

Many of the ethnographies written by Canadian researchers are excellent. They provide rich accounts of the deviant worlds of people such as road hustlers,[3] rounders,[4] and other deviant occupations and groups. The tradition for this sort of work is well-established in Canada. Buckner's *Deviance, Reality and Change,* one of the first specifically Canadian deviance texts, emphasizes the importance of what is called the "social construction of reality," in this case, the suspension of judgement and the reconstruction of actors' social worlds from the point of view of their own perceptions and situations. Although critical of traditional analyses, scholars working within this perspective still, however, tend to dwell on the worlds of what might be called "conventional" deviants: married virgins, transvestites, stutterers, rounders, prostitutes, skid row bums, drug addicts, homosexuals, mental patients — in short, "nuts, sluts and perverts." By focusing on the daily world of deviants — their subcultures, routines, and *modus operandi* — such work may succeed in "humanizing" and "normalizing" deviants to some degree. And, in this sense, a social constructionist approach represents an advance over the more traditional ways of looking at these same phenomena. But it has little to say about the reasons why groups are defined as deviant: the historical basis for these definitions, the contemporary political economy of deviance, and the politics of the social creation of deviance/non-deviance distinctions.

This kind of particularistic and ahistorical approach can be strongly contrasted with the one adopted by Clairmont in his analysis of the emergence of a "deviance service center" in Halifax's black community.[5] By using records reflecting the economic and political history of the city, he is able to provide us with insights into the processes that led, over time, to the definition of the black community as "deviant" and to its consequent role within the social ecology of the city as a whole. Cook's critical analysis of the emergence of Canadian narcotics legislation is similar: rather than exclusively focusing on those factors which shape the personal identities or subcultures of narcotics users, Cook places these facts within the larger socio-political context.[6] She concludes that class, race, and status considerations played a paramount role in determining which type of drugs were legalized and which were criminalized.

Clairmont's study of Africville is part of a collection of articles which adopts what is called a "labelling perspective" towards deviance in Canada.[7] On the whole, its stance is more critical than that assumed by most other currently available collections or texts.[8] It does, for instance, contain articles on the politics of deviance and on collective action undertaken by deviants to alter their status and social situation. But its principal focus is on the labelling process, itself, and its effects on members of deviant groups.[9] Larger political and economic questions are not emphasized.

Hagan's *The Disreputable Pleasures* represents a continuation of the same sort of provincial orientation in Canadian work. In the prologue, he notes that two strong assumptions are implicit in the title. First, that in any society most behavior is defined as either acceptable or unacceptable, as "reputable" or "disreputable." And, second, that most disreputable behavior involves an element of pleasure, whether real or imagined.[10] However, despite these promising and, apparently, fresh beginnings, the thrust of the book is about crime. After defining deviance and counting various kinds of deviant behaviors, Hagan spends two chapters interpreting deviance and crime from the point of view of consensual and conflict theories. He posits the notion that there are consensus "crimes" and conflict "crimes" which are best seen through the lenses provided by their respective theories. Although Hagan's understanding of conflict theory. — particularly Marxist conflict theory — is open to question,[11] his book does provide us with a glimpse into the nature and implications of some of its liberal variants. His notion of a distinction between consensus and conflict crimes, however, fails to answer serious questions posed by both Marxist and non-Marxist criminologists who do not adopt a correctionalist perspective.

CORRECTIONAL CRIMINOLOGY

The dominant theme in Canadian criminology has been "correctionalism": a concern with stopping crime and correcting offenders rather than understanding or interpreting behavior. Even the most cursory glance at the *Canadian Journal of Criminology* (or its predecessor *The Canadian Journal of Criminology and Corrections)* reveals that the lion's share of its space is devoted to reports about treatment programs, measures taken to reduce recidivism, community corrections, juvenile programs or other applied research. It emphasises studies of "practical" problems. This is undoubtedly partially due to the fact that far and away the largest share of funding for Canadian criminology comes from governments.

In a recent paper, Hackler notes that this close link between government funding and the type of research undertaken by Canadian criminologists could lead to serious distortions in the development of the field. "The current commercialization of criminological research," he concludes, "may foster a group of merchants skilled at pacifying ministers and easing certain governmental stresses, but this does not necessarily generate useful knowledge for the future."[12] His book *The Prevention of Youthful Crime: The Great Stumble Forward* strongly criticizes the link between delinquency policy and evaluative research. The continuing need for program evaluation, he maintains, leads to a pattern in which investigators are given numerous small grants for evaluating relatively minor programs; each of which is supposed to dramatically ease the "delinquency problem." It goes without saying that the results of these programs are almost universally disappointing since both the programs and the subsequent research focus on changing offenders. Thus, in Canada as in the United States,

> modern delinquency research has primarily extended and emphasized early positivists' work which primarily emphasized hypothesis testing, the active collection of data (questionnaires, interviews), measurement and scientific methodologies, and a nearly exclusive focus on the criminal behavior of individual actors.[13]

The so-called "community corrections movement" provides a good current example of the consequences of the unquestioning duplication of U.S. policies in Canada. Recent studies suggest that community-based correctional programs — such as probation, parole, group homes, or pre-delinquent and pre-criminal programs — increase the number of citizens under direct state control without any increase in rehabilitation, safety, reduction of incarcerated inmates, economic savings, or safety for the community. These putatively liberal programs apparently have a number of conservative consequences. Not the least of these is that they encourage a continued focus on deviants, rather than the sources of deviance: emphasis on community-based programs diverts attention from the need for fundamental changes in society and in the criminal justice system.[14]

This correctionalist orientation is also apparent in most of books on criminology widely read or used in Canada. McGrath's *Crime and Its Treatment in Canada,*[15] for instance, is a standard resource book on Canadian criminology which has largely been written by practitioners in a descriptive, atheoretical tone. It is cut from the same cloth as Kirkpatrick and McGrath (*Crime and You*), Silverman and Teevan (*Crime in Canadian Society*), and Vaz and Lodhi *(Crime and Delinquency in Canada).*[16] These texts take both the social system and criminal justice system as given. Thus, in their terms, the criminologist's task is simply to describe how these systems work and, to a limited degree, evaluate the "effectiveness" of policies pursued in terms of the latter. Basic assumptions implicit in either of these systems are not to be questioned. The most recent example of this is *Criminal Justice in Canada: An Introductory Text* which is the first text in the area. Advertised as a non-ideological piece of work, its ideology can be gleaned from its commissions and omissions. It accepts the consensus correctionalist view of law and crime and fails to address issues of white-collar or organizational crime. It largely ignores the ethnic, class and ideological conflict surrounding crime and criminal justice, while applying a "systems approach" in a simplistic and mechanistic fashion.[17]

This same kind of unquestioning attitude is evident in the work of the Law Reform Commission of Canada. Goode, a law professor, notes the pervasive influence on the thinking of members of the commission of a dual ideology which combines "liberal positivism" with a "value consensus" model.[18] Thus, throughout the Commission's reports it is assumed that the vast majority of Canadians share common values and that the criminal law — both in theory and practice — reflects these common values. It follows from this that (a) "real crimes" are ones which violate our moral sensibilities, (b) the offenses designated in the Criminal Code violate our moral sensibilities, and that, therefore, (c) the Criminal Code reflects "real" crimes.[19]

Given these beliefs, it is instructive to see what harms are not included in the commission's definition of "real crime" as well as those that are. Regulatory offenses, for example, are not considered to be "real crimes," even though violation of some regulations may injure or kill people. A number of researchers have recently pointed out that the death of an employee due to the negligence of an employer, or the death of a consumer who has eaten contaminated food that was knowingly sold, fits our general understanding of what is meant by the term "murder."[20] Nevertheless, our legal system treats violence of this kind quite leniently. As one Canadian criminologist notes, if our laws and criminal justice agencies truly reflected public attitudes:

> There would be fewer unemployed alcoholics in jails, and fewer working class children in reform schools... There would be more car dealers, drug manufactuers and supermarket managers in prison or paying heavy fines.[21]

The new approach to thinking about crime which is reflected in this perspective will be discussed at some length in a later section of this article. At this juncture, however, suffice it to say that ideology appears to play an important role in determining what is deemed to be crime and, consequently, what criminologists study. There is abundant evidence that, until recently at least, Canadian criminologists have largely confined themselves to things conventionally treated as "crime" by the legal profession.

IDEOLOGY AND CRIME

It should not surprise us that ideology is a cornerstone of criminological thought. As Miller says

> [My]... major contention... is that ideology and its consequences exert a powerful influence on the policies and procedures of those who conduct the enterprise of criminal justice, and that the degree and kinds of influence go largely unrecognized. Ideology is the permanent hidden agenda of criminal justice.[22]

Like other academicians, most criminologists go about their work secure in a set of basic assumptions and premises under which they operate. Reasons observes that

> ... it is easy to immerse onself in doing criminology without understanding the influence of the historical and contemporary milieu upon one's perspective. Therefore, one might study offenders all his life without questioning how the specific behavioral acts become criminalized or the subsequent processing of such actors in the criminal justice system. In fact, this has been a major oversight of criminologists.[23]

There has been an increasing recognition of the role of ideology in science generally,[24] and specifically in criminology[25] in recent years. This is important to bear in mind because, since World War II, there have been at least two competing schools of criminology: the conventional or "consensus" school and what has come to be called the "conflict school." Chambliss presents the assumptions and principal conclusions of these two perspectives in the form of a diagram, as on page 159.

Here Chambliss contrasts "order" and "conflict" theories of crime. The order perspective contends that criminal law reflects the common good and controls criminals. By contrast, the conflict perspective sees ruling class interests as the source of criminal law and its purpose as the maintenance of class dominance. According to order theorists, criminal behavior is due to inadequate socialization and its principal effect is to establish moral boundaries. Conflict theorists see class divisions as the chief cause of criminal behavior and the reduction of class strains as its primary consequence.

Two Canadian criminologists have recently studied the extent to which these different perspectives are reflected in criminological writings in Canada, the United States, and the United Kingdom.[26] They concluded that conflict criminology is most evident in the U.S., less so in Canada, and least apparent in the U.K. The authors content that the emergence of the conflict perspective in Canada in recent years reflects ideological changes in Canadian society — such as the Québec liberation movement, the politicization of native or poor people, and other largely powerless groups.

In her book, *Ideological Perspectives in Canada,* Marchak argues that there are two versions of the Canadian reality:

> One of these describes Canada as a liberal democracy governed by representatives elected by a majority of adult citizens. The society is maintained by a stable and self-sufficient free-enterprise economy staffed by reasonably happy and affluent workers. The second describes Canada as a society ruled by a hereditary oligarchy and multinational imperialist corporations, maintained by a large and increasingly impoverished working class.[27]

The first of these versions of reality has been, as we have seen, the dominant one presented in Canadian studies of deviance and crime. However, the second is beginning to gain adherents.

TABLE 7-1
Order and Conflict Theories of Crime

	Criminal Law		Criminal Behaviour	
	Cause	Consequence	Cause	Consequence
Conflict Paradigm	Ruling class interests	Provide state coercive force to repress the class struggle and to legitimize the use of this force	Class divisions which lead to class struggle	Crime serves the interests of the ruling class by reducing strains inherent in the capitalist mode of production
Order Paradigm	Customary believes that are codified in state law	To establish procedures for controlling those who do not comply with customs	Inadequate socialization	To establish the moral boundaries of the community

*Adapted from Chambliss, 1974.

Whose Law? What Order?

In *Crime Control: The Urge Towards Authority* Tepperman explicitly acknowledges that his view of crime was shaped by the "new" criminology, by radical politics, and by phenomenology. This is clear at the outset: in the critical stance he adopts towards the larger social and historical factors shaping Canadian perspectives on crime, in his reference to a "vast machine" producing and then punishing deviance, and in his chapters on organized crime, public perceptions of criminality, and crime and social inequality. These clearly set his text apart from the mainstream of Canadian writing on crime and deviance. Yet even Tepperman fails to adequately treat the key issue which is at the center of the conflict school: the relationship between law and power.

Questioning the legal order is not prevalent in Canadian society. In fact, ready acceptance and even adulation for those in authority is far more common. How many countries in the world have a representative of their national police as their unofficial symbol? Of course, it could be argued that we should not question the law. Isn't it for all Canadians? Both rich and poor are prohibited from panhandling, being drunk in public, disturbing the peace, stealing clothes or food from stores, or sleeping in alleys, on park benches, on the steps of buildings or in suburban shopping malls.[28]

According to the Law Reform Commission of Canada:

> Our criminal law, like any decent law, aims towards humanity. The sort of things prohibited — acts of violence, dishonesty and so on — are acts violating common sense standards of humanity.[29]

I submit that real students of law should question such statements and not just blindly accept them. This is implicit in the approaches adopted by many practitioners in the relatively new sub-discipline referred to as the "sociology of law." As such, it is relatively rare in Canada.

The sociology of law movement is primarily a post-World War II phenomenon. It has spawned several journals and encouraged the study of the emergence of law, its operation, and changes in it. Most of the handful of Canadian studies in the sociology of law have been preoccupied with pointing out the differences between the stated aims and actual operation of the Canadian criminal justice system. Grossman's *Police Command* is an example of this kind of gap research since it goes beyond idealizations of the police to a more intense and empirically-based analysis of the administrative and organizational context in which police work takes place.[30] Hogarth's classic study of the Canadian court system, *Sentencing As a Human Process* — another study in this genre — provides some of the only theoretically acute and empirically supported insights we have into the actual operation of the Canadian judicial system. Waller's *Men Released From Prison* extends this kind of work to deal with the consequences of early release from prison.[31]

Beyond this we have several articles which attempt to assess the significance of larger factors such as race, ethnicity, social class, sex and age on the administration of Canadian justice. However, most are hampered by an atheoretical approach which does not allow them to place these variables in a meaningful socio-historical context. For example, a recent review of research on natives and the law in Canada notes that

> At present many criminologists working in this area seem to be bound hand and foot by a number of quantitative research techniques which, while they no doubt provide beneficial insights into the nature of decision-making, nevertheless threaten to stifle any reasonable sense of proportion. It is, by any standards, most disappointing that only one Canadian criminologist, Charles Reasons, has assumed the burden of constructing a broad theoretical framework which explicitly considers the socio-political dimensions of the relationship between native peoples and Canadian criminal justice.[32]

The framework Reasons[33] constructs is based on the distinction between consensus and conflict models and incorporates socio-political research and ethnic relations theory. Both methodologically and ideologically, it goes beyond the typical study of crime and race. Its critical analysis of dominant institutions is particularly important. The fact that many Canadian studies of crime are methodologically narrow and ideologically subject to liberal reformism has meant that few students have critically looked at the law and legal institutions in an historical and political way. One is hard pressed to find such research in Rosenberg's voluminous, *Canadian Criminology: An Annotated Bibliography.*[34]

While there have been several studies of police and policing in Canada, it remained for a journalist and a political scientist to write the first critical history of the R.C.M.P. In their *Unauthorized History of the RCMP,* Brown and Brown provide insights into the political functions performed by Canada's national police force *vis-a-vis* larger political and economic events.[35] Recent revelations by the McDonald Commission — and in recent writings such as Mann and Lee's *RCMP vs The People* and Shearing's *Organizational Police Deviance*[36] — are not surprising given this historical context. However, the nearly sacred status of the R.C.M.P. has meant that these revelations are usually taken to be "out of place" or "out of character" for this venerable institution.

THE STATE, CRIME AND LAW

As we noted earlier, there are few Canadian studies of the historical and official context in which law emerges. One notable exception is Greenaway and Brickey's *Law and Social Control in Canada.*[37] In the introduction, co-editor Brickey points out that the "critical perspective" adopted in the book differs in a number of ways from the functionalist "value consensus" approach toward law. It is rooted, he argues, in the writings of Marx, and as a result, takes the state and its operations as an important subject for criminological research. The book includes various articles which range from "reformist" to "radical" in tone. Topics include such issues as the origins and political uses of "constructive contempt" rules, rape laws, drug laws, prison laws, juvenile justice laws, Depression-Era unemployment "prisons," and the larger issue of legitimized repression under capitalism.

Another pioneering work in the Canadian sociology of law is McDonald's *The Sociology of Law and Order*.[38] It provides an excellent socio-historical analysis of the emergence and subsequent growth of the two principal paradigms in contemporary criminology and sociology: the consensus and conflict perspectives. It then goes on to a socio-political analysis of the intellectual basis of the law and order mentality.

In McDonald's earlier work she explored the conventional wisdom about crime in Canada. Here she tests propositions derived from these two bodies of theory using data from a range of nation-states. Using the structure of each nation-state as her independent variable, she empirically assesses a number of forms of conventional wisdom — such as the belief that increased literacy and wealth lead to a decrease in crime. McDonald concludes that, contrary to received wisdom,

> Successful development of the welfare state did not lead to a reduction in social problems and an eventual reduction of political crime rates. Rather, the expansion of the welfare state meant also the expansion of the infrastructure for formal control measures.[39]

This leads her into an extended discussion of the state's contributions to the growth of crime.

Goff and Reasons' *Corporate Crime in Canada* is one of the few Canadian case studies of the socio-historical foundations of a body of law: Canadian anti-combines or anti-trust legislation and its practical application within a political context. Besides providing one of the few critical, in-depth analysis of any area of Canadian law, *Corporate Crime in Canada* recognizes that a theory of the state is important to any understanding of how law works under specific historic and material conditions. Sections concerning "State Interests and the Study of Crime" and "State Interests and Anti-Combines Legislation," albeit brief, are initial attempts to address this significant issue. Goff and Reasons conclude that "laws are ineffective not only because of the government's lack of interest in pursuing corporate offenders, but also because they are incompatible with an efficient, growth-oriented, internationally competitive capitalism."[40]

In the *New Criminology,* the British authors argue that the task is broader still. Criminology, they contend, must be committed to social change:

> It should be clear that a criminology which is not normatively committed to the abolition of inequalities of wealth and power, and in particular, of inequalities in property and life-chances, is inevitably bound to fall into correctionalism.[41]

The development of a true political economy of crime in Canada is a necessary step towards understanding what role criminology, as a sub-discipline, might play in social change generally. Quinney has provided a Marxist analysis of the political economy of crime in the United States in his book *Class, State and Crime,* which gives us some indication as to how this could be done here. According to Quinney, the basic question in the Marxist analysis of crime is "What is the meaning of crime in the development of capitalism?" More importantly, what is the nature and development of law under capitalism? How do successive stages in the development of an economic base under capitalism set the stage for the creation of certain bodies of law? How do changes in the relations of production effect class relations? And, most importantly, how do legal relations between classes reflect patterns of class domination?

In *Law and the Rise of Capitalism,* Tigar and Levy,[42] provide an incisive analysis of the emergence of law and legal ideology as a concommitant of the rise of the bourgeoisie to power. After this rise, lawyers and legal training become particularly important in all Western governmental structures. By comparison, there is much less reliance on formal written law in the People's Republic of China and many other socialist countries than in the United States.[43]

Comparative analyses of capitalist and socialist societies need to be undertaken when studying the role played by the state in the emergence and development of Canadian law and crime. For example, a study of legislation on corporate competition in four western capitalist nation-states discovered both ideological and operational similarities and differences.[44]

Recently, a Canadian and American criminologist have combined to provide a collection of cross-national readings from the conflict perspective, *The Sociology of Law: A Conflict Perspective.*[45] Their book seeks to develop a "cross-national analysis of the socio-political basis of law in various ideological settings" through articles about law and legal practice in both capitalist and socialist nation-states.

The importance of studying state ideology is brought home in a recent article, "Ideological Changes and the Legal Structure: A Discussion of Socialist Experience" where the author concludes that

> since in the long run, economic reality puts up barriers to prevent legal regulation from being effective, the study of socio-economic reality, of specific class interests, and of the mechanisms that are effective in the relationship between ideology and legal regulation, is extraordinarily important. This is even more the case when the problem is that of social reconstruction and planning, and the use of 'the law' to expedite social change.[46]

There are recent indications that the basis is being established for the development of the type of general political economy of Canada we need as a backdrop for the creation of a political economy of law and crime. Panitch maintains that this is due, in part, to the increased role of the state in post-World II capitalism, the failure of elected government to effect substantial change, industrial class conflict such as strikes, increased understanding of how Canadian democracy exists under American hegemony, and finally the failure of the concepts and theories of political science to address and explain many contemporary political questions.[47] Panitch further argues that a fully developed theory of the state in capitalist society must specify the various institutions that make up the state, show the linkages between the state and class inequality, and point out the functions of the state under the capitalist mode of production. The central task, Panitch explains, is to explore the nature and forms of legitimation used by the state in maintaining "social order."

> Legitimation is being used here not in the sense of state propaganda or statements by politicians that seek to rationalize capital accumulation in terms of its benefits for the whole community, but rather in the sense of concrete state activities such as welfare measures, anti-combines legislation, redistributive taxation, union protection, and governmental consultation with labour representatives. We are speaking of policies directed at the integration of the subordinate classes in capitalist society either through the introduction of reforms which promote social harmony or through the co-optation of working-class leaders via tripartite consultations with government and business — giving them the semblance of power without the substance — so as to employ them as agencies of social control over their members.[48]

CRIMES OF DOMINATION

A good way to begin this task is by assessing the nature and magnitude of harms committed by the upper classes against society. While there is a fairly well-established tradition of research on white collar crime in the United States,[49] there are few studies in Canada.[50]

Criminologists traditionally refer to upperworld crime or crime at the top as "white-collar crime," that is, crime committed for personal gain by a person in a position of trust. Much of this literature has emphasized individuals and their needs, goals, attitudes, and behavior. This traditional approach to the study of white-collar crime, however, ignores the ever increasing significance of organizations in our daily lives: it fails to adequately consider the physical harms which arise as a consequence of organizational offenses and does not deal with the special characteristics of illegal behavior in organizational settings:

> Organization crimes are illegal acts of omission or commission of an individual or a group of individuals in a legitimate formal organization in accordance with the operative goals of the organization, which have serious physical or economic impact on employees, consumers or the general public.[51]

By distinguishing between traditional white collar and organizational crimes, we recognize the daily impact which private and public organizations have upon our lives as workers, consumers and members of the general public. In this fashion, the behavior of individuals is placed within the context of the organization. For example, while the employee who embezzles from the employer is guilty of a white-collar offense, the same

TABLE 7-2

Organizational Crimes: A Typology

Victim	Nature of Offense		
	Economic	Human Rights	Violent
Employee	Failing to remit payroll deductions, pension fund abuse, violating minimum wage laws and other labor laws.	Restrictions on political activity, dress and demeanor, union activity, public disclosure, e.g., Ellsberg and Pentagon papers.	Deaths and injuries in workplace, industrial disease, e.g., asbestos.
Consumer	Price fixing, monopolization, false advertising	Misuse of credit information, restrictions on credit based on political, sexual, racial & class bias.	Poor inspection, unsafe products, case, e.g., Ford Pinto thalidomide
Public	Bribery, misuse of public funds, cost overruns, oil spills.	Illegal surveillance, wiretaps, abuse of power by police, CIA, FBI, RCMP, military, e.g., Watergate.	Police homicides, hazardous wastes, air and water pollutions, nuclear energy, e.g., Three Mile Island.

employee may be involved in price fixing or misleading advertising as part of the policies, practices and/or procedures of the organization. In the latter offenses, the white-collar offender is carrying out organizational goals. Such a distinction forces one to think about making organizations changes or controlling organizational behavior rather than attempting to redress simple individual actions. For example, sanctioning a police officer for illegal entry or illegal mail opening may not, by itself, provide a remedy for the practice if the organizational goals and practices of the police system reinforce such behavior.

As the distinction between white-collar and organizational crime emerged,[52] varying types of organizational offenses have been noted. Schrager and Short[53] identify three types of victims of organizational behavior based upon their relationship to the production of goods and services: (1) employees, (2) consumers, and (3) the general public. I have divided organizational offenses into three categories: (1) economic crimes, (2) human rights crimes, and (3) violent personal injury crimes.[54] Combining both victims' characteristics and the nature of the offense yields a conceptual typology for categorizing organizational crimes.[55]

VIOLENT PERSONAL INJURY CRIMES: AN EXAMPLE

While there is obvious physical danger and harm from some "street crimes" — such as murder and assault — the belief that organizations' crimes are not violent is false. For example, Ford Motor Company has lost several civil suits and was under indictment in Indiana for reckless homicide and criminal recklessness as a result of the design of the Pinto's fuel tanks. More specifically, court testimony revealed that Ford's corporate officers calculated that the costs of changing unsafe gas tanks were nearly three times the expected costs of suits arising due to deaths and injuries which might be sustained by the public.[56] The following chart is based on a Ford internal memo of 1972 which calculated *benefits* which would accrue from not making changes to their Pinto gas tanks compared to the costs of making such changes. It was obviously cheaper to continue to build an unsafe automobile. Further, it has recently been revealed that over the last two decades Ford Motor Company has sold 26 million vehicles with defects in their automatic transmission causing at least 70 deaths, 1100 injuries and 3700 accidents. A design improvement costing about three cents per car would have prevented most of the carnage.[57]

Thus, the policies and practices of the organization patently put profit ahead of saving of the lives of consumers. Another example is the 1976 fire in Hamilton's Wentworth Arms Hotel which killed six people. Subsequent investigation disclosed some 30 safety violations, including the Hotel's procedure of turning off the fire alarm at night to prevent false alarms. An internationally known student of white-collar crime states that "commercial

TABLE 7-3

Profit Over Life

Benefits	Savings:	180 burn deaths, 180 serious burn injuries, 2,100 burned vehicles
	Unit Cost:	$200,000 per death, $67,000 per injury, $700 per vehicle
	Total Benefit:	180 x (200,000) + 180 x (67,000) + 2100 ($700) = $49.5 million
Costs	Sales:	11 million cars, 1.5 million light trucks
	Unit Cost:	$11 per car, $11 per truck
	Total Cost:	$11,000,000 x ($11) + 1,500,000 x ($11) = $137 million

Source: The *Sunday London Times,* February 12, 1978, p. 1.

fraud kills more people than are murdered by acts that come to be listed as criminal homicide in the U.S. and drug companies among others have falsified test results in order to market unsafe products.''[58] Cosmetics, oral contraceptives, synthetic hormones, microwave ovens, childrens' sleepwear, pesticides, cleaning solutions and solvents, and X-rays, among numerous other consumer goods, have been found to be unsafe and poorly regulated and/or marketed.[59] Whether it be in manufactured products, services, or accommodations, violence against the consumer may be the result of an organizations's policies and practices.

The general public has been subjected to a variety of physical harms, principally through pollution, hazardous substances and maintenance of unsafe structures. There are numerous substances illegally emitted into the air and potentially hazardous, if not lethal.[60] Methylmercury is a dangerous by-product of industrial pollution which results in cerebral and visual pathway damage.[61] For example, mercury poisoning from the Dryden Chemical plant in Northwestern Ontario is evident in the native population.[62] Arsenic poisoning of the general population of Yellowknife, Northwest Territories is largely the consequence of two gold mining operations.[63] The U.S. military not only sprayed more than 10 million gallons of Agent Orange — containing dioxin, "one of the world's deadliest chemicals"[64] — on the "enemy" in Vietnam, but also on its own soldiers. The U.S. Army also sprayed Winnipeg some 36 times in 1953 as part of a chemical warfare experiment. Although the substance might have been dangerous to babies and, clearly, the ill or asthmatic, after 27 years there is no effective legal recourse.[65] Nader states, "much more is lost in money and health through pollution than crimes of violence, yet only the latter is defined officially as violence."

Workers are daily assaulted on the job through unsafe working conditions and unhealthy chemicals. Occupational hazards are the third leading cause of death behind heart disease and cancer.[66] Many of these deaths are preventable through control of the environmental level of dangerous substances. Lloyd Tataryn's book, *Dying for a Living: The Politics of Industrial Death,* documents the massive coverup by the asbestos industry, since the 1930s, of its knowledge of the hazardous effects of asbestos. While this may well become the subject of civil suits, criminal action is not possible despite the premeditated and violent nature of the actions involved.

Apart from any moral argument, it is possible that current criminal law may be relevant here. Glasbeek and Rowland[67] make a case for the application of criminal negligence, duties of master to servant, assault, criminal breach of contract, traps likely to cause bodily harm, causing mischief, common nuisance, conspiracy and murder sections of the Canadian Criminal Code to these kind of violations of health and safety laws.

CONCLUSION

The study of crime and deviance in Canada has a long way to go before it sheds its provincial and parochial orientation. Rather than looking south or overseas for discarded or outmoded theories and understandings to apply to deviants, Canadian students of crime and deviance should be drawing from emerging studies concerning critical theories of the state and political economies of crime and deviance. Then it is a matter of applying such notions to the historically specific and politically particular areas of Canadian society that deserve study.[68]

NOTES

[1]Greenaway, 1980: 262.
[2]Prus and Irini, 1980: 1.
[3]Prus and Sharper, 1977.
[4]Letkemann, 1973.
[5]Clairmont, 1974.
[6]Cook, 1969.
[7]Haas and Shaffir, 1974.
[8]E.g., Boydell, Grindstaff, and Whitehead, 1972; Vaz,, 1976.
[9]Sociologists use the term "labelling" to refer to the process or processes through

which groups of individuals come to be socially designated as "deviant." See Howard S. Becker, 1963.

[10]Hagan, 1977: 1.

[11]Beirne, 1979.

[12]Hackler, 1979: 199.

[13]Gallaher and McCartney, 1973: 80.

[14]Reasons, 1976; Chan and Ericson, 1981; Hylton, 1981.

[15]McGrath, 1976.

[16]Kirkpatrick and McGrath, 1976; Silverman and Teevan, 1975; Vaz and Lodhi, 1979.

[17]Klein, Griffith and Verdun-Jones, 1980.

[18]Goode, 1976. See also Parker, 1983.

[19]Law Reform Commission of Canada, 1976.

[20]Schrager and Short, 1980.

[21]McDonald, 1976: 233.

[22]Miller, 1974: 20.

[23]Reasons, 1974: 6.

[24]Kuhn, 1970.

[25]Reasons, 1975.

[26]Bloom and Reasons, 1978. More specifically, they established empirical measures of the use of these theories in professional articles appearing in selected journals in each of these countries from 1945 to 1974.

[27]Marchak, 1975: viii.

[28]Anatole France: "The law in its divine majesty prohibits equally the rich man and poor man from sleeping under bridges or begging bread in the streets." *The Red Lily*.

[29]Law Reform Commission of Canada, 1976: 7.

[30]See White, this volume, for a discussion of policemen as an occupational group.

[31]Waller, 1974.

[32]Verdun-Jones and Muirhead, 1979-80: 18.

[33]Reasons, 1977.

[34]Rosenberg, 1977.

[35]Brown and Brown, 1975.

[36]Mann and Lee, 1979; Shearing, 1981.

[37]Greenaway and Brickey, 1978.

[38]McDonald, 1976.

[39]McDonald, 1976: 189.

[40]Goff and Reasons, 1978: 132.

[41]Taylor, Walton, and Young, 1973: 281.

[42]Tigar and Levy, 1977.

[43]Pepinsky, 1975.

[44]Reasons and Goff, 1980.

[45]Reasons and Rich, 1978.

[46]Kulcsar, 1980: 80.

[47]Panitch, 1977: viii.

[48]Panitch, 1977: 19.

[49]Geis and Stotland, 1980; Clinard and Yeager, 1980.
[50]Goff and Reasons, 1978; Snider, 1978; La Prairie, 1979; Reasons, 1981.
[51]Schrager and Short, 1978: 411-12.
[52]Gross, 1978, 1980.
[53]1978.
[54]Reasons, 1981; Reasons and Perdue, 1981.
[55]Reasons, 1982.
[56]Jacobson and Barnes, 1978; Ford, 1978.
[57]Branan, 1980.
[58]McCaghy, 1976: 213-14.
[59]The Environmental Defense Fund, 1980.
[60]The Environment Defense Fund, 1980.
[61]Pierce, 1972.
[62]Singer and Rodgers, 1975.
[63]Tataryn, 1979.
[64]Winnipeg, 1980.
[65]Winnipeg, 1980.
[66]Reasons, Paterson and Ross, 1981.
[67]Glassbeek and Rowland, 1979.
[68]A recent plea for such analysis is found in McMullen and Ratner, 1982.

Bibliography

Becker, Howard S. *Outsiders: Studies in the Sociology of Deviance.* New York: Free Press, 1963.
Beirne, Piers. "Empiricism and the Critique of Marxism on Law and Crime." *Social Problems* 26 (1979): 373-85.
Bloom, Dianna M. and Charles E. Reasons. "Ideology and Crime: A Study In the Sociology of Knowledge." *International Journal of Criminology and Penology* 6 (1978): 19-30.
Boydell, Craig L., Paul C. Whitehead and Carl F. Grindstaff. *The Administration of Criminal Justice in Canada.* Toronto: Holt, Rinehart and Winston of Canada, 1974.
Branan, Karen. "Killer Reverse Roams the Highways, Victim Warns." *The Calgary Herald* (August 7, 1980): El.
Brown, Lorne and Caroline Brown. *An Unauthorized History of the RCMP.* Toronto: James Lorimer and Company, 1975.
Buckner, H. Taylor. *Deviance, Reality and Change.* Toronto: Random House, 1971.
Chambliss, William. *Functional and Conflict Theories in Crime.* New York: MSS Modular Publications, 1974.
Chan, Janet B. L. and Richard V. Ericson. *Decarceration and the Economy of Penal Reform.* Toronto: Centre for Criminology, University of Toronto, 1981.
Clairmont, Donald. "The Development of a Deviance Service Centre." In Jack

Haas and Bill Shaffir, eds. *Decency and Deviance.* Toronto: McClelland and Stewart, 1974.

Clinard, Marshall B. and Peter C. Yeager. *Corporate Crime.* New York: The Free Press, 1980.

Cook, S. J. "Canadian Narcotics Legislation, 1908-1923: A Conflict Model Interpretation." *Canadian Review of Sociology and Anthropology* 6 (1969): 36-46.

Environmental Defense Fund and R. H. Boyle. *Malignant Neglect.* New York: Vintage Books, 1980.

Ermann, M. D. and R. J. Lundman. *Corporate and Governmental Deviance: Problems of Organizational Behavior in Contemporary Society.* New York: Oxford University Press, 1978.

Filiatreau, J. "Ford is Indicted On Criminal Counts Over Pinto Deaths." *Globe and Mail* (September 14, 1978): A1, 6.

Gallaher, J. F. and J. L. McCartney. "The Influence of Funding Agencies on Juvenile Delinquency Research." *Social Problems* 21 (1973): 77-90.

Geis, Gilbert. "Victimization Patterns in White Collar Crime." In I. Drapkin and E. Viana, eds. *Victimology: A New Focus, Volume V: Exploiters and Exploited: The Dynamics of Victimization.* Lexington, Ma.: Lexington Books, 1975.

Geis, Gilbert and Ezra Stotland. *White-Collar Crime: Theory and Research.* Beverly Hills: Sage Publications, 1980.

Glasbeek, H. J. and S. Rowland. "Are Injuring and Killing At Work Crimes?" *Osgoode Hall Law Journal* 17 (1979): 507-94.

Goode, M. R. "Law Reform Commission of Canada — Political Ideology of Criminal Process Reform." *The Canadian Bar Review* 54 (1976): 653-74.

Goff, C. H. and C. E. Reasons. "Corporations in Canada: A Study of Crime and Punishment." *Criminal Law Quarterly* 18 (1976): 468-98.

Goff, C. and C. Reasons. *Cororate Crime in Canada.* Scarborough: Prentice Hall, 1978.

Greenaway, W. K. "Crime and Class: Unequal Before the Law." In John Harp and John R. Hofler, eds. *Structured Inequality in Canada.* Scarborough: Prentice Hall of Canada, 1980.

Greenaway, W. K. and S. L. Brickey. *Law and Social Control in Canada.* Scarborough: Prentice Hall of Canada, 1978.

Gross, E. "Organizational Crime: A Theoretical Perspective." In N. Denzin ed. *Studies in Symbolic Interaction* 1 (1978): 8.

_____. "Organizational Structure and Organizational Crime." In G. Geis and E. Stotland, eds. *White Collar Crime: Theory and Research.* Beverly Hills: Sage Publications, 1980.

Grossman, Brian A. *Police Command.* Toronto: Macmillan, 1975.

Haas, Jack and Bill Shaffir. *Decency and Deviance.* Toronto: McClelland and Stewart, 1974.

Hackler, James C. *The Prevention of Youthful Crime: The Great Stumble Forward.* Toronto: Methuen Publications, 1978.

_____. "The Commercialization of Criminological Research in Canada." *Canadian Journal of Criminology* 21 (1979): 197-99.

Hagan, John. *The Disreputable Pleasures.* Toronto: McGraw-Hill Ryerson, 1977.

_____. "Deviance." In Robert Hagedorn, ed. *Sociology.* Toronto: Holt, Rinehart and Winston of Canada, 1980.

Hogarth, John. *Sentencing As A Human Process.* Toronto: University of Toronto Press, 1971.

Hylton, John. "The Growth of Punishment: Imprisonment and Community Corrections in Canada." *Crime and Social Justice* 15 (1981): 18-28.

Jacobson, P. and J. Barnes. "66m in Damages: The Car That Carried Death in the

Boot." *The Sunday Times* (February 12, 1978): 4.

Johnson, J. M. and J. D. Douglas. *Crime At The Top: Deviance in Business and the Professions.* Philadelphia: J. B. Lippincott Co., 1978.

Kirkpatrick, A. M. and W. T. McGrath. *Crime and You.* Toronto: Macmillan, 1976.

Klein, J., C. Griffith and S. Verdun-Jones. *Criminal Justice in Canada: An Introductory Text.* Vancouver: Butterworth and Co (Western Canada), 1980.

Kuhn, T. S. *The Structure of Scientific Revolutions.* Chicago: University of Chicago Press, 1970.

Kulscar, Kalman. "Ideological Changes and the Legal Structure: A Discussion of Socialist Experience." *International Journal of the Sociology of Law* 8 (1980): 61-81.

LaPrairie, Carol Pitcher. "The Development of Sanctions for Market Manipulations in Ontario." *Canadian Journal of Criminology* 21 (1979): 275-292.

Law Reform Commission of Canada. *Our Criminal Law.* Ottawa: Information Canada, 1976.

Letkemann, Peter. *Crime as Work.* Englewood Cliffs: Prentice-Hall, 1973.

Liazos, A. "The Poverty of the Sociology of Deviance: Nuts, Sluts and Perverts." *Social Problems* 20 (1972): 103-120.

Mann, Edward and John Alan Lee. *RCMP vs The People.* Don Mills, Ontario: General Publishing Co., 1979.

Marchak, Patricia. *Ideological Perspectives on Canada.* Toronto: McGraw-Hill Ryerson Ltd., 1975.

McCaghy, C. H. *Deviant Behavior.* New York: Macmillan Publishing Co., 1976.

McDonald, Lynn. *The Sociology of Law and Order.* Montreal: Book Center, 1976.

McGrath, W. T. *Crime and Its Treatment in Canada.* Toronto: Macmillan, 1975.

McMullen, John L. and R. S. Ratner. "Radical versus Technocratic Analyses In The Study of Crime: Critique of Criminal Justice in Canada." *Canadian Journal of Criminology* 24 (1982): 483-94.

Miller, Walter B. "Ideology and Criminal Justice Policy: Some Current Issues." In Charles E. Reasons, ed. *The Criminologist: Crime and the Criminal.* Pacific Palisades, California: Goodyear Publishing Co., 1974.

Panitch, Leo. *The Canadian State: Political Economy and Political Power.* Toronto: University of Toronto Press, 1977.

Parker, Graham. *An Introduction to Criminal Law.* Toronto: Methuen, 1983.

Pearce, F. *Crimes of the Powerful: Marxism, Crime and Deviance.* London: Pluto Press, 1976.

Pepinsky, Harold E. "Reliance on Formal Written Law, and Freedom and Social Control in the United States and the People's Republic of China." *The British Journal of Sociology* 26 (1975): 330-42.

Pierce, R. E. "Aklyl Mercury Poisoning in Humans: Report of an Outbreak." *Journal of American Medical Association* 220 (1972): 1439-42.

Prus, Robert and C. R. D. Sharper. *Road Hustler.* Toronto: Gage Publishing, 1979.

Prus, Robert and Styllianoss Irini. *Hookers, Rounders and Desk Clerks.* Toronto: Gage Publishing, 1980.

Quinney, R. *Class, State and Crime.* New York: David McKay Company, Inc., 1977.

_____. *Criminology.* 2nd ed. Boston: Little, Brown and Co., 1979.

Reasons, Charles E. *The Criminologist: Crime and the Criminal.* Pacific Palisades, California: Goodyear Publishing Company, 1974.

_____. "Social Thought and Social Structure: Competing Paradigms in Criminology." *Criminology* 13 (1975): 332-65.

_____. "Toward Community Based Corrections." *Crime and/et Justice* 4 (1976): 108-114.

_____. "Native Offenders and Correctional Policy." *Crime and/et Justice* 5 (1977):

255-66.

_____. "Crime and the Abuse of Power: Offences and Offenders Beyond the Reach of the Law." In Peter Wickman and Timothy Darley, eds. *White-Collar and Economic Crime*. Lexington, Mass.: Lexington Books, 1981a.

_____. "Organizational Crime." In M. Rosenberg, R. Stebbins, and A. Turowetz, eds. *The Sociology of Deviance.*, New York: St. Martins Press, 1982.

Reasons, Charles E. and Colin H. Goff. "Corporate Crime: A Cross-National Analysis." In Gilbert Geis and Ezra Stotland, eds. *White-Collar Crime: Theory and Research*. Beverly Hills: Sage Publications, 1980.

Reasons, Charles E., Craig Paterson and Lois Ross. *Assault on the Worker: Occupational Health and Safety in Canada*. Toronto: Butterworths, 1981.

Reasons, Charles E. and Robert M. Rich. *The Sociology of Law: A Conflict Perspective*. Toronto: Butterworths, 1978.

Reasons, Charles E. and William Perdue. *The Ideology of Social Problems*. Palo Alto, Calif.: Alfred Mayfield, 1981.

Reiman, J. H. *The Rich Get Richer and the Poor Get Prison*. New York: John Wiley and Sons, 1979.

Richards, John and Larry Pratt. *Prairie Capitalism: Power and Influence in the New West*. Toronto: McClelland and Stewart, 1979.

Rosenberg, Gertrude. *Canadian Criminology: Annotated Bibliography*. Ottawa: Solicitor General of Canada, 1977.

Schrager, L. S. and J. F. Short, Jr. "Towards a Sociology of Organizational Crime." *Social Problems* (June 1978): 407-19.

_____. "How Serious a Crime? Perceptions of Organizational and Common Crimes." In G. Geis and E. Stotland, eds. *White Collar Crime: Theory and Research*. Beverly Hills: Sage Publications, 1980.

Schwendinger, H. and J. Schwendinger. "Defenders of Order or Guardians of Human Rights?" *Issues in Criminology* 5 (1970): 123-57.

_____. "Social Class and the Definition of Crime." *Crime and Social Justice* 7 (1977): 4-14.

Shearing, C. D. *Organizational Police Deviance*. Toronto: Butterworths, 1981.

Silverman, Robert A. and James J. Teevan. *Crime in Canadian Society* Toronto: Butterworths, 1975.

Singer, C. and B. Rodgers. "Mercury: The Hidden Poison in the Northern Rivers." *Saturday Night* (October, 1975): 15-22.

Snider, D. L. "Corporate Crime in Canada: A Preliminary Report." *Canadian Journal of Criminology* 20 (1978): 142-68.

Tataryn, L. *Dying for a Living*. Deaneau and Greenberg Publishers, 1979.

_____. "Winnipeg Sprayed 36 Times." *The Calgary Herald* (May, 16, 1980): A9.

Taylor, Ian, Paul Walton and Jack Young. *The New Criminology: For a Social Theory of Deviance*. New York: Harper and Row, 1973.

Tepperman, Lorne. *Crime Control*. Toronto: McGraw-Hill Ryerson, 1977.

Tigar, Michael E. and Madeleine R. Levy. *Law and the Rise of Capitalism,* New York: Monthly Review Press, 1977.

Vaz, Edmund W. *Aspects of Deviance*. Scarborough: Prentice-Hall, 1976.

Vaz, Edmund W. and Abdul Q. Lodhi. *Crime and Delinquency In Canada*. Scarborough: Prentice-Hall, 1979.

Verdun-Jones, Simon N. and Gregory K. Muirhead. "Natives in the Canadian Criminal Justice System: An Overview." *Crime et/and Justice* 78 (1979-80): 3-21.

Waller, Irvin. *Men Released From Prison*. Toronto: University of Toronto Press, 1974.

CHAPTER 8

Industrial, Work, and Organizational Sociology in Canada

Terrence H. White

INTRODUCTION

Few changes affect a society as dramatically as industrialization. This shift from agriculture or mercantile trade and small, individualized craft production to the mass production of industrial goods has significant impacts on most aspects of societies. Urbanization increases as rural populations uproot in search of work and crowd into locations around factories. A wide variety of social problems accompanies increasing population densities. Traditional institutions and value patterns experience strains and stresses as the nature and meaning of work alters with the transition to narrower, more specialized, responsibility-diluted jobs.

These developments are among the central concerns of industrial sociologists in their research and theorizing. As industrial development becomes more established, however, these same sociologists are likely to narrow their interests to the operations of specific worksites, to examine the relationships between work and other facets of people's lives, or to study specific occupations and professions. Some researchers may become especially concerned with the nature and operations of the organizations in which people work. This tradition of industrial or organizational research has had a long history in sociology, and Canadian researchers have been actively involved in exploring these questions, particularly as they relate to industrialization and work.

This chapter is an overview of Canadian sociological research on industrialization, work, and organizations. This review will not be able to deal with all facets of these issues. Instead, it will attempt to provide a sense of the variety of interests involved and to assess the strengths, weaknesses, and omissions of these efforts so far.

INDUSTRIALIZATION

Industrialization, as we have suggested, involves a fundamental shift from methods of production based on human energy to greater and greater reliance on machines in factory settings. Only a few sociologists have written broad descriptive analyses of industrial development in Canada. Rinehart, for instance, uses a social historical perspective to assess the pre-industrial period and the circumstances underlying the gradual emergence of an industrial system.[1] One consequence of the rural nature of Canadian society in the mid-1800s with its basic division of labor, he suggests, "was simply that a greater proportion of people in pre-industrial Canada exercised control over the means and ends of production than is the case in modern society." Consistent with this, "the way people worked and the way they defined work were quite different from what prevails in Canadian society today."[2]

Toward the end of the 1800s, industrialization was increasingly evident in central Canada. Manufacturing establishments proliferated. Conditions in many of these early factories were grim with six 12-hour days as the usual workweek, little concern for safety measures, child labor, and numerous other differences from what is considered normal today. Discipline was often severe, with work rules "forbidding talking, leaving one's work-station, lateness, absenteeism, laxness, and spoilage. Rules were enforced through fines, dismissals, and physical coercion."[3]

In a more detailed analysis, Smucker[4] looks at a number of facets of industrialization and provides particular insights into the sources of the rise of foreign ownership as a feature of Canadian industrial life. He shows that the particular interests of elites — as well as government actions, such as tariffs — affected the patterns assumed by industrial development in Canada. John A. Macdonald's National Policy (1879), for instance, instituted protective tariffs to assure revenue for the east-west routes of the railroads and to stimulate industrialization. But, as an unanticipated consequence:

> all analysts agree that the tariffs set the stage for a 'branch plant' economy, as foreign producers set up their own plants in Canada in order to escape the mandatory costs imposed by the tariffs. There was little attempt to control the ownership of these enterprises. The only concern seemed to be the unification of the Canadian economy in the interests of elites who were following a course of 'finance' capitalism rather than 'industrial' capitalism.[5]

While Smucker and others have laid the groundwork for examining this kind of broad historical pattern, there are still a variety of relatively untouched and fruitful areas for sociological research into the overall form assumed by industrialization in Canada. Such analyses would be enriched by social historical descriptions of the impacts these changes had on individuals and on social institutions — that is, the human costs of the early factory system.[6]

Québec

Despite the relative dearth of general analyses of industrialization in Canada, there have been a large number of studies of specific industries and regional aspects of industrialism. Many of the earliest efforts were focused on Québec. Hughes,[7] in contrast with earlier studies of Québec rural villages unaffected by industrialization and urbanization,[8] looks at a village in a well-settled farming area that was being transformed into a major textile manufacturing center. The establishment of large industries in this region, and their control by English-speaking entrepreneurs disturbed almost every institution and tradition in the community. Summarizing his impressions, Hughes says:

> French-Canadians are in the course of making their adjustments to the latest and, thus far, the most revolutionary of changes set going in their midst by their English compatriots. For unlike the military conquest of the eighteenth century and certain commercial invasions of the past, the industrial revolution of the present moves masses of people from country to city, upsets the equilibrium of the classes, strikes at the very content and aims of education, and threatens a way of life that has, in the past, given comfort and deep satisfaction to its followers.

This, and other studies of small town and rural Québec,[9] provide graphic illustrations of the profound impacts of industrialization on individuals and the organizations with which they are connected.

Not all the consequences of industrialization, of course, were negative. Although many observers viewed such developments as threats to the French-Canadian way of life, over time it became apparent that there were ironic benefits that even helped in preserving cultural patterns. As Taylor[10] observed, a system of land tenure where only one son takes over the farm (primogeniture) leaves other family members with few options but to immigrate — in Québec, to the New England states or other parts of Canada. But the population outflow resulting from this rather narrow option "dwindled to almost nothing early in the twentieth century when industrialization itself began to offer the means of absorption and so helped stabilize the rural system of succession."[11]

It appears that the relatively low initial rate of growth in industrialization in Québec was not directly related to its cultural environment, but "was a mere regional manifestation of the overall economic evolution of the North American Continent."[12] French-speaking Quebecers, however, played only a slight role in the direction and management of early manufacturing in the region. Taylor's research suggests that Québec's highly traditional and family-based culture created little interest in, and low levels of aptitude and preparation for, entrepreneurial positions in manufacturing. His comparative studies of English and French-speaking entrepreneurs reveal that

A typical French-Canadian industrial entrepreneur is likely to be educated at a somewhat lower level, with a different orientation from that of his English-speaking counterpart; that he is less concerned with growth and more insistent on the exclusive nature of his ownership and control; and that he shows a lesser readiness to use a simple business calculus in ordering his business behavior... In short, by tradition, temperament, and training, he clings to a different world of business from that which predominates in North American society.[13]

As a result, since the 1930s numerous studies "have shown the privileged position which the English-speaking population enjoys in Québec and the unfavourable status of French Canadians."[14] Combined with the use of English as the technical, business and industrial language in Québec, this pattern put French speakers at a competitive disadvantage in career advancement.[15] As the "silent revolution" — educational reform, institutional and value changes — progressed, the nature of work-life in Québec took on a unique dual character. According to Guindon, "language has been working as a sorting device in the allocation of people in English and French workplaces. The institutions dependent on the provincial state became French workplaces and the corporate world remained an English workplace."[16]

Other Impacts

Sociologists observe that an important pre-condition to successful industrialization is that a given host society have a favorable value-set. Max Weber and others have argued that the values associated with the "Protestant Ethic" provide a fertile ground in which industrialism can develop. According to this perspective, "a man's vocation is considered to be a divine calling, the virtues of thrift, honesty, hard work and ambition are thought to be proofs of salvation, and prosperity [is] welcomed fondly as a mark of providential favours."[17]

Crysdale sees four stages in the evolving values espoused by Canadian Protestant churches. Before 1900, with industrialization in its infancy, the Protestant ethic and *laissez-faire* economics were the model. Next, in the first two decades of the 1900s, the churches favored socialism, with the view that only the state could ensure an equitable distribution of economic gains. The period from the end of World War I to the end of World War II saw a shift away from individualism toward a crusade for state intervention in the poverty and disarray of the Depression. The last phase dates from the mid-1940s: "Realism has tended to replace idealism, and the churches now for the most part appear willing to settle, somewhat uneasily, for proximate justice in the imperfect orders of the day. 'Interim' ethics is favoured as against absolute moralism."[18]

Other studies have examined specific impacts of industrialization on communities and regions.[19] Although industrialism has been with us for over a century, there are still areas that are just now experiencing it, while others are already going through de-industrialization. Little has yet been published, but sociologists are currently examining the social impacts of industrial development in Canada's boom areas — such as Fort McMurray and Cold Lake, Alberta. Studies like these should provide valuable insights into the complexities involved in dealing with large influxes of people and providing them with necessary social and physical facilities.

OCCUPATIONS AND PROFESSIONS

Another long-established focus of Canadian industrial and organizational sociology has been the study of occupations and professions.

Occupations

Vincent, for instance, in describing his participant observation study of police constables in a middle-sized city,[20] vividly describes how the routine nature of much police work is punctuated by moments of danger. He argues that this, coupled with the necessity for dealing with a sometimes unsympathetic or unappreciative public, binds policemen together into a tightly knit occupational community. The additional fact that policemen must comprehend complex laws and exercise split-second judgments, he concludes, creates circumstances that often lead to stress and result in such personal difficulties as addiction problems, family or marital strains, and so on.[21]

Studies of lumberjacks in Québec by Fortin and Gosselin and Tremblay have been described by Rocher "as the first milestone of industrial sociology in French Canada."[22] Their research shows how technological change transformed part-time farmers into full-time lumberjacks. They attribute the considerable dissatisfaction among members of this newly evolved occupation to the rigidity of the formal structures of lumbering enterprises, as well as to frustrations stemming from conflicting demands of work and families.

White[23] describes another evolving occupation: oil scouts in the petroleum industry. These industrial spies provide their employers with information about the activities of competing firms. When exploration was limited to a few small geographic regions, scouts could obtain information from farmers or skulk on the perimeter of drill sites gathering clues as to the nature and success of competitors' ventures. But now it is impossible to obtain comprehensive information except through cooperation. The way in which competitors cooperate, while maintaining their own company's interests, provides insights into the effect of changing structural circumstances on occupational roles.

Other researchers have compared Canadians to members of similar occupations in other countries. Mills,[24] for example, has done research on
chiropractors in Canada and the United States. Measures of their service
orientation and theoretical knowledge suggested that, in general, Canadian
chiropractors "tended to be more professionally oriented."[25]

Other occupations which have been studied in this way include
businessmen;[26] professors;[27] real estate agents;[28] managers;[29] scientists;[30]
social workers;[31] advertising personnel;[32] miners;[33] and nurses.[34]

Professions

Professions, the 'elite' occupations, are distinguished by the fact that
(a) entry into them is limited through rigorous recruitment standards; (b)
they involve specialized, normally university-based, training; (c) control
over their practice is exercised by members, often through formal licensing;
(d) they evolve mechanisms for policing the standards of practice of
members; and (e) they often have governing bodies which administer professional activities and represent them, as a whole, to other professions, the
state and the public. Industrial sociologists are not only concerned with the
details and dynamics of individual professions, but also with attempts by
occupations to professionalize and to achieve the benefits arising from professional status.

Most studies of professions in Canada — as with those of other occupations — are quite descriptive. Brazeau,[35] for instance, has explored the
work situations of physicians. He shows the importance of social networks
and contacts for establishing and maintaining a practice. He also looks at
physicians' activities in the institutions which comprise the community's
medical system and how these affect their relative success within the medical
hierarchy. Others have written about lawyers,[36] nurses,[37] and dentists.[38]

Professionals are normally self-employed. But with the trend towards
large-scale organization, members of some professions are increasingly
becoming employees. Hall observes:

> When one turns attention to the position of the engineer in present-day society the
> model of a professional man serving a set of clients is almost totally inapplicable. Of the
> electrical engineers (who are most dependent of all engineers on salaried employment in
> the city), the proportion in independent practice is approximately 1%. The remaining
> 99% are strictly employees. This state of affairs has become abundantly apparent to
> many members of this occupational group. They realize not only that they are salaried
> workers, who are hired in large numbers by a few powerful employers, but also that col-
> lective bargaining is their appropriate relationship to their employers. However, this
> realization does not necessarily diminish their desire for professional status and for the
> prestige accorded to professional work.[39]

This analysis raises questions about the appropriateness of defining
professions in terms of the independence or autonomy of practitioners.

Occupational Prestige

Research on occupational prestige provides useful clues as to the relative social importance of various occupations and professions in Canada.[40] Blishen[41] used 1951 census data to arrange 343 occupations according to the average income and educational levels of their members. These occupations were then grouped into seven classes based on 'relative prestige.' Looking at ethnicity, he found that persons of British origin were overrepresented in the two highest classes, and those of French origin in the lowest two.

Nosanchuk[42] and Hunter[43] use Pineo and Porter's[44] data on occupational prestige and find a high degree of correspondence between anglophones and francophones in their prestige rankings of various occupations. Specific differences do occur: francophones tend to rate occupations related to medicine and construction higher, and education and government lower, than anglophones.

Other studies have looked at sex differences and report that sex has a bearing on prestige rating: "We found," Guppy and Siltanen[45] say, "that the average occupational prestige score for males was 5.0 units higher than that for females." Occupations with a high proportion of women workers have lower prestige ratings, generally, than those dominated by males — even though females are rated higher than males in female-dominated occupations. Blishen and Carroll[46] note that income differentials occur between males and females within occupations: "women gain little income by being incumbents in male-dominated occupations, while even in female-dominated occupations, nearly three times as many men as women earn higher incomes."

Eichler (1977) maintains that because it involves work, housewifery should be regarded as an occupation. In an interesting study, she included it as an occupation along with 92 others and asked her subjects to rank it relative to the others. One subsample was given a list of occupations and no specification was made as to whether the role occupant was a male or a female. Another subsample was given the same list, but the role occupant was identified as male. The final subsample was asked to rank female-specified occupations, e.g. "female doctor." Again, the list of the 92 occupations was the same.

What she finds is that "housewife" ranked fifty-second in prestige when *no* sex was specified, and fifty-second out of 88 occupations when *female* housewife was specified. It dropped to eighth lowest when the role occupant was identified as male. Relating these findings to the occupational prestige of women working outside the home, she observes that "the majority of women who choose a paid occupation over being a housewife cannot expect an increase in their occupational prestige and may, indeed, experience a loss of prestige when entering the labor market after being a housewife."[47]

Much Canadian research on occupational prestige has tended to be concerned with determining the relative levels of prestige accorded various occupations, and then observing whether differences in status can be explained by variables such as ethnicity or sex. Little work has gone beyond this level: we have only a sparse understanding as to why people rate one occupation higher than another, and why these ratings tend to be consistent within a given society.

WORK

Particularly since the famous studies of Western Electric in the 1940's,[48] industrial sociologists have spent much of their time examining all aspects of work and people in their specific jobs. As compared with other life activities, work is usually something people do because they have no alternative if they wish to achieve and maintain a desired standard of living. This is not to say that many do not enjoy their work or would not continue to do it even if they were financially secure. But for most, work is a non-voluntary activity. Key elements in work, which distinguish it from service and freetime activities, are that it is normally a non-voluntary activity, involves specified tasks, and people are paid for doing it. Life situations — for example, housework — do not always include all of these elements. What housewives do is "work" by almost any standard, but most do not receive regular remuneration for it.

Work can mean different things to different people and industrial sociologists have been intrigued by the range of meanings attributed to it. Instrumentalists are primarily concerned with extrinsic rewards — the money and security provided by work. Others are also concerned with the nature of the work itself — its intrinsic features, such as whether it is interesting, challenging, or draws on particular skills. Knight[49] reports that while material benefits were most important to production workers' relationships with companies, "a fairly substantial minority... has retained some concern for work's intrinsic rewards. Instrumentalism may prevail, but it does not overwhelm."[50] Beattie's[51] study of middle-level managers in the federal public service found a similar dual concern for both intrinsic and extrinsic features of work, although those with higher educational levels were more interested in intrinsic features of their work situations.

Westley and Westley[52] argue that increased levels of education and affluence have generated expectations that in many instances cannot be met by conventional, narrow and rigid work arrangements.[53] The tension between expectations and realities increasingly results in shifts in the meaning and value of work.[54] Practical efforts to deal with these tensions will be discussed later in this chapter.

Satisfaction

Closely related to the meaning of work is the satisfaction people derive from it. There have been numerous Canadian studies looking at the relationship between working conditions and peoples' positive feelings of job satisfaction,[55] and negative feelings of alienation at work.[56] A rather interesting spinoff of this research has been considering how work-related attitudes relate to attitudes and behavior off the job.

Non-Work Linkages

There are three main possibilities in the linkage between work and non-work life: in their free time workers may compensate for the lack of social contacts and discretion in their work, or the experiences of their work may spill over into their free time, or there may be no relationship between the two. Meissner[57] reports that, in a study of 206 industrial workers engaged in manufacturing wood products on Vancouver Island, most were engaged in constraining jobs and had minimal social contact with others on the job. Off the job, they tended to have low involvement in community activities and organizations. In other words, he found support for the "spill over" hypothesis:

> The design of industrial work creates or prevents opportunities for the development or maintenance of discretionary and social skills. When choice of action is suppressed by the spatial, temporal, and functional constraints of the work process, worker capacity for meeting the demands of spare-time activities which require discretion is reduced. When work is socially isolating, workers reduce their exposure to situations in which they have to talk, and also spend less time in organized and purpose-directed activities. They make up for it and spend a lot more time fishing on the weekend, and pushing the shopping cart through the supermarket on weekdays. Lack of opportunity to talk on the job is associated with dramatically reduced rates of participation in associations, that is, in activity commonly believed to help integrate individuals into the community.[58]

In a large-scale study of participation rates in outdoor recreation, persons in higher prestige occupations participated in significantly more activities — and did so more often — than those in lower prestige occupations. But, more detailed analyses of these data showed that occupation was relatively unimportant as a predictor of outdoor recreation when compared with other variables such as age, education, and income levels.[59]

Even though there has been comparatively little Canadian research on the relationship between job and non-job behaviors, there has been even less related to attitudes.[60] Additional research is certainly needed so that we may be able to more fully assess the impacts of job behavior on off-the-job activities and attitudes. Given the trend toward shorter work weeks in Canada, greater understanding of the work/nonwork relationship is essential.

Technology

Understanding technology is vital for industrial sociologists. "The technology of a workplace," Meissner maintains, "consists of its tools, machines, parts, and materials; the equipment used to move these parts and materials from place to place; and the buildings and parts of buildings which house all these things and the people working with them."[61] He further suggests that technologies consist of two basic components: conversion and transfer processes. Conversion processes involve changing materials from a raw state into (eventually) a finished good or service. In order to effect conversion, it is often necessary to send materials from one location to another — that is, to engage in transfer processes. After detailed analyses of secondary data (case studies involving a wide range of production methods), Meissner generates a typology of eight different technologies: handling, handwork, machine work, machine work-sequence, assembly line, hand and machine line, remote control, and automation. This typology represents an improvement and extension of earlier ones,[62] but has largely been ignored by Canadian researchers.

Other Research Areas

Some other themes related to work which Canadian researchers have explored include the language of work, immigrants' experiences, unemployment, and hazards or safety. Over the years there has been a series of studies showing how francophones have been disadvantaged in Québec business and industry where English is the working language.[63] This activity reached a peak in 1969 with the publication of the reports of the Royal Commission on Bilingualism and Biculturalism.

In an assessment of Greek immigrants, Nagata[64] finds that those with low skill levels felt job satisfied and believed that they were more prosperous and secure in their work here than in Greece. But, higher skilled workers were less satisfied because they had often experienced difficulties with having their work credentials fully recognized or appreciated in Canada.[65]

Cuneo[66] presents a case study of the 1941 Canadian Unemployment Insurance Act and traces the dynamics between labor's support for and businesses' opposition to it. Butler[67] looks at the "marginal work world" in Atlantic Canada in order to determine whether there is truth to the myth that large numbers of households in the region live off welfare. In a preliminary analysis he finds no support for this myth.[68] In other studies, Lucas[69] reports on miners in a coal mine cave-in, and Leyton[70] on the social and personal consequences of radiation and silicosis among miners in a fluorspar mine.

PREPARATION FOR WORK

In the previous section, we looked at a number of areas of study related to people at work. Considerable effort has also been devoted to determining how people make particular occupational choices in the first place and how they then prepare for these through training and education. "Finding our own place in the occupation structure," Breton says, "is like an elaborate game of individual and social leap-frog in which events, opportunities, obstacles, and socio-metric circumstances are internalized, thereby modifying perceptions, attitudes, and values."[71] He attempts to sort out the various effects in a comprehensive survey of Canadian high school students. He reports that students ranking high in mental ability who are English-speaking, interested in the work itself and not just the rewards from it, and who live in large communities are more likely to have more specific career goals than those who do not have these traits.[72]

In a study of recent graduates at four Ontario Universities, Harvey[73] asked what the most important factor was in respondent's choice of an ideal career. Fourteen per cent were primarily concerned with financial rewards and security, 44.2 per cent were looking for careers where they could work with people, and 40.3 per cent thought that the nature of work, itself, was most important in their selection of an ideal career. Since his respondents were recent graduates, job searching had been a vital activitiy for many of them. Of the various methods tried, he found that over one-third approached employers directly on their own, one-fifth relied on newspaper or other advertisements, while only one-tenth used university employment services as their most important search technique.[74]

One of the most significant studies of the linkages between schools and work in Canada was done by Hall and Carlton.[75] They interviewed teachers and administrators at all levels of a community's school system — including a college and a university — together with employers, and graduating high school students. Employers criticized the current permissive trends which allow students to avoid the more difficult courses but at the same time, the researchers observe that "in the vast variety of openings employers make exceedingly little use of the academic and technical skills of the secondary school student."[76] From the students' perspective, "office and factory working was a shock... School has not prepared them for sustained work carried on at a rapid pace."[77] Other studies in this general area have looked at why people choose to enter certain specific occupations: such as science,[78] dentistry[79] or academia.[80]

Women

The increasing numbers of women joining the labor force in recent years has sparked sociological interest in tracking women's occupational choices and career contingencies. Brinkerhoff[81] has systematically pursued these questions and hypothesizes "that women's [occupational] choices are influenced by perception of the ease of entrance *and* the perceived occupational rewards."[82] Girls in his sample of grade eleven students were more likely to be innovative in their choices — that is, to choose occupations outside those where females are conveniently concentrated, such as office-clerical jobs — if they were from families with higher socio-economic status. Also, educational levels. Interestingly, he observes that innovativeness in occupational choice is unrelated to whether or not mothers work.

Breton does not explore the innovativeness of high school females' occupational preferences but, instead, is concerned with whether they even have an occupational goal. "Girls with working mothers," he reports, "are somewhat less likely to be undecided about the pursuit of a career than others. One exception to this overall result is that those who rank high in mental ability appear unaffected by the employment status of their mother."[83] Also, English-speaking girls and those whose fathers have less education are more likely to want to pursue a career.

WOMEN AND WORK

Historically, of course, women have always been a significant factor in most societies' work forces.[84] Usually, however, early industrial sociologists ignored any systematic study of their roles and problems. But with a growing proportion of women in the labor force, and with the sensitivity to these issues generated by the women's movement, there has been additional impetus towards correcting this deficiency.

Reviewing the reasons why women work, Connelly[85] suggests that most attempts to explain higher rates of female participation are rooted in a traditional model of women's roles and what she refers to as a "consumer's choice perspective." "The consumer choice perspective," she notes, "views women as free to choose between paid employment, leisure, volunteer work, or work in the home. The major assumption underlying the consumer choice model is the existence of an opportunity structure. If one accepts this assumption, women's labor force participation becomes a matter of personal choice."[86] Data indicate that a majority of working women are married and that their husbands most frequently earn low incomes. Connelly questions whether, under these circumstance, the consumer's choice model has any relevance: she argues that a majority of working women are employed in order to supplement their husbands' low earnings. She concludes that

... as the standard of living in Canada rises married women whose husbands earn low incomes must work outside the home to maintain their relative standard of living. That is, married women don't work in order to close the gap between rich and poor families. Rather they work to prevent the difference from increasing.[87]

Boyd[88] reminds us of "the forgotten minority" in her research on working women who are divorced or separated. Data show that, for most, employment provides their major source of income. "Contrary to previous decades, women are increasingly entering the labor force and increasingly they are assuming major bread-winning roles."[89] A large number of recent studies have focused on the pay differentials between men and women doing similar work and on how women remain relatively segregated in a few occupations with lower pay scales.[90]

Impacts of Work

With large numbers of women in the work force, it is noteworthy that there has been little Canadian research on the impacts of this activity on their other roles as mothers, wives, or whatever. In one of the few examples available, Lashuk and Kurian[91] were concerned with how work affected full and part-time working wives' performance in other roles. Contrary to their expectations, they failed to find that the marital relationship suffers when the wife is employed. Also, there were no significant differences between employed and non-employed groups in their relationships with their children, in feelings of inadequacy as mothers, or in psychosomatic complaints.

Meissner, Humphreys, Meis, and Schen[92] looked at the time budgets of a sample of working couples as a test of two alternative hypotheses about ways in which housework can be managed in "dual career" families; adaptive partnership or dependent labor. According to the adaptive partnership model, roles in the family adapt so as to distribute equally the workloads of its primary members. For instance, if a wife takes a job outside the home, then her husband would be expected to take on an equal share of the housework to compensate for her newly increased responsibilities. But, the dependent labor model predicts that the husband would not increase his share of the workload because "the economic function of the household formed on marriage is the servicing of men (and the preparation of children) as resources for the corporate organization of production." In other words, the outside work a women undertakes is likely to be done as an overload, in addition to her other duties as mother and wife. Testing these two models, they found:

> that as the wives' job hours increase: (1) their hours of regular housework decline without being made up for because their husbands' housework remains virtually at the same low level of some four to five hours a week; and (2) despite the successively more compressed hours of housework, the wives' total workload increases a great deal while their husbands' declines slightly. When men's workload and regular housework are

plotted against their own job hours and compared with the data for women, men always work less than women in each of the strictly comparable conditions.[93]

Other studies have looked at a wide range of topics[94] including the working status of immigrant women,[95] the interest of women in unions and unionization,[96] and women's attitudes towards certain conditions of work such as autonomy.[97] Future research is likely to continue to emphasize pay and career differentials between men and women, as well as providing insights into newly emerging concerns such as sexual harassment at work. Much of the early research in this area, however, tended to be investigative rather than theoretically based. While useful in establishing the nature of working situations in which women are located, the apparent lack of a general model has meant that much of this research is disjointed. Usually small and isolated samples have meant that generalizability of findings is restricted. Increased use of longitudinal or time series designs would provide valuable insights into how women cope with their changing worlds and often discriminatory circumstances.

CAREERS

When we meet someone for the first time in Canada, it usually is not long before someone asks what you do for a living. The work that a person does influences a whole host of other things including not only their own social status and life chances, but quite often their family's as well. Earlier we discussed research on occupational prestige. Another somewhat related issue is whether people from certain backgrounds are improving their occupational standing as compared with earlier generations of their family. These studies provide information on whether occupational structures are relatively open — based on achievement — or relatively closed — based on "ascription," family connections, lineage, or whatever.

Sociologists measure this characteristic of a society by tracing career patterns and comparing a respondent's occupation with that of father or grandfather.[98] Such data indicate whether there has been, and, if so, the extent of, inter-generational occupational mobility.

Harvey and Charner, for instance, report that "a university degree is still a good guarantee for a person from a lower socio-economic background to obtain an occupational attainment higher than his father."[99] The tight labor market, however, makes it more difficult for those from middle and upper socio-economic backgrounds — in spite of a university degree — to improve or even maintain the equivalent of their father's position. Nevertheless, most studies of Canadian occupational structures have found a fairly high degree of inter-generational mobility — either positive or negative.[100]

On a more individual level, Canadian industrial sociologists have not provided much insight into individual career patterns within various occupational or organizational settings. Relevant research of this kind might examine the career strategies people follow: variations in careers as a function of the size and country of ownership of their employer's firm,[101] and so on.

In an early study, Ross[102] looked at the impact on businessmen's careers of participation in community philanthropic activities. She finds that such involvement is a major facilitating activity for individual career advancement, that is, the rise of a person to top executive positions in charitable campaigns is related to their rise in the business hierarchy.

Dimick and Murray report on the routes to senior management in different types of organizations. "The intermediate sized companies put more emphasis," they discovered, "on the production/operations and marketing /sales areas as preparation for people who would occupy the first and second levels of the executive ranks. The large companies, while also drawing on these backgrounds, also emphasized previous experience in the cross-functional areas we have labelled 'administration'."[103] They noted that the rapid economic expansion of the 1960s and early 70s produced much faster career movement for executives — roughly one advance every four years — as compared with a more recent average of one every six or seven years.

Most Canadian studies of career patterns have focused on those of management-level personnel.[104] White's report on the mobility aspirations and strategies of production workers is an exception to this rule.[105] Even though a seniority system of promotion was in effect in the plants he sampled, he found substantial numbers of workers who not only were interested in advancement, but many who also claimed to be actively pursuing that objective within their organizations. Supervisors were seen as important figures in facilitating advancement, and one strategy employed by interested workers was "an impression management scheme, *visibility,* whereby a worker presented visual cues to his supervisor that he believed... [would] enhance his position as a competent individual, capably performing his present duties and suitable for promotion to a higher, more demanding position."[106] Following this strategy, workers would save the more demanding aspects of their jobs until their supervisor was around and then perform them with such skill that few people would fail to be impressed.

More recently, Knight's analysis of data collected by Loubser and Fullan confirms this finding that blue collar workers are extremely interested in personal advancement and mobility.[107] This provides a powerful argument against confining studies of career attitudes to those of managers, administrators or professionals.

ADDITIONAL AREAS OF INDUSTRIAL RESEARCH

While the topics we have examined thus far have been those where the

greatest amount of research has been done, no overview of Canadian studies of work or industrial organization would be complete without reference to several other topics. Unions and strike activity, for example, have long been established topics within industrial sociology. But over the years these have tended, perhaps surprisingly, to receive relatively little attention by Canadian sociologists.

Unions

An early study of this kind by Shepard describes the transition of a Toronto clothing workers' local from an older, and predominantly Jewish, membership who fought for union rights to younger, less committed members who "lacked the sense of struggle and community of culture and interest out of which the union was born."[108] Union leaders sought to adapt to this changing constituency by encouraging youthful members to seek office, keeping channels of communication open, and by developing recreational programs.

In a rather creative piece of work, Smucker looks at ideological themes and shifts in the Canadian Labour Congress as revealed by a content analysis of presidential addresses between 1898 and 1974. Earlier addresses show the evolution of the Congress from a social movement to a more formalized institution — "a shift toward justifying the institution and away from the forward thrust of a social movement when tactics are of crucial importance."[109] Another noticeable trend in the speeches was a move away from an emphasis on programs aimed at influencing governments, to a concern for increased economic benefits. "It is as if the presidents," Smucker says, "became locked into a rhetoric of 'more' without taking account of other options for changing the structure of management-labor relations."[110]

In the same vein, Marchak looks at some of the myths about women in unions which suggest that women are less committed to the labor force and hence, less interested in unions.[111] In a survey of white-collar workers in British Columbia, she observes that potential union involvement is actually higher among women because of their disadvantaged position in terms of income and job control.

White studied breakaways and the formation of autonomous unions by Canadian affiliates of American-based international unions in the 70s.[112] He argues that these occurrences can only be partially explained by resurgent Canadian nationalism. Instead, he maintains, it is more fruitful to seek an explanation in the notion of "relative deprivation," as it has been applied to social movements.[113]

Strikes

Some Canadian sociologists have recently begun to examine the possible causes and consequences of strike activity. Based on strike data for Ontario between 1958 and 1967, one study reports finding clear relationships between the size of operations and the frequency and duration of strikes. More specifically, "as the size of establishments increases, so does the probability of strikes"; and "as organization size increases, there is a tendency for the median duration of the strike in days to decrease."[114]

Huxley argues that government legislation has probably been a contributing factor to the length of the longest walkouts:

> the intensive involvement of the Canadian state in attempting to regulate industrial conflict has had important consequences for the shape of strike activity. State intervention has reduced the number of authorized strikes over such issues as union recognition and rights disputes. More important, state regulation was a significant factor in accounting for the relatively long average duration of strikes.[115]

One of the ways in which government legislation affects strike patterns, for instance, is that by prohibiting strikes until the end of a bargaining period, it reduces uncertainty for the company. Companies can, thus, plan with some certainty for this eventuality, and may be in a position to stockpile goods that will reduce the harmful impacts of a short strike on its markets or sales. The union's main strategy, under these circumstance, is to prolong the walkout with the intention of, over time, reducing the company's flexibility. "This pattern of protracted strikes," says Huxley, "appears to have been accepted by employers in Canada in preference to what was perceived as the more disruptive alternative: frequent, less predictable stoppages."[116]

Other writers have been concerned with what effects strikes have on working-class consciousness.[117] Using secondary data derived from industry strike records, Smith notes that "strikes occur most often under conditions most propitious for their success; in particular, under conditions of full employment and where legislation is more supportive of unions."[118] This means that time lost through strikes is most prevalent in industries where wage levels are already higher and where wage increases can be passed on to consumers. "Relatively well-paid auto workers," Smith observes, "spend much more time on strike than do (often female) wretchedly-paid clothing workers."[119] Thus, while they may increase the class consciousness of those involved in them, strikes are likely to engender divisive antagonisms and result in widening gulfs within the working class. From a Marxist perspective, one could probably agree with Smith's conclusion that "A strike wave, then, may be rather less a threat to capitalist hegemony than is sometimes thought."[120]

ORGANIZATIONS

Canadian sociologists situated in places other than business schools have, at best, made modest contributions to theory and research on organizations. While economists and social critics have pointed out the domination of our economy by foreign owners, sociologists have largely ignored its impacts, if any, on the structure and operations of our business and industrial organizations. As a rule, organizational context has been taken as given, while the attitudes and behavior of individual members within these organizations have been carefully examined. Even where organizations, themselves, have been used as central units of analysis, much of the literature has been neither imaginative nor pace-setting.

Bureaucracy

Weber's early writings on bureaucracy have served as a point of departure for many organizational researchers. Jones, for instance, was interested in the relationship between one aspect of organizational structure — role differentiation — and the extent of consensus and cohesion among members.[121] He used a sample drawn from seven departments in a manufacturing concern and measured role differentiation in each by noting the number of different occupations and skill levels present. High consensus among members on questions of job satisfaction, working conditions, supervision, the company, and rewards was present when a department's role differentiation was low. Contrary to expectations, the intensity of social bonds or group cohesion among members was unrelated to role differentiation.

Government bureaucracies have served as sites for numerous studies of all aspects of their structure and operations. Sheriff's monograph provides an excellent synthesis of a vast amount of Canadian and international literature on public administration and bureaucracies.[122] Specific examples of work in this genre include Porter's[123] early research on senior public servants and the bureaucratic elite. He found that, among other things, "the analysis of the social class and ethnic origins of the senior officials suggest that the bureaucracy is more closed than open." Beattie and others[124] have also looked at a number of characteristics of senior federal bureaucrats including their salary levels. Although it appeared that education was more important for advancement than seniority for this group, negative effects of career discrimination were reflected in lower salaries for comparably qualified francophones.[125]

Solomon examined how the Canadian Army adapted to rapidly changing conditions largely outside its control.[126] These shifts included almost continual technological innovation and improvements, and changing patterns in recruitment. Extensive formal rules and procedures typical of large bureaucracies made it difficult for the Army to adjust to these changing circumstances effectively. He describes the informal channels of communication that developed and were employed by the Army to deal with cumbersome rules and bureaucratic structures. An informal system of written communications referred to as "D.O." — or "demi-official" — were used to streamline operations and were not included in the regular filing system:

> These informal processes enable the organization to get its daily business done effectively and with dispatch, within the framework of formal rules and regulation but with sufficient flexibility to modify the otherwise rigid application of formalized policy.[127]

Another topic Solomon dealt with here was how the Army socialized individual recruits into its collective discipline.[128]

Organization Size

Sociologists have observed that as organizations grow in size they become more rule-bound, less adaptive, and tend to stifle initiative. In a study of the juvenile courts, Tepperman finds that as they become larger, and the density of their volume of work and interactions increases, the necessity for coordination results in greater bureaucratization:

> Bureaucratization of decision-making in a large organization emerges in opposition to norms of 'individualized' treatment, as a response to the scale of operations and the potential for conflict among decision-makers. With such bureaucratization, large organizations (in this case, juvenile courts) become more like one another in their decisions; their responsiveness to ascribed differences among clients (specifically, sex differences) decreases; and techniques of expediting the flow of clients are perfected, without noticeable benefit to the recipients of organizational services. This analysis of the emergence of bureaucratic decision-making implies that (1) 'individualized' decision-making is unlikely to survive increases in the scale of organizational operations; and (2) 'bureaucratized' decision-making may develop as an unanticipated consequence of growth.[129]

This issue of organizational size and its social consequences was the focus of several studies undertaken for the Royal Commission on Corporate Concentration.[130] One of these considered individual alienation and found only a weak relationship between organization size and reported feelings or behavior that might be interpreted as alienation.[131] In another commission study, White found "that organization size alone is not a major determinant of individual attitudes and behaviours. Size may increase the probability that certain structural arrangements are present, but what is more important is how people in their actual behaviours adapt or fail to adapt to these potential situations."[132] Using data from a sample of production workers, positive relationships were observed between organization size and a number of measures of worker attitudes and behaviors. But, the results which looked at the relative importance of various predictors were more important: organization size was found to be a minor and relatively unimportant predictor. Individual career opportunities within the organization, style of supervision, and opportunities to use one's skills were all stronger predictors of various measures of the positive health of labor relations than organization size.

Environments and Change

The last decade has witnessed an increasing focus on issues related to organizations and their environments among organizational sociologists. Some Canadian work bears on this subject.

Hall and Carlton, for example, studied the interrelationships between schools and the processes of social change in community and societal environments. They give a good account of school system adjustments to the public push for raising average levels of individual schooling and making post-secondary education more accessible. Commenting on how bureaucratic educational institutions at all levels have responded, they note that "schools are neither so consciously creative nor malleable as we might imagine: they tend to move slowly, pulled along by the drift of the larger society while exerting some small pressures and resistances of their own."[133]

In other studies, Lucas[134] describes the interrelationships between the community and organizations in single-industry towns. Kelner, Haour, Court, and Voineskos,[135] look at the impacts on a well-established, traditional mental hospital when it is moved to a new facility, and Craig[136] defines some behavioral guidelines as to what might be expected of multinationals if they wish to be viewed as good corporate citizens.

Corporations

Corporations have been the center of much attention, particularly by students of elites. Boards of directors and the interlocking directorships between major corporations have been used as a means of locating important business elites.[137] Less emphasis has been placed on examining the patterns of control within corporations.[138]

Smucker reviews the manner in which management has manipulated ideological themes in order to perpetuate the authority and control of employers.[139] Looking at a 70 year period, he examined topical themes in the official publication of the Canadian Manufacturers' Association, *Industrial Canada*. Management control largely remains intact today, but he observes shifts in how it is expressed:

> The strategy of management with regard to individual workers evolved from a behavioural model in which better physical surroundings and economic incentives were stressed, psychological testing was advocated, and educational programs were supported, to an emphasis upon cooperation, good communications, and teamwork.[140]

A few researchers have looked at where power and control lies within corporations. Is it with the board of directors or with management? A study of directors and managers indicates that who exercises control over major decisions often depends on corporate circumstances. Ownership, for instance, was found to be a key factor influencing control. "If ownership is concentrated on a parent subsidiary basis," says White,[141] "control tends to be exercised through management links. When ownership is largely by managers, they are likely to retain direct control. If, on the other hand, ownership is by non-manager shareholders, then the board will have varying degrees of control in corporate decision-making, depending on the concentration of that ownership."

A second important factor relating to directorate control was the composition of the board. Where it contains some directors who are not dependent on the corporation — they are neither employees, nor major owners, etc. — the board is much more likely to perform a control function in corporate decision-making than when it is composed solely of insiders. This tendency is even more pronounced for independent or parent corporations than for subsidiaries.

In a study of some Canadian managers in a subsidiary of a large multinational oil corporation, House[142] argues that parent corporations do not tend to stifle local initiative. Instead, a deliberate strategy of group decision-making and entrepreneurial expression is fostered and training is provided for managers climbing up the hierarchy. In this way, House believes that parents not only encourage Canadian entrepreneurship, but nurture and co-opt it to their own ends: "The collectivization and cooptation of entrepreneurial decision-making is a major occupational innovation of the multinational corporation, basic to its economic power and success."[143] Beyond this, Marchak[144] provides an excellent examination of the concept of the corporation and how large foreign-owned firms impact on Canadian workers.

An alternative legal form under which business can be conducted is the cooperative. Although not widely used in many parts of Canada, it is prevalent enough that more should be known about its operations. Craig[145] provides a study of cooperatives "whose activities have moved beyond the confines of the country in which they originated." His use of case studies presents useful insights into their operations.

We began this section by refering to Weber's writings on bureaucracy. Over the years since he wrote, the principal criticism of bureaucratic forms of organization has centered on their inflexibility, which tends to retard adaptation to turbulent environments. Matejko suggests that bureaucratic order acts as an anaesthetic on creative activity, and may even protect and foster mediocrity.[146] Bureaucracies, he contends, lay greater stress on loyalty to the organization than to professional qualifications and merit when hiring or promoting employees. "The harmful effects of bureaucracy," according to Matejko, "and its progressing maladaptation to modern society make it probable that it will wither away."[147] While bureaucracies have been part of social reality for several thousand years — and although it is probably an overstatement to suggest that they will wither away — serious efforts are now being made to seek alternative organizational forms.

QUALITY OF WORKING LIFE

Noticeable shifts have occurred in the composition of the labor forces in Western countries during the last decade. Westley and Westley[148] were among the first Canadian observers to point out that young workers — under 35 years of age — now constituted a majority. They were entering the labor force, moreover, with very high levels of education, receiving high and rising incomes, and doing so under circumstances of record full employment and societal norms strongly emphasizing consumerism. These factors resulted in increased expectations about what work should be, and tended to include a desire for interesting and challenging tasks, responsibility, and opportunities to use one's skills and to develop new ones.[149] At the same time, however, the reality was that many jobs were narrow, specialized, repetitious, and provided few opportunities for the use of the talents of this "new" or "emerging worker."

Where there is this poor fit between individual qualifications and expectations and the nature of the job, there is a tendency for people to "turn off" and adopt a more instrumental view of work. The job, in other words, becomes regarded simply as a means to an end — a way of getting money to do the things *off the job* that are of real interest. Under these conditions, a minimal or declining commitment to work may be reflected in absenteeism, lost or shoddy production, disinterest, low levels of satisfaction, and "burnout."

Another trend, that often relates very closely to the situation being described here, is the substantial increase in the number of women entering the labor force.[150] This has frequently resulted in multiple-income families and decreasing numbers of workers who are the sole means of support for their households.[151] This has created new flexibility for many workers and — in a state of relatively high employment — may contribute to high turnover rates as workers shift about from job to job in search of better conditions or rewards.

These changes in the values and behavior of workers are impacting on organizations in many ways, and bureaucratic structures and traditions often create rigidities that make adequate responses difficult, if not impossible.

Industrial Democracy

Casting about for alternatives to our present system one that almost always emerges in a favorable light is the European system of "industrial democracy.'' Although there are numerous variations, industrial democracy is essentially a scheme that attempts to provide an organizational framework within which workers assume a more active role by participating in the joint operation of certain facets of a corporation's or establishment's affairs.[152] Proponents of this approach to labor relations base their support on the view that all members of an organization should have a reasonable and a representative say in the control and direction of their destinies while at work. They argue that this control should be not only over the particular jobs at which people work, but over the larger organization as well.

In a survey of manufacturing employees, White[153] found substantial numbers who would be willing to participate in decisions affecting their own immediate work routines or jobs, but far fewer felt comfortable with the prospect of participating in decisions affecting the larger operations of the company. Whitehorn[154] conducted a unique comparative study between a sample of Canadian workers and a group functioning in an industrial democratic setting in Yugoslavia. It is always difficult in cross-cultural studies to control for differences in cultural values, but Yugoslavian respondents were considerably higher in job satisfaction, and after assessing other comparisons, he concludes, ''my findings suggest that participation in worker's self-management is associated with lower alienation levels, and one might consequently begin to infer that no substantial amount of frustration from participation in self-management bodies seems to be present.''[155]

Sociotechnical Design/Redesign

It is unlikely that a legislated approach — such as industrial democracy — will gain much of a foothold in North America. Instead, the underlying principles of participation are being incorporated in a more systematic approach to job and organization design/redesign that is currently known as ''Quality of Working Life,'' or QWL. This approach is a practical, joint problem-solving attempt to apply social science knowledge of organizations and people at work to restructure organizations and jobs with a view towards improving the fit between peoples' changing values regarding work and the realities of their work settings.

Usually a central component of this approach is a sociotechnical perspective.[156] If an organization is to get anything done, it must rely not only on the technology and work processes of its *technical system,* but also on the people or its *social system.* Most organizations have tended to focus their efforts on the technical system and have taken the social system more or less for granted. Extrinsic rewards often have been used as a means of convincing members of the social system to accept the demands and necessities of the technical system. But an important and growing consequence of the societal trend we have been describing is that people are requiring organizations to give more consideration to their social systems and to the better use of human resources.

Job enlargement, job enrichment,[157] and other earlier interventions have had a more limited effect than sociotechnical approaches such as QWL. Westley[158] contrasts job enrichment with sociotechnical systems methods and sees job enrichment as an isolated, individual, and psychological approach. A sociotechnical approach, on the other hand, subsumes job enrichment and supplements it with utilization of semi-autonomous teams, value changes, and joint labor-management problem-solving.

Recent Canadian experience in this practical and applied endeavor has been important and pace-setting.[159] Very few industrial and organizational sociologists, however, are as yet involved, and research and publishing efforts thus far are woefully inadequate. This is an area where Canadians can have a significant scholarly and practical impact if the present opportunities are seized.

CONCLUSION

This chapter has reviewed Canadian research relating to industrial, work, and organizational sociology. It is apparent that a wide variety of studies have been done on various aspects of occupations and professions, work, and recently, working women. But it is equally apparent that very little work has been done specifically in the area of organizational sociology.

Most research by Canadian industrial sociologists has been concerned with manufacturing or production workers. Given that only a small portion of the labor force is employed in these types of jobs, future studies ought to devote more attention to office and service workers. In addition, it is clear that more work is needed on employees approaching retirement age, and how they and their organizations adjust to prospective separation; on the increasing presence of handicapped persons in work settings; and on all facets of work organization in isolated worksites.

Methodologically, much industrial and organizational research in Canada up to this point has relied on data gathered through questionnaires. In order to provide greater depth and understanding, researchers need to adopt a wider range of research strategies, such as the analysis of historical documents,[160] participant observation (which was a common approach in early industrial sociology),[161] and more comparative, time series analyses than are currently employed. A comparative base — either within or between studies — can only be achieved if greater care is taken in the selection and description of samples and if appropriate controls — such as type of technology[162] — are introduced. Improved attention to these details will increase the probability that future studies will move away from strictly anecdotal accounts towards being interrelated with other research in a more systematic fashion.

One of the reasons for the paucity of organizational research in Canadian sociology is the small number of persons specializing in formal and complex organizations. Perhaps, the appeal of current practical and applied endeavors — for instance, in organization design/redesign or Quality of Work Life — will generate more interest in this area.

On balance, Canadians have generated a significant body of literature in the areas of industrial and work research, and the breadth of issues addressed in recent publications bodes well for future development and continuing contributions to knowledge in these fields.

NOTES

[1]Rinehart, 1978.
[2]Rinehart, 1978: 29
[3]Rinehart, 1978: 34.
[4]Smucker, 1980.
[5]Smucker, 1980: 71.
[6]Cross, 1974.
[7]Hughes, 1943.
[8]Miner, 1939.
[9]Gold, 1975; Hughes, 1938.
[10]Taylor, 1960b
[11]Taylor, 1960b: 63.
[12]Faucher and Lamontagne, 1964: 268.
[13]Taylor, 1960a: 52.
[14]Rocher, 1964: 333; Royal Commission on Bilingualism and Biculturalism, 1969.
[15]Brazeau, 1958; 1964.
[16]Guindon, 1978: 238.
[17]Crysdale, 1961: xii.
[18]Crysdale, 1961: xii.
[19]Richardson, 1952; Butler, 1979; Sinclair and Westhues, 1974.
[20]Vincent, 1979.
[21]Westley, 1970; Kelly and Kelly, 1976.
[22]Rocher, 1964: 340.
[23]White, 1983.
[24]Mills, 1966; 1968.
[25]Rootman and Mills, 1977: 190.
[26]Ross, 1954.
[27]Robson, 1978; Ambert, 1976.
[28]House, 1977b.
[29]Beattie, 1972; McKie, 1974; Dimick and Murray, 1978.

[30]Mulkay, 1968; Inhaber, 1975.

[31]Greenaway, 1976.

[32]Elkin, 1977.

[33]Lucas, 1960; 1969.

[34]Ross, 1961; Lucas and MacLean, 1970.

[35]Brazeau, 1961.

[36]Giffen, 1961.

[37]Ross, 1961; Lucas and MacLean, 1970.

[38]McFarlane, 1964; Hall, 1965.

[39]Hall, 1961: 107-108.

[40]Burshtyn, 1968; Baxter and Nosanchuk, 1975; Blishen and McRoberts, 1976.

[41]Blishen, 1958.

[42]Nosanchuk, 1972.

[43]Hunter, 1977.

[44]Pineo and Porter, 1967.

[45]Guppy and Siltanen, 1977: 329.

[46]Blishen and Carroll, 1978: 356.

[47]Eichler, 1977: 156.

[48]Mayo, 1945; Roethlisberger and Dickson, 1939.

[49]Knight, 1979.

[50]Knight, 1979: 32.

[51]Beattie, 1977.

[52]Westley and Westley, 1971.

[53]Burstein et al., 1975; White, 1979b.

[54]Rinehart, 1978.

[55]Loubser and Fullan, 1970; Williamson and Gartrell, 1976; White, 1977.

[56]Fullan, 1970; Archibald, 1976; Rinehart, 1978; Matejko, 1976; Whitehorn, 1979.

[57]Meissner, 1971.

[58]Meissner, 1971: 260.

[59]White, 1975b: 197.

[60]Harvey, 1974a; White, 1981.

[61]Meissner, 1969: 13.

[62]Woodward, 1965; Blauner, 1964.

[63]Brazeau, 1958, 1964.

[64]Nagata, 1977.

[65]Richmond, 1967.

[66]Cuneo, 1979.

[67]Butler, 1979.

[68]Clairmont and Wien, 1974.

[69]Lucas, 1960; 1969.

[70]Leyton, 1975.

[71]Breton, 1972: 3.

[72]Breton and MacDonald, 1967; 1968; Harvey and Harvey, 1970.

[73]Harvey, 1974a; 1974b; Harvey and Charner, 1975.

[74]Harvey, 1974a: 108.

[75]Hall and Carlton, 1977.

[76]Hall and Carlton, 1977: 277.

[77]Hall and Carlton, 1977: 31.

[78]Mulkay, 1968.

[79]McFarlane, 1964.

[80]Robson, 1978.

[81]Brinkerhoff, 1977; Brinkerhoff and Kunz, 1972; Brinkerhoff and Corry, 1976.

[82]Brinkerhoff, 1977: 288.

[83]Breton, 1972: 71.

[84]Abella and Millar, 1978; Acton, Goldsmith and Shepard, 1974.

[85]Connelly, 1977.

[86]Connelly, 1977: 11.

[87]Connelly, 1977: 25.

[88]Boyd, 1977.

[89]Boyd, 1977: 67.

[90]Archibald, 1970; Ambert, 1976; Armstrong and Armstrong, 1975; Blishen and Carroll, 1978; Hall, 1964; Judek, 1968; Marchak, 1973b.

[91]Lashuk and Kurian, 1977.

[92]Meissner, Humphreys, Meis and Schen, 1975.

[93]*Ibid.*, at 429.

[94]Eichler, 1975.

[95]Boyd, 1975.

[96]Marchak, 1973a.

[97]White, 1973.

[98]I use the terms "his," "father," and "grandfather" here advisedly: until recently, too few women were in the labor force to use women's occupations in this way.

[99]Harvey and Charner, 1975: 140.

[100]For example, de Jocas and Rocher, 1957; Rocher, 1964; Goyder and Curtis, 1977; Dofny, 1969; 1977.

[101]See Marchak, 1979.

[102]Ross, 1954.

[103]Dimick and Murray, 1978: 379.

[104]See Beattie and Spencer, 1971.

[105]White, 1974.

[106]White, 1974: 129.

[107]Knight, 1979; Loubser and Fullan, 1970.

[108]Shepard, 1949: 251.

[109]Smucker, 1976: 165.

[110]Smucker, 1976: 171.

[111]Marchak, 1973a; 1974.

[112]White, 1975a: 292.

[113]White, 1975a.

[114]White, 1977: 25.

[115]Huxley, 1979: 236.

[116]Huxley, 1979: 236.

[117]For example, Rinehart, 1971.
[118]Smith, 1978: 463.
[119]Smith, 1978: 465.
[120]Smith, 1978: 470.
[121]Jones, 1968.
[122]Sheriff, 1976.
[123]Porter, 1958: 495.
[124]Beattie and Spencer, 1971; Beattie, Desy and Longstaff, 1972; Beattie, 1977.
[125]See Beattie and Spencer, 1971: 481-88.
[126]Solomon, 1954a; 1954b.
[127]Solomon, 1954a: 536.
[128]Solomon, 1954b; Jones, 1961.
[129]Tepperman, 1973: 346.
[130]See Murray and Dimick, 1978.
[131]Gartrell, 1977.
[132]White, 1977: 8.
[133]Hall and Carlton, 1977: 259.
[134]Lucas, 1971.
[135]Kelner, Haour, Court, and Voineskos, 1975.
[136]Craig, 1974.
[137]See Porter, 1965; Clement, 1975, 1977.
[138]See Berkowitz, Chapter 10 of this volume: "Corporate Structure, Corporate Control, and Canadian Elites."
[139]Smucker, 1977.
[140]Smucker, 1977: 277.
[141]White, 1978: 51.
[142]House, 1977a.
[143]House, 1977a: 10.
[144]Marchak, 1979.
[145]Craig, 1976: i.
[146]Matejko, 1979.
[147]Matejko, 1979: 11.
[148]Westley and Westley, 1971.
[149]Burstein, et al., 1975.
[150]See Elkin, Chapter 3 of this volume: "Family Studies in the Canadian Context."
[151]See White, 1979b: 4.
[152]See Matejko, 1979.
[153]White, 1972.
[154]Whitehorn, 1979.
[155]*Ibid.*, at 213.
[156]See Matejko, 1975.
[157]See Rainville and Guerin, 1978.
[158]Westley, 1979.
[159]White, 1979b.
[160]Smucker, 1976; 1977.

[161]See Roy, 1954; 1960.
[162]See Meissner, 1969.

Bibliography

Abella, Irving and David Millar, eds. *The Canadian Worker in the Twentieth Century.* Toronto: Oxford University Press, 1978.

Acton, Janice, Penny Goldsmith, and Bonnie Shepard, eds. *Women at Work: Ontario 1850-1930.* Toronto: Canadian Women's Educational Press, 1974.

Ambert, Anne-Marie. *Sex Structure.* Don Mills: Longman Canada, 1976.

Archibald, Kathleen. *Sex and the Public Service.* Ottawa: Queen's Printer, 1970.

Archibald, Peter W. "Using Marx's Theory of Alienation Empirically." In R. F. Geyer and D. R. Schweitzer, eds. *Theories of Alienation.* Leiden: Martinus Nijhoff, 1976.

_____. *Social Psychology as Political Economy.* Toronto: McGraw-Hill Ryerson, 1978.

Armstrong, Hugh and Pat Armstrong. "The Segregated Participation of Women in the Canadian Labour Force, 1941-1971." *Canadian Review of Sociology and Anthropology* 12 (1975): 370-84.

Baxter, E. H. and T. A. Nosanchuk. "The Learning of the Occupational Hierarchy." In Robert M. Pike and Elia Zureik, eds. *Socialization and Values in Canadian Society.* Vols. I and II. Toronto: McClelland and Stewart, 1975.

Beattie, Christopher. "Why People Work: Middle-Level Men at Mid-Career in the Federal Public Service." In C. Beattie and S. Crysdale, eds. *Sociology Canada: An Introductory Text.* 2d ed. Toronto: Butterworths, 1977.

Beattie, Christopher and Byron G. Spencer. "Career Attainment in Canadian Bureaucracies: Unscrambling the Effects of Age, Seniority, Education and Ethnolinguistic Factors on Salary." *American Journal of Sociology* 7 (1971): 472-90.

Beattie, C., J. Desy and S. Longstaff. *Bureaucratic Careers: Anglophones and Francophones in the Canadian Public Service.* Ottawa: Information Canada, 1972.

Blauner, Robert. *Alienation and Freedom.* Chicago: University of Chicago Press, 1964.

Blishen, Bernard R. "The Construction and Use of an Occupational Class Scale." *Canadian Journal of Economics and Political Science* 24 (1958): 519-31.

Blishen, Bernard R. and Hugh A. McRoberts. "A Revised Socioeconomic Index for Occupations in Canada." *Canadian Review of Sociology and Anthropology* 13 (1976): 71-79.

Blishen, Bernard R. and William R. Carroll. "Sex Differences in a Socioeconomic Index for Occupations in Canada," *Canadian Review of Sociology and Anthropology* 15 (1978): 352-71.

Boyd, Monica. "The Status of Immigrant Women in Canada." *Canadian Review of Sociology and Anthropology* 12 (1975): 406-16.

_____. "The Forgotten Minority: The Socioeconomic Status of Divorced and Separated Women." In P. M. Marchak, ed. *The Working Sexes: Symposium Papers on the Effects of Women at Work*. Vancouver: Institute of Industrial Relations, University of British Columbia, 1977.

Brazeau, E. Jacques. "Language Differences and Occupational Experience." *Canadian Journal of Economics and Political Science* 24 (1958): 532-40.

_____. "The Practice of Medicine in Montreal." In B. R. Blishen, F. E. Jones, K. D. Naegle, and John Porter, eds. *Canadian Society: Sociological Perspectives*. Toronto: Macmillan, 1961.

Brazeau, E. Jacques. "Language Differences and Occupational Experience." In Marcel Rioux and Yves Martin, eds. *French Canadian Society*. Toronto: McClelland and Stewart, 1964.

Breton, Raymond. *Social and Academic Factors in the Career Decisions of Canadian Youth*. Ottawa: Department of Manpower and Immigration, 1972.

Breton, Raymond and John C. MacDonald. *Career Decisions of Canadian Youth: A Compilation of Basic Data*. Ottawa: Manpower and Immigration, 1967.

Breton, Raymond and John C. MacDonald. "Occupational Preferences of Canadian High School Students." In B. R. Blishen, F. E. Jones, K. D. Naegele, and John Porter, eds. *Canadian Society: Sociological Perspectives*. Toronto: Macmillan, 1968.

Brinkerhoff, Merlin. "Women Who Want to Work in a Man's World: A Study of the Influence of Structural Factors on Role Innovativeness." *Canadian Journal of Sociology* 2 (1977): 283-303.

Brinkerhoff, Merlin B. and P. R. Kunz. "Some Notes on the Measurement of Perceived Barriers to Occupational Aspirations." *Rural Sociology* 37 (1972): 436-44.

Brinkerhoff, Merlin B. and David J. Corry. "Structural Prisons: Barriers to Occupational and Educational Goals in a Society of 'Equal' Opportunity." *International Journal of Comparative Sociology* 17 (1976): 261-74.

Burshtyn, H. "A Factor-Analytic Study of Occupational Prestige Ratings." *Canadian Review of Sociology and Anthropology* 5 (1968): 156-80.

Burstein, M., N. Tienhaara, P. Hewson, and B. Warrander. *Canadian Work Values*. Ottawa: Manpower and Immigration, Information Canada, 1975.

Butler, Peter M. "Earnings and Transfers: Income Sources in Atlantic Canada and Their Relationship to Work Settings." *Canadian Review of Sociology and Anthropology* 16 (1979): 32-46.

Clairmont, D. H. and E. C. Wien. "Segmentation, Disadvantage and Development: An Analysis of the Marginal Work World, Its Linkages With the Central Work World and Its Role in the Maritime Provinces." A Working Paper in the Marginal Work World Research Program. Halifax: Institute of Public Affairs, Dalhousie University, 1974.

Clark, S. D. "The Canadian Manufacturers' Association: Its Economic and Social Implications." In H. A. Innis, ed. *Essays in Political Economy*. Toronto: University of Toronto Press, 1938.

_____. *The Canadian Manufacturers' Association*. Toronto: University of Toronto Press, 1939.

Clement, Wallace. *The Canadian Corporate Elite: An Analysis of Economic Power*. Toronto: McClelland and Stewart, 1975.

_____. *Continental Corporate Power*. Toronto: McClelland and Stewart, 1977.

Connelly, M. Patricia. "The Economic Context of Women's Labour Force Participation in Canada." In P. Marchak, ed. *The Working Sexes: Symposium Papers on the Effects of Sex on Women at Work*. Vancouver: Institute of Industrial Relations, University of British Columbia, 1977.

Craig, John G. "What is a Good Corporate Citizen?" *Canadian Review of Sociology and Anthropology* 11 (1974): 181-96.

————. *Multinational Co-operatives: An Alternative for World Development.* Saskatoon: Western Producer Prairie Books, 1976.

Cross, Michael S. *The Workingman in the Nineteenth Century.* Toronto: Oxford University Press, 1974.

Crysdale, Stewart. *The Industrial Struggle and Protestant Ethics in Canada: A Survey of Changing Power Structures and Christian Social Ethics.* Toronto: Ryerson Press, 1961.

Cuneo, Carl J. "State, Class, and Reserve Labour: The Case of the 1941 Canadian Unemployment Insurance Act." *Canadian Review of Sociology and Anthropology* 16 (1979): 147-70.

de Jocas, Yves and Guy Rocher. "Inter-Generation Occupational Mobility in the Province of Quebec," *Canadian Journal of Economics and Political Science* 23 (1957): 58-66.

Dimick, D. E. and V. V. Murray. "Career and Personal Characteristics of the Managerial Technostructure in Canadian Business." *Canadian Review of Sociology and Anthropology* 15 (1978): 372-84.

Dofny, Jacques and Muriel Garon-Audy. "Mobilites Professionelles au Quebec." *Sociologie et Societe* 1 (1969): 272-301.

————. "Occupational Mobility in Quebec, 1954 and 1964." In C. Beattie and S. Crysdale, eds. *Sociology Canada: An Introductory Text.* Toronto: Butterworths, 1977.

Eichler, Margrit. "Sociological Research on Women in Canada." *Canadian Review of Sociology and Anthropology* 12 (1975): 474-81.

————. "The Prestige of Occupation Housewife." In P. Marchak, ed. *The Working Sexes: Symposium Papers on the Effects of Women at Work.* Vancouver: Institute of Industrial Relations, University of British Columbia, 1977.

Elkin, Frederick. "French-Canadian Nationalism and Occupational Dilemmas." In C. Beattie and S. Crysdale, eds. *Sociology Canada: An Introductory Text.* Toronto: Butterworths, 1977.

Faucher, Albert and Maurice Lamontagne. "History of Industrial Development." In Jean-Charles Falardeau, eds. *Essais sur la Quebec Contemporain.* Quebec: Les Presses Universitaires Laval, 1953.

————. "History of Industrial Development." In Marcel Rioux and Yves Martin, eds. *French Canadian Society.* Toronto: McClelland and Stewart, 1964.

Fortin, Gerald and Emile Gosselin. "La Professionalisation du Travail en Foret." *Recherches Sociographiques* 1 (1960): 33-60.

Fortin, Gerald et Louis-Marie Tremblay. "Les Changements d'Occupations dans Une Paroisse Agricole." *Recherches Sociographiques* 1 (1960): 467-95.

Fullan, Michael. "Industrial Technology and Worker Integration in the Organization." *American Sociological Review* 35 (1970): 1028-39.

Gartrell, John W. *Organization Size and Alienation.* Royal Commission on Corporate Concentration Report No. 27. Ottawa: Supply and Services Canada, 1977.

Gary, Carl. *Administrative and Curriculum Change in a Canadian Community College.* Montreal: Canadian Sociology and Anthropology Association, 1975.

Giffin, P. J. "Social Control and Professional Self-Government: A Study in the Legal Profession in Canada." In S. D. Clark, ed. *Urbanism and the Changing Canadian Society.* Toronto: University of Toronto Press, 1961.

Gold, Gerald. *Saint Pascal: Changing Leadership and Social Organization in a Quebec Town.* Toronto: Holt, Rinehart and Winston, 1975.

Goyder, John C. and James E. Curtis. "Occupational Mobility in Canada over

Four Generations." *Canadian Review of Sociology and Anthropology* 14 (1977): 303-19.

Greenaway, W. K. "Faith and Science in the Professional Ideology of Canadian Social Caseworkers." *Canadian Review of Sociology and Anthropology* 13 (1976): 106-13.

Guindon, Hubert. "The Modernization of Quebec and the Legitimacy of the Federal State." In D. Glenday, H. Guindon, and A. Turowetz, eds. *Modernization and the Canadian State.* Toronto: Macmillan, 1978.

_____. "The Modernization of Quebec and the Legitimacy of the Canadian State." *Canadian Review of Sociology and Anthropology* 15 (1978): 227-45.

Guppy, L. N. and J. L. Siltanen. "A Comparison of the Allocation of Male and Female Occupational Prestige." *Canadian Review of Sociology and Anthropology* 14 (1977): 320-30.

Hall, Oswald. "Sociological Research in the Field of Medicine: Progress and Prospects." *American Sociological Review* 16 (1951): 639-44.

_____. "The Place of the Professions in the Urban Community." In S. D. Clark, ed. *Urbanism and the Changing Canadian Society.* Toronto: University of Toronto Press, 1961.

_____. "Gender and the Division of Labour." Report of The Round Table Conference on the Implications of Traditional Divisions Between Men's Work and Women's Work. Ottawa: Department of Labour, Women's Bureau, 1964.

_____. *Utilization of Dentists in Canada.* Ottawa: Queen's Printer, 1965.

Hall, Oswald and Bruce McFarlane. *Transition from School to Work.* Ottawa: Queen's Printer, 1963.

Hall, Oswald and Richard Carlton. *Basic Skills at School and Work.* Toronto: Ontario Economic Council, 1977.

Harvey, Edward and Lorna R. Harvey. "Adolescence, Social Class, and Occupational Expectations." *Canadian Review of Sociology and Anthropology* 7 (1970): 138-47.

Harvey, Edward. *Educational Systems and the Labour Market.* Don Mills: Longman Canada, 1974a.

_____. *Educational Employment of University Arts and Science Graduates.* Toronto: Queen's Printer, 1974b.

Harvey, Edward B. and Ivan Charner. "Social Mobility and Occupational Attainments of University Graduates." *Canadian Review of Sociology and Anthropology* 12 (1975): 134-49.

Haug, Marie and Jacques Dofney, eds. *Work and Technology.* Beverly Hills: Sage Publications, 1977.

Hitchman, Gladys Symons. "Occupational Decision-Making, Career Aspirations and Preparation for Labour Force Participation: The Case of Male and Female Doctoral Candidates." In P. Marchak, ed. *The Working Sexes: Symposium Papers on the Effects of Women at Work.* Vancouver: Institute of Industrial Relations, University of British Columbia, 1977.

House, J. D. "The Social Organization of Multinational Corporations: Canadian Subsidiaries in the Oil Industry." *Canadian Review of Sociology and Anthropology* 14 (1977a): 2-14.

_____. *Contemporary Entrepreneurs: The Sociology of Residential Real Estate Agents.* Westport, Connecticut: Greenwood Press, 1977b.

Hughes, Everett C. "Industry and the Rural System in Quebec." *Canadian Journal of Economics and Political Science* 4 (1938): 341-49.

_____. *French Canada in Transition.* Chicago: University of Chicago Press, 1943.

Hunter, A. A. "A Comparative Analysis of Anglphone-Francophone Occupational Prestige Structures in Canada." *Canadian Journal of Sociology* 2 (1977):

179-93.

Huxley, Christopher. "The State, Collective Bargaining and the Shape of Strikes in Canada." *Canadian Journal of Sociology* 4 (1979): 223-39.

Inhaber, N. "Location and Employment of Canadian Scientists, 1967-72." *Canadian Review of Sociology and Anthropology* 12 (1975): 594-605.

Jones, Frank E. "The Socialization of the Infantry Recruit." In B. R. Blishen, F. E. Jones, K. D. Naegele, and John Porter, eds. *Canadian Society: Sociological Perspectives.* Toronto: Macmillan, 1961.

_____. "Structural Determinants of Consensus and Cohesion in Complex Organizations." *Canadian Review of Sociology and Anthropology* 5 (1968): 219-40.

Judek, Stanislaw. *Medical Manpower in Canada.* Ottawa: Queen's Printer, 1964.

_____. *Women in the Public Service: Their Utilization and Employment.* Ottawa: Queen's Printer, 1968.

Kelly, William and Nora Kelly. *Policing in Canada.* Toronto: Macmillan, 1976.

Kelner, M. J., M. K. Haour, J. P. M. Court and G. Voineskos. "Environment and Mental Health: The Impact of New Buildings on the Programs and Organization of a Psychiatric Hospital." *Canadian Review of Sociology and Anthropology* 12 (1975): 193-205.

Knight, Graham. "Work Orientation and Mobility Ideology in the Working-Class." *Canadian Journal of Sociology* 4 (1979): 27-41.

Lashuk, Maureen Wilson and George Kurian. "Employment Status, Feminism and Symptoms of Stress: The Case of a Canadian Prairie City." *Canadian Journal of Sociology* 2 (1977): 195-204.

Leyton, Elliott. *Dying Hard.* Toronto: McClelland and Stewart, 1975.

Loubser, J. and M. Fullan. *Industrial Conversion: Workers' Attitudes to Change in Different Industries.* Ottawa: Queen's Printer, 1970.

Lowe, Graham S. "The Rise of Modern Management in Canada." *Canadian Dimension* 14 (December, 1979): 32-38.

Lucas, Rex H. *Men in Crisis: A Study of a Mine Disaster.* New York: Basic Books, 1969.

_____. *Minetown, Milltown, Railtown.* Toronto: University of Toronto Press, 1971.

Lucas, Rex H. and H. D. Beach, eds. *Individual and Group Behaviour in a Coal Mine Disaster.* Disaster Study #13, Washington: National Academy of Sciences — National Research Council, 1960.

Lucas, Rex H. and Catherine D. MacLean. *Nurses Come Lately.* Etobicoke: The Quo Vadis School of Nursing, 1970.

Marchak, Patricia M. "Women Workers and White-Collar Unions." *Canadian Review of Sociology and Anthropology* 10 (1973a): 134-47.

_____. "The Canadian Labour Force: Jobs for Women." In Marylee Stephenson, ed. *Women in Canada.* Toronto: New Press, 1973b.

_____. "Women Workers and White-Collar Unions." In R. Breton, ed. *Aspects of Canadian Society.* Montreal: Canadian Sociology and Anthropology Association, 1974.

_____. ed. *The Working Sexes: Symposium Papers on the Effects of Sex on Women at Work.* Vancouver: Institute of Industrial Relations, University of British Columbia, 1977.

_____. *In Whose Interests: An Essay On Multinational Corporations in a Canadian Context.* Toronto: McClelland and Stewart, 1979.

Marsden, Lorna and Edward Harvey. "Equality of Educational Access Reconsidered: The Postsecondary Case in Ontario." *Interchange* 2 (1971): 11-26.

Marsden, Lorna, Edward Harvey and Ivan Charner. "Female Graduates: Their Occupational Mobility and Attainments." *Canadian Review of Sociology and*

Anthropology 12 (1975): 383-405.

Matejko, Alexander J. *The Social Technology of Applied Research.* Meerut, India: Sadhna Prakashan, 1975.

_____. *Overcoming Alienation in Work.* Meerut, India: Sadhna Prakashan, 1976.

_____. "From the Crisis of Bureaucracy to the Challenge of Participation." In R. P. Mohna, ed. *Management and Complex Organizations in Comparative Perspective.* Westport, Connecticut: Greenwood Press, 1979.

Mayo, Elton. *The Social Problems of an Industrial Civilization.* Cambridge, Mass: Harvard University Press, 1945.

McFarlane, Bruce A. *Dental Manpower in Canada.* Ottawa: Queen's Printer, 1964.

McKie, D. C. *An Ontario Industrial Elite: The Senior Executive in Manufacturing Industry.* Ottawa: Queen's Printer, 1974.

Meissner, Martin. *Technology and the Worker.* San Francisco: Chandler, 1969.

_____. "The Long Arm of the Job: A Study of Work and Leisure." *Industrial Relations* 10 (1971): 239-60.

Meissner, Martin, E. W. Humphreys, S. M. Meis, W. J. Schen. "No Exit for Wives: Sexual Division of Labour and the Cumulation of Household Demand." *Canadian Review of Sociology and Anthropology* 12 (1975); 424-39.

Mills, Donald L. *Study of Chiropractors, Naturopaths and Osteopaths in Canada.* Ottawa: Queen's Printer, 1966.

Mills, Donald L. and Irving Rootman. "Law and Professional Behavior: The Case of the Canadian Chiropractor." *University of Toronto Law Journal* 18 (1968): 170-78.

Miner, Horace. *St. Denis, A French-Canadian Parish.* Chicago: University of Chicago Press, 1939.

Mulkay, M. J. "A Study of Some Prospective Scientists." *Canadian Review of Sociology and Anthropology* 5 (1968): 181-91.

Murray, V. V. "Interaction Patterns and Felt Own Power in a Simulated Work Situation." *Canadian Review of Sociology and Anthropology* 4 (1967): 219-41.

Murray, V. V. and D. E. Dimick. *Personnel Administration in Large and Middle Size Canadian Businesses.* Royal Commission on Corporate Concentration Report No. 25. Ottawa: Supply and Services Canada, 1978.

Nagata, Judith A. "Greek Working-Class Immigrants in Toronto." In C. Beattie and S. Crysdale, eds. *Sociology Canada: An Introductory Text.* Toronto: Butterworths, 1977.

Nosanchuk, Terrance. "A Note on the Use of the Correlation Coefficient for Assessing the Similarity of Occupational Rankings." *Canadian Review of Sociology and Anthropology* 9 (1972): 357-65.

Perry, Robert L. *Galt, U.S.A.* Toronto: MacLean-Hunter, 1971.

Pineo, Peter C. and John Porter. "Occupational Prestige in Canada." *Canadian Review of Sociology and Anthropology* 4 (1967): 24-40.

Porter, John. "Higher Public Servants and the Bureaucratic Elite in Canada." *Canadian Journal of Economics and Political Science* 24 (1958): 483-501.

_____. *The Vertical Mosaic.* Toronto: University of Toronto Press, 1965.

_____. "Post-Industrialism, Post-Nationalism, and Post-Secondary Education." *Canadian Public Administration* 14 (1971): 32-50.

_____. "Educational and Occupational Opportunity in the Canadian Mosaic." *Canadian Counsellor* 8 (1974): 90-105.

_____. *The Measure of Canadian Society.* Toronto: Gage, 1979.

Rainville, Jean-Marie and Gilles Guerin. "Facteurs Explicatif de la Satisfaction dans le Travail." *Canadian Review of Sociology and Anthropology* 15 (1978): 16-29.

Richardson, Stephen, A. "Technological Change: Some Effects on Three Canadian

Fishing Villages." *Human Organization* 11 (1952): 17-27.

Richmond, Anthony. *Post-War Immigrants in Canada.* Toronto: University of Toronto, 1967.

Rinehart, James W. "Affluence and the Embourgeoisement of the Working Class: A Critical Look." *Social Problems* 19 (1971): 149-62.

_____. "Contradiction of Work-Related Attitudes and Behavior: An Interpretation." *Canadian Review of Sociology and Anthropology* 15 (1978): 1-15.

_____. *The Tyranny of Work.* Don Mills, Ont.: Longmans of Canada, 1975.

Robson, Reginald A. H. "Sociological Factors Affecting Recruitment in the Academic Profession." In B. R. Blishen, F. E. Jones, K. D. Naegle, and John Porter, eds. *Canadian Society: Sociological Perspectives.* Toronto: McClelland and Stewart, 1978.

Rocher, Guy. "Research on Occupations and Social Structure." In Marcel Rioux and Yves Martin, eds., *French Canadian Society.* Toronto: McClelland and Stewart, 1964.

Roethlisberger, F. J. and W. J. Dickson. *Management and the Worker.* Cambridge, Mass.: Harvard, 1939.

Rootman, Irving and Donald L. Mills. "Professional Behaviour of American and Canadian Chiropractors." In C. Beattie and S. Crysdale, eds. *Sociology Canada: An Introductory Text.* Toronto: Butterworths, 1977.

Ross, Aileen D. "Philanthropic Activity and the Business Career." *Social Forces* 32 (1954): 274-80.

_____. *Becoming a Nurse.* Toronto: MacMillan, 1961.

Roy, Donald F. "Efficiency and 'The Fix': Informal Intergroup Relations in a Piecework Machine Shop." *American Journal of Sociology* 60 (1954): 255-66.

_____. "'Banana Time': Job Satisfaction and Informal Interaction." *Human Organization* 18 (1960): 159-68.

Royal Commission on Bilingualism and Biculturalism. *The Work World.* Book III of Report of the Royal Commission on Bilingualism and Biculturalism. Ottawa: Queen's Printer, 1969.

Shepard, Herbert A. "Democratic Control in a Labor Union," *American Journal of Sociology* 54 (1949): 311-16.

Sheriff, Peta. "Sociology of Public Bureaucracies, 1965-1975." *Current Sociology* 24 (1976): 1-175.

Sinclair, Peter R. and Kenneth Westhues. *Village in Crisis.* Toronto: Holt, Rinehart and Winston, 1974.

Smith, Michael R. "The Effects of Strikes on Workers: A Critical Analysis." *Canadian Journal of Sociology* 3 (1978): 457-72.

_____. "A Comment on Knight's Work Orientation and Mobility in the Working Class'." *Canadian Journal of Sociology* 4 (1979): 155-61.

Smucker, Joseph. "Reformist Themes in the Canadian Labour Congress." *Sociological Focus* 9 (April, 1976): 158-73.

_____. "Ideology and Authority." *Canadian Journal of Sociology* 2 (1977): 263-82.

_____. *Industrialization in Canada.* Scarborough: Prentice-Hall, 1980.

Solomon, David N. "Sociological Research in a Military Organization," *Canadian Journal of Economics and Political Science* 20 (1954a): 531-41.

_____. "Civilian to Soldier: Three Sociological Studies of Infantry Recruit Training." *Canadian Journal of Psychology* 8 (1954b): 87-94.

Taylor, Norman W. "French Canadians as Industrial Entrepreneurs." *The Journal of Political Economy* 68 (1960a): 37-52.

_____. "The Effects of Industrialization: Its Opportunities and Consequences Upon French-Canadian Society." *Journal of Economic History* 20 (1960b):

639-47.

_____. "The French-Canadian Industrial Entrepreneur and His Social Environment." In Marcel Rioux and Yves Martin, eds. *French Canadian Society.* Toronto: McClelland and Stewart, 1964.

Tepperman, Lorne. "The Effect of Court Size on Organization and Procedure." *Canadian Review of Sociology and Anthropology* 10 (1973): 346-65.

_____. "Demographic Aspects of Career Mobility." *Canadian Review of Sociology and Anthropology* 12 (1975): 163-77.

Tremblay, Marc-Adelard. "Les Tensions Psychologiques Chez le Bucheron: Quelques Elements d'Explication." *Recherches Sociographiques* 1 (1960): 61-89.

Vincent, Claude L. *Policeman.* Toronto: Gage, 1979.

Weaver, Harold R. and Ronald B. Parton. "Replication and the Contamination of Relational Variables." *Canadian Review of Sociology and Anthropology* (1979): 237-38.

Westley, William A. *Violence and the Police.* Boston: M.I.T. Press, 1970.

_____. "Problems and Solutions in the Quality of Working Life." *Human Relations* 32: 2 (November, 1979): 113-23.

_____. and Margaret W. Westley. *The Emerging Worker.* Montreal: McGill-Queen's University Press, 1971.

White, Terrence H. "Workers' Attitudes about Industrial Democracy." *Canadian Personnel and Industrial Relations Journal* 19 (1972): 39-42.

_____. "Autonomy in Work: Are Women Any Different?" In M. Stephenson, ed. *Women in Canada.* Toronto: New Press, 1973.

_____. "Production Workers and Perceptions of Intra-Organization Mobility." *Sociological Inquiry* 44 (1974): 121-29.

_____. "Canadian Labour and International Unions in the Seventies." In S. Clark, J. Paul Grayson and Linda Grayson, eds. *Social Movements in Canada.* Toronto: Gage, 1975a.

_____. "The Relative Importance of Education and Income as Predictors in Outdoor Recreation Participation." *Journal of Leisure Research* 7 (1975b): 191-99.

_____. *Organization Size as a Factor Influencing Labour Relations.* Royal Commission on Corporate Concentration Report No. 33. Ottawa: Supply and Services Canada, 1977.

_____. *Power or Pawns: Boards of Directors in Canadian Corporations.* Don Mills: CCH, 1978.

_____. "Boards of Directors: Control and Decision-Making in Canadian Corporations." *Canadian Review of Sociology and Anthropology* 16 (1979a): 77-95.

_____. *Human Resource Management - Changing Times in Alberta.* Edmonton: Alberta Department of Labour, 1979b.

_____. "Occupational Adaptation to Environmental Complexities: The Case of Oil Scouts." In A. Wipper, ed. *Sociology of Occupations and Professions.* Toronto: Macmillan, 1983.

_____. "The Relative Importance of Work as a Factor in Life Satisfaction." *Relations Industrielles* 36 (1981): 179-91.

Whitehorn, Alan. "Alienation and Industrial Society: A Study of Workers' Self-Management." *Canadian Review of Sociology and Anthropology* 16 (1979): 206-17.

Williamson, David R. and John W. Gartrell. "Employee Work Attitudes and Work Behaviour in Canadian Business." Ottawa: Economic Council of Canada, 1976.

Woodward, Joan. *Industrial Organization: Theory and Practice.* London: Oxford, 1965.

CHAPTER 9

Elitism, Fragility, and Commoditism: Three Themes in the Canadian Sociological Mythology

Y. Michal Bodemann

INTRODUCTION

Joe Clark, not only a short-lived Canadian Prime Minister, but also a would-have-been political scientist, has made at least one meritorious contribution to his academic discipline: he shared with us his vision of Canada as a "community of communities."

A vision, a myth indeed. But like other ideological representations of the social order, this myth stands in peculiar tension to its reality. Indeed, social myths are products of the interpretive patterns available to given social classes. As such, they not only reflect the imagined order of these classes, but they also supply us with clues as to the real class nature of the society of which these interpreters are a part.

More important, however, hegemonic classes use these myths in order to bolster their predominance. Social myths fulfill this role only because they do, indeed, relate to real, concrete societies — but only in that they conceal and distort the actual relations which constitute it. As such, they are ideological.

Modern social science, insofar as it serves ruling classes, presents the added difficulty that its myths — unlike Plato's "noble lie" — appear in an a-mythical, scientized form. A detailed critical analysis, therefore, has to point to the key themes of this imagined order, discuss its relationship to a given concrete society, and interpret its principal distortions. Moreover, since social science in the service of ruling classes is hegemonic, its perceptions tend to spill over into anti-establishment social science. As critical scholars, we must therefore be critical regarding our own work, as well.

In the chapter which follows, I will sketch some key elements of the Anglo-Canadian social mythology. And while social science tends to set itself apart from everyday conceptualizations, it should become clear that some of these themes are shared by popular and scientific ideology alike: (1) the view of Canada in terms of commodities (or the commoditist view, for lack of a better word); (2) the view of Canada as fragile and in need of a protective shield; and, growing out of this, (3) the necessity to relegate power to a circumscribed elite. As we will see, these are very broad themes which are interwoven and which subsume a number of narrower ones.

THE COMMODITY VIEW OF SOCIAL RELATIONS

There is a difference between Canada and the U.S. that is even evident in their respective national symbolism. The Canadian dollar bill depicts Canada as a piece of real estate, i.e., in territorial terms: *ad mari usque ad mare.*[1] *E pluribus unum,*[2] the American equivalent, expresses the transformation of disparate human elements into a consensual entity. This difference is expressed in a similar fashion in the two flags: while the Stars and Stripes enshrines a theme in the political history of the U.S., the Maple Leaf represents the universe of Canadian staples and simultaneously, their naturalistic suspension.

This blatant commoditism in the Canadian national consciousness extends to its social science. The popularity of the staples theory is, of course, a very obvious instance of this view of Canada as a piece of real estate. More important, Canadian sociologists and their popularizers have projected this image onto Canada's human population. In contrast to the American eagle — symbol of imperial, aggressive strength — we have the Canadian beaver as an allegorical representation of what Her Majesty's Canadian subjects are meant to be: diligent, industrious, tranquil, apolitical — "stalwart peasants" in Sifton's words[3] — well nourished but with few independent thoughts or questions of their own.

As early as 1908, J. S. Woodsworth, deeply concerned about the "mixed multitude" of immigrants who were "being dumped into Canada by a kind of endless chain," graded the "quality" of various immigrant groups,[4] and his associate, J. W. Sparling, worried that "the civilization and ideal of Southeastern Europe are not transplanted to and perpetuated on our virgin soil."[5]

This view of Canada's population as a *human staple* sees its sociological refinement most prominently in the work of S. D. Clark — whose approach, as I will try to show, has had a considerable impact on present day Canadian sociology. In his *The Developing Canadian Community,* first published in 1962,[6] Clark develops his view of Canada as a society basically in equilibrium — albeit a precarious one — which periodically had to contend with disturbances from the outside (the U.S.) or from its periphery (the frontier). Clark contends that Canada, moreover, has been a society which depended on good leadership, especially for its "lower-grade" populations.

Thus, in the Maritimes, Clark argues, the "persistence of [ethnic] diversity made impossible any real cultural unity."[7] The isolation of the Acadians in that region and a lack of economic opportunities, but also "the ease with which agricultural operations could be carried on... destroyed a spirit of enterprise and made them content with their drab existence."[8] Those Acadians who were induced to move to Prince Edward Island "were unwilling to engage in the difficult task of clearing the land";[9] and the economically dependent character of Halifax "was enhanced by the type of colonists brought out to found the settlement in 1749."[10] These poor quality immigrants were, again, the Acadians, as well as Germans, "hopelessly incapable of supporting themselves in the New World."[11] By contrast, however, the influx of a "number of families from New England served to promote a local fishing industry."[12]

At least in part, Clark maintains, this heterogeneity of largely low-grade populations has led to a preponderance of crime, destitution, and vagrancy in the region, and to "undue reliance on state welfare."[13]

Clark further highlights the low quality of certain population groups by emphasizing their need for responsible and strong leadership. He contends, for example, that German immigrants lacked "ministers of their own persuasion"[14] and the maritime region as a whole appears to have needed "the support of a true social elite."[15] Migrants from New England, by contrast, brought with them, in the form of town meetings and their "congregational association," an effective social organization which necessitated less leadership, and thus made a positive contribution to the development of the region.

Now one might suppose that the Highland Scots (lacking "the experience and resourcefulness of the American settlers")[16] or the Loyalists, would be on the same level with Germans, Acadians, and *coureurs de bois*. Surprisingly, however, Clark finds that these groups were nevertheless able to "adjust their habits to new needs"[17] and hence could make substantial contributions as pioneers.

What emerges from Clark's analysis, then, is a notion of two basic categories into which Canada's population can be sorted: the downtrodden masses of varying origins, and the people with the proper pedigree or background. The former, of non-Anglo-Saxon stock, can only make a contribution to Canadian development if they are provided with firm, moral leadership. Without it, they drain Canada's resources and weaken the country. The latter group, however, which has the proper pedigree — Scots, Loyalists, and so on — can do without these authoritarian structures because they have internalized them: they have healthy patterns of social organization and "strict codes of honesty and morality."[18]

FRAGILITY AND THE ELITIST "SOLUTION"

This theme appears over and over again. As we noted, Clark views the frontier as a threat to societal stability; notably because it also attracted unstable, lower-quality human material. As a result, the situation could only be kept under control if religious guidance were provided for immigrants. Thus, while Methodism greatly contributed to the consolidation of the frontier in Upper Canada, the "cutting off of the supply of Methodist Episcopal preachers" led to conflict between religious groups and, hence, a weakening or moral leadership.[19]

Disturbances in the social organization of the frontier also occur because of the increasing polarization of its class structure. Consequently, the rising proletariat experienced "cultural disenfranchisement" because of the "increasing divorce between religious leadership and the unfortunate classes."[20]

Clark's model, of course, encounters something of a dilemma when he begins dealing with groups which, despite the fact that they are under firm religious leadership, pose economic and political problems for the emerging Canadian state. Paramount here is the class position of French Canadians and the political problems associated with them. Since French Canadians have had strong religious leadership, Clark must seek the source of their lack of progress elsewhere. Here he alludes to the psychological make-up of the French Canadian upper class which he sees as "on the whole inept in promoting new forms of economic enterprise."[21]

In other situations where his theories or models run afoul of the historical evidence, Clark maintains that other institutions — such as social work agencies or trade unions — act as the functional equivalents of churches in providing leadership for the Canadian underclass, thus keeping it under control. And where leadership is absent, as in the West before 1914, "the vigilance of the Mounted Police and the predominantly British background of the population checked the growth of crime."[22]

Again, two categorically different types of people populate Canada — ethnic immigrants and francophones on the one hand, and British stock on the other. Ethnic immigrants tend to create problems. Some may possess "the character of mobility" and can be absorbed by the new frontiers, but not so others: "... within the recesses of the cities there accumulated a growing number of people who possessed neither the desire nor the ability to move. The city selected the failures out of the streams of overseas immigrants."[23]

A Contemporary Alternative

A year after Clark's core argument was published in 1942, another important contribution to Canadian sociology appeared: Everett Hughes's *French Canada in Transition*. The differences between the approaches taken by Clark and Hughes are remarkable enough to be of interest to us here.

Even the titles of Clark's and Hughes's publications indicate something about the nature of these differences. Clark's principal work during this era is entitled *The Social Development of Canada*. Hughes speaks instead about *French Canada in Transition*. Clark, then, clearly delineates boundaries — Canada bounded by its frontiers. He is, moreover, principally concerned with the statics of internal cohesion and control. Hughes speaks, dynamically, about "transition" — the transformation of Québec from a rural-based to an urban-industrial society.

This difference in global orientation carries over into the way in which each author perceives the key issues facing Canadian society at the time: while Clark is concerned about leadership and the control of social disturbances, Hughes observes the interaction of different nationalities and the articulation of power relationships among them. While Clark is interested in establishing a Canada within firm boundaries and settled frontiers,[24] Hughes sees Québec in a dynamic relationship with its surrounding area — English Canada *and* the United States. He even questions, in the face of the Canadian and American internal diversity, the traditional conception of the nation-state.[25]

Both Clark and Hughes draw a distinction between the dominant WASP and subordinate non-WASP population — in this case the French. But where Clark endows the former with the superior moral fiber and the latter with deficiencies in social organization, Hughes portrays, without moral opprobrium, the social structure of the two national groups and the dramatic changes in their joint society. Much the same difference in perspective carries over into their later work: Clark's *The Developing Canadian Community* and Hughes's *Where Peoples Meet.*

History as a Social Forum

The image of Canada Clark portrays is remarkably static. His work, as a result, clearly reflects or even typifies the three central themes in the Canadian social mythology:

(1) *Commoditism:* Clark is obsessed, in the staples tradition, with the frontier, and pays little attention to changes in the industrial production affecting Canada's cities and towns. Moreover, in the Woodsworthian tradition, he treats the immigrant masses as a staple — quality graded in terms of their utility to the Canadian state.

(2) *The precarious nature of Canadian society, due to external forces:* this theme is reflected in Clark's treatment of the interaction between the "settled" portions of the country and the frontier, as mentioned above, and in what he sees as the recurring threat of being swallowed up by the U.S.

(3) *Elitism:* while Clark concludes that WASPs, the dominant Charter group, are properly adapted to Canada — presumably because their

authoritarianism has been internalized — francophones and ethnic immigrants are a liability unless they can be provided with proper leadership. Indeed, no disruptions even by oppressed or exploited groups really pose a threat to the state as long as there are leaders who direct these groups' frustrations into proper channels.

Commoditism

Clark, of course, was not alone in propounding these views of Canadian society. In important ways, these three interwoven themes were prefigured in J.S. Woodsworth's *Strangers Within Our Gates*:[26] as in Clark, there are the "strangers" and the "we" — and there are certainly "gates" where "we stand on guard" because of the fragility of the society. Clark, however, gave these themes their quintessential sociological expression — in effect, creating a dominant perception of Canadian society which is still very much with us today.

As with Clark and his predecessors, for instance, even younger writers such as Bell and Tepperman seem to blame Canada's overall fragmentation on the internal institutional deficiencies of its constitutive cultures. Moreover, on the basis of these deficiencies, they seem prepared to concede that a presumably "classless elite" is needed to intercede between and among different groups — or rather, to maintain control over them — and all of this is put forward in a way which is strongly reminiscent of Clark.

Fragility

The notion of Canada's "fragility" is especially apparent in some recent writings. As Bell and Tepperman[27] put it

> Troubled by national disunity, Canadian writers have fallen into speaking the language of doubt when describing their Society. A group of Western and Maritime intellectuals brooded over the "burden of unity"; at the same time their colleagues from Ontario asked the ominous question, Must Canada Fail?... According to other writers, Canada is a "nation unaware" of its past and uncertain of its future: our legendary capacity for survival stands threatened by internal strains, "divided loyalties" and foreign "dominance."[28]

Elitism

Given this "fragility," strong leadership is needed to keep the Canadian ship of state on course. Bell and Tepperman conclude, for instance, that, in the absence of a true national culture, and as long as Canada is culturally and regionally segmented, we must resign ourselves to the fact that "elites will always have to interpret these segments to one another."[29]

Following Clark, Bell and Tepperman — albeit more subtlely — reproduce the dichotomy between the WASP elite and "Ethnocanadians."[30] In *Roots of Disunity,* Bell and Tepperman want to do away with the "class connotation" of the notion of a Canadian mosaic. But, in the process, they rely on the state apparatus to set limits to diversity and to thwart the political autonomy of these groups:

> The Federal Government needs to do more than support ethnic cultural activities; it must also promote the democratic values that nourish multicultural harmony and justice. But conversely, it must also protect the society against cultural anarchy... and it must therefore teach the Canadian identity to newcomers.[31]

Finally, Bell and Tepperman accept the factual necessity for an elite which integrates Canada's disparate cultures: "If Canadians of different regions and backgrounds spoke directly to one another, they would not need to be spoken for."[32]

This idea, of course, is fully consistent with Clark's general framework. What is most striking about this is that while Bell and Tepperman appear quite willing to cede the job of running the country to this "elite," *The Roots of Disunity* makes *no effort whatsoever* to discuss the actual historical role of the Canadian elites in this "disunity." Later in this chapter I will argue, in contrast to Bell and Tepperman, that these elites have promoted a "particular ideological outlook"[33] and it is precisely the presence, rather than absence, of this hegemonic view in Canada which is the root source of what some analysts see as a "lack of national identity."

MARXIST, CRITICAL, AND LIBERAL COUNTER-CURRENTS

This particular set of views or framework is not, of course, shared by all Canadian sociologists. It can, however, be taken as representative of some kind of contemporary "Toronto School" of Canadian sociology. Another perspective — which might well be termed the "Carleton School" — is best represented by the work of John Porter, Wallace Clement, and a number of others. In most important respects, it may be seen as the negative image of the Toronto School — and, in this sense at least, shows the mark of its dependence upon the former.

Where the New Toronto School is concerned with "order," the Carleton School is preoccupied with "power." Where Clark is concerned with the "quality" of Canada's various sub-populations, Porter reveals the class basis of the mosaic. Where Clark endows Canadians of British origins with superior value systems,[34] Porter — and following him, Clement — demonstrate that the higher social standing of White Anglo-Saxon Protestants is a direct result of their privileged access to power relative to Canadians from other backgrounds.[35] While Bell and Tepperman finally, and sometimes self-doubtingly,[36] accept the abstract necessity for an elite role in Canada — in part to protect us from the United States — Clement and his associates analyze the nature and structure of the elite and concretely examine its relationship to the elites in the United States.

While the work of Porter and Clement and other critical writers is a vast improvement over that of the New Toronto School, it is not without its difficulties. There is, for instance, a marked "economism" in the Canadian Marxist literature, i.e., a tendency to look for simple correspondences between changes in the modes and means of production and changes in ideological or political forms. There is also a tendency towards class reductionism, towards a weak analysis of bourgeois ideology, and, hence, towards an unsatisfactory conception of power.

Glenday, Guindon and Turowetz's[37] introduction to the section on ethnicity and marginality in *Modernization and the Canadian State,* for instance, avoids a discussion of the assimilation of immigrant groups into the dominant culture in favor of a description of "how various levels of the state have contributed to the exclusion of certain ethnic groups from a share in the benefits...."[38] In general, of course, this is an entirely legitimate and proper concern. We are entitled to raise some questions, however, when a concern for the material well-being and economic role of groups such as blacks, Japanese and native peoples dwarfs all other considerations. Glenday *et al.*'s principal argument with respect to northern native peoples is that, while "the federal state attempted to transform 'native culture and society," it left this group with "no guarantees that they will materially benefit from the exploitation of the North."[39] They deal with the Japanese in British Columbia almost exclusively in terms of the economic threat they were perceived as posing — which is why "the state hoped to exclude Japanese Canadians by placing them in small isolated communities."[40] In general, all these groups have the choice of ethnic identification or a loss in their "life chances:" "A sense of community, where it exists, acts against their possible inclusion in the procurement of benefits from economic growth."[41]

This kind of overwhelmingly and crudely economic interpretation of these ethnic communities is all the more astonishing given the fact that, in the case of the native peoples, they are first and foremost fighting for their legal-political rights in the face of a concerted effort by the Canadian state to commit *ethnocide* — to destroy native culture and social identity. We see a clear example of this in the forced education of Inuit children in boarding schools in the south. As long ago as 1966, Hobart and Brant[42] pointed out that the Danish approach of utilizing native teachers and small schools in local communities had largely succeeded in helping to preserve Greenland's social structure and identity, whereas Canadian policy had led to forced assimilation and alienation of northern children from their home cultures. In the face of evidence of this kind — and Hobart and Brant's findings have been echoed by those of other researchers during the last 17 years — it is clear that Canadian policy is intended to lead to the complete destruction, rather than preservation, of the Inuit way of life. Economic issues are secondary.

There are parallels in the case of the Japanese Canadians. Economic competition undoubtedly played some role in determining the approach taken by the state in dealing with them. But the central problem for WASP hegemony posed by the Japanese in British Columbia was the political strength inherent in a tightly clustered, socially segregated community aspiring for middle class status. Japanese Canadians were politically decapitated during World War II, I submit, in much the same way that German Canadians were when it was felt that British dominance had to be symbolically re-affirmed during and after World War I.[43] The difference, of course, is that the forced disperson of the Japanese was more than a matter of political decapitation: what was aimed at was nothing less than the complete destruction of the Japanese national identity in Canada. As MacKenzie King put it so succinctly:

> They will have to settle in such a way... that they do not present themselves as an unassimilable colony which might again give rise to distrust, fear and dislike... the sound policy and best policy for the Japanese Canadians themselves is to distribute their numbers as widely as possible throughout the country where they will not create feelings of racial hostility.[44]

There is a parallel here to the fate of the old black communities in the Maritimes. The destruction of entire settlements, as Clairmont and Magill document in great detail for "Africville," coincided suspiciously closely with the assertion of a new black consciousness in the United States.[45]

A similar tendency towards crude economic interpretations of Canadian society and, as the author recognizes,[46] towards class reductionism, can be found in Grayson's reader which explicitly offers "Marxist Perspectives on Canada." Although the section on ideology covers nearly one quarter of the entire book, not one of the articles attempts to do for English Canada what Marcel Rioux did for Québec: present an analysis of Anglo-Canadian ideology, *per se.* In fact, the essays on ideology in English Canada tend to apply to North America or capitalist societies as a whole,[47] and the volume fails to discuss ethnicity, religion and is quite deficient in its analysis of political power in Canada. It is self-evident that any collection tends to have strengths and weaknesses, and this collection in particular reflects accurately what is strong and what is weak in Marxist sociological writing on Canada.[48]

This economistic bias is by no means limited to, broadly speaking, Marxist approaches. Reitz's[49] otherwise rich study, for example, appears to attribute ethnic segregation and group cohesion to an elaboration of economic and cultural factors.[50] He finds that "economic segregation creates common economic interests, which foster greater group cohesion in the less preferred ethnic groups."[51] In approximately 250 pages he devotes only four or five to political factors in ethnic group cohesion. Reitz believes that the most oppressed groups are the ones who are generally not very interested in political participation:

> It is one of the ironies of political life in formally democratic societies that the people who suffer the greatest deprivation both economic and social are often those who participate least in the political affairs of the society.[52]

But, then, for the mass of the population, political participation is not a rational, only a "symbolic" form of behavior:

> ... after all, the effect of any one person on political outcomes is small.[53]

Moreover:

> ... except for political elites and leaders in political movements, each person's own position is affected most directly and obviously by effects in the economic arena.[54]

What Reitz is suggesting, then, is that *real* political action issues only from leaders — national elites and leaders of political movements. Political participation by the masses, by contrast, is a rather meaningless, symbolic ritual.

Apart from this elitist view, Reitz subscribes to a voluntaristic conception of politics. Far from being forcibly excluded from political life, the most oppressed groups do not "want" to participate in political affairs. Their passivity, for Reitz, is therefore "ironic." Despite an extensive discussion of ethnic institutions, Reitz neglects the role played by state apparatuses in the formation — and, as we have seen, liquidation — of national groups. He also ignores, for example, the extensive literature on ethnic political patronage. No wonder, then, that he is unable to suggest what may have caused the "vertical" nature of the Canadian mosaic in the first place.

THE DOMINANT TREND

Thus far, I have sketched out what I believe to be three key themes in the conservative social philosophy of English Canada: its commoditism, its notion of "fragility," and its paternalistic elitism. I have suggested that these currents, since they were dominant in Canadian sociology until well into the 1960s, have spilled over into Marxist and liberal approaches. It should not be denied that, as in the case of the staples approach, syntheses between these perspectives have produced useful insights.

At the beginning of this essay I argued that social myths stand in peculiar tension to actual social reality: they legitimize and conceal actual relations and, as such, present a distorted view of society. Here I will briefly discuss how this relates to our three themes.

Relation 1. We have seen that the sense of Canada as a fragile, disunited, failing, and generally precarious community is very apparent in contemporary treatments. This same concern can clearly be traced back to the work of S. D. Clark, among others. Most authors who convey this precariousness, be they conservative, liberal, or left of center, tend to argue — the leftists in a Fabian-elitist fashion — that only a benign, yet firm leadership can liberate the country from the threat of imminent disintegration.

This precarious sense of community is remarkable in light of the fact that the Canadian state has, over the past one hundred or so years, proven to be an astonishingly robust entity — obvious obstacles to this resilience notwithstanding. These obstacles are well known: the depenence on the U.S., the narrow belt of settlement from east to west, regional disparities, the co-existence of two national and numerous ethnic groups, and so on.

Yet despite the odds against it, the Canadian state, rather than being progressively weakened, has come out of every crisis stronger and more powerful. The "October Crisis" is a clear example. Canada was founded through conquest. But, compared to the U.S., it did not suffer a civil war. Compared to capitalist states in Europe, it did not have to have recourse to fascist rule in order to preserve bourgeois hegemony. It did not split in two, as Denmark and Norway or Germany did. It did not disintegrate like Austro-Hungary or show the instabilities of Italy or France. Considering its relative youthfulness, it has been far more successful than the Mother Country in appeasing or subduing regional or class antagonisms. Thus, I would argue that it is precisely the apparent *disunity* of Canadian society that strengthens its state in a number of important ways.

Relation 2. In one sense — the most evidently ideological one — this heterogeneity and disunity has been used to generate a sense of precariousness and thus legitimize a species of elitism — the intervention of the ruling class in spheres of decision-making which, in other countries, are left to elected or corporate bodies. Moreover, here this intervention is carried out by a rather monolithic ruling class fraction — a densely linked, WASP, corporate and political elite group.

Apart from this ideological use of the notion of disunity, there are other ways it is mobilized in order to exert control. As Clement has shown, corporate and political elites are numerically overrepresented in Québec and Ontario, but scattered in other provinces. These scattered elites, as Leo Panitch observed, use "the provincial state to express their interests."[55] By contrast I argue that, rather than weakening the central state structure, these regionally refracted conflicts within the bourgeois class in fact strengthen the federal state by calling for its, however lopsided, mediation. Since class fractions are able to articulate their intra-class conflict — and conflict with the central state apparatus — in provincial terms, they continually reproduce regional and provincial institutions or consciousness. This mechanism can thus be viewed as the regionalistic form in which class conflict (and largely intra-ruling class conflict) is articulated.

There are, however, still other mechanisms through which classes are balkanised, and these, again, directly relate to the perception, by Clark and his followers, of the lower classes as politically emasculated groups, as mere commodities.

On the ideological level, this balkanisation of the lower classes expresses itself today in the state ideology of multi-culturalism; a strategy which was imprinted into the Canadian social formation with the conquest of New France. The conquest was not a "social decapitation," as Stanley Ryerson[56] has pointed out — the old French ruling class remained — but it was a *political* decapitation which basically reflected the colonial practice of home rule whereby a subjugated population is free to regulate its internal affairs as long as they do not conflict with the interests of the colonial power. As Pitt declared:

> In lower Canada, as the residents are chiefly Canadians, their assembly, etc. will be adapted to their peculiar customs and prejudices.[57]

What emerged in practice in French Canada was the institutional monopoly held by the Catholic Church and the political disenfranchisement of the *habitant* in this transplanted version of the *Ancien Regime.*

I contend that this form of home rule is intrinsically state-supporting and conservative — in conformity with the state allegory of the beaver. Home rule disenfranchises a population politically, in exchange for some form of cultural or religious autonomy, and is thus a constitutive characteristic of the Canadian social structure. It is no accident that Hutterites, Mennonites and other communal religious groups — socially introverted and apolitical — were so whole-heartedly welcomed to Canada; together with conservative religious peasant immigrants from all over Europe. All of these groups had the freedom to be *"maitres chez eux,"* and, at the same time, were blocked from effective participation in national political life and from entrance into the national ruling class.

Icelandic immigration to Manitoba provides a good illustration of how this home rule system operates.[58] Shortly after settling in Manitoba in 1875, the new immigrants "established a republic of New Iceland in the interlake region of Manitoba north of Winnipeg."[59]

> During this early period of settlement, New Iceland was essentially an independent political entity. A constitution drawn up in 1878 made New Iceland virtually a republic of its own, with internally controlled legal and political structures and mechanisms and the right to do everything possible to retain Icelandic traditions and the continued use of the Icelandic language.[60]

One imagines such largesse on the part of the Canadian state. One wonders whether any other modern state would have tolerated this situation. The fact, however, is that this "republic" did not constitute an external challenge at all: it had no chance of real independence and its immigrants were principally interested in cultural and educational autonomy — which was not only tolerated, but encouraged by the province of Manitoba and the federal state. Even the Icelandic newspapers, rather than formulating independent political positions, faithfully reflected party divisions at the national level. Since the Icelandic community had, in fact, no political autonomy, it is no surprise that, in their settlement "debate over the Trinity supplanted... other issues which created both factionalism and cohesion in communities in Iceland."[61]

Relation 3. This pattern of home-rule generated acephalous, politically passive, or conformist communities throughout Canada. While particularly visible in the peculiar consolidation of immigrant groups, this pattern is not restricted to them. In an insightful study of the rural town of Hanna, Alberta, for example, Burnet shows how, in contrast to towns in New England, Alberta towns of this kind did not develop their own peculiar forms of political expression, and "village government [was] thought to be too unimportant to be of concern."[62] This weakness in the internal political structure of the local community was underlined by internal cleavages: the fracturing of classes along ethnic lines and divisions between town and country which discouraged collective action *vis-à-vis* outside companies or the provincial and federal governments.[63] In Hanna, not unlike Québec before the Quiet Revolution, the lives of the German-Russian population were dominated by conservative clergymen, and their social organization reflected their life under feudal domination.

As Clement observes,[64] Lucas makes a similar case with regard to the single-industry community he describes in *Minetown, Milltown, Railtown.*[65] This single-industry community was characterized by "total control and paternalism exhibited by the companies,"[66] buttressed by the RCMP. This extends to the point where the company and the town hierarchy sets rules which prohibit wives from going out to work, determine what type of dance may be held, or where residents can shop. As one informant put it:

> ... community interest is dangerously low. I think that the basic reason that men don't take a more active part in civic enterprises in this city is that they are afraid of their bosses or of supervisors who might be on the same board with them on some community project.[67]

Lucas concludes that "the citizen of a single industry community has the feeling that he has no control over his destiny."[68] This sense of fatalism also appears to explain the "lack of militant unionism in most of these communities."[69]

Relation 4. This strategy, then, which splits large sectors of Canadian society — parts of the middle class, the industrial working class and the farmers — into politically passive, conservative communities conforms with former Prime Minister Clark's vision of Canada as a "community of communities" and has important consequences for the nature of the Canadian social formation.

The price paid for this form of domination is, most of all, the lack of *genuine* national culture — but not as Bell and Tepperman and others have claimed, lack of a national ideology. It is undoubtedly correct that Canada's economic and political dependence on the U.S. has diminished its ability to control American dominance in the cultural sphere. What has often been overlooked, however, is the fact that, by turning over cultural autonomy to a myriad of ethnic, religious and regional enclaves in exchange for political acquiescence, the state abandoned, by definition, the attempt to develop an all-encompassing national and popular culture. As Creighton cynically notes, "imitation and plagiarism [have] become deep-seated Canadian instincts; economic and political dependence [have] grown into a settled way of life."[70]

It is therefore not surprising that despite excellent achievements, there is no characteristically Canadian tradition in any of the arts; all self-advertisements to the contrary. The work of the Group of Seven, for example, held as part of the "Canadian cultural heritage" is an obvious import of European expressionism and stands in clear contrast, for example, to autonomous artistic expression in the United States. The same could be shown for other cultural domains, including academic disciplines: rarely is there more than a thin upper layer that could pass as characteristically Canadian.

Relation 5. The absence of a national culture, however, does not imply absence of a national political ideology, which is a necessary instrument in support of the hegemony of any ruling class. I have discussed an academic state-supportive ideology here. This ideology is linked with the two key elements of the national ideology at large.

In contrast to the United States, which presents a pronounced ideology revolving around individual liberties as expressed in the U.S. Constitution, Canada's national ideology has the remarkable characteristic of appearing devoid of content — witness the emptiness of the national anthem, the wholly pragmatic language of the B.N.A. Act, devoid of any sense of a national mission, or the following remark by John Diefenbaker, which Layton calls "an exhortation to pursue an empty and undefined national objective."[71]

> Catch the vision! Catch the vision of the kind of Canada this can be! I've seen this vision, I've seen this future of Canada. I ask you to have faith in this land and faith in our people.[72]

I contend that, in Canada, the sense of a national mission — the idiom that typically characterizes a national ideology — is replaced by the idiom of actual political rule itself. This is most vividly expressed in the fact that, while Americans swear allegiance to their constitution, Canadians swear loyalty to a monarch.

Tied in with this professed loyalty to a foreign monarch is the colonial character of the political order and its idiomatic expression. The Mother Country may no longer be a significant factor in Canadian politics, but the legitimacy of the Canadian state is still expressed through an artificial attachment to Britain.

Thus, any British crime story, or British gossip and trivia — from Buckingham Palace to a sleepy town in Scotland — is elevated by the Canadian newsmedia, especially the C.B.C., to the level of the political, while dramatic political developments in countries which have furnished large proportions of Canada's ethnic population are rarely covered at all, reinforcing the powerlessness of these groups and their depoliticized status.[73] Earlier, I discussed the dichotomization of the population into "ethnocanadians" and Canadians of British origin. The depoliticized status of these groups is also apparent from their role in public appearances. Whereas, in the U.S., St. Patrick's Day, Columbus Day, Israel Independence Day, etc. are occasions for expression of ethnic solidarity — albeit in a generalized American cultural context[74] — such parades are extremely rare in English Canada, where they tend to have a distinctly British flavor.

This dichotomy into ethno — and anglo — Canadians, so important in the national political culture at large, is also visible in the fields of literature and religion. Literature, for example, is still a distinctly anglo monopoly. Whereas Jews have furnished a disproportionately large and prominent contingent of writers in other western countries, their contribution in Canada appears particularly small — and rather restricted to "less serious" writing, such as the satirical work of Mordecai Richler; and satire aptly reflects this social and political marginality.

As far as religion is concerned, Clark has rightly pointed out that there is a clear distinction between the churches on the one hand — typically those of the two charter groups — and the sects on the other, which are prevalent in rural areas in the West and in working and lower-middle class neighbourhoods. It is the churches to which a political role is attributed, whereas sects are in the domain of the apolitical. Hence the quasi-political role assumed by the Catholic clergy and more so, the Anglican priests or rabbi's columns in the editorial pages of the *Globe and Mail,* or the prominent role of the Timothy Eaton Memorial Chapel in Toronto.

We can see here as well the difference between Canada's relationship to its churches, and the relatively strict separation of church and state in the United States. It is precisely this separation of the two which integrates its ethnic and other communities to a much greater degree than could be possible in Canada.

This rough outline of the key elements of the Canadian social mythology should help to demonstrate that Canada's elites do not simply react defensively *vis-à-vis* the colossus to the south, in ideological terms as well, but that this class has produced a *genuinely Canadian* form of domination with its corresponding ideology. The political disfranchisement of the Canadian people, "ethnic" or "Anglo-Saxon" in origin, and their alleged political apathy and actual cultural ghettoization can therefore only be eliminated with the elimination of the present form of rule by the Canadian ruling elite, and the form of state in which it is expressed.

NOTES

[1]"From Sea to Sea."
[2]"From Many, One."
[3]Porter, 1965: 66.
[4]Woodsworth, 1908: 203.
[5]Sparling, in Woodsworth, 1908.
[6]Key parts of this work previously appeared in his *The Social Development of Canada,* 1942.
[7]Clark, 1968: 41.
[8]Clark, 1968: 43.
[9]Clark, 1968: 44.
[10]*Ibid.*
[11]Clark, 1968: 45.
[12]Clark, 1968: 44.
[13]*Ibid.*
[14]Clark, 1968: 46.
[15]Clark, 1968: 45.
[16]Clark, 1968: 65.
[17]*Ibid.*
[18]*Ibid.*
[19]Clark, 1968: 76.
[20]Clark, 1968: 80.
[21]Clark, 1968: 173. The psychological make-up of diverse ethnic groups is expressed very explicitly in another context, that of the "Gold Rush Society" of British Columbia: "Displays of tolerance on the part of the British peoples served only to aggravate the strained relationships by giving the Negroes an undue sense of their importance and thereby irritating even more the American populace... The Chinese constituted something of a despised race in the mining society, though their general inoffensiveness provided little occasion for acts of vituperation." Clark, 1968: 89ff.
[22]Clark, 1968: 102.
[23]*Ibid.*
[24]With pitifully few references to Canada's colonial status and its relationship to the U.S.
[25]Hughes, 1943: ix.
[26]1909.
[27]Bell and Tepperman, 1979.
[28]Bell and Tepperman, 1979: 3.
[29]Bell and Tepperman, 1979: 158.

[30]A term propagated by Johnny Lombardi, a leading multicultural entrepreneur.

[31]Bell and Tepperman, 1979: 90.

[32]Bell and Tepperman, 1979: 158.

[33]Bell and Tepperman, 1979: 98.

[34]Clark, 1976: 78ff.

[35]Note, however, the difference between Anglo-Canadian and Québec Marxist approaches. For example, Clement writes of the "corporate elite," while Jorge Niosi *(La Bourgeoisie Canadienne,* 1979) deals with the broader conception of the power of its various class segments, as well as their ideological outlook. It is self-evident that the former shows a certain economistic tendency while the latter is far more interested in questions of power and ideology.

[36]In their discussion of co-operative regionalism, "a positive form of regionalism made possible through political decisions made by those who have the authority to commit their communities to collective action" (their quote from Jacob and Toscano, 1964) the authors state at one point, "the elitist bias of the approach poses problems on occasion. However, focusing on political decision makers makes good sense when analyzing cooperative regionalism in *this* country" (193ff., their italics).

[37]Glenday, Guindon, and Turowetz, 1978.

[38]Glenday, Guindon, and Turowetz, 1978: 297.

[39]Glenday, Guindon and Turowetz, 1978: 298.

[40]Glenday, Guindon and Turowetz, 1978: 297.

[41]Glenday, Guindon, and Turowetz: 297.

[42]Hobart and Brant, 1966.

[43]"I desire to put the objections of the people of British Columbia in concrete form: they object to the Asiatic: Because they usually get a grip on the country they enter. Because, while they may come here as hewers of wood and drawers of water, they do not remain in a servile position. Because they are incapable of assimilation. Because they are strangers to our civilization... Because we want to preserve the British type in our population." (Duncan Ross, Member for Yale-Cariboo, on December 16, 1907 in the House of Commons) Canada Debates, 1907: 743. Quoted in Reitz, 1970.

[44]Canada Debates, 1944: 5917.

[45]This destruction of community need not be on the basis of ethnicity, but can be directed at backward European communities as well: Planners of the Newfoundland government "even concluded that resettlement 'tends to offer a wider scope for the development of better citizens.' The same emphasis occurs in Canada's overall regional development strategy: in their efforts to better the economic situation of poor people, our economic planners have developed a model which makes economic sense, but which fails to take into consideration the social costs involved.

[46]Grayson, 1980: 158.

[47]Allan Smith's discussion of the "self-made man" in Canada and Dorothy Smith's analysis of sexist biases against academic women easily apply to the U.S. as well. The essay by Layton on Canadian bourgeois ideology and the Graysons' study on class concepts in the English Canadian novel again bring out North American (western capitalist) features, and fail to point out what is *specifically* Canadian about these conceptions.

[48]A similar criticism could be levelled against P. Marchak (1975) who again provides little sense of the *political* nature of the Canadian state, and who only obscures it in the cliché of ruling classes.

[49]Reitz, 1980.

[50]1980: 88.

[51]*Ibid.*

[52]1980: 226.

[53]Reitz, 1980: 226.

[54]*Ibid.*

[55]Panitch, 1977: 11.

[56]Ryerson, 1960: 204.

[57]Quoted in Ryerson, 1960: 228.

[58]Mathiasson, in Elliott, 1979.

[59]Mathiasson, in Elliott, 1979: 195.

[60]Mathiasson, in Elliott, 1979: 199.

[61]Mathiasson, in Elliott, 1979: 204.

[62]Burnet, 1947: 63.

[63]For similar observations on an Ontario town, see Sinclair and Westhues, 1974.

[64]Clement, in Glenday, Guindon and Turowetz, 1978.

[65]Lucas, 1971.

[66]Lucas, 1971: 106.

[67]Lucas, 1971: 157.

[68]*Ibid.*

[69]*Ibid.*

[70]Creighton, 1971: 356.

[71]Grayson, 1980: 224.

[72]John Diefenbaker, March 10, 1958.

[73]For example, the news of the capture of the Yorkshire Ripper was the CBC's headline news throughout the day in question. The highly dramatic murder of a general of the Italian *carabinieri,* on the other hand, was barely mentioned. The B.B.C. by contrast, reported in detail on the Italian story, and the Ripper case became very quickly a secondary news story.

[74]Apart from the notion of the melting pot itself, this generalization is clearly apparent in the United States. For St. Patrick's Day, for example, Jewish bakeries in Boston bake green bagels which would be quite inconceivable in the ambience of Toronto.

Bibliography

Adachi, Ken. *A History of the Japanese Canadians in British Columbia.* Toronto: Japanese Citizens Association, 1956.

Anderson, Alan B. and James S. Frideres. *Ethnicity in Canada: Theoretical Perspectives.* Toronto: Butterworths, 1981.

Avery, Donald. "Continental European Immigrant Workers in Canada, 1896-1919: From 'Stalwart Peasants' to Radical Proletariat." *Canadian Review of Sociology and Anthropology* 12 (1975): 53-64.

Bainbridge, William S. and Rodney Stark. "Church and Cult in Canada." *Canadian*

Journal of Sociology 7 (1982): 351-66.

Balakrishnan, T. R. "Changing Patterns in Ethnic Residential Segregation in the Metropolitan Areas of Canada." *Canadian Review of Sociology and Anthropology* 19 (1982): 92-110.

Bell, David and Lorne Tepperman. *The Roots of Disunity.* Toronto: McClelland and Stewart, 1979.

Bercuson, D. J., ed. *Canada and the Burden of Unity.* Toronto: Macmillan, 1977.

Boissevain, Jeremy. *The Italians of Montreal: Social Adjustments in A Plural Society.* Royal Commission on Bilingualism and Biculturalism. Study 7. Ottawa: Information Canada, 1970.

Breton, Raymond, J. G. Reitz, and Victor F. Valentine. *Cultural Boundaries and the Cohesion of Canada.* Montreal: IRPP, 1980.

Brody, Hugh. *The People's Land.* New York: Penguin, 1975.

Burnet, Jean. "Town-Country Relations and the Problem of Rural Leadership." *Canadian Journal of Economics and Political Science* 13 (1947): 395-409.

Cardinal, Harold. *The Unjust Society: The Tragedy of Canada's Indians.* Edmonton: Hurtig, 1969.

Clairmont, Donald. "The Development of a Deviance Service Centre." In Jack Haas and Bill Shaffir, eds. *Decency and Deviance.* Toronto: McClelland and Stewart, 1974.

Clairmont, D. H. and D. W. Magill. *Africville.* Toronto: McClelland and Stewart, 1974.

Clairmont, D. H. and E. C. Wien. "Segmentation, Disadvantage and Development: An Analysis of the Marginal Work World, Its Linkages With the Central Work World and Its Role in the Maritime Provinces." A Working Paper in the Marginal Work World Research Program. Halifax: Institute of Public Affairs, Dalhousie University, 1974.

Clark, S. D. *The Developing Canadian Community.* Rev. ed. Toronto: University of Toronto Press, 1968.

_____. *The Social Development of Canada.* Toronto: University of Toronto Press, 1942.

_____. *The Suburban Society.* Toronto: University of Toronto Press, 1966.

Creighton, Donald. *The Story of Canada.* Toronto: Macmillan, 1971.

Crysdale, Stewart. "Social and Occupational Mobility in Riverdale: A Blue-Collar Community." In W. E. Mann, ed. *Canada: A Sociological Profile.* Toronto: Copp Clark, 1968.

Darroch, A. Gordon. "Another Look at Ethnicity, Stratification, and Social Mobility in Canada." *Canadian Journal of Sociology* 4 (1979): 1-25.

de Jocas, Yves and Guy Rocher. "Inter-generational Occupational Mobility in the Province of Quebec." *Canadian Journal of Economics and Political Science* 23 (1957): 58-66.

Elliott, Jean L. *Minority Canadians 1: Native Peoples and Minority Canadians.* Toronto: Prentice-Hall, 1971.

_____. *Minority Canadians 2: Immigrant Groups,* Toronto: Prentice-Hall, 1971.

_____. *Two Nations, Many Cultures: Ethnic Groups in Canada.* Scarborough, Ont.: Prentice-Hall, 1979.

Forcese, Dennis. *The Canadian Class Structure.* Toronto: McGraw-Hill Ryerson, 1975.

Glenday, Daniel, Hubert Guindon, and Allan Turowetz, eds. *Modernization and the Canadian State.* Toronto: Macmillan, 1978.

Grabb, Edward G. "Canada's Lower Middle Class." *Canadian Journal of Sociology* 1 (1975): 295-312.

Grayson, J. Hall, *Class, State, Ideology and Change: Marxist Perspectives on Canada.* Toronto: Holt Rinehart and Winston, 1980.

———. "Male Hegemony and the English Canadian Novel." *Canadian Review of Sociology and Anthropology* 20 (1983): 1-21

———. "The Canadian Novel and the Class Structure." *Canadian Journal of Sociology* 6 (1981): 423-45.

Hall, Oswald. "The Place of the Professions in the Urban Community." In S. D. Clark, ed. *Urbanism and the Changing Canadian Society.* Toronto: University of Toronto Press, 1961.

Hobart, Charles and C. S. Brant. "Eskimo Education, Danish and Canadian: A Comparison." *Canadian Review of Sociology and Anthropology* 3 (1966): 47-65.

Hughes, Everett C. "Industry and the Rural System in Quebec." *Canadian Journal of Economics and Political Science* 4 (1938): 341-49.

———. *French Canada in Transition.* Chicago: University of Chicago Press, 1943.

Ishwaran, K. *Family, Kinship and Community: A Study of Dutch Canadians.* Toronto: McGraw-Hill Ryerson, 1977.

Joy, Richard. *Languages in Conflict: The Canadian Experience.* Toronto: McClelland and Stewart, 1972.

Krauter, Joseph and Morris Davis. *Minority Canadians: Ethnic Groups.* Toronto: Methuen, 1978.

Lieberson, Stanley. *Languages and Ethnic Relations in Canada.* New York: Wiley, 1970.

Lucas, Rex H. *Minetown, Milltown, Railtown.* Toronto: University of Toronto Press, 1971.

McCrorie, James N., ed. *Canadian Review of Sociology and Anthropology.* (A Special Issue on Quebec) 15: (1978).

———. "Change and Paradox in Agrarian Social Movements: The Case of Saskatchewan." In Richard Ossenberg, ed. *Canadian Society: Pluralism, Change and Conflict.* Scarborough: Prentice-Hall, 1971.

McGee, H. F. *The Native Peoples of Atlantic Canada.* Toronto: McClelland and Stewart, 1974.

Marchak, Patricia. *Ideological Perspectives on Canada.* Toronto: McGraw-Hill Ryerson, 1975.

Niosi, J. *The Economy of Canada.* Montreal: Black Rose, 1978.

Panitch, Leo, ed. *The Canadian State: Political Economy and Political Power.* Toronto: University of Toronto Press, 1977.

Porter, John. *The Vertical Mosaic.* Toronto: University of Toronto Press, 1965.

Reitz, J. G. *The Survival of Ethnic Groups.* Toronto: McGraw-Hill Ryerson, 1980.

Richmond, Anthony. *Post-War Immigration to Canada.* Toronto: University of Toronto Press, 1967.

Royal Commission on Bilingualism and Biculturalism. *Report, Vol I.: Introduction and the Official Languages.* Ottawa: The Queen's Printer, 1968.

———. *Report, Vol. II: Education.* Ottawa: The Queen's Printer, 1968.

———. *Report, Vol. 3a and 3b: The Work World.* Ottawa: The Queen's Printer, 1969.

———. *Report, Vol. 4: The Other Groups.* Ottawa: The Queen's Printer, 1969.

Rioux, Marcel and Yves Martin, eds. *French Canadian Society.* Vol. I. Toronto: McClelland and Stewart, 1964.

Tepperman, Lorne. *Social Mobility in Canada.* Toronto: University of Toronto Press, 1973.

Tremblay, Marc-Abel and Walton Anderson, eds. *Rural Canada in Transition.* Ottawa: Agricultural Economics Research Council of Canada, 1966.

Ujimoto, Victor. "The Pre-War and Post-War Japanese Community in B.C." *Canadian Review of Sociology and Anthropology* 13 (1976): 80-89.

Valee, F. G. and Norman Shulman. "The Viability of French Groupings Outside Quebec." In Mason Wade, ed. *Regionalism in the Canadian Community, 1867-1967.* Toronto: University of Toronto Press, 1969.

Wade, Mason, ed. *Regionalism in the Canadian Community, 1867-1957.* Toronto: University of Toronto Press, 1969.

Wellman, Barry. "The Community Question: The Intimate Networks of East Yorkers." *American Journal of Sociology* 84 (1979): 1201-31.

Woodsworth, James S. *Strangers Within Our Gates: Or, Coming Canadians.* Toronto: F. C. Stephenson, 1907.

CHAPTER 10

Corporate Structure, Corporate Control, and Canadian Elites

S. D. Berkowitz

BACKGROUND

When John Porter first published *The Vertical Mosaic* almost 20 years ago, it seemed to capture the essence of Canadian society. While thoroughly sociological in form and content, it appealed to a far wider audience than normally reached by academic work. It was brightly written and clearly argued. It avoided elaborate scholarly qualifiers. It addressed the hard questions in any societal-level study — the source and extent of class, power, and group differences — and provided answers. It used data, but did not hide behind it. As a result, it was reviewed in the popular press as well as in academic journals. Within a few years, the broad outlines of its analysis of Canadian society were so widely accepted that journalists and politicians could refer to it without explanation.

What *The Vertical Mosaic* had done more than anything else was to shatter the *myth* of Canada as a middle class, consensual and popular-democratic society in which individuals' aspirations are only limited by their abilities and energies. What it created as an alternative, however, was an image of Canadian society which is fundamentally and seriously flawed. And, like its predecessor, this image will probably not be easily put to rest.

The core of Porter's argument in *The Vertical Mosaic* is that social ranking is "ubiquitous" in all societies.[1] In urban industrial societies of the western type, social differentiation takes the form of class stratification.[2] Within this class-based system, further differentiation occurs because of the necessity for coordination among separate, but interrelated, institutional arenas.[3] To the extent that we can identify these semi-autonomous spheres, we can uncover power roles within each of them. Occupants of these roles constitute the elites within each specific institutional realm.[4] *The Vertical Mosaic* identifies four groups corresponding to institutional sub-systems which have historically played an important part in Canadian society: economic, political, administrative or bureaucratic, and ideological elites.[5]

While Porter emphasizes that the nature of the relationships among them cannot be determined *a priori,* he observes, empirically, that Canada's economic elite has often been dominant in the past and that the other elites have accommodated to this fact. For this reason, I take Porter's theoretical and empirical contentions regarding corporate power and the economic elite to be the core of his model and will focus on them here. In each of the sections which follow we will examine a few issues related to the structure and institutional control of the large business corporations which dominate the Canadian economy. Many of these questions are raised directly in *The Vertical Mosaic.* Others have been the subject of extensive research by analysts following in Porter's footsteps. Since it has been so influential, where possible we will begin by discussing *The Vertical Mosaic's* statement of a particular problem. Where it is not, we will use the neo-Porterian formulation instead. We will then look at how Porter and/or his disciples develop this question and the conclusions they reach regarding it. This will be followed by a brief discussion of the particular issue at hand and how it relates to the system of power-holding we call an "elite structure." The final section will attempt to sketch an overall picture of the role played by corporations and corporate elites in Canadian society and to point out theoretical and substantive questions that still remain to be answered.

CONCENTRATION OF ECONOMIC POWER

The crux of Porter's interpretation of Canadian social structure lies in his notion of "the concentration of economic power." Porter contends that the Canadian economy is dominated by less than 200 large corporations whose decisions and indecisions have a formidable and pervasive impact on the rest of the society. These corporations employ hundreds of thousands of people whose lives and careers depend on their policies and practices. They shape perceptions of the world, mold tastes, and help fix the criteria by which we judge ourselves. They play a critical role in setting goals for the educational system, have a significant impact on federal and provincial legislation and may act to raise or lower social barriers between groups. They determine, in important respects, which regions of the country will prosper and which decline. In short, they form the single most important institutional nexus in advanced capitalist societies such as Canada.

The men[6] who operate these corporations — their chief officers and directors — constitute an "economic elite":

> In the Western type of industrial society the concept of an economic elite derives its validity from the concentration of economic power within a relatively few corporations which become linked to one another and to the principal financial institutions through interlocking directorships.[7]

Beyond these purely economic ties, the directors and officers of dominant corporations share social characteristics and common life experiences. From these they are able to forge a collective identity:

> Frequency of interaction, homogeneity in social background, and class continuity all lead to common outlook and common attitudes and values about the social system and the place of corporate enterprise in it. The fact that the corporate elite hold important positions beyond the corporate world means that they are in a position to make their ideology pervade the entire society until it becomes identified with the common good.[8]

While Porter's "economic elite" is ultimately rooted in the corporate system, then, it has firm bases in other institutional structures as well. This is essential to his argument:

> An elite group is...something more than a statistical class, so it is [also] necessary to provide evidence that the economic elite exhibits a degree of social homogeneity.[9]

Just as in C. Wright Mills's analysis of the U.S. a decade earlier,[10] Porter's *economic elite* is the only one of the four that, to a significant degree, is also bound together by strong sources of social and cultural identity. Hence, while each of the other elites exercises considerable power within its own functional domain, when conflicts arise Porter observes that the views of core elements within the economic elite tend to prevail.

Chapters eight and nine of *The Vertical Mosaic* are largely taken up with this twin task of demonstrating (a) that economic power in Canada is concentrated in a small number of large corporations, and (b) that the officers and directors of these corporations constitute a cohesive social group. In describing the results of a study of economic concentration he conducted in 1955, Porter concludes that among "establishments employing more than 500 hands" one could isolate "183 dominant corporations."[11] Beginning with these firms:

> ...it was possible to show that in the period 1948-50, from which the basic data were drawn, these dominant corporations were responsible for 40 to 50 per cent of the gross value of production in manufacturing, 63 per cent of the total value of metal production, 90 per cent of railway transportation, 88 per cent of the gross earnings of telegraph and cable services, 82 per cent of the revenue of Canadian air carriers, 83 per cent of telephone revenues, and 60 to 70 per cent of the hydro-electricity produced by privately owned companies, as well as a large but undetermined proportion of other industries such as minerals, fuels, water transportation, and retail distribution.[12]

These are impressive statistics. Data of this kind — and *The Vertical Mosaic* provides a great many of them — tend to shock ordinary readers. Most of us live in worlds where the common reference point for the notion of a "business" is a corner grocery store or local manufacturing firm. So when someone asserts that "a large but undetermined proportion" of retail sales and "40 to 50% of the gross value of production in manufacturing" is concentrated in some 200 firms, we tend to react with concern or awe or both. This, of course, is precisely what Porter wants us to do.

On closer inspection it is quite unclear how we ought to treat these data analytically — and Porter does not do more than present us with raw numbers. We need some kind of basis for comparison. Are these figures "high" or "low"? If so, by what standard? More importantly, what *behavioral* consequences can we anticipate from them? In other words, if Porter is using these data as a measure of "economic power," how can we tell when this power is being exercised?

Economists who subscribe to the dominant "structure-conduct-performance" paradigm are principally concerned with one form of economic "power": the ability of sellers or buyers to dominate *specific* markets for goods or services.[13] When there are large numbers of buyers and sellers in a particular market, so the theory goes, no seller or buyer can exercise undue influence because others will take up the slack: sellers will offer their wares at lower prices or buyers will be willing to pay more for them.[14] Hence, market power can only exist when there are so *few* buyers or sellers that individual economic actors can have a direct impact on prices.[15]

There are several analytically important considerations which follow from this statement of the problem. First, in *unconcentrated* markets sellers and buyers cannot reap benefits simply due to market power. Where a market is concentrated, they can. Market power distorts corporate income (a) by allowing concentrated sectors to draw additional resources out of the rest of the economy and (b) by facilitating the accumulation of assets in that set of firms (or other economic units) best able to exercise this power.[16] Second, since market power is a property of an economic actor (or group of actors) within a specific market, it is senseless to speak about "concentration" without closely defining a context. Parts of a given economy may be highly concentrated — even monopolized or oligopolized — while others may be quite competitive. Since the impact of highly concentrated industries on other sectors of the economy depends on a variety of additional factors, "overall" or "average" measures of concentration can mean a variety of different things. Finally, the sheer size of firms (or other economic units) is not a critical determinant of their market conduct: their size relative to others is much more important. Thus, we have to be extremely careful in constructing bases for comparison.

While there are superficial similarities between this neo-classical interpretation of economic power and the way Porter approaches the topic, the differences are important. First, Porter usually talks about "economic concentration" at the level of the economy as a whole. In practical terms, this means that his model cannot deal with effective competition, i.e., the actual constraints and conditions faced by particular firms in given markets. This is significant because it is these practical conditions that determine prices, the allocation of income among industries, and so on. Second, by moving to this global level Porter has left those spheres of economic activity for which we have the most analytically interpretable results. This implies that, in most instances, the best he can hope to do in a rigorous fashion is to *describe* the conduct of actors within portions of the economy. His *explana-*

tions must be imported *ad hoc.* Third, since Porter's model precludes dealing with effective competition or utilizing rigorous analytic techniques, he cannot base his conclusions on some well-defined model of allocative efficiency. This is critical because the use of the term "power" implies the power *to do something.* If, as Porter suggests, the primary consequence of the exercise of "economic power" is a reallocation of income shares, he must show that the actual distribution differs significantly from that which would obtain under optimal conditions. Finally, Porter's statistics are based on a number of different measures of economic activity (e.g., "gross value of production," "revenue," "per cent...produced") whose relationship to one another — and to interpretations of market conduct — are by no means self-evident. Porter makes no effort to justify their use in this context.

While limited in scope, then, the neo-classical notion of economic power has the advantage that it can be readily *operationalized*[17] and measured. Since it is specific to a given market-context, analysts need only determine three things: the boundaries of the market, the number of actors or effective units it contains, and their relative share of assets, sales, shipments — or whatever else a given theoretical model stipulates as a measure of the effective interplay of market forces.

For instance, let us assume that we were interested in determining how much of an impact the largest tool manufacturers have on the rest of the industry in which they operate. By identifying the proportion of all shipments originating with each firm, we can construct a *distribution* similar to those sociologists use to represent household income. But since corporations are legal fictions there is no intrinsic reason why any firm "ought" to have a share of the total; i.e., we assume that the number of corporations within an economy is artificial in a way that the number of people in a population is not. For this reason, economists usually focus on only those firms which are most critical theoretically, i.e., the market actors who account for the largest share of activity. The conventional way to do this is to calculate the proportion of all shipments (or assets or whatever) attributable to the top four, top eight or top 20 participants. In our hypothetical case, if the top four firms in the "hardware, tool, and cutlery manufacturing" industry[18] shipped 25 per cent of all goods in a given year, then we would report the "top four concentration ratio" as "25" for that period. If the top eight shipped 37 per cent, the comparable top eight number would be "37" — and so on. By comparing the top four, top eight, and top 20 figures for several different industries, we can then establish their relative degree of concentration or openness.[19]

This type of statistic makes good intuitive sense because it draws attention to precisely that aspect of market activity — the interplay of numbers of participants and market share — which is critical to models of the conduct and relative power of effective economic units.

Dominant Corporations

Similar claims cannot be made for Porter's method of determining the "dominant firms" he uses in examining trends in the economy. He provides no satisfactory explanation, for example, as to what exactly "dominant corporations" dominate. When pressed, his answer is "the economy." But, if so, how? Dominant corporations are certainly large, but we know that by definition: they are selected on the basis of "size." So to argue that they are "dominant" *because* they are large is tautological. If, as Porter suggests, we ought to treat corporations as dominant when they account for a disproportionate share of industrial activity, then we must be careful since, using his method, an industry group may include any number of "dominants." Thus, we have no easy way of comparing the "shares" he reports across industry groups. If two corporations together accounted for 50 per cent of shipments in a given industry, most people would agree that that industry was highly concentrated. If 22 firms did, we might not be so impressed.

From a social scientist's point of view, the important thing here is that Porter does not standardize observations in some analytically meaningful way. In summarizing evidence gathered by the Royal Commission on Canada's Economic Prospects,[20] for instance, he concludes that:

> Eleven leading manufacturing industries with a total net value added in 1954 of $2,049.6 million were examined. Sixty-four firms accounted for $1,345.2 million (or 65 per cent) of net value added in these industries. After duplicates were eliminated and subsidiaries were consolidated with parent firms, fifty-six firms were left, forty-nine of which were dominant corporations. The seven which were not on the list were relatively small producers in their industries, and were included by the commission investigators only to make up the six largest firms.[21]

While he does not make this explicit, Porter's obvious *contrast conception* here is an economy in which each producer accounts for the same proportion of the total value added.[22] This, in itself, is unrealistic in that it assumes *no* barriers to entry, i.e., that new and old market entrants will be on precisely the same footing.

We can gain some insight into what is at work here by comparing Porter's presentation of these data with the more standard form. Assume that his final 49 firms are evenly distributed among industries. This yields an average of 4.5 firms per industry. Since halves are difficult to deal with, let us give Porter the benefit of the doubt and round down.[23] Seen in this way, the average top four concentration ratio for value added in these industries is 65. This is high, but not execssive. Moreover, since value added calculations closely reflect scale of industrial production, we suspect that some large-scale industries (e.g. autos) have numbers in the nineties — and this drags the average upwards.[24] So, in some cases, the top four ratios must be much lower — say in the forties. Once again, these are not statistics we should get very excited about since (a) four or five large producers and a number of small ones are quite sufficient to form an open market and (b) given the relatively small demand for some goods in Canada (e.g., refrigerators) this number of producers is probably *larger* than it ought to be strictly on the basis of economies of scale.[25]

When translating his figures in this fashion, one should of course bear in mind that Porter is not genuinely interested in the economic consequences of corporate concentration. While his discussion of the issue begins with some broad references to "problems of monopoly" and the relatively ineffective ways Canadian anti-combines legislation attempts to deal with them, Porter's overriding purpose is to convince us that there are broad social consequences of corporate wealth-holding. His arguments regarding economic concentration, then, are really a surrogate for more detailed treatments of a series of complex social and political issues: the role of large-scale organizations in industrial societies, the relationship between corporate and governmental power under advanced capitalism, interest group formation, and so on. Rather than taking these questions on directly, he brings them in through the back door as part of his discussion of "the concentration of economic power."

This shows through clearly in the rather exotic ways Porter goes about operationally defining "dominant corporations." He first determines the one per cent of the 33,447 manufacturing "establishments" (productive units) which accounted for the largest share of total production in 1948.[26] These establishments are then mapped together into 218 firms.

> In some industries although there were one or two firms with an establishment employing more than 500 the industry was not highly concentrated. Such was the case, for example, with the secondary textile industry.... Although there were some large firms in the wool textile industry [they were dropped because] it was not highly concentrated, and at the same time it was relatively unimportant in the total economy.... The printing and publishing industry was excluded because the power of these firms does not lie so much in their use of economic resources as their ability to influence opinion.... After subtracting from the 218 corporations those in the less important industries there were left 162 firms.... Of these...eight were too small to be considered dominant corporations. In their place on the list of dominant corporations were put ten firms all of which had gross assets of more than $10 million.[27]

Porter continues in this fashion until he comes up with his list of 183 "dominants." Note that companies are added to or dropped from this set on the basis of criteria other than their direct role in the economy. Since his ultimate goal is to articulate a relationship between corporate power and broader forms of social influence or control, Porter runs the risk of contaminating his principal variable whenever he does this. Excluding certain industries because they are "relatively unimportant," for instance, distorts the size distribution for "dominant" firms. Including other firms because of the size of their assets — despite the fact that they play no strategic role in the industries within which they operate — probably has a similar effect. Moreover, since he does several of these kinds of things simultaneously, we have no clear way of establishing their *net measurement effects*: the impact they have on the variable (firm dominance) Porter constructs using his list of dominant firms. The result is a methodological morass from which it is very difficult to extract clear empirical results.

Unfortunately, these methodological difficulties have now become almost a standard feature of Canadian sociological research on corporate power. For instance, in *The Canadian Corporate Elite* Wallace Clement provides an initial definition of "dominant corporations" in 1972 which emphasizes their size:

> To identify the economic elite it is...necessary to specify both the largest, or what will be called *dominant,* corporations and positions within these corporations which are uppermost.[28]

Later, however, he specifies "dominants" in terms of their *effects* on others:

> There are roughly three levels operating within the economy: those "dominant" corporations powerful enough to set the "tone" and direction of particular segments of the economy and together the general direction of the entire economy; the "middle range" economic powers which conform to the "tone" established by the dominants but which generally benefit from doing so and are not powerful enough to contradict the direction of the dominants; those who are affected by the policies and direction of each of the above, like small businessmen and consumers.[29]

Here Clement is stipulating that, irrespective of size, "dominant corporations" are those which play a specific "dominating" role *vis-à-vis* other economic actors:

> ... the 'domination effect'... means that 'firm can alter for its own benefit the structure of competitive or allied firms'.... Dominant firms, then, are those which exercise the 'domination effect.'[30]

These two ways of defining leading corporations — one based on a simple attribute (size) and the other on a relational property (power or influence over others) — are, of course, quite different and would, in the limiting case, yield dramatically different results. The most strategically-placed firm in a non-capital intensive industry, for instance, might be quite "small" — in terms of assets, sales, shipments, or whatever — relative to even a moderate-sized firm in an industry with higher scale requirements. Within industry boundaries, a firm which is small in terms of assets might well play an important brokering role for the others and hence wield enormous power. As I have argued elsewhere,[31] there is no *necessary* correspondence between aggregative and structural characteristics of economic actors and, consequently, it is dangerous to draw inferences about structural dimensions from the variable properties of aggregates.[32]

Clement's confusion of structural and aggregative dimensions of power comes through most clearly when he begins to use these definitions operationally. Interestingly, he recognizes some of the limitations of Porter's approach:

When, for example, "valued added" or "number of hands employed" is used to indicate relative concentration, they are necessarily biased towards production-based companies and, even within these companies, towards particular ways of producing profits. For instance, "number of hands employed" is biased towards labour-intensive industries and understates the power of capital intensive operations.[33]

However, fundamental methodological problems remain:

If it can be agreed that increased revenues or profits, and with that, control over sources of capital, is the goal of capitalism, then it is more appropriate to focus on the goal than the means. More general statistics such as assets, revenue or net income cut across all sectors and, since oriented toward the actual goals of capitalism, are more appropriate to a focus on general economic power.[34]

Here we can see one of the problems of the Porter-Clement method in stark relief. Since, for Clement as for Porter, the specification of a set of dominant corporations is simply a way-station en route to the discovery of a "corporate elite," Clement has no clear model to inform his selection process. Thus he is forced to resort to *ad hoc* justifications for his use of particular criteria in choosing the firms in his sample. The notion of the "goals of capitalism" which Clement throws out here is completely exogenous: he neither prepares the reader for a discussion of general conditions of capital formation nor subsequently integrates this concept into his interpretation of corporate power. His rationale, moreover, will not meet even rudimentary tests of consistency. Do "increased revenues or profits" really eventuate in "control over sources of capital"? A corporation can obviously be *completely* owned and controlled by a parent company — or even a single stockholder — and, at the same time, highly profitable. Increasing profitability will not alter its "control over...sources of capital" one iota. Moreover, a company can have huge revenues and still incur heavy losses. In the long run, this *is* indeed likely to alter its "control over resources": such corporations stand a good chance of winding up in the hands of their creditors! By contrast, investment banks often have comparatively modest asset bases, but wield power due to the structured opportunities they have for using what Louis Brandeis refers to as "other people's money."[35] This power is a byproduct of their strategic location in a network of corporate relationships, and not the "size" of any attribute Clement might specify.

In any case, a far more robust theoretical justification is necessary before a model could hope to account for even rudimentary aspects of the relationship between forms of capital-holding and intercorporate control. This cannot simply be intuited from a set of abstract "goals." Clement, as Porter before him, is insensitive to the dynamic aspects of an economy. In practical terms, this means that both Porter and Clement are often unaware of the intricacies involved in reconstructing the interplay between corporate organization, corporate performance, and business behavior.

Interlocking Directorates

Having determined a set of "dominants," both Porter and Clement then turn to the directors and officers who, they maintain, play a socially critical role in translating the concentrated wealth and influence of these corporations into tangible forms of social and political power. This is an important juncture in both of their models: corporations themselves, they seem to argue, have only indirect impacts on the societies in which they operate. In order to understand the broader effects of large business corporations on life in western industrial societies, they submit, we must come to grips with the immediate influence of the men who shape and direct the activities of these corporations: the "economic elite." In the process, general *institutional* power becomes transformed into *personal* power.

In Porter's version of the argument, the mechanisms which allow for the exercise of this personal power remain relatively obscure. For Porter, the members of the corporate elite are powerful because they have undergone the "right" social experiences, have become tied to the "leading" economic institutions, and participated in the "correct" decision-making contexts. They have disproportionately dominated important channels of communication between functional realms. In sum, their power rests on their preponderance within certain social roles and institutional locations.

Clement puts the case somewhat differently. While he repeats Porter's "preponderance" argument, he also maintains that corporate elites are able to exercise influence — to monopolize decision-making, control communications, etc. — because they can draw upon the power implicit in structural ties between formal organizations. Thus, while interlocking directorates — ties formed when individuals sit on the board of directors of more than one corporation — only play a small and episodic role in the body of evidence Porter brings forward, they become a major focus in Clement's work.

Clement begins by identifying 1,454 positions in 113 "dominant" corporations which were occupied by Canadian residents in 1971.[36] An additional 301 positions were held by persons living outside Canada. After a brief summary of some of the attributes of persons occupying these positions,[37] Clements proposes that we view the interlocks between these positions as a measure of the ability of corporations to communicate with, and therefore influence, other corporate actors. In particular, Clement is fascinated by the large number of interlocks formed by banks and other financial institutions — both among themselves, and with industrial corporations:

> In 1951 Porter found that the nine largest Canadian banks had 55 interlocks with the ten largest Canadian insurance companies. In 1972 the largest five Canadian banks, when interlocked with the eight independent Canadian controlled dominant insurance companies, produced a total of 51 interlocks. Since insurance companies are prohibited

from interlocking with other insurance companies and banks with other banks, each bank and each insurance company can only interface once. In 1951, 90 interfaces (10 banks times nine insurance companies) produced 55 interlocks; in 1972, only 40 interfaces (five banks times eight insurance companies) produced 51 interlocks representing a substantial increase in the "density" of interlocking between dominant Canadian banks and insurance companies.... Finance has the strongest relationship with each of the other sectors both in terms of density and actual interlocks. In addition to the .71 relationship with utilities, finance has a .62 relation with manufacturing, .59 with resources but only .37 with trade.[38]

While this focus on corporate *structure* represents a considerable advance over the fascination with *individual* characteristics which dominates Canadian elite studies — much of *The Canadian Corporate Elite* included — it is clear that Clement is insensitive to some elementary properties of his data. Thus, much of his discussion of the phenomenon of interlocking directorates, while well-intentioned, is a methodological and, hence, substantive jumble.

I have dealt elsewhere with a number of formal problems with the way Clement handles these data.[39] A few examples will suffice here. First, as we observe above, Clement uses the term "interface" to mean "an opportunity to interlock with." Clement wants to count these "interfaces" so that he can establish a benchmark for his calculation of "density": actual interlocks over "opportunities." The difficulty, of course, is that banks and insurance companies — or other corporations — can interlock more than once, i.e., when more than one man sits on both boards. We know that Clement has not taken this fact into account in calculating "interfaces." Clement does not tell us whether he has counted more than one "interlock" between firms in establishing the numerator for his "density" measure. From the context, it appears that he has.[40] Thus (a) Clement has ignored an important property of interlocks in the second term in his ratio — multistranded ties or what is called "multiplexity" — and (b) he has incorporated it into the first. The ratio of one to the other which he constructs is, therefore, meaningless.

Second, by using his own notion of "density" Clement runs the risk that unwary readers will confuse his use of the term with the standard, and mathematically precise, interpretation of the concept in the literature.[41] This is especially unfortunate since the "densities" he reports (e.g., .62, .71) are quite high. Thus we are left with the impression that Canadian banks and insurance companies form part of a highly interwoven and closely articulated communications network. Oddly, Clement himself indicates at another point that this is not exactly correct:

> Not all dominant insurance companies are equally interlocked with the dominant banks. The three foreign controlled insurance companies have only eight interlocks with the five giant banks and four of these are between Standard Life (UK) and the Bank of Montreal. Sun Life, the largest insurance company, has a total of 14 interlocks with the dominant banks including four with each of the Royal Bank and the Canadian Imperial Bank and five with the Bank of Montreal; in other words, 70 per cent of the directors of

Sun Life also hold a dominant bank directorship.[42]

Here we see that Clement thinks that multiplexity *is* important ("four of these are between...") while the second term in his ratios ignores it. Moreover, if we adopt the logic of his notion of "interfaces," i.e., we treat all ties between banks and insurance companies as either "made" or "not made" (binary), we can see that some insurance companies are far less closely connected to the banks than others. This is a potentially interesting fact to which Clement has paid little attention because his methods obscure it.

Finally, given that both the number of firms and number of directors per firm varies significantly from area to area within an economy, Clement's calculations of the "density" of ties between sectors — e.g., "finance" and "resources" — are difficult to interpret. One cannot, of course, have a large number of interlocks with a small board: the upper limit is fixed by the number of directors on the smaller board. Since "sectors," as Clement treats them, are simply aggregates of varying numbers of firms with varying board-sizes, those with small numbers of firms and small board sizes — such as "trade" — cannot be closely tied to others if one uses simple number of ties as a measure of closeness of contact.

Errors of this kind are so plentiful in *The Canadian Corporate Elite* that it is extremely difficult for a reader aware of them to take much of the book seriously. Clement's examples of how interlocking directorates are used are well taken. Indeed, they provide us with a "feel" for the phenomenon that is not often found in the literature. But, unfortunately, he rests much of his case on data analyses, such as those presented here, which are simply too crude and ill-considered to be of much validity.

Clement is not alone, of course, in analyzing interlocking directorates. Scott[43] summarizes over a hundred empirical studies which, in whole or in part, deal with the implications of interlocking for the interpretation of corporate structure. Fennema and Schijf[44] examine several methodologically sophisticated articles, published both before and after *The Canadian Corporate Elite*, which are concerned with precisely the kinds of problems Clement encountered. Symptomatically, he ignored them: as a rule, Canadian research on interlocking directorates has lagged behind that in other countries. Thus, while Canadians, belatedly, often cite new theoretical and methodological trends, they have not tended to pioneer in the development or application of new techniques.

There are exceptions. For instance, in 1976 Ornstein[45] published a paper which systematically examined the relationship between the size, composition and patterns of interlocking of the boards of directors of 248 of the largest corporations operating in Canada in 1973. While not entirely new in its approach — Waverman and Baldwin[46] had explored similar issues — it was unusually careful in examining not only the strength of relationships, but why they were present.

In the same year, Berkowitz *et al.* completed a study of Canadian corporate structure for the Royal Commission on Corporate Concentration[47] which included a detailed examination of the extent to which "director/officership" and ownership ties in Canada reinforced or supplemented one another. On the basis of this, they were able to differentiate or "detect" groups of firms operating under common control ("enterprises") from amidst the mass of closely interlocked corporations in certain key Canadian industries.

In 1977, Carroll, Fox and Ornstein circulated a paper which utilized the "smallest space mappings"[48] Levine had applied in an earlier study of bank-corporation interlocking.[49] While Levine had examined the structured relationships between (U.S.) corporations as mediated by banks, Carroll, Fox and Ornstein dealt directly with corporation-to-corporation ties.[50] They first computed (a) measures of integration among firms in their data.[51] With these in mind, they (b) generated a "smallest space" mapping — a kind of multidimensional picture of all relationships among firms compressed into a best-fit "image." Finally, they (c) attempted to partition their network into distinct sub-sets of corporate actors. Carroll, Fox and Ornstein discovered a number of interesting things. First, the network of directorship interlocks they created could not be readily subdivided into easily recognizable sub-groupings. This contradicted Clement's assumption that interlocks were simple indices of discrete communities of interest within a larger network of elite ties. Second, they found no pronounced cleavage between "foreign" and domestically-controlled firms. As we will see in detail in the next section, this "cleavage" is an essential part of Clement's argument. Finally, Carroll, Fox and Ornstein found tentative evidence to support the view that the dominant integrative role in the Canadian economy was played by *Canadian*-controlled — and *not* foreign-controlled — financial groups.

In addition to representing a distinctly more sophisticated treatment of interlock data than those put forward by Clement, then, Carroll, Fox and Ornstein reached decidedly different substantive conclusions. This is especially interesting since the techniques they used — measures of integration, smallest space mapping, and partitioning or clustering — are ideally suited to testing precisely those hypotheses about Canadian corporate structure which Clement suggests throughout his work.[52] As we will see later, this is often the case: when many often-repeated conclusions about the Canadian corporate system are subjected to rigorous empirical tests, they turn out to be "myths."

INTERCORPORATE CONTROL

The question of "intercorporate control" has probably been one of the most hotly debated in Canada in recent years. When Porter wrote *The Ver-*

tical Mosaic, the question of foreign control of Canadian industry was not the burning issue it was to become only a few years later. For a variety of technical reasons, it was also not possible to appreciate the full impact of foreign control/ownership on the economy.[53] Indeed, throughout the book, Porter gives the effects of foreign ownership relatively short shrift except where they can be seen to have a measurable impact on corporate concentration[54] or on the defensive strategies adopted by firms in avoiding foreign takeovers.

The publication of the Watkins Report (The Task Force on the Structure of Canadian Industry)[55] in 1968 engendered greater awareness of the question, but, once again, the data it was based upon were incomplete.[56] Within a few years, however, with the greater availability of information, both the issue of foreign ownership and the larger question of the centralization of economic power in Canada were fully joined.

Foreign Domination

Clement's *The Canadian Corporate Elite* takes the issue of foreign impacts on the Canadian economy far more seriously than Porter. In fact, in an important sense, it is the point upon which his entire analysis turns. His stratification of elites into "indigenous," "comprador," and "parasite" sub-groups,[57] for instance, is based on a variant of the "core-periphery" or "metropolis-hinterland" model in which different nation-states take up roles within an international capitalist economy. The role played by a country within this global system then determines its internal system of stratification — including divisions within its elite:

> Although it will be emphatically argued in subsequent chapters that Canada's economic system is not separate or detached from a wider capitalist system, it is none the less [sic] valuable to examine Canada's place within the wider system and analyze the implications of this for Canadians. For now it is sufficient to note that the issue of whether Canada is "dominated" by U.S. capitalists or in a "junior partnership" with them is at least as problematic and much more complex than these simple assertions suggest. While this [?] is probably correct for what will later be called the comprador elite, it does not accurately describe the traditional indigenous elite. The indigenous elite is better understood as being in an alliance with foreign capital as a full partner resulting from an historical division of labour.[58]

Note here that Clement extends what is essentially a geographic or spatial metaphor to social groups, i.e., he generalizes from core and peripheral areas to core-tied ("comprador") and periphery-tied ("indigenous") elites. According to the model he adopts, "internal contradictions" among "dominant class fractions" result from the process of the "uneven development of capitalism" in "dependent" regions.[59]

There are several reasons why it is particularly interesting that Clement applies this model to the Canadian case. First, by treating Canada as an "imperialized" country, Clement ties his analysis of foreign domination back into the work of the Toronto School — especially Innis's — and, simultaneously, links it to a more theoretically explicit model of development. This is useful because, as I argued in the introductory chapter, the Toronto School avoided truly general theory construction. At the same time, modern core-periphery theorists have characteristically paid little attention to the concrete economic and social mechanisms through which "dependency" is developed and sustained. By explicitly relating these two bodies of work to his problem Clement has built an important bridge between Toronto School enthusiasts — such as R. Laxer,[60] J. Laxer,[61] Watkins,[62] and Hutcheson,[63] — and the work of a more self-conscious international theory group.

Second, while Clement encompasses work by a number of writers with intellectually modest goals who dealt with the issue of Canadian-American economic relations immediately before *The Canadian Corporate Elite* was written — such as Levitt,[64] and Naylor,[65] — it extends their arguments by placing them in the larger context of a complex set of international economic ties. This is, in one sense, quite interesting: the "debate" over foreign ownership was cycling back and forth over the same ground at the time — with fewer insights added as it "progressed." But Clement does not follow up on the consequences of this notion of a "global" capitalist system. At best, his injunction that we study Canada in the context of the world economy is a kind of academic pietism: when it comes down to concrete cases, Clement either resorts to a tried-and-true focus on bilateral exchanges between Canada and the U.S. or dredges up Toronto School platitudes about Canada exchanging British Colonialism for American neo-Colonialism. He makes no attempt to use the notion of multi-lateral economic ties analytically.

Finally, Clement recognizes that Canada does not fit easily into either the unconventional ("core-periphery") or the conventional ("modernization") model:

> It is often argued that multinationals bring extensive investment into capital poor areas, either geographically defined or developmentally defined, but the example of Canada suggests otherwise. Between 1960 and 1967, new capital inflow from the U.S. amounted to $4.1 billion but counter to this, outflows in the form of remittances to U.S. parents amounted to $5.9 billion, a net outflow of capital from Canada to the U.S. of $1.8 billion.... The argument that U.S. investment comes to Canada because capital is scarce...runs counter to the evidence... [it] indicates that mostly Canadian capital, or capital generated from retained earnings by Canadian operations of foreign firms, finances large amounts of foreign investment.[66]

Rather than reject his assumption that Canada is a classic "dependent" or "modernizing" country, Clement assumes that the models are flawed. This, once again, is unfortunately typical of much of the work by sociologists on Canadian economic development: they seem bound and determined to "fit" Canada into one of the prevailing models on the basis of a cursory reading of the data and, at the same time, to ignore important results obtained by those using these same models. Thus, the "fits" involved are often quite superficial. For instance, the same argument about the indigenous generation of investment capital that Clement puts forward can, in general terms, be made with regard to "developed-dependent" countries in Latin America.[67] Both the "developmentally defined" (modernization) and "geographically defined" (core-periphery) models recognize that there is a pattern associated with investment which will generate a different balance of flows at different stages in the process. The differences between the two schools have to do with how one interprets the observed use of retained earnings or indigenous capital for reinvestment and the net outflow of payments in the "mature" phase: modernization theorists — and here Rostow[68] is probably the best example — see it as a prelude to "takeoff." Core-periphery theorists see this pattern as evidence of continuing dependency.

The historical evidence on the subject is mixed. Some "developed-dependent" countries have broken out of this status. The United States itself, for instance, was a net capital debtor until after World War I. Others, like Chile or Argentina, have not. In retrospect, whether or not countries have been able to break out has depended, in large measure, on the magnitude and sectoral sources of capital outflows. The Canadian literature has dealt with these questions only superficially.

What is most striking here is that, whether they follow one school or another, the overwhelming majority of Canadian researchers concerned with the impact of foreign corporate control on the Canadian economy have done no serious analytic work with data on capital flows. Like Clement, they simply present their data, intone platitudes, and think that this is sufficient. It is not. In most cases, the interactions and effects of foreign investment within an economy — in particular, a "mature" one — are varied and complex. Usually they are so complex that we need elaborate and detailed models to separate them out. They cannot simply be determined by "eyeballing" raw numbers.

For instance, J. Laxer argues that the principal effect of American foreign investment has been to retard and reduce Canada's manufacturing capacity, relegating it to the status of a service economy:

> As Canada has moved more completely into the American economic orbit, the nature of the American impact on the manufacturing sector has altered. Since World War II Canada's manufacturing industries can increasingly be characterized as warehouse assembly operations which rely on imports of technology, machinery and parts and components. Moreover, as U.S. investment in Canada has more and more derived from the reinvestment of profits made in Canada and from loans on the Canadian money market, the net flow of dividends out of Canada has surpassed the inflow of new foreign investment....
>
> A striking feature of Canadian manufacturing is the relatively small percentage of the country's work force it employs. In 1965 only 24.5 per cent of the paid non-agricultural work force in Canada was employed in manufacturing. By 1971, the

percentage had dropped to 21.3 per cent.

Among Western countries, only Greece and Ireland have a lower percentage of their work force employed in manufacturing. For the United States the comparable figures are these: in 1965, 29.7 per cent of the paid non-agricultural work force was employed in manufacturing; in 1971 the figure was 26.3 per cent.[69]

With these and similar statistics as a base, Laxer goes on to argue that Canada is being "de-industrialized" and that this "de-industrialization grows out of the nature of Canadian capitalism and its relation to American capitalism."[70]

What is most striking here is the rather one-dimensional way Laxer looks at the problem — almost as if he had the "answers" before he compiled the data. There are, in any case, a variety of factors which might explain them. First, multinational companies act so as to minimize taxation.[71] Since they are in a good position to shift profits from one country to another by varying the transfer prices associated with non-traded goods (a fender for a GM automobile, for instance), they can affect a series of book transfers which result in higher rates of dividends and other income, i.e., they can borrow money in Canada rather than reinvesting income that parent corporations claim back in the form of dividends and other income. Since Canadian corporate tax rates are, for certain industries, consistently higher than in the United States, there is an incentive to do this.

Second, technology transfers — a machine tool sent to Canada by a U.S. parent, for instance — are usually reckoned at some relatively arbitrary book value. If, during the period in question, an increasing proportion of U.S.-to-Canada transfers were in the form of capital goods — and Laxer himself suggests that they might have been — and, at the same time, there were incentives towards minimizing these stated values, then the *apparent* rate of external investment would decline. Since Laxer locates the greatest shift in flows in the high technology area, this is a real possibility.

Finally, changes in patterns of capital investment must be viewed over a long time period. Capital recovery may occur in some industries in as little as three to five years. In most cases, it takes much longer. Thus, in considering aggregate data which lump all investments together, we must look for cyclic patterns before resting our case on data drawn from one specific time period. There are standard statistical techniques — similar to those used in calculating seasonally adjusted unemployment — which can be used to do this where long time series data are available.[72]

In any event, Laxer presents no convincing evidence for the belief that changes in the pattern of American capital investment in Canada are part of some larger strategy for shifting production back to the United States. First, note that the apparent proportionate decline in paid non-agricultural workers is higher (3.4 per cent in the United States than in Canada (3.2 per cent). The apparent relative decline (decline as a proportion of the total) is two percent higher in Canada during the period in question — nothing with which to go running to the newspapers.

Second, the period Laxer has chosen was one in which there was a marked increase in the proportion of women in the labor force in both countries. Since proportionately fewer women are employed in manufacturing, this, in itself, would tend to reduce the proportion of the total labor force in manufacturing — despite an enormous increase in employment, generally.

Third, the reason women were able to enter the labor force in such numbers was that there had been a secular trend towards the growth of the service and government sectors of both economies. Part of this, at least, built on itself: as women entered the labor force they generated a demand for services to replace part of their household labor, e.g., laundry services, fast food franchises. This, in turn, led to further growth of service sector employment — in some cases for women — and so on.

Finally, in recent years there has been a multilateral — not simply a bilateral — shift towards a pattern in which workers in various countries sub-assemble components at different stages in the production process. This long-term trend is the result of (a) an increasing international division of labor and (b) variations in labor costs.[73] This is a fact of life which *all* western industrialized countries, not simply Canada, must face. In many cases, these shifts are the result of contractual arrangements rather than, as Laxer might suspect, decisions by multinationals to "relocate" production.

My point, of course, is not that Laxer's conclusions are wrong — some may well be right — but that we have no way of assessing them given the limited nature of his analysis. Unfortunately, the number of studies which have looked at the impact of foreign investment on Canada with the care that it deserves are few and far between. And almost none have been conducted by sociologists or political scientists. Economists — such as Safarian,[74] Rosenbluth,[75] Caves, Porter, Spence and Scott,[76] Eastman,[77] Globerman,[78] Gorecki,[79] Mathewson and Quirin,[80] and Reuber and Roseman[81] — have looked at some of these issues in a systematic and sustained way. But, especially in recent years, many of these studies have been too narrowly focused to encompass larger sociological concerns such as the impact of foreign investment on the structure of the workplace, elite systems, and so on. There is a clear gap in the general sociological literature which needs to be filled.

Centralization of Power

The ultimate goal of any study of corporate power, of course, is to locate the centers of that power and to circumscribe the group(s) that wield it. *The Vertical Mosaic* and *The Canadian Corporate Elite* both find the source of economic power in Canada in a set of large private business corporations. The men occupying the upper reaches of these corporate hierarchies are the ones best situated to wield this power. Porter:

> The economic elite of Canada has been defined...as the 985 Canadian residents holding directorships in the 170 dominant corporations, the banks, insurance companies, and numerous other corporations not classed [sic] as dominant.[82]

Clement:

> The corporate elite is.... that set of positions known as senior management and directors within dominant corporations...[Since] the elite is defined as the [role occupants of the] uppermost positions only within dominant corporations, not all corporations... the corporate elite may then be said to correspond to the "big bourgeoisie."[83]

Both Porter and Clement stress that, in order to function as an elite, it is necessary for this group to be bound together by common backgrounds, social ties, and life experiences.[84] Common patterns of birth and residence facilitate this. Both Porter and Clement observe that their elites are overwhelmingly located in Central Canada — particularly in Montreal and Toronto — although at least some elites may be found in other regions. Clement systematically explores the birthplace of members of this elite, discovering that Central Canada is over-represented relative to the population as a whole.[85] These distributions mirror those for Canadian business enterprises and corporate wealth.

The Canadian "economic elite" or "corporate elite," according to both authors, is overwhelmingly anglophone, of British origin and Protestant religion[86]. It is disproportionately drawn, both Porter and Clement maintain, from the upper-middle and upper classes.[87] Private school education and private club membership are common among members of the group.[88] They are disproportionately university educated for people in their age-cohorts[89] and tend to have been trained in technical specialties or in law, commerce and finance.[90] Their children tend to intermarry, they grace one another's tables, and they interact in a variety of other informal ways. Thus they form, both authors agree, a coherent social group. This group tends to exclude — to varying degrees — French speakers, Jews, and other ethnics.

Moreover, in recent years, the economic base for the power of this group has grown through mergers, acquisitions and other consolidations of capital. According to Clement, major consolidations of Canadian capital occurred during and after the First World War and in the 1950s.[91] In the 1960s, the expansion of the activities of foreign-owned multinationals led to a corresponding increase in the power of "comprador" elites connected with them.[92] This also led, however, to a weakening of the social boundaries around the corporate elite because access to positions in Canadian subsidiaries of multinationals was controlled by non-Canadian parent firms.[93]

On balance, then, the Porter-Clement analysis of economic power in Canada circumscribes a group which closely resembles that identified in various Canadian regionalisms: what the Saskatchewan populist calls "those snotty bastards down East," the Newfoundlander "those rich Mainlanders," and the Québécois nationalist "les Anglais." This is one reason why both books are so popular: they play into and lend academic legitimacy to "what we already know." Both are, in this sense, good journalism but bad sociology because, as a scientist, it is a sociologist's job not simply to present interesting distributions, but to show *why* they occur: to tease out the essential underlying features of social structure which lead to the construction of the world as we observe it. Both books fail to do this in a number of ways.

First, only the most deliberately naive would expect that those persons occupying key positions in the Canadian economic structure would be randomly drawn from the population. Even without strong institutional constraints, the general structure of societies, skill requirements, times of immigration, and so on would yield a non-random distribution of certain group traits — in the absence of specific elite-generated pressures and mechanisms. The faculty of the department of sociology at the University of Toronto in 1972 — the same year for which Clement gathered his elite data,[94] and hardly what one would call a branch of the economic elite — was 56.6 per cent WASP, 3.8 per cent French, 26.4 per cent Jewish, and 13.2 per cent other ethnic. Thus, in a year in which Clement reports that the general population was 44.7 per cent WASP, the proportion among sociologists was 11.9 per cent more. Whereas 28.6 per cent of the general population was French, the percentage among sociologists was 24.8 per cent less. Jews were only 1.4 per cent of the total population, but 26.4 per cent of sociologists. Other ethnics were 25.3 per cent of the Canadian population, but 13.2 per cent of the sociology faculty. In the same year, the economic elite, according to Clement, was 86.2 per cent WASP, 8.4 per cent French, 4.1 per cent Jewish and 1.3 per cent other ethnic.[95]

What are we to make of these data? Toronto sociologists decidedly over-represented certain groups and under-represented others. But why? Are they subject to the same familial and economic pressures which Clement claims forged the economic elite into an exclusive club over a period of 200 years? By contrast with the economic elite, the Toronto sociology department had expanded rapidly in the 1960s. It was much younger: over two-thirds of its members were under 50, while 70 per cent of the corporate elite were over that age.[96] Many sociologists had recently migrated to Canada. Thus, we would expect the department to disproportionately represent non-Charter groups.

We can begin to appreciate this if we reduce the *number* of Jews proportionate to their percentage in the general population, and increase the number of other ethnics in the same fashion; holding the number of WASPS and French constant. In this fashion, we generate an artificial faculty of size 46 in which 65.2 per cent are WASP, 4.3 per cent French, 2.2 per cent Jewish and 28.3 per cent other ethnic. The results of this procedure are shown in Table 10-1, top next page.

TABLE 10-1

Distributions of Ethnicity Within Various Groups

Econ. Elite	Sociologists	Gen Pop.	Sim. 1	Sim. 2
WASP 86.2%	56.6% (30)	44.7%	65.2%	85.7%
French 8.4	3.8 (2)	28.6	4.3	6.7
Jews 4.1	26.4 (14)	1.4	2.2	4.7
Other 1.3	13.2 (7)	25.3	28.3	2.9

This begins to look more like the distribution of Clement's corporate elite. It we then rescale the age distribution among sociologists to fit that of the corporate elite, and recalculate an ethnic distribution on this basis, we generate an artificial group of size 35 which is 85.7 per cent WASP, 6.7 per cent French, 4.7 per cent Jewish, and 2.9 per cent other ethnic. In this distribution. French-speakers are under-represented relative to the corporate elite and other ethnics over-represented. This is to be expected since Clement's data includes elites in Montreal as well as Toronto.

This procedure reveals that, by "fitting" constraints, we can generate a distribution for another group which closely mirrors the ethnic background of Clement's corporate elite — but without any of the specific assumptions he makes about the forces determining the composition of that group. Since the factors at play in our experiment had an impact on the composition of *both* groups, they cannot be intrinsic to the corporate elite but must have been related to general changes going on in Canadian social structure, i.e., changes in patterns of immigration, age structure within institutions, etc.

Second, Porter and Clement have an obligation as scientists to doubt the conclusions of their own research, i.e., not simply to "make a case," but to weigh and assess alternative explanations. There is no evidence of even a slight sensitivity to this question in their examinations of the mechanisms leading to the creation and centralization of power within the WASP-dominated, Eastern establishment group they identify. Clement's treatment of the role played by Jews in the corporate elite is, perhaps, the most obvious example in *The Canadian Corporate Elite* of how advocacy can get in the way of scientific objectivity.

Clement assumes that, as in Porter's assessment, Jews are marginal to any system of socio-economic power in Canada. Thus, in describing the corporate elite he begins by telling us that there are "*only* 32 Jewish-Canadians" included in his corporate elite.[97] Later he cites a 1939 study by Rosenberg to justify the assertion that "[Jews'] participation [in the corporate system] is, for the most part, peripheral to the economic elite and located in the high risk sectors of trade and real estate."[98] Clement, however, has a problem: in the case of every other ethnic group — especially WASPs — he has rested his case on the fact that a given group is either "over-represented" or "under-represented" in the corporate elite relative to the general population. As Clement himself tells us, Jews constitute only 1.4 per cent of the general population, but 4.1 per cent of the elite group. Put another way, the Canadian corporate elite contains just under three times the number of Jews we would expect at random — or we can view them as 200 per cent over-represented.

This fact is hard to ignore, but Clement tries:

> A closer examination of the firms with which they are associated explains why they are 4.1 per cent of the elite and only 1.4 per cent of the population. Of the 32 Jews, 28 are associated with one of the five long established corporations in the beverage industry, three in trade and one primarily in real estate. These are tightly-held family firms with only six families accounting for 25 of the 32 Jewish members of the elite. Outside these family firms, Jews have much less economic power in dominant financial corporations, holding only five of the dominant bank directorships (2.4 per cent) and two dominant insurance company directorships (1.2%). In other words, their representation in financial corporations is well below their proportion of the entire economic elite.[99]

What is most disturbing here is that, when Clement speaks about other large family holdings — such as the Irving's or Sifton's — he does not treat them as "only" family capital: when WASPs control whole industries in some region, it is taken as evidence of enormous personal power. When Jews do, it is seen as a *prima facie* case of marginal status.

If there is a single inviolate rule of science it is the notion that one should let the data have their say. Clement is breaking this rule with impunity. The "long established corporation in the beverage industry" Clement refers to above is, of course, Distillers-Corporation Seagrams Ltd. The family involved is the Bronfmans. We know from data published by Statistics Canada[100] that the Bronfmans control literally dozens of corporations in a wide range of financial and industrial areas. Yet, they are only noted episodically in Clement's account. Other highly significant Jewish families are not even mentioned — including one which is now gradually buying lower Manhattan from the natives. When Clement talks about Jews outside of these "family firms,"[101] he notes that they "only" hold "five of the dominant bank directorships" for "2.4 per cent" of the total. Once again, this is 170 per cent of what we would expect them to hold at random.

This goes beyond stubborness: it takes a real commitment to one's model of WASP exclusiveness to persist in the face of this kind of evidence that families like the Bronfmans wield enormous financial power on both sides of the border. The costs are also clear: Clement has failed to detect one of the most important interfaces between Canadian and American capitalism.

Finally, both Porter and Clement have failed to provide readers with a realistic context within which to view the trends towards centralization of power which they observe. We know, for instance, very little about the demography of their corporate elites.[102] Thus, when they talk about intermarriages, we have little idea how likely they are. We have anecdotal accounts of club membership, but, once again, little sense of the opportunity structure surrounding them. Clement, in particular, seems to be extremely concerned with the "place" of Canadian capitalism within a worldwide scheme. Yet, is this an issue with any practical referents: is the American real estate developer who is dealing with the Bronfmans, for instance, really concerned about whether, in the abstract, Canadian capitalists are "junior partners" or acting out a role in an historic division of labor? The practical questions surrounding foreign ownership or centralization of power have to do with what economists refer to as "welfare effects": who derives what benefits from what sets of arrangements and who bears the costs. The costs and benefits of centralizing production within a few firms are, for example, not self-evident. They require some considerable study since they vary a great deal from industry to industry and from market to market within the economy. Similarly, the tradeoffs between concentration and dispersal of economic decision-making within a vast country such as Canada are not matters for speculation, but ought to be treated in a theoretically and empirically consistent way. If sociological approaches to these issues are to get the attention they deserve, then Canadian sociologists must not simply use their models as a way of reinforcing their biases or popular prejudices.

Neither of these issues — foreign domination nor the centralization of economic power — are, of course, simply scholarly preoccupations: both the remnants of the Diefenbaker Conservatives and the present Liberal government have accommodated to the concern of what had once been "fringe" groups over foreign domination of the economy. Witness, for instance, the creation of the Foreign Investment Review Agency and the establishment of Petro-Can. The "centralization of power" issue has been with us, in one form or another, since the days of the "Family Compact" and the "Chateau Clique." It has been the recurring theme in regional confrontations over resources,[103] transfer payments to the provinces, and, most recently, amending formulae for the constitution. There is no doubt that it provided a major impetus for the striking of the Royal Commission on Economic Union and Development Prospects for Canada (the "McDonald Commission"). It is, therefore, "natural" that these issues should become major foci in an assessment of the Canadian elite structure. However, it is interesting that the analytical content of most treatments of these questions in the Canadian social science literature is so weak. Despite the fact that the data assembled by Statistics Canada for its *Structural Aspects of Domestic and Foreign Control in the Manufacturing, Mining, and Forestry Industries* has been available for over five years, for instance, social scientists are almost unaware of their existence. I submit that these are not "anomalies" — that the basic approach to the study of Canadian elites must be substantially revised. In the course of examining why and how this should be done, some of the strengths and weaknesses of modern Canadian sociology will become clear.

CONCLUSION: Toward A Structural Theory of Canadian Corporate Elites

It is ironic that what has been hailed as "the most Canadian of books," *The Vertical Mosaic,* should be so closely wedded to its American counterparts. Its basic analytic framework is not much different from that in C. Wright Mills' classic study of American society, *The Power Elite,* which was published some nine years earlier.[104] As such, it owes much to Weber's notions of power and social organization, to Mosca and Pareto's treatments of elites, and to a kind of domestic North American populism in which one sees the "big guys" — usually in the "East" — as the major source of domestic woes and foreign entanglements.[105]

This is also true of *The Canadian Corporate Elite.* While Clement tends to borrow the rhetoric of neo-Marxist writers — such as Frank or Domhoff — his basic overall analytic schema is not much different from Porter's: "elites" are still defined as functional groups thrown up by institutional hierarchies and closely identified with dynamics in each of several relatively autonomous social and cultural spheres. The basic thrust of argument in both books is to show that certain social groups disproportionately monopolize access to key positions within these institutions and important channels of communication between them.

What is missing from all of this is a sense of social structure. Access to favoured goods in a society — such as wealth, prestige and power — is governed by a series of structures at different levels of the system.[106] These vary from society to society: there is no particular reason why the barriers which impede access to certain favoured goods in one should act in the same way in another. In fact, given that societies may have widely varying institutional histories, it is extremely unlikely that any two will structure inequality in precisely the same way.

In Britain and France, for instance, accents act as a sorting mechanism to discriminate classes and regions from one another. As in George Bernard Shaw's famous tale, persons without "appropriate" accents are barred from certain circles. This is, to some extent, true in the United States as well.[107] But no one has shown that accents are used in this way in Canada, and it is unlikely that they would be given the newness of most upper class social circles. However, there are undoubtedly other signals that perform the same function. No doubt, for instance, French Canadians without pronounced French overtones in their speech or Jews without "Jewish" inflections find it easier to function in the *haute monde* than those with these traits.

By borrowing heavily from their American counterparts, both Porter and Clement — perhaps inadvertently — have fallen into assuming that certain features of social structure in Canada operate in substantially the same way as they do in the United States. The American educational system, for instance, is large and varied. Some colleges and universities function as national institutions: they draw their student body from across the country and around the world. They clearly see their role as training "the next generation of leaders," within each locale, for the tasks involved in running the system. Competition for places in these institutions is fierce, since each applicant knows that only a few will be chosen from a given city or state. Other American educational institutions clearly exist to serve some regional or local clientele. These schools are easier to get into and the branches of government which often support them are usually successful in pressuring administrators into accepting a large number of local sons and daughters. Thus, while their student bodies may include a sprinkling of out-of-state or foreign students, the primary base for the student population is within a limited, local geographic locale. Still other institutions — usually state colleges — are not only geographically limited in focus but really specialize in some few forms of highly specialized training geared to the needs of a local area. Some institutions are private, some public, some closely affiliated with religious denominations, some are closely tied to particular industries or companies. Thus, precisely where one goes within this panoply of possibilities is quite important and will have strong implications for his or her future careers and life chances.

The college and university system is structured quite differently in Canada. Most students prefer — and provincial legislatures have agreed — to attend university in their home cities. As we noted in the first chapter, until very recently this has meant that a single institution, the University of Toronto, had all but monpolized the lion's share of teaching in English Canada. Within Québec, McGill had functioned the same way for anglophones. Both institutions, as a result, have been huge and entrance requirements, in American terms, comparatively low.[108] Student bodies, as a result, are quite heterogeneous with respect to both abilities and class background.

When the members of Porter's and Clement's elites were growing up, these institutions were probably more elite than they are today. At the same time, students had fewer options. Thus, when Porter says that "Of the 118 [men] born and educated in Canada, 42 graduated from McGill science and engineering faculties, 35 from Toronto, and 4 from Queens,"[109] he implies a great deal more than he ought to: "This common educational background can make for homgeneity of social type."[110] While this may be true for the 1929 graduates of, say, MIT or Caltech, it is at least unproven that it is as meaningful here. Even a cursory examination of the subsequent careers of the graduates of Toronto and McGill in these years would reveal a far wider scatter of paths than those of elite American scientific institutions.

Clement commits the same error. When he talks about the lawyers in his corporate elite, he says:

All the lawyers are trained in Canada with half attending Osgoode Hall and about one fifth going to each of the University of Toronto and McGill; Dalhousie, University of Manitoba, Laval and University of Montreal are also important.

There are 113 law schools in the United States. They are elaborately stratified and rated. Students, moreover, are aware of this and of the career implications of attending one or the other. During the period when the American counterparts of the Canadian economic elite were the appropriate age, there were between 90 and 100 such schools. At the time that most of Porter or Clement's elite were attending law school, there were only two in the province of Ontario. McGill was the only wholly anglophone law school in Québec. Since Canadian law schools have tended to be quite oriented to their own provincial bodies of law — i.e., they see their task as training lawyers rather than educating jurists — it makes sense to attend a school within one's own province. Thus, Clement is not saying very much in this paragraph that we did not know by definition: the distribution of elites among law schools is undoubtedly very close to a random one for all English-speaking law students at the time. All lawyers of the appropriate age — those practicing on Bay Street and those in storefronts on Roncesvalles — would have had similar educational backgrounds in a way that American lawyers of the era would not.[111]

The point, then, is that, however Canadian elites are filtered out, these kinds of institutions do not do it and it is a false inference to assume that they do. Porter and Clement are probably on firmer ground when they view private school education as an elite-shaping experience,[112] but, once again, the term covers a myriad of different things in Canada and we have no precise way of sorting this out as one does in the United States.

If educational careers are not the mechanism through which elites are socialized and shaped in Canada, what is? Probably the family system. While both Porter and Clement deal, in a passing way, with the influence of particular families on the careers of their members, neither deals with family systems *qua* systems.

What is obviously needed is a study of the "structuration" of class in Canada comparable to those done by Berkowitz[113] and Bertaux[114] — for the United States and France, respectively — in which capital formation and family structure are explicitly related to one another. Given the history of "family compacts" in Canada, this approach is likely to yield even richer insights into the process in Canada than it did in other cases. Niosi,[115] in what is probably the best single study of the structural dynamics of the Canadian economy, begins this process by identifying ethnically-tied capital pools in Québec. But Niosi was principally concerned with the question of finance *vs.* industrial capitalism and his discussion of the issue is necessarily limited. A more extensive treatment would have to go beyond this to the kind of level where we no longer are simply reifying popular conceptions and misconceptions — unfortunately, the point at which most Canadian studies of economic elites are at present — to a fuller understanding of the dynamics underlying the Canadian system of capital mobilization.

NOTES

[1]Porter, 1965: 7-9.

[2]Porter, 1965: 9-15.

[3]Porter, 1965: 201.

[4]Porter, 1965: 201-30.

[5]Porter, 1965: 522.

[6]The term is used advisedly here.

[7]Porter, 1965: 231.

[8]Porter, 1965: 305.

[9]Porter, 1965: 231.

[10]Mills, 1956.

[11]This notion of a "dominant" corporation will be discussed in detail, below.

[12]Porter, 1965: 233.

[13]Bain, 1959.

[14]For a general discussion of the properties of competitive equilibria, see Vickrey, 1965: ch. 5.

[15]Bain, 1959, presents a cogent argument for why this must be the case.

[16]Scherer, 1970.

[17]That is, translated into things we can observe.

[18]In practical terms, "industries" or "industrial sectors" are used to determine market boundaries. We will examine this assumption, in detail, later in this essay.

[19]These numbers can be combined together into what is called a "Herfindahl index." See Scherer, 1970.

[20]Brecher and Reisman, 1957.

[21]Porter, 1965: 235.

[22]There is an "inequality measure," the Gini index, which compares actual or obtained distributions of something with perfect equality of this kind. Interestingly, Porter does not calculate Gini indices.

[23]The usual practice, of course, would be to round up — yielding 5 firms per industry and weakening Porter's case.

[24]This was subsequently confirmed for concentration ratios based on value of shipments. See Berkowitz *et al.*, 1976.

[25]There is an extremely interesting question here which, unfortunately, goes beyond the scope of this essay. However, for purposes of discussion consider this hypothesis: Many Canadian manufacturing firms are subsidiaries of American parents. Because they interact with one another on a world-wide scale, each of these parents feels that it has to protect its Canadian part of its global market share. Thus, parents are willing to operate less than optimally efficient Canadian subsidiaries in industries where there are more producers than the Canadian economy, alone, would justify.

[26]Porter, 1965: 571-72.

[27]Porter, 1965: 572-73.

[28]Clement, 1975: 5. Emphasis mine.

[29]Clement, 1975: 30.

[30]Clement, 1975: 31. Clement is citing Perroux, 1971: 56-61.

[31]Berkowitz, 1980.

[32]For a more complete elaboration of this point, see Berkowitz, 1982.

[33]Clement, 1975: 127.

[34]Clement, 1975: 127.

[35]Brandeis, 1913. Note that in Clement's later treatment of American corporate structure (1977) he almost completely ignores investment banks and sometimes confuses them with commercial ones.

[36]Clement's final selection criterion for these corporations included both assets and sales. See Clement, 1975: 125-50.

[37]Note that, while not *incompatible* with an interest in the impact of institutional ties on communication, this type of aggregative analysis contributes little to our understanding of the *structure* of a corporate system, *per se.*

[38]Clement, 1975: 156-61.

[39]Berkowitz, 1980.

[40]Note that he compares interlocks in his 1971 data with Porter's and that Porter does not treat ties as binary. Also see the paragraph cited below.

[41]Mitchell, 1969.

[42]Clement, 1975: 156-57.

[43]Scott, 1979.

[44]Fennema and Schijf, 1978/79.

[45]Ornstein, 1976.

[46]Waverman and Baldwin, 1973.

[47]Berkowitz *et al.*, 1976.

[48]Guttman, 1968.

[49]Levine, 1972.

[50]Carroll, Fox, and Ornstein, 1982.

[51]The 100 largest firms.

[52]See Berkowitz, 1982.

[53]Brecher and Reisman, 1957, began exploring this issue. At the time — and until Statistics Canada began publishing these data in detail in *Inter-Corporate Ownership* — it was often not possible to determine the exact proportion of a Canadian subsidiary's assets held by its foreign parent(s). Moreover, until the late 1960s it was often all but impossible to disentangle the operating statistics of subsidiaries from those of their parents.

[54]"Where there is no Canadian participation in a productive instrument called a corporation there is little difference between that situation and one where ownership is completely in the hands of one person or a group within the country. In these terms there is no difference between T. Eaton Company and General Motors of Canada. Nor does it seem to matter much from the point of view of the operation of the economic system whether these large pieces of private property are in the hands of Canadians or people of other nations." Porter, 1965: 246.

[55]Task Force on the Structure of Canadian Industry, 1968.

[56]Indeed, until the publication of the 1975 edition of *Inter-Corporate Ownership* (1978) a method was used for determining proportion of foreign ownership which tended to *understate* foreign control. Statistics Canada now provides two statistics to

reflect these different aspects of the problem. See Berkowitz *et al.*, 1976, for a detailed discussion of the issue.

[57]Clement, 1975: 36.

[58]Clement, 1975: 33.

[59]Frank, 1967.

[60]Laxer, 1973.

[61]Laxer, 1970; 1973.

[62]Watkins, 1973.

[63]Hutcheson, 1973.

[64]Levitt, 1970.

[65]Naylor, 1972.

[66]Clement, 1975: 109.

[67]Fuentes, 1963.

[68]Rostow, 1971.

[69]Laxer, 1973: 129.

[70]Laxer, 1973: 146.

[71]Caves, 1982; Adams and Whalley, 1977; Aharoni, 1966; Brooke and Remers, 1970.

[72]Hamburg, 1970.

[73]A friend of mine in Canada recently wrote a book for a British publisher which was typeset in India.

[74]Safarian, 1966.

[75]Rosenbluth, 1970.

[76]Caves, Porter, and Spence with Scott, 1980.

[77]Eastman, 1964.

[78]Globerman, 1975.

[79]Gorecki, 1980.

[80]Mathewson and Quirin, 1979.

[81]Reuber and Roseman, 1972.

[82]Porter, 1965: 274.

[83]Clement, 1975: 5-6.

[84]Porter, 1965: 231; Clement, 1975: 5. "To demonstrate that a particular elite is also a social group requires that its structure be specified, that members of the group interact and are related to one another sufficiently to say they exhibit solidarity, cohesiveness, coordination, and consciousness of kind."

[85]Sixty-eight percent of Clement's elite was born in central Canada. See Clement, 1975: 224-25.

[86]Porter, 1965: 285-90; Clement, 1975: 231-40.

[87]Porter, 1965: 291; Clement, 1975: 224-30.

[88]Porter, 1965: 283-85, 304-305; Clement, 1975: 240-47, 247-49.

[89]Porter, 1965: 289-85; Clement, 1975: 240-43.

[90]Porter, 1965: 274-79; Clement, 1975: 240-42.

[91]Clement, 1975: 80-102, *passim*.

[92]Clement, 1975: 109-12.

[93]Clement, 1975: 112-6.

[94]My source here was the 1973-74 academic calendar since it was compiled during

1972.

[95]Clement, 1975: 232, 237.

[96]Clement, 1975: 218.

[97]Clement, 1975: 237. Emphasis mine.

[98]Clement, 1975: 238.

[99]Clement, 1975: 237-38.

[100]Statistics Canada, 1978.

[101]When Clement uses the term in this context, it sounds like it refers to a mom and pop grocery.

[102]See Tepperman, 1977.

[103]See Kinzel, 1978.

[104]Mills, 1956.

[105]Berkowitz, 1976.

[106]Berkowitz, 1982.

[107]Kavaler, 1960; Wechter, 1937.

[108]At the time I taught there, the minimum entrance requirements for the University of Toronto were high school graduation and a 65 grade point average from an Ontario high school. This is the equivalent of a "D" average in the United States, and would qualify a student for entrance into only the very lowest rungs of the system.

[109]Porter, 1965: 277.

[110]*Ibid.*

[111]Smigel, 1969.

[112]Porter, 1965: 283-85, 292, 295, 342, 528; Clement, 1975: 4, 6-7, 73, 91, 96, 176, 178, 180-81, 185, 188, 190, 192-95, 277, 240-47, 251, 267, 269, 272, 307ff, 308.

[113]Berkowitz, 1976.

[114]Bertaux, 1977.

[115]Niosi, 1978.

Bibliography

Adams, J. D. R. and J. Whalley. *The International Taxation of Multinational Enterprises in Developed Countries.* Westport, Ct.: Greenwood, 1977.

Aharoni, Y. *The Foreign Investment Decision Process.* Boston: Division of Research, Graduate School of Business Administration, Harvard University, 1966.

Allen, M. P. "The Structure of Interorganization Elite Co-Optation: Interlocking Corporate Directorates." *American Sociological Review* 39 (1974): 393-406.

Alsegg, R. J. *Control Relationships Between American Corporations and Their European Subsidiaries.* New York: American Management Association, 1971.

Arabie, P., S. A. Boorman and P. R. Levitt. "Constructing Blockmodels: How and Why." *Journal of Mathematical Psychology* 17 (1978): 21-63.

Arrow, K. J. "Vertical Integration and Communication." *Bell Journal of Economics* 6 (1975): 173-83.

Bain, J. S. *Industrial Organization.* New York: Wiley, 1959.

Baba, M. "Foreign Affiliated Corporations and Concentration in Japanese Manufacturing Industry." In M. Ariga. *International Conference on International Economy and Competition Policy.* Tokyo: Council of Tokyo Conference on International Economy and Competition Policy, 1975.

Baranson, J. "Technology Transfer Through the International Firm." *American Economic Review* 60 (1970): 435-40.

_____. "Technology Transfer: Effects on U.S. Competitiveness and Employment." In U.S. Department of Labor, *The Impact of International Trade and Investment on Employment.* Washington: U.S. Government Printing Office, 1978.

Barnet, R. J. and R. E. Muller. *Global Reach: The Power of the International Corporations.* New York: Simon and Schuster, 1974.

Baum, D. J. *The Banks of Canada in the Commonwealth Caribbean: Economic Nationalism and Multinational Enterprises of a Medium Power.* New York: Praeger, 1974.

Bearden, J., W. Atwood, P. Freitag, C. Hendricks, B. Mintz, and M. Schwartz. "The Nature and Extent of Bank Centrality in Corporate Networks." Paper presented at the annual meetings of the American Sociological Association, 1975.

Berkowitz, S. D. *An Introduction to Structural Analysis.* Toronto: Butterworths, 1982.

_____. "Structural and Non-Structural Models of Elites: A Critique." *Canadian Journal of Sociology* 5 (1980): 13-30.

_____. "Markets and Market Areas." In S. D. Berkowitz and B. Wellman. *Structural Sociology.* Cambridge and New York: Cambridge University Press, forthcoming.

Berkowitz, S. D., P. J. Carrington, Y. Kotowitz and L. Waverman. "The Determination of Enterprise Groupings Through Combined Ownership and Directorship Ties." *Social Networks* 1 (1978/79): 391-413.

Berkowitz, S. D., P. J. Carrington, J. Corman and L. Waverman. "Flexible Design for A Large Scale Corporate Data Base." *Social Networks* 2 (1979): 75-83.

Berkowitz, S. D., Y. Kotowitz, and L. Waverman. "A Design for a Large-Scale Data Analysis System for Corporate Information." Toronto: Institute for Policy Analysis, University of Toronto, 1977.

Berkowitz, S. D., Y. Kotowitz, and L. Waverman, with B. Becker, R. Bradford, P. J. Carrington, J. Corman, and G. Heil. *Enterprise Structure and Corporate Concentration.* Royal Commission on Corporate Concentration Technical Study No. 17. Ottawa: Supply and Services Canada, 1976.

Bertaux, D. *Destines personnels a structure de classe.* Paris: Presses Universitaires de France, 1977.

Bhagwati, J. N. and R. A. Brecher. "National Welfare in An Open Economy in the Presence of Foreign-owned Factors of Production." *Journal of International Economics* 10 (1980): 103-15.

Booth, E. J. R. and O. W. Jensen. "Transfer Prices in the Global Corporation Under Internal and External Constraints." *Canadian Journal of Economics* 10 (1977): 434-46.

Bornschier, V. "Multinational Corporations and Economic Growth: A Cross-National Test of the Decapitalization Thesis." *Journal of Developmental Economics* 7 (1980): 191-210.

Brandeis, L. "The Endless Chain: Interlocking Corporate Directorate." *Harpers Weekly* (December 6, 1913): 13-15.

Brecher, I. and S. S. Reisman. *Canada — U.S. Economic Relations.* (Study done for the Royal Commission on Canada's Economic Prospects, Appendix D) Queen's Printer, 1957.

Breton, Albert. "The Economics of Nationalism." *Journal of Political Economy* 72 (1964): 376-86.

Brooke, M. Z. and H. L. Remers. *The Strategy of Multinational Enterprise: Organisation and Finance.* New York: Elsevier, 1970.

Burns, J. O. "Transfer Pricing Decisions in U.S. Multinational Corporations." *Journal of International Business Studies* 11 (1980): 23-39.

Burt, R. S. "A Structural Theory of Interlocking Corporate Directorships." *Social Networks* 1 (1978/79): 415-35.

_____. "Diaggregating the Effect on Profits in Manufacturing Industries of Having Imperfectly Competitive Consumers and Suppliers." *Social Science Research* 8 (1979): 120-43.

Canada, Government of. *Foreign Direct Investment in Canada (Gray Report).* Ottawa: Information Canada, 1972.

Carrington, P. J. "Horizontal Co-optation Through Corporate Interlocks." Ph.D. dissertation. Toronto: University of Toronto, 1981.

_____. "Anticompetitive Effects of Directorship Interlocks." Paper Read at the Annual Meeting of the Canadian Sociology and Anthropology Association, Halifax, 1981.

Carroll, W., J. Fox, and M. Ornstein. "The Network of Directorate Interlocks Among the Largest Canadian Firms." *Canadian Review of Sociology and Anthropology* 19 (1982): 44-69.

Caves, R. E. "Causes of Direct Investment: Foreign Firms' Shares in Canadian and United Kingdom Manufacturing Industries." *Review of Economic Statistics* 56 (1974): 279-93.

_____. *Multinational Enterprise and Economic Analysis.* Cambridge and New York: Cambridge University Press, 1982.

Caves, R. E., M. E. Porter and A. M. Spence with J. T. Scott. *Competition in The Open Economy: A Model Applied to Canada.* Cambridge, Mass.: Harvard University Press, 1980.

Chase-Dunn, C. "The Effects of International Economic Dependence on Development and Inequality." *American Sociological Review* 40 (1975): 720-38.

Clement, Wallace. *The Canadian Corporate Elite.* Toronto: McClelland and Stewart, 1975.

_____. *Continental Corporate Power.* Toronto: McClelland and Stewart, 1977.

De Bodinat, H. "Influence in the Multinational Corporation: The Case of Manufacturing." Boston: D.B.A. dissertation, Harvard University, 1975.

Dooley, P. C. "The Interlocking Directorate." *American Economic Review* 59 (1969): 314-23.

Dhingra, H. L. "Patterns of Ownership and Control in Canadian Industry: A Study of Large Non-Financial Private Corporations." *Canadian Journal of Sociology* 8 (1983): 21-44.

Eastman, H. C. "The Canadian Tariff and the Efficiency of the Canadian Economy." *Papers and Proceedings of the American Economic Association* 54 (1964): 437-48.

Eastman, H. C. and S. Stykolt. *The Tariff and Competition in Canada.* New York: St. Martin's, 1967.

Evans, P. *Dependent Development: The Alliance of Multinational, State and Local Capital in Brazil.* Princeton: Princeton University Press, 1979.

Fennema, M. and H. Schijf. "Analyzing Interlocking Directorates: Theory and Methods." *Social Networks* 1 (1978/79): 297-332.

Flowers, E. B. "Oligopolistic Reactions in European and Canadian Direct Investment in the United States." *Journal of International Business Studies* 7 (1976): 43-55.

Frank, R. H. *Distributional Consequences of Direct Foreign Investment.* New York: Academic Press, 1967.

Fuentes, C. *Whither Latin America.* New York: Monthly Review Press, 1963.

Gale, B. T. "Market Share and Rate of Return." *Review Economic Statistics* 54 (1972): 412-23.

Gartrell, J. *Organization Size and Alienation.* Royal Commission on Corporate Concentration Technical Report No. 27. Ottawa: Supply and Services Canada, 1977.

Globerman, S. "Technological Diffusion in the Canadian Tool and Die Industry." *Review of Economic Statistics* 57 (1975): 428-34.

_____. "Foreign Direct Investment and 'Spillover' Efficiency Benefits in Canadian Manufacturing Industries." *Canadian Journal of Economics* 12 (1979): 42-56.

Gorecki, P. K. "The Determinants of Foreign and Domestic Enterprise Diversification in Canada: A Note." *Canadian Journal of Economics* 13 (1980): 329-39.

Greene, J. and M. G. Duerr. *Intercompany Transactions in the Multinational Firm.* New York: Conference Board, 1970.

Greenhill, C. R. and E. O. Herbolzheimer. "International Transfer Pricing: The Restrictive Business Practices Approach." *Journal of World Trade Law* 14 (1980): 232-41.

Guttman, Louis. "A General Non-metric Technique for Finding the Smallest Co-Ordinate Space for a Configuration of Points." *Psychometrika* 33 (1968): 469-506.

Hamburg, Morris. *Statistical Analysis for Decision Making.* N.Y.: Harcourt, Brace and World, 1970.

Horst, T. "The Industrial Composition of U.S. Exports and Subsidiary Sales to the Canadian Market." *American Economic Review* 62 (1972): 37-45.

Hutcheson, J. "The Capitalist State in Canada." In R. Laxer, ed. *(Canada) Ltd.* Toronto: McClelland and Stewart, 1973.

Jenkins, G. P. "Taxes and Tariffs and the Evaluation of Benefit from Foreign Investment." *Canadian Journal of Economics* 12 (1979): 410-25.

Jenks, Leland H. *The Migration of British Capital to 1875.* N.Y.: Alfred A. Knopf, 1927.

Kavaler, Lucy. *The Private World of High Society.* N.Y.: David McKay, 1960.

Knickerbocker, F. T. "Market Structure and Market Power Consequences of Foreign Direct Investment by Multinational Companies." Washington: Center for Multinational Studies, 1976.

Kopits, G. F. "Dividend Remittance Behavior Within the Industrial Firm: A Cross-Country Analysis." *Review Economic Statistics* 54 (1972): 339-42.

Larner, R. J. "Ownership and Control in the 200 Largest Non-Financial Corporations, 1929 and 1963." *American Economic Review* 56 (1966): 777-87.

Laxer, J. *The Energy Poker Game: The Politics of the Continental Resource Deal.* Toronto: New Deal, 1970.

Laxer, J. and D. Jantzi. "The De-Industrialization of Ontario." In R. Laxer, ed. *(Canada) Ltd.* Toronto: McClelland and Stewart, 1973.

Lessard, D. G. "Transfer Prices, Taxes, and Financial Markets: Implications of Financial Transfers Within the Multinational Corporation." In R. G. Hawkins, ed. *Research in International Business and Finance: An Annual Compilation of Research.* Greenwich, Ct.: JAI Press, 1979.

Levitt, C. *Silent Surrender.* Toronto: Macmillan, 1970.

Levine, J. H. "The Sphere of Influence." *American Sociology Review* 37 (1972): 14-27.

Litvak, I. A. and C. J. Maule. "The Multinational Corporation: Some Perspectives." *Canadian Public Administration* 13 (1970):.

Lubitz, R. "Direct Investment and Capital Formation." In R. E. Caves and G. L. Reuber, eds. *Capital Transfers and Economic Policy: Canada, 1951-62.* Cambridge, Mass.: Harvard University Press, 1971.

Marfels, C. *Concentration Levels and Trends in the Canadian Economy, 1965-1973.* Royal Commission on Corporate Concentration Technical Report No. 31. Ottawa: Supply and Services Canada, 1976.

Mathewson, G. F. and G. D. Quirin. *Fiscal Transfer Pricing in Multinational Corporations.* Toronto: University of Toronto Press for the Ontario Economic Council, 1979.

McManus, J. C. "The Theory of the International Firm." In G. Paquet, ed. *The Multinational Firm and the Nation State.* Don Mills, Ont.: Collier-Macmillan Canada, 1972.

Mills, C. W. *The Power Elite.* New York: Oxford University Press, 1956.

Mitchell, J. Clyde. *Social Networks in Urban Situations.* Manchester: Manchester University Press, 1969.

Naylor, R. T. "The Rise and Fall of the Third Commercial Empire of the St. Lawrence." In Gary Teeple, ed. *Capitalism and the National Question in Canada.* Toronto: University of Toronto Press, 1972.

Niagara Institute. *Corporate Social Performance in Canada.* Royalk Commission on Corporate Concentration Study No. 21. Ottawa: Supply and Services Canada, 1977.

Niosi, J. *The Economy of Canada.* Montreal: Black Rose, 1978.

Ornstein, M. "The Boards and Executives of The Largest Canadian Corporations." *Canadian Journal of Sociology* 1 (1976): 411-37.

Ornstein, M. "Interlocking Directorates in Canada: Evidence From Replacement Patterns." *Social Networks* 4 (1982): 3-35.

Orr, D. "The Industrial Composition of U.S. Exports and Subsidiary Sales to the Canadian Market: Comment." *American Economic Review* 65 (1975): 230-34.

Owen, R. F. "Inter-industry Determinants of Foreign Direct Investments: A Perspective Emphasizing the Canadian Experience." Princeton: Economic Finance Section, Princeton University, 1979.

Park, Libbie and Frank. *Anatomy of Big Business.* Toronto: Progress, 1962.

Porter, J. *The Vertical Mosaic.* Toronto: University of Toronto Press, 1965.

Redlich, Fritz. *The Molding of American Banking: Men and Ideas.* N.Y.: Johnson Reprint Co., 1968.

Reuber, G. L. and F. Roseman. "International Capital Flows and the Takeover of Domestic Companies by Foreign Firms: Canada, 1945-61." In F. Machlup, W. S. Salant and L. Tarshis, eds. *The International Mobility and Movement of Capital.* New York: Columbia University Press for NBER, 1972.

Richards, J. and L. Pratt. *Prairie Capitalism: Power and Influence in the New West.* Toronto: McClelland and Stewart, 1979.

Richardson, R. J. " 'Merchants Against Industry': An Empirical Study of the Canadian Debate." *Canadian Journal of Sociology* 7 (1982): 279-95.

Rosenbluth, G. "The Relation Between Foreign Control and Concentration in Canadian Industry." *Canadian Journal of Economics* 3 (1970): 14-38.

Rostow, W. W. *The Stages of Economic Growth.* Cambridge: Cambridge University Press, 1971.

Safarian, A. E. *Foreign Ownership of Canadian Industry.* Toronto: McGraw-Hill, 1966.

———. *The Performance of Foreign-Owned Firms in Canada.* Washington and Montreal: Canadian-American Committee, 1969.

Saunders, R. S. "The Determinants of Productivity in Canadian Manufacturing Industries." *Journal Ind. Econ.* 29 (1980): 167-84.

Scherer, F. M. *Industrial Market Structure and Economic Performance.* 2d. ed. Chicago: Rand McNally, 1970.

Scott, J. *Corporations, Classes and Capitalism.* London: Hutchinson, 1979.

Smigel, Erwin O. *Wall Street Lawyer.* Bloomington: Indiana University Press, 1969.

Statistics Canada. *Industrial Organization and Concentration in the Manufacturing, Mining and Logging Industries.* Ottawa: Information Canada, 1973.

_____. "Structural Aspects of Domestic and Foreign Control in the Manufacturing, Mining and Forestry Industries, 1970-1972." Ottawa: Statistics Canada, 1978.

_____. "Domestic and Foreign Control of Manufacturing Establishments in Canada, 1972." Ottawa: Statistics Canada, 1977.

Stuckey, J. A. "Vertical Integration and Joint Ventures in the International Aluminum Industry." Cambridge, Mass.: Ph. D. dissertation, Harvard University, 1981.

Task Force on the Structure of Canadian Industry, *Foreign Ownership and the Structure of Canadian Industry (Watkins Report).* Ottawa: Privy Council Office, 1968.

Tepperman, Lorne. "Effects of the Demographic Transition Upon Access to the Toronto Elite." *Canadian Review of Sociology and Anthropology* 14 (1977): 285-93.

Van Loo, F. "The Effect of Foreign Direct Investment in Canada." *Review Economic Statistics* 59 (1977): 474-81.

Vickery, W. S. *Microstatistics.* New York: Oxford, 1956. Harcourt Brace & World, 1965.

Watkins, M. "Resources and Underdevelopment." In R. Laxer, ed. *(Canada) Ltd.* Toronto: McClelland & Stewart, 1973.

Waverman, L. and R. Baldwin. "Determinants of Interlocking Directorates." Working Paper No. 7501. Toronto: Institute for Policy Analysis, University of Toronto, 1975.

Wechter, Dixon *The Saga of American Society: A Record of Social Aspiration, 1607-1937.* N.Y.: Charles Scribner's Sons, 1937.

White, T. *Organization Size As A Factor Influencing Labour Relations.* Royal Commission on Corporate Concentration Technical Report No. 33. Ottawa: Supply and Services Canada, 1977.

Williamson, O. E. *Corporate Control and Business Behavior.* Englewood Cliffs, N.J.: Prentice-Hall, 1970.

Author Index

Subject Index